# The Future of the International Monetary System

This book is dedicated to the memory of
Curzio Giannini

# The Future of the International Monetary System

*Edited by*

Marc Uzan

*Founder and Executive Director, Reinventing Bretton Woods Committee, New York, USA*

**Edward Elgar**
Cheltenham, UK • Northampton, MA, USA

HG
3881
.F8716
2005

© Marc Uzan 2005

All rights reserved. No part of this publication may be reproduced, stored in
a retrieval system or transmitted in any form or by any means, electronic,
mechanical or photocopying, recording, or otherwise without the prior
permission of the publisher.

Published by
Edward Elgar Publishing Limited
Glensanda House
Montpellier Parade
Cheltenham
Glos GL50 1UA
UK

Edward Elgar Publishing, Inc.
136 West Street
Suite 202
Northampton
Massachusetts 01060
USA


A catalogue record for this book
is available from the British Library


ISBN 1 84376 805 4

Printed and bound in Great Britain by MPG Books Ltd, Bodmin, Cornwall

# Contents

University Libraries
Carnegie Mellon University
Pittsburgh, PA 15213-3890

*v*

# Contributors

**Lorenzo Bini Smaghi** Director General, International Financial Relations, Department of Treasury, Rome, Italy

**Henk J. Brouwer** Executive Director, De Nederlandsche Bank, Amsterdam, Netherlands.

**Michael Buchanan** Co-Director of Global Macro Research, Goldman Sachs.

**Sergio Edeza** President and CEO of the Philippine Export–Import Credit Agency (PhilEXIM), former Treasurer, Republic of the Philippines.

**Allen Frankel** Head, Secretariat of the Committee on the Global Financial System, Bank for International Settlements, Basle, Switzerland.

The late **Curzio Giannini** formerly Deputy Director, International Department Banca D'Italia, Rome, Italy.

**Ricardo Gottschalk** Fellow, Institute of Development Studies, University of Sussex, Brighton, UK.

**Robert Gray** Chairman, Debt Financing Advisory Group, HSBC Investment Bank, London, UK.

**Stephany Griffith-Jones** Professional Fellow, Institute of Development Studies, University of Sussex, Brighton, UK.

**Andrew G. Haldane** Director, International Finance Division, Bank of England, London, UK.

**Pierre Jaillet** Deputy Director, General-Economics and International, Bank of France, Paris, France.

**Harold James** Professor of History, Princeton University, Princeton, NJ, USA.

**Vijay Joshi**   Fellow, Merton College, Oxford, UK.

**David Leblang**   Professor of Political Science, University of Colorado, Boulder, CO, USA.

**Daniel Marx**   Former Secretary of Finance, Buenos Aires, Republic of Argentina.

**Adam McKissack**   Manager, IMF Unit, Department of Treasury, Canberra, Australia.

**John Murray**   Advisor to the Governor, Bank of Canada, Ottawa, Canada.

**Martin Parkinson**   Executive Director, Macroeconomic Group, Department of Treasury, Canberra, Australia.

**Wouter Raab**   Director, Foreign Financial Relations, Ministry of Finance, The Hague, The Netherlands.

**Lord Skidelsky**   Professor, Department of Economics, Warwick University, UK.

**Marc Uzan**   Executive Director, Reinventing Bretton Woods Committee, New York, USA.

**E.J. van der Merwe**   Chief Economist, Reserve Bank of South Africa, Pretoria, South Africa.

**John Williamson**   Senior Fellow, Institute for International Economics, Washington, DC, USA.

**Jeromin Zettelmeyer**   Senior Economist, International Monetary Fund, Washington, DC, USA.

# 1. The International Monetary Convention Project: the search for a new equilibrium in the international monetary system

**Marc Uzan** F33

The Reinventing Bretton Woods Committee was founded in 1994 to study the changes needed in economic institutions if they are to be effective in this new environment. Unlike similar efforts underway, the Committee's work is based on the premise that whereas the emergence of a regional focus of economic power is a phenomenon that is relatively well understood, the shift in the relative weight of private versus public capital flows in the world economy is less so.

The establishment, 60 years ago, of the International Monetary Fund (IMF) and the World Bank was the most important achievement of international cooperation following the Second World War. The IMF was the guardian of the Bretton Woods regime of fixed exchange rates, and its essential mission immediately after the war was to seek foreign exchange rate stability and a balance of payments equilibrium through three instruments: short-term financing, policy surveillance and capital controls. The World Bank supported reconstruction and development through long-term finance and mobilization of private capital through risk transfers.

Over the past 60 years, the world has witnessed tremendous changes in its political and economic regimes, largely altering the environment in which international financial institutions (IFIs), including the IMF and the World Bank, pursued their activities. After the collapse of the Bretton Woods regime in 1971, the fixed exchange rate system gave way to a floating exchange rate system. As a result of spreading liberalization of capital controls, the free flow of capital became a fact of life, and was often volatile and massive. These changes in the economic and financial environment appeared to have made the missions of the Bretton Woods institutions more complex.

The waves of financial crises that have spread across the world since 1995 generated a consensus that fundamental reform was required in the

*1*

international financial system. The existing mechanisms created in 1944 at Bretton Woods were inadequate for preventing and managing crises in the dramatically changed world of the 21st century and a significant reform was needed to update the Bretton Woods institutions. This debate has taken place under the heading the 'international financial architecture': the international community has passed through phases in thinking about appropriate future changes. Some initial, radical thoughts such as a global central bank or a world financial authority, while worthy of some consideration, have been rejected as impractical. Subsequently, a coalescence of thinking on more pragmatic measures occurred to prevent financial crises from occurring and to better manage them when they do occur. A set of initiatives on desirable medium-term initiatives worthy of pursuit includes: improved transparency and disclosure, measures to strengthen financial systems in emerging markets, strengthening prudential regulation in the developed countries, sequencing or temporary limitations on capital account liberalization, more involvement by the private sector in crisis prevention/management, strengthening and reforming the IFIs with augmented resources and more contingency financing programs together with the private sector, and more appropriate exchange rate regimes in emerging market countries.

To move this agenda forward, the G7 since 1995 has adopted a pragmatic path of change. The group has maintained its strong commitment to an open global economy, supported by free movement of capital, technology and skill, and reinforced by increasingly liberalized foreign trade and investment regimes as the most desirable course to maintain global growth under stable conditions. It proposed an approach which involves the establishment of comprehensive *standards*, representing best global practices toward which all countries participating in the global system would strive.

In 2004, almost five years after the Asian crisis, the fact that deep crises have continued to occur, most recently in Turkey and Argentina, indicates clearly that the international financial system in place needs further changes. Indeed, it can be argued that the depth of the Argentine crisis may be an indication that the system is in a phase of transition and that a radical transformation is about to emerge. On top of these issues, net private capital flows to emerging economies have fallen sharply since 1997 to the extent that if these flows do not recover, a greater role would need to be played by official liquidity and development finance.

In that context, the international financial community seems confused about the way forward. The uncertainty with the current economic and geopolitical situation, and the aftermath of the sovereign debt restructuring mechanism leaves the architects of the 21st century in disarray and concerned about the breakdown of the Bretton Woods consensus, which had convinced leaders that a new set of cooperative monetary and trade arrangements was a prerequisite for world peace and prosperity. In this current landscape, discussion of the design of a new international financial architecture has its limits unless we go back to the key principles and the political legitimacy of the Bretton Woods system. The world of global finance needs to move beyond the technical intractability of bond documentation to a more ambitious agenda. What should be the articles of an agreement today for a new IMF under the quasi-universal acceptance of floating exchange rates or monetary union? What should be the role of an international monetary fund in a world where private capital flows are more dominant? Which institution can provide the leadership to provide a roadmap for reform with a new mandate of political legitimacy? What are the incentives for the creditors and debtors to establish the right forum to manage financial crises? Would it be desirable and feasible for the international community to have a broader agenda that would include the key subjects on reform of the international financial system, including systemic issues? Can we look at an ambitious agenda and transform it into a body with the potential to make a truly valuable contribution to meaningful reform of the international financial system?

Would it be desirable and feasible to have a broader agenda that would include the key subjects on reform of the international financial system, including systemic issues and representation, particularly at the IMF discussions about revisions to quota allocations? Such allocations should represent the country's position in the international economy as well as improve the effectiveness of international institutions, which are necessary to ensure a strong and stable global financial system. There should be a move toward a governing structure that is more representative and a relative allocation of member quotas that reflects the changes underway in the world economy – so that each country's standing and voice is more consistent with its relative economic and financial strength.

Can the international financial community take over an ambitious agenda and transform the body into one with the potential to make a truly valuable contribution to meaningful reform of the international financial system?

On the eve of the 60th anniversary of the Bretton Woods institutions and with the sense of radical change that is starting to emerge, there is a clear need to shape and adapt the IMF to new challenges and thus provide a new political legitimacy. The debate of crisis resolution and the discussion underway for a sovereign debt restructuring mechanism or a voluntary approach from the private sector should not prevent the official sector and the international financial community from going back to the key underpinnings of the creation of the Bretton Woods institutions and reinforcing the political legitimacy of the IFIs.

After two years of debate exploring the possibility of a sovereign debt restructuring mechanism, the international community has decided at this stage to adopt a more market-driven approach through the use of collective action clauses in bond documentation and possibly a code of good conduct clarifying the principles and responsibilities of stakeholders in a context of a debt restructuring. Nevertheless, the debate is not over, and the Argentine restructuring is likely to have implications for the techniques and burden sharing of debt restructuring. What will its implications be for the role of the International Monetary Fund, whose lending has become increasingly concentrated on a few emerging market members that received exceptional access to fund resources? This Fund-supported program will be prolonged and extended over a number of years. Could this trend impair the revolving nature of IMF lending? Are there other aspects of the expansion of private capital flows that are potential sources of systemic risk and deserve closer scrutiny?

This book is the first in a series aimed at reflecting the current thinking among the international financial community on the way forward for managing the global financial system. There have been more questions than answers. As a new generation of policymakers will be taking over the responsibility of international financial stability, they will have to face new challenges as complex as those faced by previous generations. The integration of China into the international monetary system will clearly be one of them. Will they be dealing with a world with fewer currencies? Will they set up new institutions or will they realize that a new Bretton Woods will be the outcome of the long search for a new international financial architecture?

The contributions (excluding Chapter 15) were originally presented at the International Monetary Convention, Madrid, 13–14 May 2003, organized by the Reinventing Bretton Woods Committee and the Spanish Ministry of Finance. We would like to gratefully acknowledge the financial support for this conference from the Ministry of the Economy of Spain.

PART I


The Future Evolution of the International
Monetary and Financial System

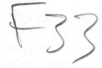

## 2.  The IMF and the challenge of relevance in the international financial architecture

### Martin Parkinson and Adam McKissack[1]

---

## INTRODUCTION

The end of the 20th century, and beginning of the 21st, has proven to be something of a watershed period for the International Monetary Fund (IMF). The string of major crises of the past decade, and the associated reassessment of how to maintain international financial stability, saw significant questioning of the role of the Fund.[2] The resulting soul searching – and the acknowledgment by the Fund and its shareholders of the need for change – has led to a substantial refocusing of its activities onto its core responsibilities in the last five years.

This change has not been without pain, but more change is needed still. The IMF must continue to evolve as the world changes, in order to retain its relevance to the international financial system. But its evolution must be around its core responsibilities. It must avoid having its focus fragmented by straying into areas better dealt with by other parts of the international financial architecture.

This need for further change provides an opportune time to reconsider the evolution of the IMF's role since it was established in the 1940s and to ponder some of the challenges ahead. Despite criticism, the Fund retains a central role in today's international financial architecture, suggesting that the evolution to date has been broadly viewed as successful. However, the choices it makes now in response to pressures for further change will help determine whether it remains equally relevant over the next half century.

While the actions of the Fund are important, the debate about its role is not simply about what the institution should, or should not, do. It is also about what the national government shareholders of the IMF expect from the Fund as an institution and their commitment to the role they bestow upon it. The appropriate role of, and the interactions among, the various institutions within the international financial architecture also bears on the debate. The shareholders of the Fund comprise virtually all countries in the world; its future effectiveness is, therefore, the responsibility of the international community writ large.

## ORIGINAL ROLE OF THE IMF

The IMF was established in 1944 to promote international financial stability in the post-Second World War reconstruction period. The Fund's purpose, as set out in its Articles of Agreement (see Box 2.1), is to promote international monetary cooperation, financial stability and world economic growth. This purpose remains broadly relevant to the present day, although the means of achieving it have clearly changed.

---

### BOX 2.1   ARTICLES OF AGREEMENT OF THE IMF

#### ARTICLE I

#### Purposes

The purposes of the International Monetary Fund are:

(i)  To promote international monetary cooperation through a permanent institution which provides the machinery for consultation and collaboration on international monetary problems.

(ii)  To facilitate the expansion and balanced growth of international trade, and to contribute thereby to the promotion and maintenance of high levels of employment and real income and to the development of the productive resources of all members as primary objectives of economic policy.

(iii)  To promote exchange stability, to maintain orderly exchange arrangements among members, and to avoid competitive exchange depreciation.

(iv)  To assist in the establishment of a multilateral system of payments in respect of current transactions between members and in the elimination of foreign exchange restrictions which hamper the growth of world trade.

---

(v) To give confidence to members by making the general resources of the Fund temporarily available to them under adequate safeguards, thus providing them with opportunity to correct maladjustments in their balance of payments without resorting to measures destructive of national or international prosperity.

(vi) In accordance with the above, to shorten the duration and lessen the degree of disequilibrium in the international balances of payments of members.

The Fund shall be guided in all its policies and decisions by the purposes set forth in this Article.

At the time the IMF was established, the experience of the 1930s remained fresh in many minds. Competitive devaluations associated with 'beggar-thy-neighbor' policies were seen as a key source of instability in the international financial system. A key part of the answer to this problem, as conceived by the architects of the Bretton Woods system, was to create a system of pegged exchange rates to counter such destabilizing behavior.[3] The system provided for a set of exchange rate parities between members linked to gold or the US dollar, with the value of the dollar in turn linked to the price of gold at $US35 to the ounce.

The Fund's primary function under this system was to support the maintenance of these exchange rate parities, including by lending to members facing short-term balance of payments disequilibria. The Fund essentially acted as an international credit union. Members contributed to a pool of reserves from which countries facing balance of payments deficits could borrow to maintain their pegged exchange rate.[4]

The Articles of Agreement (Clause (V) of Article 1) arguably presume conditionality in referring to resources being made temporarily available 'under adequate safeguards'. But the nature of conditionality was not defined. Rather, it has emerged over time with the development and operation of Fund-supported programs of adjustment. The introduction of Stand By Arrangements (SBAs) in 1952 to provide medium-term assistance saw the introduction of explicit conditionality, whereby countries were required to adopt policies to resolve balance of payments difficulties in exchange for Fund support.[5] The introduction of the Extended Fund Facility in 1974 for longer-term balance of payments difficulties saw the introduction of three-year programs of conditionality covering structural, not just macroeconomic, policies relevant to the balance of payments.[6]

# CHANGING ROLE OF THE IMF

The international financial system has seen many changes since 1944. Most notably, these include abandonment of the original Bretton Woods system of pegged exchange rates in the early 1970s and the emergence of capital account crises in the 1990s on the back of rapid growth in private capital flows.

## Breakdown of the Bretton Woods System

A defining change was the breakdown of the Bretton Woods system of exchange rate parities between 1968 and 1971.[7] While no consensus exists on the reasons for the breakdown, some common factors are generally put forward. Among these are the breaking of the link between the US dollar and the monetary gold stock, as the Vietnam War and the growth in world output and liquidity strained the convertibility of the US dollar into gold. Increasing capital mobility also put strains on the system through facilitating speculation against fixed parities. Finally, greater price instability in the United States meant that the system of fixed exchange rates increasingly ran the risk of providing a transmission mechanism for higher world inflation, in turn placing pressure on parities.

Since the collapse of the Bretton Woods system, but especially since the Asian crisis of 1997–98, there has been growing acceptance of the benefits of more flexible exchange rates. Economic orthodoxy moved from regarding floating rates as a source of instability in the 1940s, to increasingly perceiving them as a means of absorbing the impact of international shocks (although acceptance of this argument is by no means universal).[8]

The 'shock absorber' role of floating rates became relatively more important with the increased output and price instability seen from the early 1970s onwards. It has become increasingly accepted that the trinity of a monetary policy directed at domestic balance, a fixed exchange rate and international capital mobility was not sustainable. That is, it was recognized that it was not possible to pursue an independent monetary policy while defending a fixed exchange rate with mobile capital, and that this limited the flexibility of policymakers in addressing issues of price and output instability.

The fact that the end of the Bretton Woods system did not mean an end to the role of the IMF is itself informative of the way in which the IMF had evolved since its inception. While the system of pegged exchange rates had proved unsustainable, countries were not indifferent to exchange volatility. Exchange rates were free to move, but desirably in an 'orderly' fashion. So the need remained strong for an institution that would promote international financial stability, including through lending to countries requiring liquidity to correct for short-term macroeconomic imbalances. However, the changing trends in the world economy clearly altered the way the Fund approached its role.

In particular, the beginning of the era of flexible exchange rates saw significant development in the concept of IMF surveillance. The Fund acquired a formal surveillance role following an amendment to its Articles of Agreement in 1978. Associated with this role, the IMF was charged with conducting surveillance over member policies. Equally, members were obliged to provide the information necessary for the conduct of that surveillance.

This reflected the broadening of the Fund's focus away from one of achieving balance of payments outcomes consistent with the relevant exchange rate towards considering issues of whether general macroeconomic policy settings were consistent with internal and external balance; identifying stresses before they had reached breaking point. This represented an evolution in the role for the Fund, but one which remains consistent with its overall purposes.

The introduction of the Extended Fund Facility in 1974, which focused on longer-term policies affecting the balance of payments, is indicative of the associated broadening in scope of Fund programs. With the broader scope of programs came increasingly sophisticated conditionality addressing the longer-term policy settings of member countries.

In retrospect, the IMF's role up to the end of the 1970s evolved in a broadly sensible fashion. The overarching purpose of ensuring international financial stability remained the same, but the assessment of the problem moved from one of exchange rate management, narrowly defined, to the compatibility of broader macroeconomic settings with orderly exchange rate behavior, and the IMF's approach moved in step with this change.

**More Recent Trends**

More recently, an important development has been the rapid expansion of private capital flows between countries and closer integration of global capital markets. While potentially beneficial for the growth of recipient countries, these developments have had a number of less benign consequences.

First, countries have become more exposed to the risk of capital account crises. The presence of large amounts of mobile private capital has increased the risk of sharp market reactions in the face of emerging economic imbalances. This has meant that the loss of confidence in domestic policies can be quite sudden and can result in dramatic reversals in capital flows, with consequent disorderly and damaging adjustment.

A second consequence has been that crises have increasingly been triggered by, and have exposed, serious structural policy weaknesses, particularly in relation to the financial sector. This has seen a distinction drawn between financial crises and 'traditional' balance of payments crises. While it would be overly simplistic to seek to draw a strict dichotomy between the two, it is clear that the strains on domestic financial systems posed by the increasing scale of capital flows have introduced a new element into modern crises. This has dragged the focus of Fund surveillance further beyond that of macroeconomic stabilization and into areas of prudential and regulatory reform in the financial sector.

An additional feature of modern crises has been the presence of contagion effects arising from the closer integration of global capital flows. This has seen the loss of confidence in one country trigger similar losses of confidence in other countries. The transmission of crises from one country to another has posed new threats to the stability of the international financial system as a whole.

The changing nature and increased severity of crises has had a number of implications for the Fund's role. It has seen a further evolution in the role of Fund surveillance. The scope of surveillance has been broadened. First, to address structural issues which pose a threat to macroeconomic stability. Second, to better and earlier detect emerging vulnerabilities, which has led to a focus on issues such as the size, maturity and currency composition of external debt.[9] The widened scope of individual country monitoring has been complemented by an increased emphasis on multilateral and regional surveillance to identify interactions and linkages that might facilitate the spread of crises.

There has also been an increased focus on the stability of domestic financial systems, particularly following the Asian financial crisis of the late 1990s. This has seen the development and broadening of a role for bodies which complement the role of the Fund. Included among these is the Financial Stability Forum (FSF), which promotes discussion among members on appropriate regulatory and prudential practices. The FSF is not alone, however, with the work of the various standard-setting bodies gaining greater attention in recent years.[10]

Increases in the size of private capital flows have also introduced a new element to crisis resolution. In 'traditional' current account crises, the challenge was to provide finance to support countries in making the appropriate domestic policy adjustments to correct the imbalance. While this role remains, the build-up of large amounts of privately held debt has meant that IMF lending and domestic policy adjustment may not be sufficient to

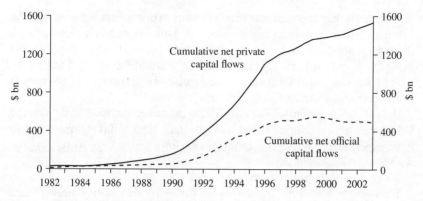

Source: Based on data from IMF, *World Economic Outlook*, September 2002.

*Figure 2.1 Emerging market economies: cumulation of capital flows*

achieve macroeconomic stability. That is, countries increasingly appear to find themselves in situations where there may be no set of domestic policies that can place them on a sustainable path without some restructuring of their debts. This has led to calls for mechanisms to better coordinate the restructuring of privately held sovereign debt in crisis situations.

The relatively reduced importance of official sector capital flows has produced a situation in which the credibility and success of Fund-supported programs, Fund lending and conditionality are at a premium. In recent years the Fund has tried to stem crises with finance that is small relative to volatile private capital flows, notwithstanding a period in which the scale of Fund interventions has grown very large by its own historical benchmarks (see Figure 2.1). Consensus also exists that, even were they large enough to do so, official sector resources cannot be used to 'bail out' the private sector. The need for Fund involvement in crisis prevention to be catalytic – to be confidence inspiring and to 'bail in' the private sector – has therefore become all the more important.

The recent period has also seen increased debate about the effectiveness of the Fund's policies in terms of crisis prevention and crisis resolution. Following the Asian financial crisis, some criticized the Fund for 'missing the signs' of the emerging crisis and for relying too much on 'old' solutions in seeking to resolve 'new' problems, for example, through relying on macroeconomic stabilization policies when many of the underlying problems were essentially structural in nature. Still others argued that the macroeconomic policy settings appropriate to the avoidance of a crisis were not those that should be pursued in the aftermath of a capital account crisis.[11] Some critics also argued that the pursuit of structural reforms as part of crisis management was inappropriate, while others believed that the Fund had no role in structural issues at all. This debate has intensified with the emergence of crises in countries that have been subject to ongoing and extensive Fund support. This has reduced the credibility of the Fund in the eyes of some commentators and raised questions about its effectiveness in both preventing and resolving modern-day crises.

Recent developments have also led to increased public scrutiny of the IMF's role and questions about its legitimacy. The Fund is considered to have experienced 'mission creep', moving into areas beyond its original mandate and areas of expertise.

At one level, these criticisms are unfair.

First, there is still no consensus on how best to identify, prevent and resolve capital account crises. Even if such a consensus had by now emerged, hindsight is blessed with 20:20 vision – it may still be too much to expect the Fund to have known this in the mid-1990s.

Second, the Fund has experienced mission creep at the behest of its shareholders, and in response to broader international opinion (for example, as represented by some non-governmental organizations), which has demanded that attention move to include structural policies in a wide range of areas only loosely related to the original purpose of the institution. These include military expenditures and environmental and gender issues. But mission creep has also arisen as the nature of the membership has changed. The membership of the transition economies in the early 1990s brought with it new sets of issues which were different from those the Fund had previously to deal with, especially in relation to structural policy and its interaction with growth and macroeconomic stability.

Similarly, the increased emphasis placed on growth and poverty reduction – at the behest of the international community – has thrown up new and different issues upon which the Fund is expected to advise. Indeed, a checklist would indicate that Fund missions should now address perhaps as many as 40 separate issues in every Article IV surveillance report. The wider the range of responsibilities placed on the Fund, the greater the risk that its focus becomes fragmented, a risk that needs to be recognized explicitly by its shareholders.

That said, there is also a legitimate basis for criticism.

It is only in recent years that the Fund has begun to engage with its critics, and to become more transparent and accountable for its surveillance and policy advice. By exposing its judgments to public gaze, the Fund can help educate the broader community and make it easier for outsiders to see and assess the types of 'on balance' judgments it is required to make – this has been good discipline for national policymakers and there is no reason to believe it will not be equally valuable for the Fund.

The progressive redefinition of the problem of how to maintain international financial stability has taken the Fund into a widening range of structural, financial and institutional issues. Having embarked on this path the challenge is knowing when to stop, since virtually every aspect of an economy can be said to be macroeconomically relevant to at least some degree. Despite the success of recent efforts to refocus the Fund on its core responsibilities, the need to avoid excessive mission creep will remain an ongoing challenge.

Almost seven years after the start of the Asian crisis, it needs to be recognized that there has been considerable evolution in the Fund's focus and *modus operandi*. This evolution must continue in response to the changing nature of the international economic and financial system. All institutions need to evolve if they are to remain effective. The question is how to get the right balance.

## FUTURE ROLE

### General Considerations

Notwithstanding recent criticisms, the Fund has an ongoing and important role to play in the international financial architecture. Its purposes as set out in its Articles of Agreement remain relevant to addressing the challenges confronting the global economy today and those likely to arise in the decades ahead. However, given the changes in the world economy of the last decade it is clear that there is a need to continue to reevaluate the nature of its role going forward.

This is a critical point. As discussed above, the Fund's role is not, and has never been, static. It was initially established to support a system of pegged exchange rates and had to adapt when this system broke down. It was established at a time of limited international capital mobility and has had to adapt to a world of large and rapid private capital flows.

While the trend toward increased capital market integration is unlikely to be reversed, appropriate exchange rate regimes have been a matter of debate for over a century. With proposals for target zones and currency unions continuing to be discussed as a means of promoting regional stability, it cannot be ruled out that fixed exchange rates will again become a more important feature of the global financial system in the future. Further, it is unclear what additional pressures the forces of globalization will place on domestic policy settings. The Fund needs to be flexible enough to continue to adapt to these, and other, trends as they develop.

The Fund's future role is, in many ways, endogenous. The role will evolve based on how it performs; specifically to how well it adapts to changes in the international environment. The Fund is likely to still exist in one form or another in the decades ahead, but whether it remains a relevant institution is a function of the decisions made now and in the future. It is one thing to survive as an institution – all national policymakers can attest to the difficulty of closing institutions and fora that have outlived their usefulness – but another to survive as a credible institution.

Credibility therefore emerges as a key issue that will shape the Fund's direction in the future. What do we mean by credibility? There are two key aspects to the concept. The first is the issue of effectiveness. Recent crises have highlighted the tension between providing funds to help bail out countries in crisis and encouraging countries, whether before, during or after a crisis, to make difficult, but necessary, domestic policy adjustments. The Fund has been seen in some quarters as too ready to dole out financial assistance without sufficient policy adjustment. Critics in the 'effectiveness camp' argue that the Fund is not doing enough to push the reforms necessary for domestic adjustment but is in some cases deferring (or even exacerbating) the necessary adjustment through its financing packages.[12]

In contrast, others argue that the Fund goes too far in seeking to impose changes to domestic policies and question the Fund's legitimacy in undertaking such a role. Critics in the 'legitimacy camp' argue that the Fund is not sufficiently accountable to its members and, as evidence, point to the lack of country ownership of the types of policies endorsed by the Fund. They would argue that a lack of legitimacy leads to an inability to achieve reform, in turn creating problems of low Fund credibility.

This would appear to place the Fund between the proverbial 'rock and a hard place'. For example, Feldstein (1998, p. 27) has argued, 'A nation's desperate need for short-term financial help does not give the IMF the moral right to substitute its technical judgments for the outcomes of the nation's political process'. Equally, though, we would suggest that a nation has no automatic right to be bailed out by the rest of the international community if it persistently pursues inappropriate policies.

There are no easy answers to this dilemma, but it is clear that the Fund needs to address issues of both effectiveness and legitimacy if it is to have credibility. In fact, the two concepts can be mutually supporting – for example, greater country ownership and broader support for the Fund among the international community may increase country and communal support acceptance of programs that recommend difficult policy choices. A fundamental challenge for the international community moving forward is to find an appropriate balance between measures that increase the Fund's effectiveness and measures to address its legitimacy.

**Streamlining Conditionality and Promoting Country Ownership**

The task of promoting ownership of policy adjustments is often more difficult the greater is the needed adjustment, which may explain perceptions of low ownership of Fund-supported programs in recent crises. Often a lack of country ownership of policy *failures* makes ownership of policy *adjustments* difficult to achieve. Indeed, it is hard to recall any government saying that its policies led to crisis, although many are happy to attribute blame to the IMF for the failure to recover from crisis.[13]

Discontent with its policy advice has led to pressures for the Fund to adopt a role more like that of an international central bank, providing swift access to finance without applying excessive policy conditionality.[14] The idea would be to play down the Fund's role of policy adviser in favor of its role as a provider of liquidity.

Against this background, the Fund has taken a number of steps to streamline conditionality and promote better ownership of Fund-supported programs. Following reviews of conditionality beginning in 2000, revised conditionality guidelines were agreed in 2002. The revised guidelines aim to ensure that policy conditions in IMF programs enhance the prospects of program success by including only those conditions that are 'critical' or 'relevant' to achieving the goals of the program. The guidelines also aim to provide greater emphasis on national ownership of IMF-supported programs.

These efforts are to be welcomed, but they are unlikely to be sufficient. We would venture that they need to be married to a focused and effective communication strategy within countries with Fund-supported programs if support for IMF policy advice is to be maximized. But is this the role of the Fund?

Governments adopt Fund-supported programs, meaning that governments should be the ones to engage with their citizens on these issues. This highlights an intractable dilemma – the very existence of the Fund may provide 'cover' for governments to pursue policies that are necessary but for which support is lacking. While we believe that governments ultimately expend scarce political capital whether they educate their populace on the need for given policies or argue 'the Fund made us do it', it has to be conceded that the IMF may be a convenient whipping boy at times. If this is the case, perhaps a lack of 'in-country' legitimacy is to be expected.

But then it makes it even more imperative that the Fund should have 'global' legitimacy. That is, when it provides policy advice it does so from a position of strength – with a good track record of effective advice and with the clearly recognized support of its membership behind the policy recommendations being made. That is, the 'they' in 'they made us do it' becomes the international community and not the Fund in isolation.

This suggests two critical issues. First, that the advice must be recognized as of high quality and appropriate for the country. Second, that the Fund should be seen to receive 'direction' and 'guidance' on its policies from a broadly representative group of members. If it is seen to dance to the tune of a small group of like-minded countries to the exclusion of others, then this global 'legitimacy' will always be under threat.

**Improved Surveillance**

We argue that the role of the Fund revolves around providing sound policy advice to members to promote macroeconomic stability and prevent the emergence of crises. Macroeconomic stability is crucial as it is a prerequisite for ensuring the effective operation of the international financial and trading systems and meeting the ultimate goals of economic growth and development. Consistent with this, the IMF should also only provide members with access to its resources where demonstrably necessary, and likely, to assist in achieving stability.

Central to the effectiveness of the Fund's policy advice is the strength of its surveillance, where surveillance encompasses both the identification of necessary policy adjustments and, equally importantly, the effective implementation of policy advice by member countries.

The current and future shape of Fund surveillance is a topic that merits detailed consideration in its own right and we will not cover it here. The important point to note is that as the nature of problems facing countries has evolved, so has Fund surveillance. Indeed, a commentator from 1993 would be astounded by the change in surveillance over the last decade. We hope to be equally astounded by the change in the shape of surveillance between now and 2013.

The formal surveillance function was introduced when the move away from the pegged exchange rate system saw more of a focus on broader macroeconomic stabilization policies. With more recent crises raising issues of longer-term solvency, this has created a need to extend surveillance to examine underlying structural problems, particularly in the financial sector. This has stretched the Fund's traditional areas of expertise and made the task of surveillance more challenging.

Since the Asian financial crisis, the Fund has introduced a range of measures to strengthen its surveillance function. These include measures to increase transparency and accountability through the voluntary publication of Article IV staff reports and program documentation, and through the publication of all policy papers. The promulgation of standards and codes has helped promote sound policies in member countries, particularly in the critical area of financial sector stability. The rapid development of the Reports on the Observance of Standards and Codes (ROSCs) and the Financial Sector Assessment Program (FSAP) – both introduced at the end of the 1990s – has been impressive. Enhanced data dissemination standards have improved the consistency and comparability of data available to the Fund while supporting the monitoring of developments within member countries. Improvements to debt sustainability assessment methodologies and to multilateral and regional surveillance, including monitoring of capital market developments, and the development of early warning systems, are all designed to assist the Fund to identify vulnerabilities in the international financial system at an earlier stage.[15]

The list of measures adopted by the Fund is long and represents a constructive response to the changing international landscape.[16] While it might be desirable for all the new initiatives to be a mandatory part of surveillance, the Fund has made a pragmatic decision to move slowly to overcome opposition among some members to the broadened scope of surveillance. It is evident that the Fund is continuing to evolve to the changing circumstances of the world economy, just as it did in the 1970s following the breakdown of the Bretton Woods system of pegged exchange rates. That said, there is more that needs be done to enhance the Fund's surveillance function.

The relationship between the Fund's surveillance function and its role in providing policy advice is central to the effectiveness of the Fund in preventing crises. Unfortunately, poor surveillance appears to have resulted in an excessive level of optimism by the Fund in relation to many members, particularly program countries. While a reluctance to make candid and critical assessments of economies may be understandable – perhaps in the hope of engendering confidence in the policies of the program country – such an approach is short-sighted and ultimately damaging to both the Fund and the member.

It is for this reason that we have championed the application of a 'fresh pair of eyes' to surveillance in program countries. The introduction of a fresh perspective will in many cases be necessary to ensure that surveillance remains objective and supports robust policy advice.

That said, we would not go as far as advocating a strict separation of surveillance from the Fund's program function. Put simply, the creation of parallel institutional edifices comprising something called 'surveillance' and something called 'programs' would, in our view, be a retrograde step. This would be more so the more 'surveillance' looked like the activities of rating agencies.

The Fund's judgments carry weight because they are, in principle, the voice of the international community, placing it in a powerful position as policy adviser. To be effective, it is important that the Fund engage in open and honest dialogue with its members. If the Fund fragments its focus by attempting to become both an entirely independent and open observer and a candid and confidential policy adviser, then it risks the breakdown of its relationship with its members.

Instead, we would argue that the fresh pair of eyes should be approached pragmatically. We could support the development of a specialist 'programs department' if that would more effectively bring cross-country experience to bear on emerging problems. But the IMF would need to establish internal arrangements to effectively ensure that the advice of that department, the relevant area department and the Fund's surveillance watchdog – the Policy Development and Review Department – was confronted. A simpler model still would see management facilitate the development of an evaluation culture in the organization by periodically augmenting country teams with 'outsiders' tasked with reviewing and evaluating the approaches being pursued.

The need for a fresh pair of eyes highlights what is the single most striking problem in the operation of the IMF – the capacity of the executive board and management to take hard decisions.

Clearly, the IMF must respect national sovereignty and it is recognized that there can be legitimate differences in approach to addressing particular economic problems. However, it is incumbent on the board and management to tell governments when risks are emerging,[17] to be rigorous in assessing requests for assistance and to refuse requests for assistance when they do not believe that the policies being pursued will contribute to achieving macroeconomic stability. Major shareholders should encourage the board to make such clear-eyed assessments and should support hard decisions rather than pursue short-term political objectives. This issue is taken up further below.

Another challenge thrown up by the evolution of surveillance is how to improve the 'traction' of policy advice. In short, how can Fund advice be made more compelling to national governments?

It is striking that the Fund has singularly failed over the last decade to encourage faster corporate and financial restructuring in Japan, to move Europe to address persistent constraints to product and labor market flexibility and, more recently, to address emerging financial sector weakness, or to convince the United States of the dangers of disorderly current account adjustment. These failures constitute a set of serious structural weaknesses that now constrain global growth, yet they have been apparent for five, and in some cases, ten or more years. This raises a question – has the failure been with the message, or simply that countries that believe they will never be borrowers feel comfortable in ignoring advice? While the Fund may have had no discernible impact on economic management in the major advanced economies, it is hard to believe that developing economies would have been able to avoid responding to Fund advice for anything like this length of time.

If Fund advice is to be legitimate, there needs to be a presumption that it will be given *appropriate* consideration by developed, emerging market and developing economies. What constitutes 'appropriate' may differ among countries and may require the Fund to develop a better appreciation of the political constraints operating in member countries at any point in time. At the least, the Fund may need to begin to think about how it can best help governments persuade their citizens of the desirability of particular policy reforms.

**Financial Support**

While the Fund's approach to surveillance has evolved since the Asian crisis, its lending activities have changed in a more radical fashion.

The Fund currently (May 2003) has resources outstanding on the General Resources Account of around 65 billion special drawing rights (SDRs). However, a substantial proportion of this amount – SDR 45 billion – is accounted for by just three countries, Argentina, Brazil and Turkey. Moreover, Brazil has the capacity to draw down a further SDR 15 billion.

In contrast to the way in which it would caution financial supervisors to avoid concentrated lending, the IMF has more of its resources concentrated in a small group of countries than at any time in its history. This concentration of risk is striking. In the event that the Fund were to find itself faced with substantial arrears this could constitute a true watershed, with profound consequences for the operation of the institution.

This concentration of resources is a consequence of the way in which the Fund has responded to capital account crises – through large packages involving exceptional access. But exceptional access carries with it risks that magnify the risks inherent in these types of crises. While such an approach may be inevitable given the changing nature of crises, it again places a premium on rigorous assessment of the likelihood of success, and the capacity to take, and stick to, hard decisions – to learn how to 'just say no'.

**Governance Issues**

As noted earlier, bolstering the IMF's role as a policy adviser is not only about the advice and actions of its executive board, management or staff. The IMF is a creature of its member governments. It is difficult, if not impossible, for the Fund to make hard decisions with respect to individual member countries without the backing of its other members. This suggests that the responsibility for ensuring that Fund surveillance and programs are effective is shared by all member countries.

The backing of national governments is key to ensuring the legitimacy of the Fund. Unless the Fund's membership has collective ownership of the types of policies it pursues, the legitimacy of these policies will always be questioned. But this need not involve the Fund stepping back from its role of policy adviser. Rather, it involves national governments, through their representation on the IMF board, supporting the Fund in giving robust policy advice and making rigorous assessments of requests for resources by the Fund. Importantly, it means governments accepting some ownership of that advice. It means not pursuing short-term 'fixes' for individual countries that undermine the future and effectiveness of the Fund. It also means being willing to operate bilaterally to reinforce Fund advice to other members.

This is admittedly not easy to achieve in practice. The desire of individual governments to use the Fund to achieve such short-term political aims is a sign of the relevance of the institution. There will always be political pressures on the board to provide assistance to countries in crisis and there is the risk of these immediate pressures forcing decisions that go against the aim of implementing sound policies in the medium term. This is a difficult tension for the board to address, but it is important that member countries avoid sacrificing Fund credibility in pursuit of short-term goals.

In this light, it is also important for the Fund to address voice and representation issues. While this means different things to different players, we believe that Fund representation should better reflect developments in global economic weight, subject to some minimum and effective representation of all members. In the current economic environment, this requires greater representation for some Asian economies, especially Korea, at the expense of reduced representation of older developed economies.

In the interest of operational effectiveness, it would be undesirable to further increase the size of the executive board although a strong case can be made for measures to assist the capacity of smaller, multi-country- or constituency-, based chairs, and especially those representing developing countries predominantly or wholly. Our own experience points to the benefit of mixed constituencies – comprising both developed and developing economies – for reasons of voice, representation and importantly, enhanced recognition of different perspectives. It is recognized, though, that this experience will not be compelling for others.

**The IMF's Role in the Overall Financial Architecture**

The legitimacy of the Fund depends not only on its internal governance and the support provided by its members, but also on 'external governance' arrangements, that is, where it is seen to sit in the overall financial architecture. Many of the challenges it faces raise issues not just of how the IMF operates but are equally relevant for the other fora and institutions that provide direction and/or assistance to the Fund.

Our premise is that the IMF should retain a central role in the international financial architecture. It should fill this role, first, because it has near universal representation.[18] Second, the IMF's mandate to promote international financial stability forms a foundation stone for the work of the other international financial institutions, and has done so since the Bretton Woods institutions were established.

In addition, the IMF also has the resources to back up its decisions, which sets it apart from other, more consultative, fora such as the G7, G20, G24, FSF, the standard-setting bodies and so on. However, an effective relationship with these representative fora is critical in maintaining and enhancing the IMF's effectiveness and legitimacy.

Groups such as the G20 will not replace the Fund – they are fora, not institutions, and lack a mandate or the resources to intervene in the international financial system in the manner of the IMF. However, they can play an important role in bringing together IMF member countries to consult on issues that are both relevant for, and go beyond, the IMF.

Notwithstanding the Fund's advantages, it cannot always easily play a consultative role, in part because issues fall outside its mandate but also because its membership is large and its processes for coordinating the views of such a broad membership are inherently unwieldy.

The Fund should not expect, or try, to be expert on all issues or represent all the needs of regional groups. The emergence of bodies such as the G20 and FSF reflect an understanding in the international community that the Fund cannot do all these things and that its governance mechanisms are relatively unwieldy and unrepresentative. Pressures for regional bodies have arisen for similar reasons. A key challenge for the Fund moving forward is to ensure that these bodies help to reinforce its role rather than seek to supplant it.

Groups such as the G20 and the Organization for Economic Cooperation and Development (OECD) would appear better suited to facilitating the exchange of views between member countries than the IMF with its diffuse membership and rigid institutional structures. Similarly, the FSF and other specialist bodies are able to harness technical expertise on a range of issues outside the Fund's traditional areas of expertise. In recent times, such bodies have made an important contribution to developing accepted practices for strengthening domestic financial systems. The presence of such consultative and technical support mechanisms can reinforce the IMF's role by shoring up support for, promoting ownership of, and enhancing the technical basis of, the types of policies it pursues. They can also help constrain the development of 'mission creep', whereby the Fund's resources are continually stretched outside its traditional areas of expertise and ensure that issues do not 'fall between the cracks' of the mandates of the Fund and other international financial institutions.[19]

But to maximize the benefits of a larger and more diverse group of players in the international financial architecture, these other fora need the support, not hostility, of the IMF. With respect to the relationship among the G20, the IMF and the World Bank, it would seem that the Bank has been the quicker of the two institutions to recognize the potential synergies and influence to be gained from extensive interaction with the G20.

Despite this, as Germain (2003) has noted, the current international architecture is perhaps more consensual than previously, in part because of this specialized division of labor (see Figure 2.2). There is also arguably greater public and academic appreciation of the issues confronting the international financial system than a decade ago. This enhanced appreciation has led to a more sophisticated dialogue regarding IMF policies – that is, the IMF's own enhanced transparency is leading to more widely shared expertise and resulting in strengthened accountability.

The issue is how to 'optimize' the guidance provided to the Fund by other groupings while ensuring appropriate accountability for all. The G7 has played the most important 'guidance' role for the Fund to date. However,

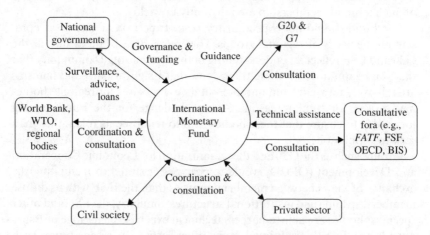

*Note:*   BIS: Bank for International Settlements; FATF: Financial Action Task Force; FSF: Financial Stability Forum; OECD: Organization for Economic Cooperation and Development; WTO: World Trade Organization.

*Figure 2.2    The IMF and the international financial architecture*

it cannot provide the Fund with great legitimacy as it only represents the interests of larger developed economies. In fact, it has been argued that guidance from the G7 has detracted from the Fund's legitimacy as its members have been seen to be pursuing their own agendas through the Fund (Meltzer 2000). Downplaying the G7 role in favor of a more representative grouping could, therefore, be an important step towards ensuring greater legitimacy and enhanced effectiveness of the IMF.

The G20 may be an effective consultative grouping able to offer valuable guidance to the Fund. G20 members account for around two-thirds of the world's population, nearly 90 percent of world GDP and almost 60 percent of the world's poor (Martin 2001). The G20 therefore represents a reasonable approximation of the IMF's membership, bringing in both developed and emerging market views and capturing well the growing influence of the fast-developing economies. As such, it is a potentially powerful tool for facilitating a dialogue between a representative group of member governments, for achieving agreement among key economies on issues of common interest, and for getting emerging concerns of these key economies (especially the non-G7 members) onto the IMF's radar. This has been shown by the G20's work in recent years identifying policy lessons for member countries in the areas of globalization, economic growth and poverty, much of which has the potential to be directly relevant to the activities of the Fund.[20]

Consequently, guidance from the G20 can support the legitimacy of Fund policies.

## CONCLUSION

It is a major achievement of the IMF, and the architects of the Bretton Woods system, that the Fund remains relevant today despite the momentous changes in the global economy since it was first established in 1944. The challenge for the Fund moving forward is to maintain that relevance in the face of significant changes to the underlying 'problems' which the institution was established to address.

There are, today, important tensions underlying the IMF's role. How does the Fund maximize its effectiveness in crisis prevention and resolution? How can it continue to improve its surveillance when so many of the recent initiatives are voluntary? Is there a case for a fresh pair of eyes? How does it best catalyse the actions of debtor countries and their creditors through sound policy advice? Does it have a role in helping members better communicate the desirability or particular policy choices? Is it possible to strengthen the capacity of the executive board to make hard decisions? Is it excessively exposed to individual countries? How can the right balance be struck between ensuring legitimacy (through measures to improve the overall architecture and governance) and improving effectiveness (through stronger surveillance and programs)? How can it ensure appropriate voice and effective representation of all members? What role can other groups, such as the G20, play in helping the Fund confront these issues?

The Fund's role has evolved. The challenges it faces going forward call for further evolution. The question is whether the international community – the Fund's shareholders – is up to the challenge.

# NOTES

1. We thank Michael Callaghan, Gordon de Brouwer, Ted Evans, Ken Henry, Neil Hyden, Maryanne Mrakovcic, Terry O'Brien and Alice Peterson for helpful comments. All errors remain our own.
2. See, for example, Feldstein (1998) and Meltzer (2000).
3. The response goes beyond the creation of exchange parities *per se* to include the other matters set out in Box 2.1 above.
4. For an interesting description of how this lending occurred during the Fund's first major financial crisis, see Boughton (2000).
5. However, as noted by Boughton (2000, p. 4), while the first SBA 'in which drawings were made conditional on the country adhering to specified policies was for Peru in 1954', this did not become standard practice until the 1960s.
6. See IMF *Annual Report* (2002).
7. The abandonment of the pegged exchange rate system was, however, a symptom of a broader problem manifest in recurring current account crises among the developed economies and successively weakening political will in favor of seeking IMF support.
8. This view is perhaps more widely held in Australia than in some other countries given its experimentation in the period after the Second World War with a wide range of exchange rate regimes. The Australian dollar was pegged to the pound sterling to November 1971, then to the US dollar to September 1974. It was subsequently pegged to the trade-weighted exchange rate – a basket peg – to November 1976, which became a crawling peg until December 1983, at which point the currency was allowed to float freely.
9. While the Fund's focus on structural issues expanded dramatically in the 1980s, it has been recognized that Fund conditionality with respect to structural issues may have 'overreached' in the 1990s. As a result, the Fund has recently emphasized that structural conditions should only be imposed in areas where an absence of structural reform will pose a threat to efforts to achieve macro stabilization.
10. See, for example, www.imf.org/external/standards/agency.htm.
11. See, for example, Stiglitz (2002). On whether the crises are really new, Boughton (2000) draws interesting parallels between the pressures on sterling associated with the 1956 Suez crisis and the experiences in Asia in 1997–98.
12. These criticisms have been made most recently in the case of the current IMF-supported program for Argentina.
13. This is particularly the case in the Asian crisis where, as noted in Parkinson et al. (2002), legitimate criticisms of the Fund's actions have not been matched by a willingness to acknowledge that some crisis-affected countries rejected warnings and refused repeated offers of assistance from the IMF until the crisis was in full flight.

14. This is by no means a new development. The IMF envisaged by J.M. Keynes was more along the lines of a global central bank, as are the lender of last resort models put forward since by Fischer (1999) and others.

15. While not established for the direct purpose of improving surveillance, the existence of the new Independent Evaluation Office (IEO) is a critical step in creating a culture which learns from experience and, as such, is likely to enhance the effectiveness of surveillance, albeit indirectly. As evidence of this, the IEO is soon to produce an evaluation of the Fund's actions during some of the early capital account crises. Not only should this help to throw some light on the validity of the 'old solutions for new problems' claim cited earlier, it may provide pointers to early signs of crisis and hence contribute to better surveillance.

16. It is somewhat ironic that the scope of surveillance – the keystone of crisis prevention – has been broadened at the same time that conditionality – the foundation of crisis resolution – has been narrowed.

17. While there is much to be gained from making such assessments public, this needs to be balanced against the likelihood of the Fund precipitating the very crisis it is attempting to prevent.

18. That said, it is worth noting that the IMF (with 184 members, and the United Nations (191), are both less representative than FIFA – Fédération internationale de football association – which has 204 members!

19. There has also been pressure in recent years for the development of regional institutions, particularly in the Asia-Pacific region. The appeal of such institutions is that they provide the scope to give regions a greater sense of ownership of outcomes in international crisis management and to fill gaps in the representativeness of the Fund, which may not be well placed to handle region-specific issues. Consequently, a regional body that plays a complementary role to the IMF can improve the credibility of the overall financial architecture and thus help reinforce the Fund's role. However, there is a danger that the development of regional institutions – particularly regional monetary funds – may have the opposite effect. If they lead to a situation of competing crisis managers or are seen as a soft alternative to the IMF, they risk undermining the credibility of the international financial architecture. (see Parkinson et al. 2002). The extent to which regional funds seek to replace, rather than complement the Fund, will reflect perceptions of the Fund's effectiveness and legitimacy.

20. See, for example, the results of the workshop on Globalization, Living Standards and Inequality held in Sydney in May 2002 (Gruen et al., 2002). A series of case studies on members' experiences with globalization have been published. Further work on globalization and the role of institution building in the financial sector is an ongoing topic of discussion at the G20.

# BIBLIOGRAPHY

Bordo, M.D. (1992), 'The Bretton Woods International Monetary System: an historical overview', NBER Working Paper no. 4033, National Bureau of Economic Research, Cambridge, MA.

Boughton, J. (2000), 'Northwest of Suez: the 1956 crisis and the IMF', Working Paper 00/192, International Monetary Fund, Washington, DC.

Boughton, J. (2001), *The Silent Revolution – The International Monetary Fund 1979–1989*, Washington, DC: International Monetary Fund.

Boughton, J. (2002), 'Why White, not Keynes? Inventing the post-war international monetary system', Working Paper 02/52, International Monetary Fund, Washington, DC, March.

Camdessus, M. (1996), 'Is the new Bretton Woods conceivable?', Address by Michel Camdessus, Société d'Economie Politique, Paris, 19 January, www.imf.org/external/np/sec/mds/1996/mds 9601.htm, accessed 4 March 2003.

Council on Foreign Relations (1999), *Safeguarding Prosperity in a Global Financial System: The Future International Architecture*, C. Hills and P. Peterson (Co-Chairs), M. Goldstein (Project Director), Washington, DC: Institute for International Economics.

Curtin, D. and S. Fisher (2000), 'Strengthening the international financial system: key issues', *World Development*, **28** (6), 1133–42.

de Brouwer, G. (2002), *The IMF and East Asia: A Changing Regional Financial Architecture*, Canberra, A.C.T.: Australia–Japan Research Centre.

Eichengreen, B. (1999), *Toward a New International Financial Architecture: A Practical Post Asia Agenda*, Washington, DC: Institute for International Economics.

Eichengreen, B. and P. Kenen (1994), 'Managing the world economy under the Bretton Woods system: an overview', in Kenen (ed.).

Feldstein, M. (1998), 'Refocusing the IMF', *Foreign Affairs*, **77** (2), March/April, 20–30.

Fischer, S. (1999), 'On the need for an international lender of last resort', revised version of a paper delivered at the joint luncheon of the American Economic Association and the American Finance Association, New York, 3 January, IMF.

Germain, R. (2003), 'Global financial governance and the problem of accountability: the role of the public sphere', paper delivered to the annual conference of the International Studies Association, Portland, OR, 25 February–1 March.

Gruen, D., T. O'Brien and J. Lawson (eds) (2002), 'Globalisation, living standards and inequality: recent progress and continuing challenges', proceedings of a conference held in Sydney, 27–8 May, J.S. McMillan Printing Group.

G20 (2003), *Economic Reform in this Era of Globalization: 16 Country Case Studies*, Washington, DC: Communications Development Incorporated.

Horsefield, J.K. (ed.) (1972), *The International Monetary Fund 1945–1965 – Twenty Years of International Monetary Cooperation*, Washington, DC: International Monetary Fund.

International Monetary Fund (IMF) (2002), *Annual Report*, Washington, DC: IMF.

Kenen, P. (ed.) (1994), *Managing the World Economy: Fifty Years After Bretton Woods*, Washington, DC: Institute for International Economics, September.

Kenen, P. (2001), *The International Financial Architecture: What's New? What's Missing?*, Washington, DC: Institute for International Economics, November.

Martin, P. (2001), 'Notes for an address by the Honorable Paul Martin, to the Royal Institute of International Affairs', Ottawa, 24 January, www.fin.gc.ca/news 01/01-009.html, accessed 4 March 2003.

Meltzer, A. (chair) (2000), 'International Financial Institution Advisory Commission Report', March, www.house.gov/jec/imf/meltzer.html, acccessed 4 March 2003.

Miyazawa, K. (1998), 'Towards a new international financial architecture', speech to the Foreign Correspondents Club of Japan, Tokyo, 15 December.

Parkinson, M., P. Garton and I. Dickson (2002), 'Regional financial arrangements: what role in the international financial architecture?', paper presented at the Conference on Regional Financial Arrangements in East Asia, Beijing University, 24–25 March.

Rugina, A.N. (2001), 'A reorganization plan of the International Monetary Fund as oriented toward conditions of stable equilibrium', *International Journal of Social Economics*, **28** (1), 141–53.

Sachs, J. (1995), 'Do we need an international lender of last resort?', Frank D. Graham Lecture, Princeton University, Princeton, NJ, April.

Schwartz, A. (1998), *'Time to terminate the ESF and the IMF'*, Foreign Policy Briefing No. 48, Cato Institute, Washington, DC.

Stiglitz. J. (2002), *Globalization and Its Discontents*, London: Penguin, Allen Lane.

30- 51

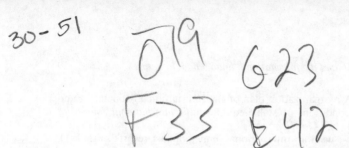

# 3. The future of the international monetary system: how long is the long run?

**John Murray**[1] / US, Canada, EMU, asia/

## INTRODUCTION

The world is getting smaller in the sense that the global economy is becoming ever more integrated and interconnected. Goods, services, capital and labor all flow more freely; and developments in any one region – whether good or bad – are more likely to influence activity elsewhere. The implications of this integrative process for the near-term evolution of the international monetary system have been the subject of considerable debate and disagreement. Many economists, however, have suggested that the long-run consequences are clear. Eventually the global economy will operate much like a traditional national economy – with a single universal currency, a single monetary authority, and a single (integrated) financial market. How one gets to this centralized state is less obvious.[2]

Fischer (2000) has noted that the transformation of the international monetary system will likely involve an intermediate step, in which the number of currencies in the world economy initially expands, after which the international monetary system will begin to shrink, until eventually only a single currency remains. Centrifugal forces will dominate in the short term, but centripetal forces will subsequently gain the upper hand, and the system will begin to collapse – much like the physical universe. At some point, in other words, economic gravity will take hold and the global economy will condense to a single integrated system.

Many observers believe that the gradual disappearance of national currencies will be matched by a similar concentration of international capital markets and the emergence of a single monetary/supervisory authority for the global economy. How responsibility for the oversight and operation of this supranational entity will be shared across numerous nation states is left open. Perhaps in the very long run, nation states as we presently know them will simply disappear. Recent experience would suggest, however, that this is another process in which the number of active participants is likely to grow much larger before it eventually collapses.

The present chapter has two primary objectives. The first is to determine where we are in terms of this evolutionary process. Is there any evidence that centripetal forces have gained the upper hand? The second objective is to gauge how long it might take us to reach the mythical long run. The next section provides a brief overview of the long-run forces that are currently at play in the global economy, and that favor greater integration and centralization in the international financial system.[3] The subsequent section follows with an analysis of recent economic developments and what they might tell us about the structural impediments that could inhibit the consolidation process. The penultimate section looks at the extent of financial integration in the North American economy, and uses this experience to draw conclusions about the speed with which the global economy is likely to shrink. The final section concludes.

The two main messages that emerge from the analysis are the following. First, the global economy is subject to significant structural rigidities that would severely limit its ability to operate effectively within a single, integrated, monetary system. Efforts to accelerate the consolidation process, therefore, through government intervention and legislated measures are likely to impose sizeable costs on the global economy. Second, while underlying economic forces may eventually push the global economy towards a centralized international monetary system, these forces appear to be operating very slowly. For example, although the Canadian and US economies are highly integrated, there is little (if any) evidence that the Canadian financial system is being effectively 'dollarized' or that Canadian capital markets are being drawn into the US vortex. Centralization, if it is occurring, is taking place at a glacial pace. This should not be regarded as cause for alarm, however. Agents are presumably acting in their own best interests, and there is no sign of widespread market failure, beyond the sort of structural rigidities and border effects that affect transactions between most national economies.

The deeper lesson that lies beneath these two messages is that policy independence should not be surrendered too readily. Any additional degree of freedom that policymakers have at their disposal should be closely guarded. Although harmonization and unification have considerable appeal based on micro-efficiency considerations, they are likely to carry significant macroeconomic costs in terms of forgone growth and excessive instability. Indeed, much of the financial instability that we have seen in recent years has been either caused or exacerbated by efforts to bind the international monetary system too tightly. The pressures that result from exogenous asymmetric shocks and significant structural differences often emerge in more costly and catastrophic forms when asset prices and private market mechanisms are not allowed to move freely. A more flexible and less interventionist approach to both currency arrangements and liquidity management could go a long way toward making the international monetary system more stable. Until such time that the preconditions for integration have been largely satisfied, a much lighter and more *laissez-faire* response is recommended. Some observers have suggested that the integrative process described above is actually endogenous, and that it is possible to accelerate the necessary structural adjustments by removing policymakers' room for maneuver. Experience to date, however, has not been encouraging.

## LONG-RUN TRENDS FAVORING CENTRALIZATION

The reason why so many economists believe we will eventually move to a more centralized or concentrated international financial system are easy to understand. Long-run trends, such as the growth of international trade and the increased mobility of capital and labor, have made national borders less relevant and made national economies more interdependent. International externalities have become more important in this context and the prospective benefits from greater cooperation have no doubt increased.

### Optimum Currency Considerations

The optimum currency criteria first described by Mundell in 1961 continue to serve as the benchmark against which most economists judge the appropriateness of alternative currency arrangements. According to these criteria, it is easy to see why the case for a common currency might have strengthened in recent years. The microeconomic benefits realized through reduced exchange rate risk and lower transactions costs clearly increase with the volume of trade, and the volume of world trade has grown at roughly twice the rate of world output for most of the post-war period. On these grounds alone, one would expect to see fewer national currencies over time.

In addition, one might expect that as economic integration and international trade increased, economies would become more similar, reducing the structural differences that might have justified separate monetary policy responses and divergent currency movements in the past.[4] Market liberalization and structural reform should also facilitate the adjustment process by making economies more flexible, thereby reducing the need for remedial macro policies. Increased factor mobility, more efficient financial markets, and greater flexibility in domestic prices and wages make flexible exchange rates redundant, providing another reason why, in the limit, separate and floating currencies might be both unnecessary and unhelpful.

**Consolidation in the Financial Sector**

Growth in world trade has been matched by an even more dramatic acceleration in international capital flows. Gross movements in financial capital across international borders now exceed the value of trade in goods and services by a wide margin. While active financial markets exist in most industrial countries, a large part of the money that is raised and the instruments that are traded in the global economy is concentrated in only two markets – London and New York. Technological advances in communication and the creation of new financial instruments have strengthened the linkages among financial markets around the world, but instead of diffusing trading activity across a greater number of countries they appear to have increased the dominance of these two centers. Significant advantages are obviously associated with agglomeration and close physical proximity. Bigger is clearly better when it comes to providing liquidity and attracting the sort of expertise that is necessary to maintain these markets and let them grow.

A similar trend has been observed with regard to financial institutions and the intermediation of household savings. While small, domestically owned, banks and insurance companies usually account for a significant share of national markets, large multinational conglomerates have become increasingly important. Concentration ratios in the financial sectors of most countries have increased dramatically, and foreign ownership has started to expand. The latter reflects, in part, the easing of foreign investment restrictions that limited foreign ownership in the past.

This trend towards greater concentration, increased foreign ownership, and ever larger international capital flows has three important implications for the efficiency and stability of the international financial system. First, it increases the susceptibility of domestic financial markets to external shocks, over which national authorities have little control. Second, it limits the ability of all but a few national authorities to effectively supervise and regulate their domestic financial markets. Third, it makes it more difficult to provide timely and effective emergency assistance when problems arise. Greater interdependence increases the need for collaborative effort both to strengthen financial supervision and to deal with any potential instability.

Local authorities do not have the resources or powers necessary to effectively monitor the activities of large complex financial institutions. Nor do they have ready access to the sort of capital that many of these institutions would require in times of crisis. National central banks are expected to serve as a lender of last resort in these situations, but if most of the assets and liabilities on an institution's balance sheet are denominated in foreign currencies, the central bank's ability to play this role could be severely constrained. The large volumes of short-term capital that can move into or out of a country at a moment's notice also pose a challenge in this regard.

Similar complications arise in terms of regulation. Although steps can be taken to help insulate domestic financial markets from external shocks, the size and strength of the international linkages often limit their effectiveness. The international financial system, one might argue, is only as strong as its weakest link. While this is obviously an exaggeration, the financial interdependencies are now large enough that every country has a stake in what its neighbors are doing. Independent action is therefore difficult, and a premium has to be put on cooperative activity and harmonization. All countries do not enter the process on an equal footing, however. Some countries, such as the United States and the United Kingdom, are expected to play a more important role and often take the lead in establishing the rules and guidelines that others are expected to follow.

## The Role of the International Financial Institutions (IFIs)

The interdependencies and systemic risks created by increased international capital mobility and greater concentration in the global financial system are not new. They were recognized by the architects of the Bretton Woods system, who established the International Monetary Fund to help deal with them, assisted by other international financial institutions such as the Bank for International Settlements (BIS), whose creation predates that of the IMF. While views differ on how successful these institutions have been in preventing or managing international financial instability, the scope and scale of their activities have clearly grown over time.

Some observers feel that the role of IFIs must continue to expand, reflecting the new realities of an interdependent world economy. Eventually the international financial system will gravitate towards a highly centralized structure in which a single central bank sets monetary policy for the entire world, a single supervisory body sets the rules and regulations for financial markets, and a single entity serves as a lender of last resort. National authorities might play a supporting role, but most of their responsibilities would be effectively subsumed by a multinational institution (or institutions) in which national authorities were one of many voices providing oversight and general direction.[5]

While this long-run vision may seem rather far-fetched and fanciful, some observers suggest that we have already gone a considerable distance in this direction. However, the existence of independent sovereign states does pose an important challenge for the creation of an effective supranational entity.

Sovereigns are understandably reluctant to cede any of their powers, even if the changing shape of the world economy makes their situation more analogous to that of a province or local government within a federal state. The economy that they are trying to manage no longer conforms to the national boundaries within which their powers are effective. It is similar, some would suggest, to an individual town or city trying to conduct monetary policy and establish a regulatory framework for the rest of a country.

Since nation states are not likely to disappear in the near future, the chances of moving towards a centralized, supranational, institution charged with these sorts of powers might seem remote. Nevertheless, some important precedents can be noted. First, and most evidently, there is the recent launch of the euro and the creation of the European Monetary Union (EMU). Twelve countries, perhaps soon to be 15 or 25, voluntarily abandoned their national currencies and transferred responsibility for setting monetary policy to a multilateral institution over which they exert little political control.

A second example is the IMF. It has been assuming an increasingly important role both as an international supervisor – via its Article IVs, the Reports on the Observance of Standards and Codes (ROSCs) and the Financial Sector Assessment Programs (FSAPs) – and as a lender of last resort. Recent efforts to define these roles more precisely and to establish credible limits, especially with regard to its lending powers, have met with mixed success, and there is clearly support in many quarters for a more ambitious mandate. Work relating to the creation of a Sovereign Debt Restructuring Mechanism (SDRM) is perhaps the most notable in this regard. While the SDRM proposal failed to gain the unanimous support of the G7 and the broader IMF membership, the initiative attracted considerable sympathy and was given more serious consideration than many observers had expected. Indeed, work continues and supporters still hope that something like the SDRM will be implemented within the next few years. Similar, though more informal, agreements are also becoming an important part of the international supervisory and regulatory system under the auspices of the BIS and the various committees that are affiliated with it. These include groups such as the Financial Stability Forum (FSF), the International Organization of Securities Commissions (IOSCO), and the Basle Committee.

The implied transfer of sovereign rights that is inherent in the SDRM is analogous to the derogation that has occurred in the context of the World Trade Organization. In the case of the WTO, countries have formally agreed to accept the decisions of an international body and to waive their rights to sovereign immunity. Another example is the International Court of Justice at The Hague. In short, there is already ample evidence that national rights and institutions have started to bend in response to the new international reality, and that the process of centralization is likely to continue. The only question that remains is how far has it gone and what steps, if any, should be taken to reinforce it.

# IS THE WORLD READY TO BE CENTRALIZED?

The fact that the global economy has gone some distance towards greater centralization and concentration does not mean that it is ready for a rapid advance in this direction. It is one thing to argue that much of what we now regard as national responsibilities for monetary policy and financial sector regulation may eventually be ceded to a multilateral authority. It is another to suggest that it should happen immediately or be vigorously promoted by political action. Some useful lessons can be learned from recent developments in Asia, Europe and the emerging market economies in terms of the present state of national economies and how amenable they might be to more centralized solutions. Just because something is inevitable – or likely to obtain in the long run – does not mean that one should enthusiastically embrace it. (Death and taxes are obvious examples.)

**Lessons from Europe and EMU**

The euro was launched in January 1999, with 12 countries eventually participating in the new economic and monetary union.[6] Although separate national currencies would continue to circulate until January 2002, the euro became the official currency of these countries as soon as it was introduced, and monetary policy became a shared responsibility conducted through the new European Central Bank. Three other members of the European Union, Denmark, Sweden and the United Kingdom, decided to delay their entry into EMU, but are still expected to join in the near future, while the ten so-called accession countries are expected to join within the next five years. Once all 25 countries have joined, a significant portion of the world's economic activity and currency will be concentrated in the EMU area.

Four years might not represent a long enough timeframe within which to judge the success of the EMU experiment. Nevertheless, certain tentative conclusions can be drawn which might be useful for our analysis. Indeed, the fact that three potential members have decided to remain outside EMU for the last four years makes the experiment even more interesting, since two of the countries have continued to operate under a flexible exchange rate while the third has pegged its exchange rate to the euro. That said, there have been surprisingly few rigorous *ex post* examinations of the European experience.

Certain benefits were bound to be realized by replacing 12 currencies with one. Estimates of net gain in terms of reduced transactions costs vary, but typically run from 0.25 to 0.5 percent of GDP. Other benefits, such as gains from reduced exchange rate uncertainty and a more competitive price system across Europe, are harder to gauge. However, interesting work by economists such as Rose (2000) and Frankel and Rose (2002) suggests that the growth in intraregional trade and investment following the adoption of a common currency could be very large – in the order of 300 percent!

Simple comparisons between the trade performance of EMU members and that of non-members are generally less encouraging. Trade among member countries appears to have *declined* over the past four years, both as a percentage of GDP and as a percentage of total trade with member and non-member countries. Other factors were no doubt at work, and it would be imprudent to draw any strong conclusions. In addition, four years is too short a period for all the long-run benefits to be realized. Nevertheless the early results suggest that some of the advantages of a common currency might have been oversold (see Figure 3.1). The fact that Denmark, Sweden and the United Kingdom have enjoyed comparable or higher growth rates in trade and output over this period is also noteworthy, although it is important to remember that this not a controlled experiment.

Some difficulties were anticipated with EMU from a macro perspective since many of the countries, particularly along the perimeter of continental Europe, were at different stages of development and had disparate structural characteristics. It is probably fair to say, however, that the experience

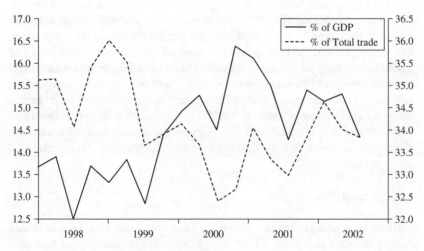

*Figure 3.1   Intra-euroland trade (€bn)*

in this regard has been more difficult than most of EMU's supporters had imagined. The one-size-fits-all approach to monetary policy has proven awkward for almost all of the participants – too tight for some and too easy for others. (There is even some debate as to whether it has been correct on average.) Ironically, it has been the countries at the center – Europe's old guard – that appear to have suffered the most. Some of this disappointing performance can be credited to an unfortunate string of events, such as the collapse of the high-tech bubble, volatile world oil prices and rising geopolitical tensions. All these shocks were endured by other industrial countries, however, without the same economic consequences. More varied and flexible monetary policy responses might have improved the situation.

The costs related to a common monetary policy were not expected to be very large when EMU was conceived. Structural differences among the member countries were not regarded as very significant, and authorities hoped that moving to a common currency would help drive the market liberalization and structural adjustment process. Structural differences among the various regions of the United States were thought to be just as large as those in Europe, and yet it did not seem to experience any serious problems because of its one-size-fits-all monetary policy. If factor mobility within Europe could be improved, and made comparable to that of the United States, customized monetary policies for each EMU member should no longer be necessary.

The structural rigidities and market impediments in Europe are evidently more serious than many had assumed. Moreover, there is nothing to suggest that the reform process has been accelerated as a result of EMU. Some progress has been made in a few countries. But the improvements have not been noticeably faster than those in other countries, outside EMU; nor have they been any faster than in the pre-EMU period. In some cases, the process appears to have gone in reverse with additional restrictions and market impediments being introduced. This is not to suggest that the EMU experiment should be abandoned or that it will not prove successful. It is still early days. The lesson that one can take from the first four years is that the preconditions for a successful EMU introduction were not as favorable as some had hoped, and that the adjustment processes associated with moving to a common currency are perhaps much longer than some had anticipated.

**Lessons from Asia**

Europe, of course, is not the only region to experience economic difficulty during the past few years. Many of the countries in eastern and southern Asia experienced a major financial crisis, and Japan has suffered through more than a decade of limited growth and (more recently) deflation. Opinions differ on the reasons for Japan's disappointing performance and the measures that might be taken to improve the situation. Two aspects of this painful period are nevertheless worth highlighting for present purposes.

The first concerns the special status that Japan enjoyed immediately prior to the sharp economic downturn in the late 1980s. Japan was regarded as a country that could do no wrong – a country that had found the formula for assured growth. While potential problems were noted, such as its restrictive trade and labor market practices, Japan was viewed as an innovative and highly flexible economy that would soon overcome the problems posed by falling real estate and stock prices. As in Europe, under somewhat different circumstances, this confidence appears to have been misplaced. Structural rigidities and market impediments seem to have been more significant than originally thought, and Japan has yet to exit from its deflationary trap.

A similar situation developed in Hong Kong following the 1997–98 Asian financial crisis. Although Hong Kong is still regarded as the proto-typical market economy, with flexible prices and wages, and a minimum of government rules and regulations, it has not been able to reverse the deflationary pressures that have depressed its output growth. Unlike Japan, which operates under a flexible exchange rate, Hong Kong has fixed the value of its exchange rate to the US dollar by means of a currency board. When domestic economic activity and local real estate prices collapsed in the late 1990s, the only means by which the necessary depreciation in the real exchange rate could be achieved was through a painful and protracted decline in domestic prices and wages. Once again, however, it appears that domestic prices were more rigid than expected, inhibiting the adjustment process and resulting in a significant drop in employment and output.

Another lesson that can be drawn from this period concerns the dangers of piecemeal or conservative policy actions in the presence of deflationary pressures. A recent study by Ahearne et al. (2002) at the US Federal Reserve noted that few, if any, economists predicted the severity or timing of the Japanese downturn. Once it had started, however, authorities would have been well advised to undertake more aggressive countercyclical measures. The risks associated with operating an economy close to the zero-inflation threshold are extremely skewed, the authors observed. The costs of using too little monetary medicine early in the downturn, and failing to avoid a liquidity trap, are much higher than those associated with overstimulating the economy and pushing inflation above its target level for a short period of time. There is an obvious advantage, therefore, to adopting a more aggressive policy stance and ensuring that deflationary pressures do not become entrenched. The latter requires prompt and decisive action, however. (Something that large committees are not known for.)

In summary, therefore, it appears that even the most flexible economies suffer from serious price and wage rigidities, and that independent policy action in the form of aggressive monetary easing and flexible exchange rate is often needed to offset negative shocks. The macroeconomic benefits associated with a floating exchange rate should be carefully preserved and not traded too readily for microeconomic benefits of a fixed exchange rate.

## The Special Needs of Emerging Market Economies

The international financial system should not be designed solely to accommodate the needs of industrial countries, of course. Even if the necessary conditions were met for a single currency and single monetary authority among the developed economies, it is unlikely that such an arrangement would suit the needs of the rest of the global community. Emerging market economies (EMEs) and less-developed countries are, by definition, at different stages of development from their industrial counterparts and therefore subject to different shocks and economic forces. Faster productivity growth in the tradables sector of an EME, for example, often leads to a real appreciation in its exchange rate. If the exchange rate is tied to that of another developed country, the only way the appreciation can be achieved is through higher domestic inflation. But if the EME is part of a currency union, and monetary policy is governed by a strict inflation target, higher inflation in the EME must be offset with lower inflation elsewhere, constraining growth and reducing economic welfare. In the absence of other effective stabilization tools that could substitute for an independent monetary policy, it is difficult to imagine a single currency system meeting the needs of all its participants, unless they have similar structures and are at a similar stage of development.

EMEs may also be special in another sense, making a speedy transition to open international capital markets unlikely. The financial crises of the 1990s raised serious questions about the wisdom of rapid financial market liberalization, and gave renewed legitimacy to the notion of 'sequencing' and temporary constraints on short-term capital flows. Through much of the 1990s, the common perception among most industrial country economists and IFI officials was that financial market liberalization should be promoted at every opportunity, and that capital controls were inevitably costly or ineffective. The positive experience of Chile, coupled with the unfortunate consequences of premature liberalization elsewhere, have done much to reverse this view, such that temporary controls on short-term capital flows have now become an important part of the new orthodoxy.

The precepts that McKinnon so effectively outlined in 1973 have been redis-covered 30 years later.

Another feature of the international financial system that economists expect to observe in the (very) long run involves the creation of a single supervisory authority, as well as a true international lender of last resort. The recent attention given to codes and standards might be regarded as a first step in this direction, along with efforts to establish the SDRM. Some observers would also like to see additional lending powers granted to the IMF, making it a more effective lender of last resort.[7] Pushing any of these initiatives too far and too fast would be a mistake, however. The focus on codes and standards is obviously appropriate and represents an important step in crisis prevention, since it is pitched at a sufficiently high level that EMEs can still adjust them to their specific needs. Trying to impose an overly prescriptive and precise set of codes and standards on all countries would, in contrast, create considerable risks.

The same thing can be said of efforts to create a more ambitious inter-national lender of last resort. While there are some economists who favor free banking in a domestic context, and therefore question the need for a lender of last resort, most people agree that this is an effective and useful function. There are risks, however, in extending this experience to the inter-national arena as a solution for EME financial crises. While 'constructive ambiguity' and a notion of lending freely but at a penalty rate might have some merit when applied to domestic banking, international financial crises present a number of unique challenges that make the lender of last resort role less practicable. Most importantly, the IMF operates under a number of constraints that its domestic counterpart does not. For example, it cannot demand collateral for any funds that it advances; nor can it ensure that policy recommendations are implemented or replace management if it is unhappy with the results. Differentiating between liquidity and solvency problems is also arguably more difficult when one is discussing countries as opposed to individual institutions. Indeed, experience has shown that the key to achieving an effective and timely resolution of crises in an inter-national setting is often to limit the amount of official lending in a clear and credible manner, as opposed to holding out the prospect of much larger but less certain funding.[8]

The common thread linking each of these examples is that the world economy is very diverse, and that visions of an international financial system structured along the lines of a national economy are far removed from the present reality. Any move to a single currency, an integrated finan-cial system, a single supervisory authority, and a true international lender of last resort will have to wait on more substantive structural change and follow a more evolutionary route.

## IS A CENTRALIZED SYSTEM INEVITABLE?

Some appreciation of just how long the convergence to a centralized system might take can be gained by examining the relationship between Canada and the United States. The Canadian–US experience is instructive for several reasons. First, Canada and the United States are two of the most highly integrated industrial economies in the world. More than 45 percent of Canada's GDP is exported, and more than 85 percent of its exports go to the United States.[9] Second, domestic and foreign capital have been free to move in and out of Canada for most of its 136-year history. The only notable exceptions to the free movement of capital have been (i) the temporary controls that Canada imposed during the First and Second World Wars; (ii) an upper limit on the percentage of foreign assets that Canadians are allowed to hold in tax exempt registered retirement plans; and (iii) the selective restrictions that Canada has imposed on foreign ownership in a few politically sensitive industries. It is also worth noting that Canada and the United States have had a free trade agreement in place since 1989.[10] In other words, the strong and essentially unrestricted economic relationship that ties these two North American countries bears a close resemblance to the type of integrated system that economists like Cooper, Mundell, McKinnon and Fischer have envisaged for the world economy at some distant date. The Canadian–US experience might therefore serve as a useful test case or guide as to whether the pressures for a centralized international monetary system are as strong as some observers think.

As some readers might know, an active debate has been raging in Canada for the last few years concerning the desirability of moving to a fixed exchange rate system with the United States. Canada currently operates under a flexible exchange rate and has done so for most of the post-war period, making it the most loyal supporter of flexible exchange rates in the industrialized world. Many Canadians, however, are convinced that forming a currency union with the United States, or moving to some other permanently fixed arrangement (such as unilateral dollarization), would yield significant benefits. Others maintain that any official decision to move in this direction is largely irrelevant since informal dollarization is already occurring, owing to Canada's close ties with the United States. Many Canadians, in other words, are convinced that the inexorable gravitation forces that were described in earlier sections of this chapter are already in motion in North America.

The material that is reported below is drawn from a larger study (see Murray and Powell 2003) that was recently conducted to shed some light on this contentious issue. Although a number of economists, journalists and other interested observers have confidently asserted that the dollarization process is well underway, no persuasive evidence has been offered to substantiate these claims.

**The US Dollar as a Unit of Account**

The first stage of the study focused on the use of the US dollar as a unit of account in Canada. Representatives at the Bank of Canada's five regional offices were asked to conduct a survey during 2002 in which 400 representative firms were asked the following four questions:

1. Does your firm quote prices to Canadian customers in Canadian dollars, US dollars, or both currencies?
2. Does your firm quote prices to foreign customers in Canadian dollars, US dollars, the local currency (if different from the US dollar), or some combination of currencies?
3. Does your firm quote salaries and wages in Canadian dollars, US dollars, or both currencies?
4. Are your financial statements quoted in Canadian dollars, US dollars, or both currencies?

Before the results were collected, there was a general presumption that most sales to foreigners (question 2) would be priced in US dollars, and that a smaller, but significant, portion of firms would also use the US dollar for sales to their Canadian customers, as well as for paying salaries and wages, and preparing their financial statements. The final results are reported in Table 3.1. A surprisingly small percentage of firms used the US dollar for anything except pricing sales to foreign customers. Even here, however, the use of the US dollar was much smaller than most had assumed. Previous studies by Krugman (1984), Black (1990) and others have highlighted the dominance of the US dollar as a world currency, and noted that many

Table 3.1   Percentage of Canadian firms quoting prices in Canadian dollars and foreign currencies

|  | CAD | USD | Both | Local |
|---|---|---|---|---|
|  | | Total responses (%) | | |
| Sales to Canadians | 81 | 5 | 14 | – |
| Sales to foreigners | 24 | 52 | 20 | 4 |
| Financial statements | 88 | 5 | 7 | – |
| Salaries and wages | 99 | 0 | 1 | – |

international transactions are denominated in US dollars even if neither party is American.

While the survey results reported in Table 3.1 simply provide a snapshot at a particular point in time, and give no information on whether use of the US dollar has been growing over time, they are nevertheless comforting (at least from a Bank of Canada perspective) and suggest that the US dollar has a very limited role in the Canadian economy. More than 80 percent of all Canadian firms surveyed used the Canadian dollar to quote prices to Canadian customers. The percentage of firms preparing financial statements and quoting salaries and wages in Canadian dollars was 88 and 99 percent, respectively. Aside from some professional athletes and a few senior executives who spend most of their time working in the United States, there is very little evidence to suggest that Canadians are regularly paid in US dollars.

### The US Dollar as a Medium of Exchange

Hard data on the extent to which the US dollar is used in Canada as a medium of exchange are also limited. While statistics are available on the value of US dollar deposits held at Canadian financial institutions, no Canadian agency collects information on the amount of US currency that Canadians actually hold or the extent to which it is used for transactions in Canada. Since most Canadians live within 100 kilometres of the US border, and day trips for shopping in the United States are common, it seems reasonable to assume that most of the US dollars held on deposit or as currency would be used for transactions outside Canada.

Figure 3.2 plots the US dollar deposits of Canadian residents as a percentage of M3, a measure of broad money. Although the percentage has been rising steadily since the early 1990s, no doubt reflecting the increased trade between Canada and the United States, it remains below 10 percent and has yet to regain the levels reached in the 1970s and early 1980s. Some sense of how significant these numbers are can be gained by comparing them to those of other countries that are truly dollarized. Argentina, for example, just prior to its 2001 collapse, had more than 70 percent of the deposits in its banking system denominated in US dollars.

Figure 3.3 reports the same M3 data as Figure 3.2, but adjusts the numbers for the growth in Canadian–US trade. Here the downward trend in dollarization is even more evident.

Another way of assessing the importance of the US dollar as a medium of exchange in Canada can be obtained from the Currency and Monetary Instruments Reports (CMIR) that the US Customs Agency has prepared since 1980. These reports are confidential, but the information is

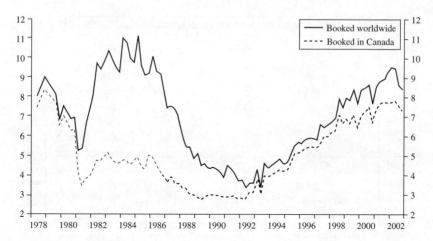

*Figure 3.2    US$ currency deposits of Canadian residents as a percentage of M3 (expressed in Canadian dollars)*

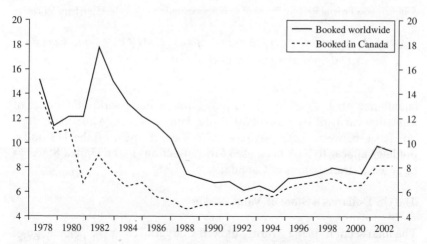

*Figure 3.3    US$ currency deposits of Canadian residents as a percentage of trade with the United States (expressed in Canadian dollars)*

occasionally made available to researchers. The purpose of the reports is to monitor individuals and businesses transporting more than $10,000 in cash across the US border. While there is reason to believe that the data are far from complete, one can nevertheless generate an approximate measure of how much US currency Canadians hold at different points in time by cumulating these inflows and outflows. Figure 3.4 plots the

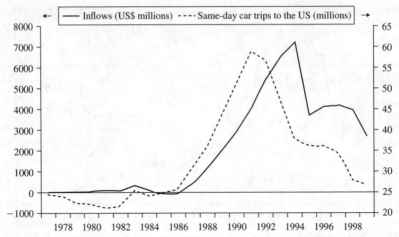

*Note:* Currency and Monetary Instrument Reports were collected by the US Customs Service.

*Sources:* US Federal Reserve Board of Governors; Statistics Canada – Car Trips VI29491.

*Figure 3.4    Cumulative net US dollar inflows (CMIR data) into Canada and same-day car trips to the United States*

cumulative net US dollar inflows into Canada along with the number of same-day car trips by Canadians to the United States. While the correspondence between these two series is not exact, most of the US dollar holdings appear to have been used for transactions in the United States as opposed to transactions in Canada.

## The US Dollar as a Store of Value

The final section of the Murray–Powell study looked at the percentage of Canadian financial assets and liabilities that were denominated in US dollars. Estimates of the currency distribution of asset holdings in Canadian mutual funds and pension plans over the 1985–2001 period are shown in Table 3.2 and Figure 3.5. While the numbers do suggest a steady upward trend, some of the increase can be credited to a change in government regulations limiting the foreign content of tax-exempt investment funds. Even if attention is restricted to investment vehicles that are not subject to any limitations, there is an evident home-country bias in the asset composition of most Canadians' portfolios. The proportion of US and other foreign currency-denominated assets is well below the efficient levels recommended

*Table 3.2   Holdings in equities and bonds of mutual, pension and other pooled funds ( distribution of portfolio assets by currency of denomination\*, %)*

| Currency group | 1997 | 1998 | 1999 | 2000 |
|---|---|---|---|---|
| Canadian dollar | 75 | 72 | 68 | 67 |
| US dollar | 13 | 15 | 17 | 19 |
| Other currency | 6 | 7 | 7 | 9 |
| Unidentified currency\*\* | 5 | 5 | 8 | 4 |
| Total (rounded) | 100 | 100 | 100 | 100 |

*Notes:*
  \*Canadian stocks and bonds are considered 100% Canadian dollars and US stocks are considered 100% US dollars.
\*\*Contains foreign assets only.

*Source:*   Statistics Canada.

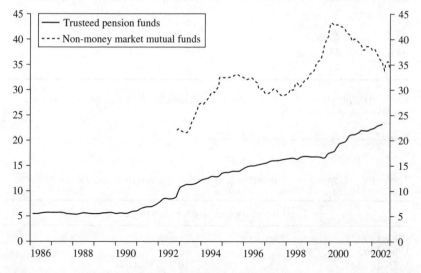

*Figure 3.5   Trusteed pension funds and mutual funds (% foreign content)*

by a simple capital asset model. It is also substantially lower than those observed in several other industrial countries – testament perhaps to the efficiency of the Canadian financial market.

Concern has also been expressed in the past about the supposed 'hollowing out' of Canadian financial markets. A number of people in the financial community have suggested that Canadian fixed income and equity markets are gradually disappearing, and that most of the funds raised by Canadian businesses are (i) denominated in US dollars, and (ii) obtained in the United States. Both the Canadian dollar and Canadian financial markets, according to these commentators, have fallen into disfavor. Tables 3.3 and 3.4 contain some data that cast doubt on this popular but mistaken view. The percentage of outstanding bonds issued by Canadian corporations in Canadian dollars has remained essentially unchanged since 1985, while the percentage of Canadian corporate equity issues placed abroad has moved within a very low and narrow range of 3–12 percent since the mid-1960s.

Most of the information provided here will be of direct interest only to a few Canadians who have participated in the dollarization debate. There

*Table 3.3    Distribution of bonds outstanding issued by Canadian corporations (%)*

|  | CAD | USD | EuroCAD* | EuroUSD | Other |
|---|---|---|---|---|---|
| 1985 | 47 | 23 | 7 | 16 | 7 |
| 1990 | 46 | 17 | 14 | 8 | 15 |
| 1995 | 43 | 35 | 8 | 6 | 8 |
| 2000 | 47 | 37 | 3 | 9 | 5 |
| 2001 | 44 | 42 | 2 | 7 | 5 |

*Note:*   *EuroCAD are CAD issues placed outside of Canada; EuroUSD are USD issues placed outside the United States.

*Source:*   *Bank of Canada Review*, Table K8.

*Table 3.4    Canadian corporate equity issues placed abroad: 1955–2000 (%)*

| | Total net corporate stock issues placed abroad (%) |
|---|---|
| 1955–1960 | 1 |
| 1961–1965 | 3 |
| 1966–1970 | 10 |
| 1971–1975 | 3 |
| 1976–1980 | 3 |
| 1981–1985 | 3 |
| 1986–1990 | 6 |
| 1991–1995 | 12 |
| 1996–2000 | 7 |

*Source:*   Bank of Canada.

is, however, a broader and more relevant message for the purposes of the present chapter. It is the following. Even in the case of Canada and the United States, two of the most highly integrated and compatible industrial economies in the world, financial system centralization seems to be proceeding at a slow pace. The gravitation pull of US markets has not had a noticeable impact on Canada's ability to maintain a separate currency or conduct an independent monetary policy. Nor has it led to a noticeable hollowing out of Canadian financial markets, despite the (virtual) absence of currency and capital controls. Indeed, questions could be raised about whether the process of financial system centralization is occurring at all.

## CONCLUSION

The international financial system may eventually gravitate towards a more centralized structure in which there is a single currency, a single supervisory and regulatory authority, and a single lender of last resort. The information reported above would seem to suggest that if this is the case, it will be a long time in coming – without more active measures by governments to bring it about. Experience in industrial countries and emerging market economies casts doubt on the usefulness of more interventionist and statist measures, however. It is not obvious that the preconditions for a move to a more centralized system have been met, or that such a move is even necessary.

A more centralized international financial system is neither desirable nor inevitable – at least for the foreseeable future. Certain regions may decide that it is in their best interest to move to such a system and, as EMU has shown, clearly have the means to do so. While there may be strong economic arguments supporting these efforts, the available evidence would seem to indicate that this is often done primarily for political rather than economic reasons. There is little evidence to support the claims that greater centralization is necessary for either efficiency or stability reasons.

## NOTES

1. The views expressed in this chapter are those of the author. No responsibility for them should be attributed to the Bank of Canada. The author would like to thank his colleagues for their many helpful suggestions and acknowledge the valuable assistance of Suzanne Le Blanc and Francine Rioux.
2. See, for example, Cooper (1984, 1990), McKinnon (1988), Eichengreen (1999) and Fischer (2000).
3. The term 'international financial system' will be used in a broad sense throughout the chapter, referring to all the financial arrangements that characterize the global economy including the international monetary system.

4.  Krugman (1993), in contrast, has suggested that increased trade might lead to greater specialization, thereby magnifying interregional differences and making independent policy responses *more* important.
5.  A country's influence over the IFI would be determined, ideally, by its relative importance in the global economy, and need not bear a close relationship to its current standing in the IMF or the BIS.
6.  Greece did not join EMU until 2001.
7.  See Fischer (2000).
8.  See Haldane and Kruger (2002) and Murray (2004).
9.  Canada also imports more US goods and services than any other country, and is its most important trading partner.
10. This agreement was extended to Mexico in 1994 and was used as a model for elements of the World Trade Organization.

# BIBLIOGRAPHY

Ahearne, A., J. Gagnon, J. Haltmaier and S. Kamin (2002), 'Preventing deflation: lessons from Japan's experience in the 1990s', Board of Governors of the Federal Reserve System, International Discussion Paper No. 729, Washington, DC, June.

Bailliu, J. and J. Murray (2003), 'Exchange rate regimes in emerging markets', *Bank of Canada Review*, Winter 2002–03, Ottawa: Bank of Canada, pp. 17–27.

Black, S. (1990), 'The international use of currencies', in Y. Suzuki, J. Miyake and M. Okabe (eds), *The Evolution of the International Monetary System*, Proceedings of a conference organized by the Institute of Monetary and Economic Studies, Bank of Japan, Tokyo: University of Tokyo Press, pp. 175–94.

Cooper, R. (1984), 'A monetary system for the future', *Foreign Affairs*, **63**, Fall, 166–84.

Cooper, R. (1990), 'What future for the international monetary system?', in Y. Suzuki, J. Miyake and M. Okabe (eds), *The Evolution of the International Monetary System*, Proceedings of a conference organized by the Institute of Monetary and Economic Studies, Bank of Japan, Tokyo: University of Tokyo Press, pp. 277–99.

Eichengreen, B. (1999), *Toward a New International Financial Architecture: A Practical Post-Asia Agenda*, Washington, DC: Institute for International Economics.

Fischer, S. (2000), 'On the need for an international lender of last resort', Essays in International Economics, Department of Economics, Princeton University, No. 220, November.

Frankel, J. and A. Rose (2001), 'Exchange rate regimes: is the bipolar view correct?', *Journal of Economic Perspectives*, **15** (2), Spring, 3–24.

Frankel, J. and A. Rose (2002), 'An estimate of the effect of a common currency on trade and income', *Quarterly Journal of Economics*, **117** (2), 437–66.

Haldane, A. and M. Kruger (2002), 'The resolution of international financial crises: private finance and public funds', *Bank of Canada Review*, Winter 2001–02, Ottawa: Bank of Canada, pp. 3–13.

Krugman, P. (1984), 'The international role of the dollar: theory and practice', in J.F.O. Bilson and R.C. Marston (eds), *Exchange Rate Theory and Practice*, Chicago: University of Chicago Press, pp. 261–80.

Krugman, P. (1993), 'Lessons of Massachusetts for EMU', in F. Torres and F. Giavazzi (eds), *Adjustment and Growth in the European Monetary Union*, New York: Cambridge University Press, pp. 241–61.

McKinnon, R. (1973), *Money and Capital in Economic Development*, Washington, DC: Brookings Institution.

McKinnon, R. (1988), 'Monetary and exchange rate policies for international stability: a proposal', *Journal of Economic Perspectives*, **2**, 83–103.

Mundell, R. (1961), 'The theory of optimum currency areas', *American Economic Review*, **53**, 657–65.

Murray, J. (2004), 'Comments' on 'Reflections on moral hazard and private sector involvement in the resolution of emerging market financial crises', in A. Haldane, *Fixing Financial Crises in the 21st Century*, proceedings of a conference hosted by the Bank of England, July 2002, London: Routledge International Studies in Money and Banking.

Murray, J. and J. Powell (2003), 'Dollarization in Canada: the buck stops there', Bank of Canada Technical Report, No. 90, Ottawa: Bank of Canada.

Rose, A. (2000), 'One money, one market: the effects of common currencies on trade', *Economic Policy: A European Forum*, **30**, April, 7–33.

PART II


The Future Source of Finance for the
Developing World and the Future of
the Sovereign Debt Market

# 4. Emerging market crises: exchange rate regimes, bond restructurings and the IMF

**Michael Buchanan**

## INTRODUCTION

The spread of crises in emerging markets and the steps taken to deal with them have an importance that goes beyond the emerging markets asset class. While the major economies may not soon repeat the UK's call to the International Monetary Fund's emergency hotline in 1976, the type of fast-moving, virulent and contagious crises the IMF has recently dealt with have had substantial impacts on global markets. These crises, and the IMF's response to them, have had an impact on not just investors and multinational corporations with direct exposure to the crisis countries, but also investors and corporates focused entirely on the major economies.

Perhaps the most dramatic impact of recent IMF policies on global markets came in the summer of 1998. The IMF's program in Russia was unable to prevent a chaotic devaluation and debt default. Financial markets, which had banked on a blank cheque for 'too nuclear to fail' Russia, lost heavily and cut back risk across the board. This was part of the set of shocks that led to large upheavals in the global financial system and fears of severe disruption to the US payments system, and prompted a substantial increase in global liquidity (including through a cut in US interest rates). Other successful and unsuccessful IMF bailouts have also affected global capital markets in a number of ways. The links can work through direct trade channels, through the balance sheets of major global banks exposed to emerging markets, and through risk appetite and credit spreads more generally. Reducing the frequency of these emerging market crises would help reduce risk in the global financial system, and reduce asset price volatility.

The IMF was on the front-line not just in Russia, but also during the Asian crisis, the Argentine default and more recently in Brazil and

Turkey. While the Asian countries that followed IMF orthodoxy rebounded strongly, so did other more maverick countries that imposed capital controls. While we find the experiences of Malaysia and Russia relatively unhelpful in assessing the merits of a more heterodox approach, we see more encouragement from Taiwan. The situation in Latin America and Turkey suggests another worrying element of the IMF orthodoxy. The IMF programs have induced countries to take on more FX (foreign exchange)-denominated or FX-linked debt. This comes partly from the direct effect of the IMF cash (which often substitutes for domestic liabilities – including local debt and local bank deposits). But it also comes through the push to keep monetary policy very tight to fight inflation. This pushes up local interest rates and encourages the government to issue in FX (many commentators have suggested that the IMF's initials stand for 'It's Mainly Fiscal' due to the IMF's preoccupation with fiscal policy, but we would suggest that 'It's Mainly FX' might also be appropriate!). This increase in FX debt leaves the economies much more vulnerable. Sometimes this can help, as Turkey in particular is finding out now.[1] But it does raise the volatility for the economy as a whole, and bondholders in particular. Hence while one source of risk has been removed in many emerging markets – that of a fixed exchange rate coupled with an open capital account – the continued reliance on FX debt leaves the asset class vulnerable to reduced global liquidity.

The IMF had put forward some new and highly controversial suggestions for how to respond to future crises and to make them less likely, but has since backed away from them. The last version of the now-mothballed IMF plan would require changes to the legal structure of financial markets in all major jurisdictions around the world, and would unilaterally alter creditor rights on existing instruments. This bold proposal received a green light from the world's finance ministers at the IMF annual meetings in September 2002, but was subsequently shunted off into the background. We stick to our long-held view that this approach is unlikely to succeed, although if the restructuring process in Argentina leads to increasingly messy litigation, the Sovereign Debt Restructuring Mechanism (SDRM) could return in the next year or so. Regardless, we would prefer to see more evolutionary progress on the procedures to be used to restructure sovereign debt under the existing legal frameworks. In the longer term, the solution should also involve a greater emphasis on developing local capital markets.

We look below at how the IMF's role in financial crisis has changed, and whether it is helping to offset or to exacerbate the recent spate of emerging markets crises. We also look at the role of capital controls in reducing the risk of crises, and whether the IMF's proposed alternative solution is the right one.

## IMF CREATED TO AVOID THE PROTECTIONISM AND DEVALUATIONS OF THE INTER-WAR YEARS . . .

The IMF was conceived at a UN conference at Bretton Woods, New Hampshire in the closing stages of the Second World War (July 1944), and came into being the following year. The main catalyst for the birth of the institution was to reduce the likelihood of 'beggar-thy-neighbor' policies adopted during the inter-war years, in which countries tried to protect their FX reserves by tit-for-tat devaluations and restrictions on imports, but succeeded only in driving down world trade and economic growth. The basic plan was to create a revolving fund that would allow current account adjustment to take place gradually, with surplus countries allowing deficit countries to borrow while they undertook reforms to gradually restore balance of payments equilibrium. This took place against a backdrop of fixed exchange rates, with the ultimate backing of gold (through the fixed US dollar price of gold).

## . . . BUT THE WORLD HAS CHANGED SINCE THEN

The world has changed significantly since then in terms of the nature and speed of financial crises, and partly in response, the IMF has increased its lending.[2] While some of the crises of the last decade have retained some elements of the crises that the IMF was originally set up to fight – including particularly substantial current account deficits and overvalued pegged exchange rates – systemic risk from the nature of international capital flows has transformed the transmission mechanism of all the crises. In general, the global trend towards freer international allocation of capital should improve the allocative efficiency of the global economy, and provide higher yields for investors.[3] The problem for some emerging markets was that the liberalization of those capital flows came at a time when they were ill prepared to monitor and regulate the systemic risk of the inflows. This led to growing fragilities in the capital account and in the banking system, which manifested themselves in a variety of ways in the Asian crisis countries, Argentina, Brazil, Turkey and Russia. In all cases, though, the result was a massive withdrawal of capital and crises of fundamentally different proportions to those the IMF was originally created to address.

## THE IMF RESPONSE – MORE CASH, LESS TIME

Small loans to fill modest flow imbalances combined with policies to gradually restore balance of payments equilibrium are not sufficient in the face of large capital outflows. Instead, there are two main alternatives open to the indebted sovereign and the official community – either reverse the outflows with lots of fast official cash and confidence-improving reforms; or close off the outflows through more direct means. The more orthodox first option was taken by Korea, Thailand, Indonesia (albeit sporadically), Turkey, Brazil and Argentina (at least prior to its default in 2001). The second path was chosen by Malaysia (in defiance of the IMF, and probably too late to have the desired effect) and forced on Russia (with IMF acquiescence). We look below at the results for the orthodox Asian countries, Latin America and Turkey, before comparing these to the mavericks Malaysia and Russia. We then consider the separate case of Taiwan, which maintained pre-existing capital controls.

## THE ORTHODOX ASIAN COUNTRIES EVENTUALLY REBOUNDED WITH IMF HELP . . .

The Asian crisis in 1997 hit countries that had suffered from trade-weighted currency appreciation (the US dollar to which they had pegged appreciated strongly against the yen from 1995 until the onset of the Asian crisis) and sizeable current account deficits. Clearly any current account deficit increases net liabilities of some sort to non-residents. This could take the form of equity stakes (foreign direct investment (FDI) or portfolio), or local currency-denominated debt flows. But what set the crisis economies apart from others was that their corporates and banks had built up large unhedged FX liabilities. Any devaluation to reduce the current account would thus increase the local-currency value of their debts, and dramatically worsen the balance sheets of these enterprises. In this sense, they faced 'multiple equilibria' – if the exchange rate stayed strong then enterprises were safeguarded, but if the exchange rate depreciated, they would be rendered insolvent. In general, this prompted a massive withdraw of capital, a sharp contraction in activity, high real interest rates and an overshooting of the exchange rate.

For the countries in the midst of the crisis that followed IMF orthodoxy – Korea, Thailand and Indonesia – net capital flows plummeted from around +2 percent of annual GDP per quarter to around −6 percent of annual GDP in the middle of 1997. The response was to hike interest rates to around 25–30 percent to defend the exchange rate. This was only partly successful, with all three currencies overshooting. The reduction in confidence and capital flows, as well as the balance-sheet effect on corporates from the depreciations, led to quarterly year-on-year falls in GDP that exceeded 10 percent in Thailand and Indonesia, and only marginally less in Korea.

In the end, these economies generally rebounded strongly and thus these programs were in some sense a success.[4] Nonetheless, the severity and speed of the crises caused a policy rethink in Washington, and there was the question of whether some of the initial downside in growth could have been avoided. After the Asian crisis, the IMF became wary of loosely pegged exchange rate regimes for emerging markets. The orthodoxy had moved to advocating a 'bipolar' world in which exchange rates should either be fully fixed (a currency board where the central bank can only create domestic money when its FX reserves increase) or fully flexible (a relatively clean float with no exchange rate target). Hong Kong has managed to maintain its position in the fully fixed corner of this bipolar world, but this was the result of strong fiscal policy, massive reserves and an unusually flexible economy that could deliver sharp declines in wages and prices. Turkey and Argentina, however, soon showed that without these impressive attributes, even backing a pegged exchange rate with a tough monetary policy rule is no panacea for the larger emerging markets.

## ... BUT MORE-INDEBTED TURKEY AND ARGENTINA DID LESS WELL

Turkey introduced a quasi-currency board regime under an IMF program in late 1999 with the type of monetary policy straitjacket demanded by the new orthodoxy.[5] Nonetheless, a sudden political spat was sufficient to catalyse a capital outflow of similar magnitude to that suffered by the Asian countries. The resulting reserve losses tightened domestic liquidity dramatically as the central bank could not sterilize the outflows under the quasi-currency board. As domestic interest rates reached untenable levels and banks neared collapse, Turkey gave in and floated. While Turkey suffered from many similarities with the Asian economies in 1997 – including an overvalued exchange rate, a weak banking system and a private sector with large unhedged short-term FX liabilities – it started with an additional handicap. Turkey already had a frighteningly high stock of public sector debt. As the private sector rushed to close its short FX position, the resulting drain on reserves was largely filled by massive amounts of IMF money. The problem for Turkey was that this left the government with a debt burden that looked increasingly unsustainable. The government then doubled its bet by swapping part of its fixed-rate domestic debt into

FX-denominated and floating-rate debt. This bet has paid off so far, but Turkey had the good fortune to go through this period during a time of abundant global liquidity.[6]

Argentina chose to adopt a currency board arrangement in 1992 to fight inflation, which was initially very successful.[7] Unfortunately, Argentina failed to improve productivity sufficiently through structural reforms, and did not use the good times to reduce its debt. Then, when the US dollar with which it had pegged its exchange rate began to appreciate, and then many of its emerging market competitors depreciated, Argentina suffered from deflation as it fought to restore competitiveness. With the economy shrinking year after year, and fiscal profligacy continuing, the market increasingly viewed the exchange rate anchor as untenable. When Argentina finally devalued in November 2001, it was in even worse shape than Turkey. With nearly all Argentina's public debt denominated in FX, the devaluation also spelled default. Worse still, the local banks had been holding much of the debt. The default (and subsequent legislative changes to loan and deposit terms) rendered the banks insolvent, and deposits had to be frozen to avoid massive withdrawals and hyperinflation. Even the corner solution of a currency board had failed to prevent a devastating crisis.

## AVOID SINKING BY FLOATING?

So the solution must be obvious – float the currency, prevent systemically risky bets by the banking system, and implement tight fiscal and monetary policies. Alas, the crisis-prone Latin American countries soon managed to counter even this approach.

Brazil had largely cleaned up its banking system in the 1990s, had moved to a flexible exchange rate regime, and had sensible authorities implementing sound policies. Yet it was brought to the edge again in 2001. Clearly, the catalyst was market fear that the sound fiscal, monetary and structural policies would not be continued after the presidential and parliamentary elections in October 2001. But market jitters are commonplace ahead of elections in many countries, and they do not all lead to the dire situation that confronted Brazil. While it is encouraging that the new government has managed to impress the market with its adherence to fiscal austerity, it has (like Turkey) been lucky to have had the chance to rebound during a period of unusually high global liquidity.

The more fundamental question thus remains – why was Brazil so sensitive that, despite avoiding all the problems commonly associated with the earlier crises, even the largest IMF program in history did not dispel expectations of default for so long? We believe the answer lies at least in part in the very nature of the IMF programs.

## CURRENT IMF APPROACH: MORE SNAKES THAN LADDERS

Despite the sporadic anti-bailout rhetoric from the Bush administration, the basic practical response of the IMF has remained the same in all these capital account crises. The IMF has continued to provide huge FX-denominated loans to governments in trouble, providing them with a ladder to climb out of their mess. Our concern with this approach is not just the well-known fear of 'moral hazard'. In addition, we worry that the increasing reliance on FX debt inherent in the IMF's approach (both directly and through its push for rapid disinflation) is itself ratcheting up the risks by increasing the number of snakes that can push a country back down again.

---

## BOX 4.1   INVESTOR MORAL HAZARD FROM IMF LENDING

Investor moral hazard occurs when the expectation of big IMF packages leads investors to overlend. The moral hazard trade was alive and well in Russia before the August 1998 default, but is not so obvious today (other than in Turkey and perhaps Uruguay for US geopolitical considerations).

- Capital flows to emerging markets have shrunk substantially in recent years. Total private flows of around $120 billion are barely a third of the mid-1990s peak,[1] and net short-term flows are negative.
- Furthermore, nearly all of the modest inflows this year are likely to come from FDI, which seems less likely to be triggered by moral hazard than other forms of inflow.
- Detailed studies have recently shown that (allowing for global conditions and country-specific fundamentals) bond spreads are not only wider since the Russia crisis, but also diverge more for a given difference in country-specific fundamentals.[2] This suggests that if there was investor moral hazard before (with investors demanding lower yields and

> not differentiating as much as they would have without the promise of an IMF bailout), then at least this is less prevalent today.
>
> *Notes*
> 1. Total flows to emerging markets are also affected significantly by global liquidity, explaining part of the cyclicality of these flows.
> 2. Dell'Ariccia et al. (2002).

The standard critique of large (and often politically motivated) IMF lending packages is that they increase moral hazard, in which the implicit insurance the IMF provides against the full brunt of an economic crisis encourages excessive risk taking. This can stem from both investors and sovereign borrowers:

- Investor moral hazard occurs when the promise of big IMF packages leads investors to overlend. The moral hazard trade was alive and well in Russia before the August 1998 default, but is not so obvious today (other than in Turkey and perhaps Uruguay for US geopolitical considerations).
- Moral hazard can also arise from the perspective of the sovereign borrower. If governments believe they can get their hands on IMF cash if needed, then they may be less likely to bite the bullet and impose unpopular reforms to reduce the risk of a crisis.[8]

In addition to these widely cited concerns, we believe there is a fundamental riskiness to the IMF's strategy of effectively swapping local currency liabilities (including government bonds and state guarantees of local currency bank deposits) for FX-denominated liabilities. This comes about not only from the direct FX loans provided to the budget by the IMF itself. It also comes about because IMF programs usually demand rapid disinflation (or more generally, tight limits on monetary policy). This reduces seigniorage revenues and so requires more debt issuance. Some of this is likely to be denominated in FX, especially if local markets cannot absorb the extra paper. Furthermore, pushing disinflation faster than the market finds credible, leads to a sharp jump in real domestic rates, further encouraging the government to issue in FX. This greater reliance on FX debt leaves a country with less room to offset a balance of payments or fiscal financing shock with real depreciation or modest monetization. Without that flexibility, the market is more likely to react significantly to the inevitable stumbling blocks on the way to normality.[9] But is there a better way?

# CAPITAL CONTROLS – USEFUL, BUT WHEN?

Malaysia famously defied the IMF orthodoxy in the aftermath of the Asian crisis by imposing capital controls in September 1998[10] and has since rebounded impressively – could this be the solution? Malaysia did manage to avoid some of the exchange rate overshooting seen in Korea, Thailand and especially Indonesia. It also enjoyed lower and less volatile *domestic* interest rates than the orthodox Asian countries (although its domestic rates were capped).

Nonetheless, there is no discernible difference in the path of GDP. Why might this have been the case? Despite Malaysia's controls, capital flows in relation to GDP were almost the same as in the orthodox Asian countries (Korea, Thailand and Indonesia as noted above). In the year before controls were imposed, total capital outflows amounted to $6.7 billion, with private short-term capital outflows even larger at a net $8.5 billion. This evidence suggests that Malaysia introduced the capital controls after significant capital had already been withdrawn, and when confidence was returning to the region. At the time, Malaysia, like all the Asian economies, was benefiting from the extra liquidity generated by a cut in US interest rates, the export boost provided by the continued information technology boom, and the sharp fall in the yen/US$ rate. As a result, the controls may have mainly served to keep the exchange rate more depreciated in real terms during the recovery stage, rather than to avoid further depreciation in the midst of the crisis. The more depreciated exchange rate allowed reserves to rise more rapidly and local interest rates to fall further than under a more orthodox approach. This analysis is perhaps a bit too simplistic, and we explore some nuances in Box 4.2. The implications, however, remain the same. Malaysia's controls have *not* had the negative repercussions suggested by many at the time, and may have helped the recovery in domestic demand. The experience does not, however, tell us in a convincing fashion what would happen to other countries that impose capital controls at the *onset* of a crisis.

Russia provides another example of a country that ditched the IMF manual and imposed capital controls, although in this case it was out of necessity rather than choice, and it included a selective debt default. After political uncertainty led to a worsening of net capital flows and a sharp rise in interest rates on local bills (GKOs), the central bank initially tried to see off the panic by pushing policy rates into triple digits, selling reserves, and securing another $11 billion from the IMF. This failed to turn confidence, and with GKO rates heading to 300 percent, the central bank started to monetize the government's obligations. This was clearly inconsistent with the exchange rate peg, and in August 1998, Russia devalued, suspended

## BOX 4.2   WHY MALAYSIAN EXPERIENCE IS NOT CONVINCING EITHER WAY

In a direct sense, the Malaysian controls *were* successful – they eliminated offshore trading in the ringgit without leading to significant evasion or the emergence of a parallel foreign exchange market. It is, however, more difficult to determine whether the controls had a real economic benefit and to infer anything for handling future crises.

- The ban on offshore trading did seem to help lower local rates given Malaysia's particular political situation. The offshore ringgit market had an important impact on local liquidity in Malaysia in the period immediately before the introduction of capital controls. Regional banks offered high interest rates on ringgit deposits to attract the ringgit out of Malaysian banks. This gave those banks a ringgit liability (to the depositors). They could then convert these funds into FX, and so create a short-ringgit position. This led to (a) much higher interest rates offshore; and (b) a draining of liquidity from the domestic banking system in Malaysia. By banning this offshore trading (by forcing all ringgit sales to go through domestic institutions), the Malaysian authorities stopped this withdrawal of liquidity, and so allowed domestic rates to come down. An important question, to which we return below, is why this spread between local and offshore ringgit rates was so high in the first place.
- Nonetheless, Malaysia's growth path after introducing these controls was not much different from the orthodox Asian countries.[1] The simplest explanation is that the controls were implemented just as confidence was starting to return to other countries in the region, and the controls came after significant capital outflows had already occurred.
- The path of offshore rates does, however, suggest that confidence was *not* improving for Malaysia as it was for Korea and Thailand. To take account of this, we could use a 'time-shifted analysis'. In other words, we could assess the merits of the controls by comparing Malaysian performance after the controls were imposed in September 1998 with Korean performance at the time it received its IMF

package around nine months earlier. Malaysia then looks great in comparison to the average of the orthodox Asian countries, and even with respect to just Korea (the best-performing of the three we look at here). Even allowing for differences in the global environment between the two periods, Malaysia seems to have done significantly better after imposing controls than did Korea after its IMF program.[2]

- We have some reservations about relying too much on this approach for broader policy implications. The rationale for comparing Malaysia's performance with that of Korea around nine months earlier is that pressures in the offshore market indicated that Malaysia was suffering from the same lack of confidence that Korea had suffered from earlier. It would thus be unfair to compare Malaysia's performance in fighting this lack of confidence by comparing it to Korea at a time when it was enjoying the benefits of a return in confidence due to its reforms. But this reasoning sounds a little circular. A significant reason for the high spread between the local and offshore markets was the threat of the very measures that Malaysia subsequently adopted. Prime Minister Mahathir bin Mohamed had made a number of inflammatory remarks on international capital flows and raised expectations that he would remove his deputy prime minister and finance minister, Anwar Ibrahim (who was seen as the government's main defender of economic orthodoxy). Singaporean banks that wanted to create short positions in the Malyasian ringgit could do so by attracting deposits (bidding up the deposit rate) in order to create a ringgit liability, and then sell the ringgit for FX. If Malaysia had not created the expectations of some kind of dramatic change in policy, it may not have faced the loss of confidence and hence the interest rate spread. In that case, the level of confidence in Malaysia would look more like that in the orthodox Asian countries. Using the 'time-shifted' approach thus risks answering a slightly different question from the one we want to answer here. It helps tell us whether Malaysia did the 'right' thing by imposing capital controls, once it had already created fear in the market that it was going to impose those very same controls. It does not tell us whether Malaysia would have performed better by credibly promising to stick to more orthodox policies, and so avoid the build-up in speculative pressure in the offshore ringgit market in the first place. Thus while the analysis is interesting, it makes the Malaysian experience less compelling as an example for solving future crises.

- The somewhat different starting conditions of the orthodox Asian countries, Malaysia and Taiwan, add to the difficulty in making comparisons. In particular, Malaysia and Taiwan had a much lower ratio of debt to exports than Korea and Thailand, and a much lower ratio of short-term debt to reserves. This should have improved both countries' performance relative to the orthodox Asian countries. This is, however, partly the *result* of controls implemented earlier (Malaysia in 1994) and throughout (Taiwan). Also, of course, Malaysia never received the huge IMF loans that the orthodox Asian countries did – it may well have done even better had its decision to impose controls been supported by the IMF's blessing and its cash.[3]

Overall, the more detailed evidence from Malaysia is helpful for understanding how controls could help achieve specific goals. We do not, however, find it fully convincing for more general cases and see the case of Taiwan as more compelling, as discussed in the text.

*Notes*
1. This is true even when we include Indonesia, which was far more erratic than Korea and Thailand. Excluding Indonesia would make Malaysian experience look even less compelling.
2. Ethan Kaplan and Dani Rodrik's 2001 working paper from Harvard University's John F. Kennedy School of Government is a detailed and compelling version of this approach.
3. Kaplan and Rodrik (2001) also make this point well. Of course, for more indebted cases in the future, the impact of the IMF cash in such a situation must also be assessed against the backdrop of the public sector debt dynamics.

payments on local debt and imposed a three-month moratorium on external payments by the private sector.

Russia had serious fiscal solvency problems given the real exchange rate and energy prices experienced in 1998 and so looked a little closer to the Latin American than the Asian countries. Nonetheless, Russia has since rebounded strongly and after several years of strong fiscal and external surpluses and robust growth it is in great macroeconomic health. But as Russia benefited simultaneously from the dramatic bounce in oil prices, the sharply lower real exchange rate, and the reduction in its debt-service burden due to the default, this does not suggest that the Latin American countries and Turkey would also have rebounded by imposing controls after the onset of their crises.

Malaysian and Russian experiences thus do not provide definitive evidence either for or against this alternative to the Washington Consensus. In both cases, controls were added after the crisis had already had a substantial impact, rather than as a way to avoid a crisis. The experiences do at least suggest that such heterodox policies, if part of a clear and well-implemented set of reforms, might not be as disruptive for as long as previously portrayed.[11]

Ensuring that capital controls are in place before any potential crisis strikes provides a more promising solution, given the contrast between Taiwan and its neighbors. Taiwan encouraged FDI so as to benefit from the productivity improvements and additional financing this form of capital inflow can bring. But it maintained controls (including stringent limits on banking system exposures) to restrict the build-up of volatile short-term capital flows and currency and maturity mismatches in the banks and corporates. Taiwan was far less affected by the collapse in confidence than the other Asian economies discussed here. The spike in interest rates and the exchange rate were more modest, and there was relatively little impact on output growth. The experience of Taiwan thus suggests that a policy of encouraging FDI (or perhaps other equity financing too), combined with controls to limit hot money flows, might provide more breathing room during negative shocks.[12] While the IMF itself has shown a willingness to consider such previously heretical proposals, it spent some time considering a quite different plan to solve the next round of emerging market crises. While it has since backed away from pushing this plan in the near term, it is still worth examining in some detail as it may return to prominence if litigation against Argentina widens significantly.

## THE IMF'S BOLD, SCARY AND NOW-MOTHBALLED SOLUTION

The official community is clearly concerned at the cost and the potential for moral hazard of the spate of packages that have been required since Mexico's bailout in 1994. The solution proposed in late 2001 by the IMF's first deputy managing director, Anne Krueger, was undoubtedly bold, if hardly new. Krueger suggested a Sovereign Debt Restructuring Mechanism

(SDRM), which requires changing the legal structure in every IMF member country to allow a supermajority of private creditors, aggregated into broad groups, to impose a restructuring on all private creditors. Minority holdouts would be barred from litigation in the jurisdiction of any IMF member country. This would not require a supermajority of holders of each instrument to vote in favor of a restructuring, as would the simpler approach of pushing for adoption of collective action provisions in all sovereign bond contracts.[13] Because this new legal framework would cram down terms on dissident creditors, subordinate existing credit to new credit, and provide a stay on litigation, it is often described as the sovereign equivalent of the US Bankruptcy Code's Chapter 11 for corporates.

In particular, the proposal envisaged that a country would be granted immunity from litigation during a temporary standstill on debt service – during this period of a few months, the country would negotiate a rescheduling that would need to be accepted by the supermajority of all its creditors. To ensure that the cash left on the table as a result of the moratorium did not rush out of the country, capital controls could be imposed. After this total ban on litigation, the supermajority of the creditors would still have the right to accept or reject any restructuring, but holdouts would not have the right to challenge the decision. The mechanism would also seek to ensure that the debtor implemented decent economic policies and did not favor certain creditor groups. It could include a preferred creditor status for any new money coming in. The hope would be that many restructurings would then take place in the shadow of this formal mechanism, as they do in the corporate context.

In its first incarnation (from November 2001), it would be up to the IMF to decide when a standstill would come into force (after a request by the debtor itself). In the version presented to the Institute for International Economics on 1 April 2001, Krueger saw the decisions being taken by the debtor and a supermajority of the creditors, and 'the Fund would not be empowered to make decisions that would undermine the enforcement of creditor rights'. The IMF's role then would be just to bring about the change in legal protection by changing its Articles of Agreement and encouraging every member to accept those changes by way of international treaty law. If IMF members totaling 85 percent of voting power approved a change in the Articles, then a treaty obligation would arise and each country's parliament would vote on whether to accept or reject the Treaty (the United States holds 17.16 percent of the total votes at the board, giving them a legal veto in addition to their more informal veto). Krueger quite reasonably saw this approach as being better than if individual laws were drawn up in each country, as it would provide a more consistent approach across jurisdictions. The IMF suggested that the SDRM should include only private claims on the sovereign issued under foreign law, and should aggregate over broad creditor classes. This proposal is in some senses 'narrow' in coverage, although it is clear that the SDRM would not be operating in isolation from domestic debt restructurings and the Paris Club.

## BUT THAT IMF MEDICINE RISKS HURTING ITS PATIENTS

The second version of the IMF plan was far better than earlier versions (which gave the IMF itself control over the decision to invoke the bank-ruptcy protection). It was designed to reduce the cost of default by making it easier to coordinate private external creditors. But the IMF has yet to establish that creditor coordination is primarily to blame for elevating the cost of default, or even that the cost of default is too high. While we doubt that many bondholders would want the bodies of defaulters to be divided and distributed pro rata among the creditors, as permitted under the law of the Twelve Tables that began in Greece during the 5th century BC, we also doubt that they would want default to be so easy that countries turn to it frequently and credit markets cease to operate effectively.[14]

Furthermore, the now-ubiquitous observation that the shift from bank to bond financing for emerging markets has made debt restructurings more difficult is not entirely obvious from recent experience. The argument runs that bonds are more difficult to restructure because it is more difficult to get agreement from a heterogeneous group of bondholders than a smaller and more homogeneous group of bankers. Yet the 1980s Latin American bank debt crisis took much longer to sort out than bond restructurings in Pakistan and Ukraine.[15] The ease of the reschedulings in Pakistan and Ukraine may have been partly due to the collective action clauses present in their bonds, which allow a supermajority of bondholders to bind in potential dissidents and so facilitate reschedulings. While these clauses are not currently present in bonds issued under New York law, the debt exchange in Ecuador showed that even without this help, bond exchanges could be completed quite quickly once a relatively credible framework is in place. These exchanges are admittedly relatively modest in comparison to the size of the overall asset class. Nonetheless, they suggest that debt exchanges themselves can be quite quick and painless once the necessary reforms to rebuild the economy are in place.

Although we would have some sympathy with the aims of the SDRM if we were building the financial system from scratch, in reality financial markets already exist, complete with bondholders who have already paid for existing instruments based on existing legal frameworks. Sovereign borrowers, who have been among the most vocal opponents of these reforms, are reliant on the willingness of bondholders to maintain exposure. If bondholders fear that the value of their claims will be impaired because default becomes easier and reforms less likely, they will demand a higher price to maintain their exposure at an extremely sensitive time for some key emerging market economies. If the SDRM were introduced, it could create an incentive for creditors to 'rush for the exits' ahead of a decision to invoke the terms of the SDRM – as a result, swings in creditor confidence could be magnified (just like the shift to FX-denominated debt). In addition, the SDRM could change the recovery value of claims in case of default. The proponents of the SDRM would argue that it accelerates the resolution of the crisis, and so improves the value of a claim against a defaulting sovereign.[16] Against this, the SDRM could also worsen the terms that the sovereign would need to offer creditors in order to secure a deal, and so reduce the value of the pre-default claim. In addition, the reduced pressure to implement unpopular reforms to avoid default would also reduce the value of a post-restructuring claim for bondholders. The net effect is thus likely to be lower prices and greater volatility if the SDRM ever became operational (unlikely), or even if it just returned to the official sector's agenda (in which case any benefits of the plan would not help offset the problems). With little prospect of implementation, we maintain our long-held view that this plan could create substantial costs for the global financial system, and waste valuable political capital.

## THE MOVE TO COLLECTIVE ACTION CLAUSES

As part of the 'deal' to defer the SDRM, the United States encouraged Mexico and Brazil to introduce collective action clauses (CACs) in their New York law bonds earlier in 2003. These were followed by a more general move to use CACs in New York law bonds by other sovereigns.

Despite widespread concern some time ago over the use of CACs, it is interesting that there is no evidence that the introduction of these clauses caused any widening in the sovereign spread. In addition, recent work by Anthony Richards (2003) at the Reserve Bank of Australia shows that a number of New York law sovereign bonds had CACs even before these highly publicized deals. This seems to have been the result of the choice of legal advisors on the deal and was largely ignored by investors (countries with New York law bonds that contain CACs included Bulgaria, Egypt, Kazakhstan, Lebanon and Qatar – at times, some of these countries are just the ones for whom issues of CACs might be more likely to have come into the spotlight; the total amount of such bonds is around $12 billion).

CACs cannot change the emerging bond world in a single stroke, as the SDRM might have done (for better or worse). Adding CACs now to new bonds does not impact the existing stock of (mainly non-English-law) bonds without CACs. Nonetheless, over time, the increasing inclusion of CACs could help achieve a smoother restructuring when the sovereign can agree a deal with the vast majority of its creditors.

'Modified CACs' could eventually do much of what the SDRM was designed to achieve. In particular, Uruguay included aggregation clauses in its debt swap in May 2003. These clauses extend normal CACs in one key way – they allow aggregation over creditor groups. Rather than allowing a supermajority of all creditors to cram down provisions on all bondholders regardless of the views of the majority of holders of each type of bond, the Uruguay provisions would lower the threshold for a supermajority on each type of bond if a supermajority of all creditors agreed. This middle-way solution is appealing. It avoids bondholders fearing that they could be in a small minority that is unfairly treated by the supermajority, but reduces the risk of litigious bondholders buying up small stakes in orphan issues to block a deal.

That said, we see absolutely no sign that Mexico or Brazil, which recently included CACs in New York law bonds, or any other sovereign, are planning to introduce aggregation clauses in their bonds. While this argument could also have been made about the simple CACs prior to the Mexico and Brazilian issues, the change of heart then was catalysed by pressure from the United States. That pressure is now absent, as it reflected a desire to put forward an alternative to the no-longer-imminent SDRM. The SDRM died too soon to help facilitate aggregation clauses.

---

## BOX 4.3   DETAILS OF THE SDRM PROPOSAL

In the build-up to the IMF annual meetings in September 2002, the IMF board released a number of papers looking at the role of collective action clauses (CACs) in bond restructurings, and on the SDRM itself. Then, during the 2002 meetings themselves, the IMF governing body the IMFC agreed that the IMF should continue to pursue the 'dual-track' approach to sovereign restructurings, that is, to work on concrete proposals to advance both the statutory approach embodied by the SDRM and the contractual approach of pushing CACs into all bonds (including New York law bonds like those Ecuador exchanged in 2000). The International Monetary and Financial Committee (IMFC) called on the IMF to present a detailed version of the SDRM by April 2003, but in the end the SDRM was sidelined at that year's IMF Spring meetings.

The detailed proposal of the IMF was in keeping with the basic thrust of the April 2002 version of the plan, which sees creditors and the debtor decide when such a stay should be introduced (not the IMF), but still requires all countries to adopt changes in the IMF Articles of Agreement, and reduces creditor rights on existing instruments. The latest thinking from the IMF is that the SDRM should include only private claims on the sovereign issued under foreign law, and should aggregate over creditor classes. The SDRM as the IMF currently envisages it, would:

- Exclude domestic debt (that is, debt issued under domestic law regardless of who holds it), on the basis that the sovereign can usually achieve a restructuring of these instruments already under its own laws, and that including it in the SDRM would create complications in the voting process, as claims are aggregated.
- Include external debt held by local institutions, although importantly the IMF recognizes the importance of ensuring that the sovereign cannot bias the results of a vote under the SDRM process by issuing debt to itself (or one of its agencies) under foreign law.
- Exclude official bilateral credits, as there is already a mechanism to restructure this debt (primarily the Paris Club).
- Be accompanied by the creation of a Sovereign Debt Dispute Resolution Forum (SDDRF) to administer claims and disputes over which class each creditor would be placed in for purposes of aggregation.

This proposal was in some senses 'narrow' in coverage, although it was clear that the SDRM would not have been operating in isolation from domestic debt restructurings and the Paris Club.

## BOX 4.4   THE BOND EXCHANGES IN PAKISTAN, UKRAINE AND ECUADOR

After the Asian crisis, the official sector presented a substantial collection of papers on how to change the global financial architecture so as to safeguard financing for emerging markets while minimizing increasing moral hazard. Until the more recent debate about the SDRM, the main part of the new financial architecture was the IMF's private sector involvement (PSI) initiative. PSI looks at ways in which private creditors can be closely involved in any significant sovereign bailout by the official sector. Under this approach, the form this PSI should take depends on the circumstances of each bailout.

- In many ways, PSI is nothing new. The 1980s debt crisis involved substantial 'haircuts' or write-downs in syndicated bank debt, sometimes in face value and sometimes in net present value (NPV) terms. This is clearly PSI. While these haircuts were agreed only after long delays, that was more to do with weak balance sheets in major international banks rather than any difficulty for the IMF in finding the right name and number to call from its creditor phonebook.
- The consequent emergence of Brady bonds and subsequent increased reliance on bonds for new financing was seen as making future restructuring of private creditors' claims more difficult. When the major 1990s crises struck, IMF managing director Michel Camdessus and US Treasury secretary Robert Rubin did not have time to update their phone book. The much broader investor community made it too difficult to get all the players into a room to negotiate. Other than in Russia's domestic and Soviet-era debt default, bondholders (as an asset class) escaped without haircuts. But with bond financing growing from a small share of total private claims that seemed too difficult to be worth the trouble of restructuring, to the bulk of private credit to emerging sovereigns, the official sector then looked for ways to broaden PSI to include restructuring of sovereign bonds.

The first countries to be subject to the new approach were Pakistan, Ukraine and Ecuador:

- In Pakistan's case, the Paris Club announced in January 1999 that its, 'comparability of treatment' provision (under which reschedulings of official Paris Club debt were to be matched by private creditors) applied equally to non-collateralized Eurobonds as to bank credits. The Paris Club picked the first guinea pig well, as Pakistan had a number of features that made it an easy test case. All the relevant bonds fell due or were 'put-able' during the Paris Club rescheduling window, all had collective action clauses (CACs, see Box 4.6), and all non-international financial institution debt was being restructured at the same time in the face of clear payment difficulties (in the aftermath of sanctions applied after the nuclear tests by Pakistan and India in May 1998). Furthermore, there were thought to be a large number of relatively sympathetic holders. While not directly used, the CACs would have allowed a supermajority of bondholders to force new payments terms on potential hold-outs. Without CACs, Pakistan would have needed to convince all bondholders to participate. If a small number of holdouts demand (and are likely to receive) full payment, other bondholders are unlikely to accept any dilution of their claim. When finally undertaken in November–December 1999, the restructuring worked smoothly – the credibility of the threat to default in the absence of the exchange perhaps helped by the military coup just weeks before the offer opened, and the process smoothed by the appointment of a top Wall Street banker as finance minister.
- Ukraine had similar collective action provisions in its bonds, and also secured a successful exchange despite concern at the time that the holding structure of its bonds was too fragmented. Ukraine used its collective action provisions in a cunning way. To use CACs directly would require a bondholders' meeting – a potentially risky strategy as, while it provides the opportunity for the sovereign to get a supermajority of its creditors to agree to cram down a restructuring of their claims on all bondholders, it also provides an opportunity for potential litigants to band together and meet any litigation threshold. This is why Pakistan did not call a bondholders' meeting, and instead relied on CACs only as a backdrop to the exchange. In Ukraine's case, as

bondholders tendered into the exchange, they allowed the government to hold on to the bonds they tendered (normally the bonds are extinguished – this required a change in the non-payment provisions of the bond). The government could then call a bondholder's meeting knowing it held most of the bonds itself, and so vote through a change in the payment schedule without the risks associated with calling a bondholder's meeting up front.

- Ecuador was not to be denied its place in history just because the Paris Club picked Pakistan to be the first guinea pig. It became the first country to default on its Bradys when it failed to pay its Discount bonds (while paying Past Due Interest bonds (PDIs)) in September 1999. The idea of this selective default was that enough (25 percent) of the Discount bondholders would vote in favor of releasing collateral – this would allow Ecuador to cure the default without having to raise new cash. Instead, enough of them (also 25 percent) instructed the fiscal agent to accelerate their claims, pushing Ecuador into default on all $6.65 billion of its bonds (Par bonds, Discount bonds, PDIs, Eurobonds) through cross-default clauses. This left Ecuador without a strategy, and so Pakistan was the first to restructure. Ecuador was different from Pakistan – it had no CACs on the payment provisions – in other words even a supermajority could not cram down restructuring terms on holdout investors. After a year of wrangling and confusion, Ecuador finally presented an offer to swap the $6.65 billion in old debt for $3.95 billion in new Eurobonds, that is, a face value reduction of 41 percent.[1] The most important part of the Ecuador deal was the use of exit consent provisions. In agreeing to tender bonds in the exchange, holders of the old bonds agreed to changes in the non-payment provisions of the bonds (which required only a supermajority rather than unanimity to change, unlike the payment provisions). These changes were designed to make the old bonds so unattractive that potential dissidents would fold. The changes removed cross-default and cross-acceleration clauses (so that default on the old bonds did not trigger acceleration on the new bonds), delisted the bonds, and reduced asset attachment options. Acceptance was also helped by the limited NPV reduction (around 40 percent, while the upper end was 80 percent), and by principal reinstatement provisions, which gave creditors the right to the pre-exchange face value claim should Ecuador default again within certain time limits. As a result, the deal was successful, although payments are continuing on the old pre-exchange bonds.

*Note:*
1.    Not all bonds are created equal, however, as Eurobonds got the best deal (no 'haircut' if swapping into a 30-year bond), and different exchange ratios were used for each bond.

## BOX 4.5    INVESTOR REACTION TO THE SDRM

Unsurprisingly, investors typically reacted very negatively to the push on SDRM, while maintaining an ongoing dialogue on the types of clauses that could be included in individual bond contracts going forward (that is, not retroactively).

- One of the main concerns stemmed from the fundamental feature of the SDRM, which is an aggregation of creditor claims into a number of creditor classes, which would then each vote on a proposed restructuring (with some super-majority rather than unanimity required to cram down the restructuring on all investors). Investors were concerned that the separation of contracts would be overridden, and their interests may thus be ignored.
- There were also some creditors who saw the SDRM as a mechanism for the IMF to strengthen its preferred-creditor status by making it easier to reduce the claims on the sovereign by the private sector.
- Others noted that given the difficulty and expense of litigating against a sovereign (especially in the United States under the Foreign Sovereign Immunities Act), litigation usually only made sense if the full value of a claim could be accelerated – and they noted that as acceleration usually requires a reasonable proportion (often 25 percent) of bondholders to vote in favor of acceleration, this means that

litigation is unlikely when only a very small number of hold-outs exists.

The bottom line for many investors was that the IMF was seen as seeking to change the enforceability of existing contracts, over the wishes of both sides to those contracts (it would be impossible for countries to opt out of the SDRM in any credible way if it was implemented).

From the official side, the reaction was more diverse. There seemed initially to be some split within the US administration on the SDRM, with then-Treasury secretary Paul O'Neill relatively supportive, while undersecretary John Taylor remains more enthusiastic about CACs. The anti-SDRM view eventually won out and the IMF shelved the SDRM, at least for now.

From the issuance countries likely to be affected, the response was negative, albeit with nuances over the timing of discussion (some countries seemed willing to at least countenance a discussion on an SDRM-like mechanism, but were still concerned that discussion had come at a time that was especially sensitive, especially for Latin American credits).

## BOX 4.6   COLLECTIVE ACTION PROVISIONS AS THEY STAND TODAY

The terms of bond contracts that can be modified take two general forms:

- *payment* provisions, which sometimes require unanimity; and
- *non-payment* provisions, which can generally be changed by a qualified majority at a bondholders' meeting (other than in bonds issued under German jurisdiction).

CACs usually refer to those provisions that allow *payment* provisions to be altered by a qualified majority. In general, the purpose of CACs is to enable a qualified majority of bondholders to restrain the ability of a minority to hold up a restructuring. More precisely, they include:

- Majority *restructuring* provisions (MRPs) allow a qualified majority to agree a change in the payment terms that would also bind a minority of dissident bondholders. The intent of MRPs is to reduce the likelihood that the majority will be unwilling to restructure if they expect the minority to get paid in full out of the resources released. An international bankruptcy court based on corporate law could achieve the same, but is unrealistic. Typically, MRPs require 75 percent of bondholders to agree a restructuring the first time a bondholders' meeting is called, dropping to 20–25 percent if a second bondholders' meeting is required to reach quorum. The stereotypical view that MRPs exist in bonds issued under UK law (and subject to UK jurisdiction) but not under US law is generally correct, but is more by convention and historical accident than requirement:
- In the UK, freedom of contract allows bondholders to either agree or exclude MRPs; convention is that they are included.
- In the United States, the general avoidance of MRPs for sovereign bonds is a product of copying the terms of corporate bonds issued under the Trust Indenture Act (TIA) of 1939. In the wake of some restructurings that saw insiders control the process and diminish the claims of minority outsiders, the TIA was enacted to force any *corporate* restructuring before judicial review. Neither the US Bankruptcy Code nor the TIA apply to sovereigns, so it is purely habit that gives rise to the general absence of MRPs under US law. Any sovereign could choose to issue bonds under US law with MRPs, as the Electricity Generating Authority of Thailand did in 1998.
- In Germany, the law generally allows no changes to either type of provision.
- In Japan, bonds have MRPs, but any restructuring could be subject to judicial review if an 'abuse of rights' could be shown.

- Majority *enforcement* provisions (MEPs) allow a qualified majority to limit the actions of the minority once a default (including cross-default) has occurred. In this context, more important than jurisdiction is whether the bond was issued under a trust deed or fiscal agency agreement. Bonds issued under a trust deed provide for a trustee with certain powers and responsibilities to act on behalf of bondholders, whereas bonds issued under a fiscal agency agreement provide only for a fiscal agent to represent the sovereign. Neither UK nor US law prohibits either a trustee or fiscal agent, but the former is only common under UK law. Bonds issued under German law do not provide for trust deeds, while Samurai bonds have specific provisions, noted below.

- Litigation can be initiated by individual bondholders under a fiscal agency agreement, but generally only by the trustee when the bond is issued under a trust deed. The trustee is required to initiate proceedings if requested by the threshold number of bondholders, and only if it fails to do so can an individual bondholder take action. In Samurai issues, proceedings can be initiated by any bondholder.

- Sharing of litigation proceeds pro rata among all bondholders is mandatory under a trust deed, while individual litigators (who must have reached the litigation threshold) can keep the proceeds to themselves if the bond is issued under a fiscal agency agreement.

- Acceleration is generally only possible on written request of 10–25 percent of bondholders under either a trustee or a fiscal agent. In Japan, acceleration requires agreement by 50 percent of bondholders.

- Majority *representation* provisions would allow a group of bondholders to represent bondholder interests in negotiations, perhaps through creditor committees. These are not currently included in any sovereign bond contract, and have been suggested as a way to assist creditor coordination.

## CREDITOR COMMITTEES

As described earlier (EMEA Economics Analyst, April, 2002), we would prefer to see a more evolutionary approach that would improve the way in which the existing legal framework handles crises. Even if all a troubled sovereign's bonds had CACs, the debtor still needs to find a way to reach agreement with most of its creditors. So some form of creditor communication is essential – the faster this happens the better for the country and its bondholders.

BOX 4.7   THE SIMILARITIES OF 19TH CENTURY
          EMERGING MARKET FINANCING TO
          TODAY

In the late 19th and early 20th centuries, the market value of
emerging market debt traded in London was substantial and
growing rapidly. In 1875, the total value was GBP 500 million, rising
to GBP 1 billion by 1905. This was equivalent to 12 percent of world
GDP (although this ratio may be biased upwards, as official statistics may have recorded less of total activity then than they do
today). At that time, the main emerging market debtors were
Argentina, Australia, Brazil, Canada, Egypt, Hungary, Mexico,
Russia, Turkey and the United States. While Australia, Canada and
the United States have graduated (notwithstanding recent currency volatility in Australia!), the others are very much with us
today. In 1999, the total volume of emerging market debt traded
was $1202 billion, equivalent to 2.7 percent of world GDP although
this excludes derivatives transactions. So in relation to the size of
the world's economies, not only was the previous era of global capitalism more open in terms of total capital flows, but also in some
senses, in terms of the volumes of debt traded.

The average spread of emerging market sovereign bonds
between 1870 and 1913 was 326 basis points (over British sovereign rates), substantially lower than today's EMBI+. But when the
usual suspects are taken in isolation, the story is altogether too
familiar. Turkey had an average spread of 1094 bps over British
rates, and spiked into the multi-thousands. While Argentina had an
average of only 330 bps, it spiked over 1600 bps. Russia, however,
was better behaved in Tsarist times than in the post-Brady era, with
an average of less than 200 bps and a maximum of less than 500
bps, although perhaps it is headed back to the Tsarist-era rates now!

Political issues were also similar – the moral hazard play was in
vogue even then. As Efraim Karsh and Inari Karsh (1999) say in
*Empires of the Sand; The Struggle for Mastery of the Middle East
1789–1923*: 'in line with their long-standing practice of using their
perennial weakness as a lever for extracting concessions from
powerful allies, the Ottomans exploited their setbacks in the First
World War to attract ever-growing material and economic support
from Germany'. So even Turkey's use of its urgent need for official
financing to avoid catastrophe is nothing new! In the end, Turkey

did not see a significant reduction in its spreads until 1884, when it cut the interest payable on existing debt.

So in many ways, the trading patterns and the emerging market crises were similar to those we see today. One aspect to change, however, is the type of instrument being traded. There is a much broader range of investment vehicles today than was the case in the earlier period.

The largest holder of long-term cross-border investments was Great Britain, accounting for a little under half of all cross-border investments in the early 20th century. At the time, about 30 percent of its investments were in government debt, 40 percent in railways, 10 percent in mining and 5 percent in utilities.

All these sectors share a fairly obvious asset base, making it easier for foreign investors to monitor. Also, the instruments were almost entirely fixed income – again, this is easier than equity for foreign investors to monitor. So in one way, the modern form of globalization, with its greater reliance on equity flows, could be more stable – if returns in the recipient country fall, so do the returns to creditors. But this is probably offset by the different nature of direct investments. While foreign investors did not buy minority equity stakes in the previous era, they did invest (even more than today) in long-term infrastructure projects, where the return could be zero unless completed – a rail track laid only half way to a destination is worthless.

## BOX 4.8   HISTORY OF CREDITOR COMMITTEES

Emerging markets financing in the 19th century in many ways looked similar to those today in terms of volumes, spreads and influences, even if the nature of the instruments was less diverse (as noted in Box 4.7). Defaults also occurred on sovereign bonds in the earlier period, and workout mechanisms were adopted to reduce the time to resolve such crises.

In the early 1800s, sovereign bondholders were represented on an *ad hoc* basis by competing committees. After Latin American defaults in the 1820s, the Council of Foreign Bondholders (CFBH) was set up in London in November 1868. The CFBH was made up of both finance houses and private bondholders, and was paid for by fees from bondholders (five years later it incorporated, and then in 1898 the Corporation of Foreign Bondholders Act was passed by the British parliament). The council stopped stock exchanges listing new Mexican issues in 1874 and new Turkish issues in 1877 until arrears were cleared. The method of the CFBH was to appoint experts to negotiate with debtor governments on behalf of the CFBH and make non-binding recommendations. Bondholders then voted on the proposals, but the vote was not binding on any bondholder. That this worked, at least until continental exchanges gained in weight and reduced the power of the CFBH, was probably mainly because bondholders had few other options then.

Other countries did similar things. The Paris Stock Exchange established the Association Nationales des Porteurs Français de Valeurs Mobilières in 1898. The only real difference to the CFBH was that committee members had to be bondholders. Belgium, Germany, Italy, the Netherlands and Switzerland did much the same. In the United States, the Foreign Bondholders Protective Council, a private, non-profit corporation encouraged by government was established in 1993. The FBPC negotiated the settlement of foreign bond defaults directly rather than through committees, but did not finalize the deal itself – this was up to the bondholders individually (although bondholders were simply assumed to accept the restructuring if they accepted payment under the new terms). The FBPC was sometimes swayed by political pressure, the quid pro quo being that the FBPC would get State Department support for its actions on other occasions.

This would include work on the ways in which creditor committees can be formed to help bring debtors and creditors together both before and after a default, and on the precise strategies used to facilitate exchange offers. This suggestion for creditor committees is hardly new – indeed, in some ways it replicates the type of creditor body prevalent before reforms in the mid-1800s in London. This earlier period is surprisingly relevant to today – the 40 years or so prior to the First World War saw *greater* cross-border capital flows in relation to GDP, and similar volumes and spreads in traded emerging market debt. As a result, some of the workout mechanisms used to restructure sovereign debt provide useful pointers for possible future coordination mechanisms. Argentine creditor groups since last year's default have complained about the lack of adequate communication with the debtor, and this was also an issue during the Ecuador default/exchange. While we do not see the *exact* form of the creditor committees that prevailed in the earlier periods as especially inspiring, we do believe that the international community would do better to focus on measures that facilitate *voluntary* creditor coordination rather than pushing the more coercive and retroactive SDRM.

## CONCLUSION

Huge IMF packages to help arrest capital account crises provide a ladder for emerging markets to overcome their problems, helping to avoid a nasty global financial shock. Because these crises are larger and faster than the traditional current account crises the IMF was established to fight, IMF funding has likewise been much larger and more front-loaded. The Asian economies had little public sector debt prior to their crises, and so were better able to climb out of their difficulties on the ladder provided by the IMF's credit. The Latin American countries and Turkey, with considerably higher initial debt burdens, remain highly vulnerable. The very nature of these IMF programs and the FX debt they encourage seems to make them more likely to find a snake and slip back down again.

The IMF's suggestion, now mothballed, was for an SDRM that would change creditor rights on existing instruments in all the major capital market jurisdictions. We see this approach as unlikely to succeed, and as creating greater uncertainty at a particularly delicate stage for several key emerging markets. We would prefer to see more evolutionary progress on the procedures to be used to restructure sovereign debt under the existing legal frameworks. To reduce the number of new crises, countries should avoid the accumulation of too much FX-denominated debt, including that provided by the IMF. This will allow them the flexibility to use a little depreciation and monetization to offset the inevitable political and other pitfalls that will befall them. In the longer term, the solution should also involve a greater emphasis on developing local capital markets.

The implication for bondholders of the IMF-related shift to FX debt is higher volatility at the riskier end of the sovereign credit spectrum. The more FX-linked and floating-rate debt a country has, the more its debt dynamics are linked to confidence. This strategy is dangerous, but it can also help, as Turkey in particular is finding out now. As confidence improves, the FX and floating-rate debt becomes cheaper (through exchange rate appreciation and lower domestic yields). In this sense, market confidence impacts on the 'fundamentals'. This reliance on risky forms of debt does, however, raise the volatility for the economy as a whole, and bondholders in particular.

## NOTES

1. See EMEA (Emerging Europe, Middle-East and Africa) Economics Analyst, 'Turkey – the ultimate confidence game', 15 November 2002, Goldman Sachs.
2. The additional lending is also related to the significantly larger membership since the collapse of the Soviet Union.
3. In some ways, the recent liberalization of capital accounts returns the global economy to the era of high net flows common during the 19th century, and many of the problems and solutions of that earlier period of free international capital flows have replicas in today's debate (including bondholder committees). See EMEA Economics Analyst, 'Emerging market financing – a retrospective as we hit our first anniversary', 16 November 2001, Goldman Sachs.
4. This was despite quite divergent implementation of reforms, including even the reforms in the banking systems that were perhaps most directly related to the onset of the crisis.
5. Turkey had a preannounced crawling peg, backed by a rigid target for net domestic assets (NDAs) of the central bank.
6. See EMEA Economics Analyst, 'Turkey – the ultimate confidence game', 15 November 2002, Goldman Sachs.
7. Argentina had a 1:1 peg with the US dollar, but its monetary anchor was somewhat more flexible than Turkey's. We see this as a decision by the Argentine government itself, rather than one forced upon it by the IMF, in contrast to many suggestions to the contrary.
8. The IMF would argue that as its bailouts involve loans that must be repaid rather than normal insurance payouts, this type of moral hazard is minimal. But for a government faced with the need to take unpopular measures up front to reduce the chance of a future crisis, the incentives are clear. The downside of some future government having to hit taxpayers for years to repay the IMF will be outweighed by the near-term risk to their own political futures, and the reforms will be delayed.
9. To try to reduce these fragilities, the IMF typically pushes for a higher fiscal surplus. At some point, however, the political infeasibility of maintaining an extremely tight fiscal policy may make the markets more wary. This further increases the real interest rate the government faces. A country with an open capital account and with substantial net FX liabilities cannot easily relax fiscal policy as confidence starts to weaken. If it monetizes, the resulting depreciation will hit the balance sheet of the banks and corporates (and the government too if it holds enough FX debt), and it may be hard to issue more debt. If it tries to place more debt, at best it will push up local rates and hurt the economy and its own revenues, and at worst it will fail and catalyse a crisis. We explore an alternative solution through permanent capital controls below.
10. Malaysia banned offshore trading in the ringgit, cut off domestic credit to foreign banks, demanded repatriation of all ringgit held overseas, and required central bank approval for all FX purchases. In most other respects, it conformed to IMF orthodoxy by cleaning up the banking sector and maintaining relatively tight fiscal policy.
11. Any imposition of capital controls does, however, increase the potential for corruption (if a control is binding, then there is profit to be made by getting around it). The implementation abilities of the government are thus crucial. For those countries still retaining capital controls, the experiences suggest that considerable caution must be used in moving towards a freer capital account.
12. Of course, companies engaged in FDI may want to hedge themselves if a crisis looms, and will no doubt find ways to take money out of the country in the same way that they are able to partly avoid the Chilean-style taxes and controls on inflows. But the impact

will be more modest than when totally unfettered flows are allowed, and where much larger imbalances have been created in domestic corporates and banks. FDI that does not sufficiently improve the export-earning capacity of the economy is, of course, subject to its own problems, as Brazil's recent experience shows.

13. See EMEA Economics Analyst, 'Sovereign Bankruptcy Mechanisms: a way out of trouble or way out of line?', April 2002, for more on the use of collective action clauses and 3 October 2002 for an update on the SDRM after the September 2002 IMF meetings.

14. We believe the IMF's focus on the SDRM to solve the supposed creditor coordination problem stems in part from the IMF taking the wrong lessons from Argentina. The Argentine default has been a tragic mess, but it is not the result of failure of creditor coordination. The real problem in Argentina is that there is not yet any coherent government strategy that private creditors could support through a debt rescheduling. By so far refusing to restart its own lending, the IMF has implicitly acknowledged this itself.

15. While the delays in the 1980s were at least in part required to give creditor banks time to improve their balance sheets before booking a reduction in the value of their claims, the impact on the borrowing countries was nonetheless real. A creditor base made up of bondholders that mark-to-market may in this sense make it easier to secure a quick rescheduling.

16. The argument is that less damage to the economy from the default means higher debt-servicing capabilities and so a higher residual value of the claim; a faster jump to a post-default scenario means a shorter period before a return to a liquid market and coupon payments.

# REFERENCES

Dell' Ariccia, G., I. Schnabel and J. Zettelmeyer (2002), 'Moral hazard and international crisis lending: a test', IMF Working Paper WP/02/181, International Monetary Fund, Washington, DC, October.

Kaplan, E. and D. Rodrik (2001), 'Did the Malaysian capital controls work?', working paper, John F. Kennedy School of Government, Harvard University.

Karsh, E. and I. Karsh (1999), *Empires of the Sand: The Struggle for Mastery in the Middle East, 1789–1923*, Cambridge, MA: Harvard University Press.

Richards, A. (2003), 'Bond restructuring and moral hazard: are collective action clauses costly?', *Journal of International Economics*, **61** (1), October , 127–61.

# 5. The future of the sovereign debt market and its implication for the international financial institutions

**Sergio Edeza**

## INTRODUCTION

The sovereign debt market is huge and the interplay between investors and issuers can be complex. This market is influenced by the different economic regimes in each issuer nation. In this chapter I shall provide some insights about its existence, while looking at developments that will give us some understanding about the future of this market.

I shall premise my analysis on the following: (i) there are two types of sovereign debt markets, each country's domestic debt market, and the cross-border or international debt market; (ii) the domestic debt market is governed by rules peculiar to every country, although similarities exist, and many rules are adopted from existing standards; (iii) a special (third) type of sovereign debt market is that of multilateral and bilateral lenders; and (iv) part of the existence of an international debt market stems from the underdevelopment of some domestic debt markets.

## THE DOMESTIC AND INTERNATIONAL SOVEREIGN DEBT MARKETS

There are many reasons why sovereigns issue in both the domestic and international debt markets.

While sovereigns issue for the purpose of funding their budgetary gaps, benchmark setting is also a reason for issuing sovereign debt papers.

Domestic debt markets are more or less captive to the rules of the sovereign issuer, while in the international debt markets the sovereign is one among many issuers playing by the same rules. The international debt market, therefore, caters to players competing within set rules that can be more advanced than in some domestic debt markets.

The extent of development of every domestic capital market may depend on the state of economic progress a country may have achieved and its demand for capital resources. It also depends on the seriousness with which a government addresses the need to develop a domestic capital market.

Overall, domestic debt markets are far larger than the international debt market where many sovereign issuers float debt instruments.

## Underdeveloped Domestic Debt Markets

Raising funds from the international market need not be a norm for sovereigns (i) if all countries have fully developed domestic capital markets, and (ii) if economic events in those countries trigger automatic adjustments in both domestic interest and foreign exchange rates. In this ideal scenario, foreign investors merely assess their investment preference, measure and price the risks, and purchase or sell debt instruments in those countries where they choose to undertake operations.

This, however, is not the case. The lack of depth in one's domestic debt market will force sovereigns to borrow in the international market. In addition, policy mistakes such as currency pegs, with no safeguard mechanisms, result in adverse trade imbalances in some countries, thus creating the need to borrow foreign currency.

The 1997 Asian currency crisis was aggravated by the fact that most of the affected countries did not have well-functioning domestic capital markets. Will the exception of controlled currency regimes, the inability to access alternative sources of capital domestically when foreign investment was withdrawn resulted in grave financial distress.

For as long as domestic markets continue to be underdeveloped, and there is a need for foreign exchange to stave off temporary negative imbalances in economies, the international debt market will exist alongside domestic debt markets.

## Globalization and Setting Standards

A world in a hurry to adopt common standards will not quickly solve the problem in countries with underdeveloped domestic capital markets. In fact, it may lead to a greater lag in the development of such markets. While standards are mostly crafted from experience and, therefore, may be good for most economies with well-defined domestic capital markets, economies with underdeveloped domestic markets may not adapt easily to such standards. This is because certain preconditions are necessary before these standards can work. Economies with stable and mature political, financial and economic systems will adapt better to global standards than those countries in the early phase of development, unless the latter are quick to address internal issues related to adopting global standards.

Globalization may be more successful if countries are pooled together in certain categories, and phase in standards according to their development needs. As countries are in different stages of economic development (not to mention political and financial maturity), so too are their own capital markets. What globalization has done is to open the world to competition in an environment where the more-developed countries are better placed to succeed. Standards will improve the rules in the international debt markets, but may not necessarily improve domestic markets. This is because sovereigns can impose their own rules within their jurisdictions.

Setting standards are desirable in order to establish order in a common market and to ensure each participant's conformity with the rules. It is gratifying to see that these standards are improving. Such standards, however, must be fair to all players involved as the market is composed of both issuers and investors. Certainly the objectives of these players may not be the same. For standards to work, each player must see them to be fair.

Recently there have been certain developments in the sovereign debt market. In particular, the adoption of collective action clauses (CACs) in the debt issuance of a number of countries such as Mexico, Brazil, Uruguay and Argentina. Speculation abounds that other countries will follow this lead. The Philippines is looking seriously at CACs and will probably follow suit within a reasonable time. As these CACs have not yet been fully tested, only time can tell whether they will lead to an improvement in the rules in the sovereign debt market, and whether the players involved perceive them to be fair.

**A Matter of Price**

The insertion of CACs, no matter how favorable or unfavorable they may be to either or both parties, should serve to strengthen the sovereign debt market. However, when changes are introduced in documents for debt issues, investors will simply impute a value and the issuer may or may not agree with such a valuation. In certain cases, the cost of every issue may be increased or lowered. Ultimately, price is the key factor, and the issuer is a price taker.

We live in a dynamic environment, and changes should be expected.

# IMPLICATIONS FOR MARKET PARTICIPANTS

The world is not perfect. Sovereigns will continue to issue debt instruments in view of financial needs arising from budgetary gaps. The dynamics of politics sometimes leads a government to make popular decisions that eventually contribute to maintaining such gaps. In addition, trade and exchange rate policies can also lead to competitiveness or lack of it. The end result may be a need for foreign exchange.

Worldwide events can lead to shifts in investment preferences from one country to another. Such changes can cause the withdrawal of capital and can result in short-term foreign exchange requirements.

While it may be an ideal solution, governments cannot refrain from borrowing simply by increasing taxes. In addition, in periods of recession, some governments may choose to engage in deficit spending to boost their economies. This, in essence results in higher funding requirements for the government and will lead to borrowing. Of course, bilateral and multilateral sources of cheap funds are accessible under certain conditions.

The issuance of debt instruments will be a matter of form, and sourcing will be from either the domestic or the international market. It should be noted also that financial products, such as debt instruments, tend to evolve. Whereas in the past simple coupon-bearing bonds were common, variants have since been developed, for example, zero coupon bonds, 'putable' and 'callable' bonds, dual currency notes, indexed and linked bonds. As the financial market continues to innovate, new instruments that cater to both the issuer and the investor will be developed by financial engineers to better suit requirements.

A growing sophistication in risk management will lead to a proliferation in financing tools. Global financial organizations are constantly improving their risk measurement systems and strategies. As a result, new instruments will be created, which will increase the number of financing tools available to sovereigns.

Rules will continue to change, for the better. Set standards and best practices change with new developments in the financial system. Global financial organizations and the constant growth in market sophistication among developed countries will guarantee the depth of the sovereign debt market. Credit crises and other negative events will lead to a further improvement in standards and a strengthening of the rules. Globalization will increase the trend towards common standards and encourage countries to adopt existing good rules based on empirical experiences.

Finally, fiscal managers will have to adapt to the ever-changing global financing landscape. Each sovereign should be able to constantly assess the elements in its economy relative to the marketplace, and look for opportunities to extract sustainable financing value. As markets develop, so do the risk parameters of domestic and global investors, and it is the duty of each fiscal manager to adapt to these changes.

90- 130

019 F34

# 6.   Sovereign debt restructuring: the future case of Argentina*
**Daniel Marx**

## INTRODUCTION

The Argentine economy is currently facing the challenge of restructuring its sovereign debt, which has been in default since December 2001. More than a year later, this issue is still pending.

Discussions on the Argentine situation in particular and debt restructuring in general are taking place within a broader international debate regarding the consequences of increased capital mobility, with special focus on emerging economies. Within the frame of these discussions one central aspect is related to what debt resolution approach the countries should adopt in the event of a crisis, and, in particular what role both the multilateral institutions and the private sector should play in these circumstances, and what should be the extent of their involvement.

In developing a general framework to deal with financial crises, the use of certain guidelines would help the resolution process. The Argentine debt restructuring will be a case where these should be spelled out more clearly. It is questionable whether multilateral institutions should put together large packages of financial assistance to finance sovereign debts that are perceived as unsustainable. It is often said that creditors should not be bailed out. The thinking behind this is that both the debtors (countries) and their creditors should learn from their past mistakes. The costs of crises should be distributed among all stakeholders. Moreover, given the growth in the amount of capital flows, official monies become insufficient to resolve the crises by themselves, implying that a higher involvement of the private sector is required.

In comparison with other recent experiences of debt crisis events, the Argentine case presents characteristics that demand a particular analysis. Not only is the amount of debt to be restructured higher, but also the universe of creditors involved is significantly larger than in previous cases. These characteristics, among others, will pose additional difficulties when it comes to having practical discussions among all the parties involved, and are likely to require a more complex treatment to achieve a successful outcome. Argentina's debt restructuring process will be relevant not only for the country itself but also because it could very well set a precedent in the new international financial architecture.

This chapter will analyse the situation and characteristics of Argentina's sovereign debt, and recommend a set of guidelines that should be in place during the restructuring process. Emphasis will be placed on the importance of making an adequate debt categorization, such as the separation of the debt into different classes and the definition of a cut-off date. These procedures will define the debt to be restructured. As we shall see below, there are some constraints – such as the privileged status of the international financial institutions (IFIs) – that do not allow the government to operate over the whole debt, placing further restrictions on the conditions imposed when the exchange offer is put together by the Argentine government.

Although the assessment will focus on the debt restructuring exercise, the solution of Argentina's sovereign indebtedness should include the ultimate goal of reestablishing public credit as an element of a broader agenda, involving sustainability of an economic growth program with proper political support and strengthened institutions. The success of the restructuring exercise would then be given by the assurance of having removed the elements that led to previous crises and establishing positive dynamics that unleashes a virtuous cycle.

This chapter proceeds as follows. The next section compares the experiences of the 1980s with more recent ones, focusing on lessons drawn from similarities with and differences from the earlier period. The third section describes the objective of Argentina's debt restructuring exercise, while the fourth section highlights the process and principles that would guide the restructuring path. The fifth section is devoted to an estimate of Argentina's current indebtedness and analyses its main characteristics. The sixth section describes features necessary to assess Argentina's payment capacity. The seventh section examines the elements required to structure the necessary exchange operation and the final section contains concluding remarks.

## CHANGING NATURE OF DEBT CRISES

If we compare the nature of the debt crises in the 1980s with the most recent ones, we can find characteristics related to both the origin of the crisis and the main features for overcoming the difficulties that differ from the current context, while there are several key resolution components that are applicable nowadays. In the following paragraphs we shall examine some of those characteristics.

In the 1980s, a crisis was often thought to be triggered by an external event that impacted on the foreign exchange position of a particular country, such as a drop in export prices, a natural disaster that could adversely affect export volumes, an increase in demand for imported supplies or even a change in a country's monetary policy that led to a dramatic increase in the international interest rates. In contrast to what happens currently, in the 1980s most sovereign debt was concentrated in a small and quite homogeneous group of creditors. These were generally foreign banks, a significant number of them from developed countries, and many having a long-term commitment in the debtor's region.

The traditional approach to handling the financing of those crises consisted of banks extending new loans to countries in difficulties with the purpose of enabling them to remain current on their up coming debt obligations. This scheme was usually called the 'new money approach'. In practice, this mechanism had certain drawbacks because some banks adopted 'free-rider' behavior, whereby they collected payments from such countries, but did not agree to extend new financing. However, this approach experienced increasing complications not only due to free riding, but also because it did not necessarily provide a stable solution. Short-term programs with IFIs did not focus on resolving structural problems; in addition there were uncertainties regarding compliance with preset quarterly targets, which in turn were often affected by external events. Such a framework was prone to generating capital outflows, leading to currency depreciation, and deteriorating solvency perception given the fact that there were debts denominated in foreign currency while interest rates on domestic currency were very high and tenors short. This vicious cycle was self-reinforcing, thus preventing the discovery of a solution to financial problems. This flaw in the incentive scheme increasingly complicated the terms of resolution. It often became a recurring difficulty.

In the light of these complications, and after a series of initiatives were considered, a new comprehensive approach to debt resolution was launched, called the Brady plan. It was predicated on debtor countries pursuing a series of programs, mainly of structural and fiscal nature, aimed at laying sound growth foundations. Developed countries, which also happened to be where important creditors reside, provided an institutional and policy framework, generating more stability, as well as moving towards more openness. This environment set the basis for more growth opportunities with associated less risk. Governments of a broad array of countries also sent strong signals to creditors that they were supporting these initiatives. (See Figure 6.1.)

Debt restructuring was another element of the program. It entailed the exchange of the then-existing claims into newly issued securities with

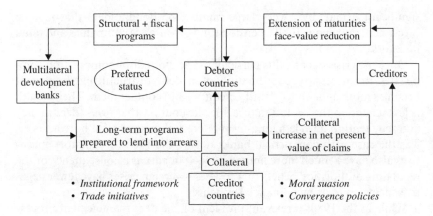

*Figure 6.1   Features of the debt resolution approach in the 1980s*

nominal reduction – whether principal or interest – and with significantly longer maturities, but with partial guarantees acquired by debtors which obtained long-term financing provided by IFIs and international governmental agencies. The success of the new approach was evidenced by the higher market prices of the new instruments compared with the old ones, despite the reduced nominal claim. The perception was that the existing problems that gave rise to payment difficulties were overcome. A drop in international market interest rates helped to this end.

Recent changes have meant that participants are quite different and the pace of events is much faster. Holdings are notably more widespread, debt instruments are liquid and capital mobility is significantly higher. The crises in the 1990s seem to be driven by the perception of agents about a deterioration in the credit standing of a particular borrower. This is usually reflected in doubts that creditors have about the willingness and/or ability of a given borrower to service its debt. Some market participants then reduced their positions, collecting at maturity or selling, an activity that tends to spread among a wide range of holders of securities. Contagion also spreads from the sovereign to the private sector, reflected in sharp increases in the cost of capital, which becomes virtually equivalent to the closure of markets. On aggregate, the result of this type of behavior is reflected in an abrupt capital flight with the consequent loss of international reserves. Experience shows that this dynamics has led to disruption on credit and capital markets, speculative attacks and banking and/or balance of payments crises.

Creditors' herd behavior is related to the new configuration of sovereign debt holders. Currently, commercial bank loans have virtually disappeared as direct forms of lending to sovereign debtors have been replaced, to a significant extent, by a very large number of bondholders that include investment and hedge funds, pension funds, insurance companies and retail investors.

Once the crisis occurs, this particular type of creditor composition complicates the necessary coordination of a debt restructuring process. It becomes more difficult to identify creditors and contact them. Their wealth is less related to the evolution of a specific country that owes them money and they tend to have less long-term interest alignment with borrowers, as was the case with commercial banks during the 1980s. Regulatory incentives also have a much more limited impact; in part as a consequence of the regulating authorities' beliefs that today's sovereign crises have fewer negative effects on their own financial systems.

While in the 1980s a relevant problem of the debt management process was the growing free-rider phenomenon, more recently the complications might arise from a growing group of holdout investors. These investors reject to participate in debt exchange offers put together by the borrower that usually contain certain reductions in the face value of principal and/or interest rates and/or more extended payment terms. Holdouts usually speculate that they could be better off because they expect to collect the entirety of the face value of their claims at maturity by not participating in debt exchange offers and maintaining their original debt instruments. This is particularly true when the failing debtor wants to be, or is in the process of becoming, current. Negotiating leverage increases when the situation regularizes. Holdout investors speculate to attach upcoming payments. Although the participation rate in the exchanges undertaken in the 1990s looks high so far (above 95 percent of restructured debt), in several cases the holdouts' strategy has been successful because they could collect their original credit at par.[1] However, in all these cases, the amount of debt to be restructured was limited when compared to total debt. Argentina is different in this respect.

In spite of the creditor's composition and the related problems, experience shows that it is possible for a debtor country to partially restructure its sovereign debt, for example, Russia, Ukraine, Pakistan and Ecuador, all of whom contemplated maturities extension. Partial deals involving Russia and Ecuador contained principal face-value reduction, while Ukraine and Pakistan reduced the corresponding interest rate. Other positive facts were that protracted negotiations were avoided (in all cases, the period between default and closing was less than 18 months) and economic recovery was generally achieved more quickly than expected.

However, as shown in Table 6.1, the Argentine case seems to be more complex than previous ones. Default is much more generalized. The amount of debt involved is larger than the sum of the other four countries, and the variety of legislation and types of instrument is significantly

*Table 6.1   Comparison of crisis features*

| Issue | Russia | Ukraine | Ecuador | Pakistan | Argentina* |
|---|---|---|---|---|---|
| Old bonds involved | 3 | 5 | 5 | 3 | 152 |
| New bonds issued | 2 | 2 | 2 | 1 | ? |
| Amount restructured (US$ bn) | 31.600 | 2.600 | 6.600 | 610 | 82.000 |
| Legislations involved | 1 | 3 | 2 | 1 | 8 |
| Exchange participation rate (%) | 98 | 95 | 97 | 95 | – |
| Minimum threshold to perform the exchange | Yes | Yes | Yes | Yes | – |
| Up-front payments (%) | 0.8 | 8.5 | 15.2 | 0.0 | – |
| Months between default and closing | 18 | 3 | 10 | 2 | – |
| Official debt/total debt (%) | 45 | 75 | 50 | 88 | 23 |
| Face-value reduction (%) | 36 | 0 | 40 | 0 | – |
| Maturity extension | Yes | Yes | Yes | Yes | – |
| Coupon reduction | No | Yes | No | Yes | – |

*Note:*   *Estimates.

*Source:*   Own analysis.

broader in the case of Argentina. Due to these complications, the Argentine situation is likely to require much more coordination between parties. A great deal of financial engineering would also be required, while associated litigation risks are higher.

## OBJECTIVE

A successful debt restructuring exercise is recognized when there are assurances that the elements that led to the previous crisis have been removed. Often, a credit event is characterized by lower means than necessary to service financial obligations. This could occur because of different factors or a combination of them: perception that the economy will not be in a position to generate necessary resources to pay back obligations, vulnerability to credit market disruptions, acknowledgment of liabilities that were previously not considered or simply signaling unwillingness to service obligations. Whatever the factor/s that are deemed to have contributed to the crisis, they have to be overcome in order to then adapt, through a debt exercise, financial terms to sustainable conditions.

From the financial point of view, in order to establish the objective of the restructuring exercise, we shall analyse the debt problem from two perspectives. The first one is how to match the stock of the current debt with the solvency conditions of the Argentine economy, while the second consists in ensuring and facilitating future liquidity, that is, credit flows necessary for the economy to consolidate its recovery process. By having a closure of the restructuring process, reestablishing payments under the restructured debt and regaining financial access, the economy will be in a condition to enter into the positive dynamics of sustained economic growth.

Given the cost associated with the process, it is key that the solution ensures that the debt problem has been resolved definitively with investors having confidence that the debt service payments will be duly made with the combination of the limited resources that will be available for this purpose and some, initially quite restricted, access to credit markets. But, at the same time, this must be implemented avoiding that, old investors believe that they have been unnecessarily harmed by the terms of the restructuring. A key expected outcome of a successful restructuring exercise should be a significant reduction in the cost of capital to all users affected by the exercise, both in the public and in the private sectors.

## THE PROCESS

To achieve a disciplined discussion among the involved parties it becomes useful to design a set of general guidelines that will govern the restructuring process. Conducive to attaining the set objective, decisions have to be made on issues such as the timing, the principles to be applied and a schedule of milestones to be achieved. It is expected that the Republic will take the initiative on all of these subjects. To obtain the desired results, these issues must also be set in accordance with internationally accepted standards.

The first element to consider is establishing the best timing to start the restructuring process. Should it be when the situation is at its worst? Or when a recovery is underway? Argentina's high political instability, alterations in judicial norms and institutional regulations, together with a particularly complicated economic situation, especially in light of the sharp depreciation in the real exchange rate and the plummeting of the activity level, have been factors of uncertainty regarding the future outlook. More precisely, in those circumstances it has been difficult to derive credible projections, thus allowing one to adequately evaluate the country's payment capacity. Given this context, the sovereign debt problem can only be resolved after addressing these shortcomings.

Nonetheless, the failure to resolve the public debt issue negatively affects, in turn, the country's possibilities for economic recovery. It becomes both cause and effect of a worrisome situation. As time goes by and the country remains in default, value is destroyed, which is particularly harmful to companies. Additionally, this negative context is reflected in a reluctance to make consumption and investment decisions, thus generating a situation with negative feedbacks. Furthermore, while the irregular condition persists, the risk of litigation and judicial action increases, as some creditors who feel that their claims are not being considered may take action in defense of their interests. Lastly, it is highly improbable that the optimal initial conditions to begin negotiations will ever, in fact, exist. In sum, putting off the solution indefinitely not only complicates the situation, but also generates additional costs for the parties involved. As such, the sooner the better, if circumstances are right.

Guidelines must be established as a way to facilitate coordinated and cooperative actions of involved parties. Experience indicates that, within such a framework, an expeditious solution will be available to the benefit of both debtor and creditors. If, as a result of the restructuring exercise, the debtor is able to extend its maturities and reduce its payments, the perception of its long-term solvency will improve. This, in turn, translates into a reduced discount rate that creditors would be willing to contemplate, resulting in a market price increase of claims. Hence the solution may be beneficial and rational to both parties.

Figure 6.2 shows a curve given by the price of a security expressed in terms of the old par claim. We assumed a hypothetical settlement including reduced principal, long tenor and low coupons, according to the conditions that are described on pages 105–8. Despite this reduction in principal and interest and extended maturities, the regularization in the macroeconomic perspectives and debt situation should produce a reduction in the relevant discount rate. The horizontal line in the figure shows the current price of existing debt while the curve shows the net present value (NPV) price evolution corresponding to different levels of discount rates. As a result, in this example, if the applicable discount rate were lower than 19 percent per annum, the new bond would have a higher price than the current one of the old claim.

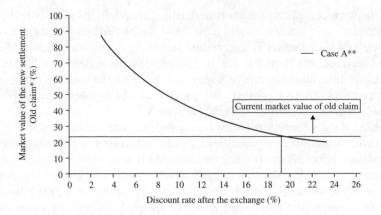

*Notes:*
 * Old Claim defined as Capital Outstanding + Past Due Interests.
 ** Specifics related to this case will be developed below.

*Figure 6.2    Rationale for agreement: an example*

A necessary step towards ensuring a certain degree of control of the process is agreeing on the clearest possible 'rules of the game' for the involved parties. To this end, it would help to define a series of specific principles that would govern the restructuring process. These must be outlined to streamline the process, improve debtor–creditor relationships, and avoid intra- or inter-creditor conflicts, which could otherwise negatively affect the likelihood of reaching an appropriate outcome. The guiding principles would be:

1.  *realism:* defining commitments according to assessed payment capacity;
2.  *fairness:* ensuring fair distribution of losses, including equal treatment among creditors of similar nature;
3.  *efficiency:* avoiding protracted discussions in order to limit further value destruction; and
4.  *communication:* providing access to relevant information to interested parties, while avoiding privileges except for sensitive information, which should be treated confidentially. Stay away from litigation, provided that good faith prevails.

In this chapter, the characteristics and implications of each of the principles outlined above will be analysed in greater detail.

# ARGENTINE PUBLIC SECTOR DEBT SITUATION

A debt restructuring exercise can only be derived from some understanding of the figures involved. The Argentine public sector debt data, including a new estimate, will be analysed as a necessary tool in order to suggest a restructuring exercise.

According to official figures, up to December 2001, the Republic's gross public sector debt totaled US$144 billion. In general terms, the origin of this debt can principally be explained by looking at three components: cumulative fiscal deficits, acknowledgment of liabilities with suppliers and pensioners, and the cost of the transition arising from the change in the pension regime (see Figure 6.3).

The most important of these three factors is the accumulation of fiscal deficits (excluding pension reform costs), which, as of the 1990s, were basically financed via the issuance of debt. The second most important is the so-called 'consolidation of different debts', including those owed to retired people and suppliers. During the 1980s and part of the 1990s, it was usual to recognize past unpaid expenses or obligations. Usually they were the result of disputes, leading to additional obligations that were acknowledged and cancelled through debt consolidation bonds. The third factor is the financing of the transition of the pension system launched in mid-1994. The Federal Republic no longer receives personal pension contributions

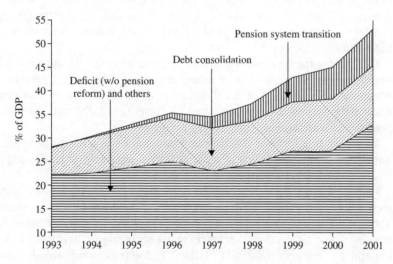

*Source:* Own analysis based on Ministry of Economy (Mecon, Ministerio de Economía).

*Figure 6.3  Debt breakdown as per origin*

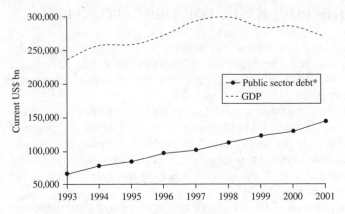

*Note:*   * Considering the year of registration.

*Source:*   Mecon.

*Figure 6.4    Evolution of public sector debt and GDP (measured in current US$ values)*

from those who opted for the individual account system (individual account or capitalization regime), but nonetheless has to continue making retirement payments for those who were totally or partially under the previous pay-as-you-go system. The cumulative effect of this element – up to December 2001 – is approximately US$30 billion (including interest). This last factor is equivalent to a partial booking of pension liabilities which most countries do not do.

Comparing the figures with respect to gross domestic product (GDP) – and using December 2001 as a reference – gross debt was 53 percent, of which the accumulation of fiscal deficits equaled 33 percent of that year's GDP, debt consolidation represented 12 percent, of GDP and the cost of pension reform another 8 points (see Figure 6.4).

When we break down the base components of this indicator, we also notice that the impact of economic slowdown is quite relevant, affecting the base on which this indicator is measured.

Official figures show that, up to September 2002, Argentina's public sector debt had shrunk to slightly more than US$129 billion, as seen in Table 6.2. This decrease between periods is explained mainly by the unilateral decision made by the government at the beginning of 2002 to announce mandatory conversion of part of the US dollar-denominated debt into local currency at a defined exchange rate. Subsequently, the AR peso devalued sharply during 2002. These figures also include some of the debt incurred with financial institutions and bank depositors as a consequence

*Table 6.2*   *Debt according to both the* Fiscal Bulletin (Boletín Fiscal) *and our estimates*

| Gross debt (US$ bn) | Dec-01 Official | Sep-02 Official | Sep-02 Revised |
|---|---|---|---|
| Total debt | 144,406 | 129,984 | 155,236 |
| *Medium and long term* | 137,660 | 105,988 | 113,916 |
| Loans | 82,603 | 57,389 | 45,085 |
|   Multilaterals | 32,362 | 31,065 | 31,065 |
|     IMF | 13,952 | 14,096 | 14,096 |
|     World Bank | 9,673 | 8,589 | 8,589 |
|     Inter-American Development Bank | 8,704 | 8,350 | 8,350 |
|     Others | 33 | 30 | 30 |
|   Official | 4,477 | 4,343 | 4,343 |
|     Paris Club | 1,879 | 1,811 | 1,811 |
|     Other bilaterals | 2,598 | 2,532 | 2,532 |
|   Commercial banks | 2,015 | 1,221 | 1,221 |
|   Others | 1,490 | 242 | 242 |
|   Guaranteed loans | 42,258 | 20,518 | 8,214 |
| Bonds | 55,057 | 48,599 | 68,831 |
|   Local currency | 1,505 | 2,348 | 2,348 |
|   Foreign currency | 53,552 | 46,251 | 46,251 |
|   Brady guarantee | – | – | (898) |
|   Revision of guaranteed loans | – | – | 21,129 |
| *Short term* | 6,746 | – | – |
| Letes | 6,746 | – | – |
| *Arrears* | – | 7,365 | 7,365 |
| Principal | – | 4,829 | 4,829 |
| Interest | – | 2,536 | 2,536 |
| *New indebtedness* | – | 16,631 | 19,344 |
| Compensation bonds | – | 11,025 | 13,470 |
|   Boden y Pagaré 2007 $ | – | 1,635 | 1,635 |
|   Boden y Pagaré 2012 US$ | – | 6,156 | 6,156 |
|   Bono Cobertura | – | 3,234 | 3,234 |
|   CER* | – | – | 1,044 |
|   Judicial injunctions* | – | – | 1,401 |
| Bonds to depositors | – | 5,414 | 5,874 |
|   Boden 2005 US$ | – | 886 | 886 |
|   Boden 2007 $ | – | 134 | 134 |
|   Boden 2012 US$ | – | 4,394 | 4,394 |
|   Boden 2013 US$** | – | – | 461 |

*Table 6.2*   (continued)

| Gross debt (US$ bn) | Dec-01 Official | Sep-02 Official | Sep-02 Revised |
|---|---|---|---|
| *Other liabilities* | – | – | 14,611 |
| Provincial debt*** | – | – | 10,611 |
| Net bank recapitalization & related | – | – | 4,000 |
| Currency in circulation | 11,981 | – | 5,168 |
| Quasi-currencies | 2,040 | – | 2,172 |
| Lecops | – | – | 907 |
| Patacones | – | – | 687 |
| Others | – | – | 579 |

*Notes:*
 * Prelimanary estimate.
 ** Assuming 5 percent swap participation.
 *** Debt with multilateral agences is included in the federal debt. Does not include revenue-sharing collateral.

*Source:*   Own analysis based on Mecon.

of the peso devaluation and asymmetric 'pesoification' on part of banks' assets and liabilities.

Nonetheless, there are some additional concepts, which have not yet been registered,[2] and must be incorporated into the analysis, revising the published debt figures:

1. Several holders of pesoified guaranteed loans (GLs) (we assume 50 percent of the December 2001 stock) could revert to their assets into US dollar claims, either by requesting the delivery of the underlying assets swapped for those GLs, which they are entitled to, or as a result of legal actions by which those holders request the re-dollarization of their claims. This is the 'revision of GLs', effect.
2. Past or future liquidation of collateral of Brady bonds reduces the stock of debt by the present value of guarantees.
3. Other liabilities taken on, such as issuance of bonds to banks and their depositors stemming from different mechanisms that began with the compensation for the effects of devaluation and was followed by payments for the difference between the *Coeficiente de Estabilización de Referencia* (CER)[3] and the *Coeficiente de Variación Salarial* (CVS)[4] adjustment mechanisms and, potentially, the payment to be made to

banks for the exchange rate difference resulting from judicial injunctions (*amparos*) filed by bank depositors.

4.  At some point, it is assumed that banks will compensate the government with the delivery of GLs in exchange for a reduction in their liabilities with the Republic or its subsidiaries, including the central bank. Those liabilities originated in financing banks paying depositors in government bonds or directly. For the purpose of making calculations, the assumed exchange factor is US$1 (of Bodens received by banks from the government) = AR$1.4 (plus CER) (of GLs delivered to the government). This factor reduces the stock of GLs and consequently the stock of debt.

5.  Partial assumption of provincial debt by the Republic, including (i) debt with local commercial banks that has been restructured (pesoified) under the *Canje de Deuda Provincial* (Provincial Debt Exchange) scheme, (ii) some of the provincial bonded debt, and (iii) debt with the Provincial Development Fiduciary Fund (*Fondo Fiduciario de Desarrollo Provincial:* (FFDP).[5] This operation does not increase net consolidated debt, but was previously not at the Federal Republic level. In exchange for taking on their debt, the Republic retains the right to withhold up to 15 percent in tax-sharing revenues from the provinces.

6.  Projected financial assistance to be granted to certain banks for their recapitalization.

Incorporating all these factors into the analysis, it is estimated that the debt would rise to approximately US$155 billion, roughly 150 percent of the current GDP.

It is very important to note that these figures neither include the effects of future contingent liabilities that would appear due to legal disputes or similar, nor consider the acknowledgment of debts with suppliers and others which are settled through the issuance of government securities.

Table 6.3, Figure 6.5 and Table 6.4 show debt breakdowns by creditor, type and/or instrument issued, currency and residence of holder. Note that:

1.  Resident holders account for 49 percent of total debt but the figure increases to 63 percent if we exclude from the base multilateral development bank (MDBs) and bilateral loans.

2.  Bonded debt was 49 percent of the total, but, if we were to add the GLs (of those holders who accepted pesoification) and 'new indebtedness' bonds (Bodens) the figure reaches 66 percent.

3.  Provincial debt assumed by the Republic represents 7 percent of total consolidated debt.

*Table 6.3 Debt breakdown per creditor, instrument, currency and residence of holder*

| Currency | IFIs | Bilaterals | Bonded debt* Bonds** | Bonded debt* GL | Bonded debt* New indebtedness | Provincial debt | Banking recap | Others*** | Total | % |
|---|---|---|---|---|---|---|---|---|---|---|
| US$ | 19,152 | 4,343 | 48,854 | 8,214 | 11,897 | – | – | 1,463 | 93,924 | 61 |
| Euro | 5,539 | – | 14,123 | – | – | – | – | – | 19,662 | 13 |
| AR$ | – | – | 2,348 | – | 7,447 | 10,611 | 4,000 | – | 24,406 | 16 |
| Yen | 4,058 | – | 2,651 | – | – | – | – | – | 6,708 | 4 |
| Others | 2,316 | – | 8,219 | – | – | – | – | – | 10,536 | 7 |
| Total | 31,065 | 4,343 | 76,196 | 8,214 | 19,344 | 10,611 | 4,000 | 1,463 | 155,236 | 100 |
| Percentage | 20 | 3 | 49 | 5 | 12 | 7 | 3 | 1 | 100 | |

*Notes:*

  *  It is worth noting that some of the provincial debt and banking recap debt would also be bonded debt.

  **  Includes estimated revision of GL and arrears.

  ***  Includes commercial banks and other loans.

*Source:*  Own analysis based on Mecon.

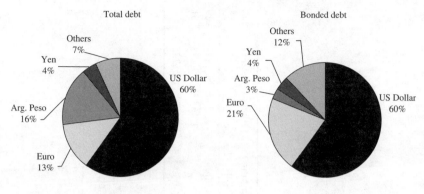

*Source:*   Own analysis based on Mecon.

*Figure 6.5    Debt breakdown per ( US$ bn)*

4.  Debt already issued due to the banking crisis (or to be issued in the future, including assumed net recapitalization) accounts for 15 percent of the total.
5.  US dollar-denominated debt represents 61 percent of the total, while foreign currency debt is 84 percent.

Another relevant aspect to consider is the payment status, as shown in Table 6.5.

Approximately 44 percent of the total debt would be performing, when adjustments were done. It includes debts owed to MDBs and the new indebtedness (Bodens) taken on with financial entities and bank depositors. It also incorporates guaranteed loans of those holders who accepted pesoification would be serviced in due time.

A debt restructuring exercise has to contemplate reprofiling existing debt. This has to include rollover of performing debt, since, as shown in Figure 6.6, there are not insignificant amounts coming due in the next few years.

Figure 6.7 clearly shows that there are a significant number of maturities over the next few years: current payment obligations total US$48.8 billion between 2003 and 2005 alone.

## ASSESSING PAYMENT CAPACITY

One aspect to consider when defining a debt position as sustainable is whether the government meets the intertemporal budget constraint without the need of later having to make brusque corrections in spending or revenues

*Table 6.4  Debt breakdown per (US$ bn)*

| | IFIs | Bilaterals | Bonded debt | GL | New indebtedness | Provincial debt | Banking recap | Others | Total | % |
|---|---|---|---|---|---|---|---|---|---|---|
| Resident | – | – | 33,668 | 8,214 | 19,344 | 10,611 | 4,000 | – | 75,837 | 49 |
| Non-resident | 31,065 | 4,343 | 42,527 | – | – | – | – | 1,463 | 79,398 | 51 |
| Total | 31,065 | 4,343 | 76,195 | 8,214 | 19,344 | 10,611 | 4,000 | 1,463 | 155,235 | |

*Source:*  Own analysis based on Mecon.

*Table 6.5   Current state of payment*

| Debt | Sep-02 | Performing | | Non-performing | |
|---|---|---|---|---|---|
| | Total debt | US$ bn | % | US$ bn | % |
| Loans | 45,085 | 42,328 | | 2,758 | |
| IFIs | 31,065 | 31,065 | | – | |
| Official agencies | 4,343 | 1,951 | | 2,392 | |
| Commercial banks | 1,221 | 916 | | 305 | |
| Other | 242 | 182 | | 61 | |
| Guaranteed loans | 8,214 | 8,214 | | – | |
| Bonds | 68,831 | 750 | | 68,081 | |
| Local currency | 2,348 | 750 | | 1,598 | |
| Foreign currency | 45,353 | – | | 45,353 | |
| Revision of guaranteed loans | 21,129 | – | | 21,129 | |
| Letes | – | – | | – | |
| Arrears | 7,365 | – | | 7,365 | |
| Principal | 4,829 | – | | 4,829 | |
| Interest | 2,536 | – | | 2,536 | |
| New indebtedness | 19,344 | 19,344 | | – | |
| Subtotal | 140,625 | 62,422 | 44 | 78,203 | 56 |
| Other liabilities | 14,611 | – | | – | |
| Provincial debt | 10,611 | n/a | | n/a | |
| Net bank recapitalization & related | 4,000 | n/a | | n/a | |
| Total | 155,236 | | | | |

*Source:*   Own analysis based on Mecon.

which could turn out to be politically and economically impracticable. Another is related to the financing costs and amounts and sources that would be available relative to the needs coming from deficits and amortizations of existing debt. This conceptualization is valid either for analysing perspectives of a performing country or for defining the path to be followed by another which has defaulted its debt and is trying to return to a regularized situation, through a debt restructuring exercise.

What seems simple in theory is much more difficult to assess in reality, as in Argentina's current situation. As a first step it would be useful to reach an understanding of a GDP growth path. From there we could derive an attainable primary surplus trajectory, bearing in mind political and social

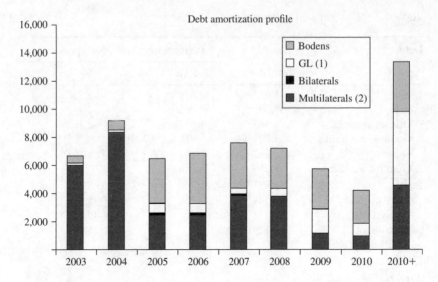

*Notes:*
1.  Considering 50 percent revision.
2.  Considering expected financing or roll overs.

*Source:*   Own analysis based on Mecon.

*Figure 6.6    Amortization schedule (performing debt)*

limitations, as well as historical considerations. To evaluate servicing capacity it is necessary to consider that the initial debt level is endogenous to the exercise and that the possible outcome is also driven significantly by the level of foreign exchange rates.

To this end, we have to take into account the real exchange rate path, particularly in light of the sharp depreciation following the crisis. As seen in Figure 6.8, recent international experience demonstrates that in all cases there is an initial 'overshooting' after a crisis occurrence,[6] which is then corrected over time in a more regularized context.

Moreover, a debt service scheme should incorporate a set of essential elements in order to achieve a successful debt operation, for example:

1.  commitments assumed should be such that future investors feel comfortable with the payment outlook – that is, they perceive that the capital structure has been adapted to the new reality – while current ones do not feel excessively penalized;
2.  a menu of options contemplating both the investors' diverse preferences and the inevitable reductions in NPV terms at a given discount

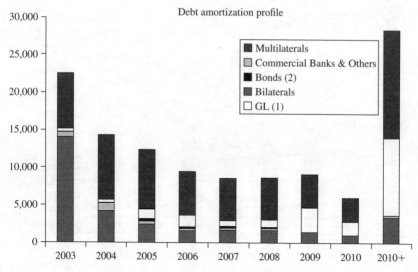

Debt amortization profile

Notes:
1. According to official figures.
2. Includes Pagarés.

*Source:* Mecon.

*Figure 6.7    Total amortization schedule (performing and non-performing)*

rate that has to be assumed – be it via face-value reductions, maturity extensions and/or interest rate cuts;
3. the maturities profile should consider, among other things: a grace period permitting the country to conclude a series of necessary reforms and to get itself back on the growth track, and a term period structure extended in such a way as to minimize refinancing risks due to liquidity problems in the international capital markets or bunching of maturities; and
4. the depth of the local capital market, bearing in mind its capacity to absorb debt and avoid the private sector crowding out; the transition from the pay-as-you-go pension regime to the current capitalization pension system, which carries along with it a temporal imbalance between revenues and perceived expenditures; and others, such as the costs associated with restructuring the banking system.

A simple exercise was performed to obtain some preliminary conclusions with respect to future repayment capacity and possible outcomes derived in terms of the payment scheme. To this end, we set up some macroeconomic

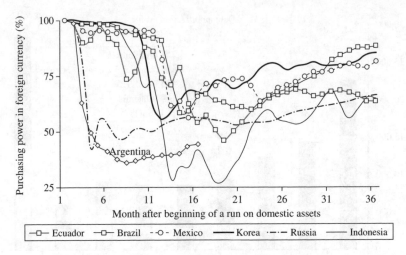

*Figure 6.8    Real exchange rate overshooting experiences*

scenarios and established a primary surplus target of 3 percent of GDP. Then, we propose a generic restructuring scheme, with a grace period for principal amortization, extension of maturities, and step-up interest rates. As a result of the exercise we obtain debt/GDP and interest payment/GDP ratios' evolution for each assumption of initial face-value reduction and macroeconomic scenario. Table 6.6 shows three macroeconomic scenarios, which differ in the real GDP growth rate and the real exchange rates.

To simulate an exercise we created a synthetic security corresponding to the average hypothetical options to be considered in an exchange. Different combinations of interest rates, tenors and principal value can be presented that would result in even more varying valuations of NPV terms, given the possibility of utilizing different discount rates. Nevertheless, the only purpose of the exercise is to simulate evolution of debt/GDP and interest payments/GDP ratios under different scenarios.

The restructuring conditions established are the following: (i) US$82 billion to refinance.[7] We assume rollover for multilateral debt and original amortization schedule for the remaining debt; (ii) the closing date is set at Q2 2004; (iii) a four-year grace period on capital; (iv) consecutive and equal amortizations until Q1 2031; (v) step-up interest rates (from 2 percent in 2004, to 5 percent in 2007); and (vi) a marginal financing rate of 6 percent.[8]

Arbitrarily, for the stated purpose and regardless of the NPV reduction, when we assume an average 35 percent face-value reduction and a 3 percent of GDP primary surplus we obtain the results shown in Figures 6.9 and 6.10. Implicit fiscal effort – according to each macro scenario – is depicted

*Table 6.6  Macro assumptions*

| Scenarios | 2002 | 2003 | 2004 | 2005 | 2006 | 2007 | 2008 | 2009 | 2010 | 2011 | 2012+ |
|---|---|---|---|---|---|---|---|---|---|---|---|
| **High (H)** | | | | | | | | | | | |
| GDP real growth | −11.0% | 4.0% | 4.0% | 4.0% | 4.0% | 4.0% | 4.0% | 4.0% | 4.0% | 4.0% | 4.0% |
| Purchasing power of AR$ | 0.44 | 0.55 | 0.60 | 0.65 | 0.75 | 0.75 | 0.75 | 0.75 | 0.75 | 0.75 | 0.75 |
| **Medium (M)** | | | | | | | | | | | |
| GDP real growth | −11.0% | 3.0% | 3.0% | 3.0% | 3.0% | 3.0% | 3.0% | 3.0% | 3.0% | 3.0% | 3.0% |
| Purchasing power of AR$ | 0.44 | 0.48 | 0.53 | 0.60 | 0.65 | 0.65 | 0.65 | 0.65 | 0.65 | 0.65 | 0.65 |
| **Low (L)** | | | | | | | | | | | |
| GDP real growth | −11.0% | 2.0% | 2.0% | 2.0% | 2.0% | 2.0% | 2.0% | 2.0% | 2.0% | 2.0% | 2.0% |
| Purchasing power of AR$ | 0.44 | 0.45 | 0.48 | 0.50 | 0.55 | 0.55 | 0.55 | 0.55 | 0.55 | 0.55 | 0.55 |

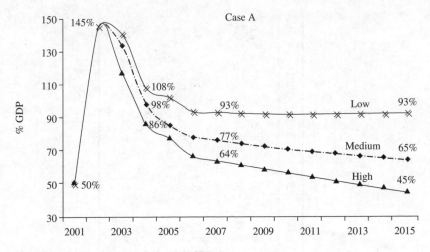

*Figure 6.9    Evolution of the debt/GDP ratio*

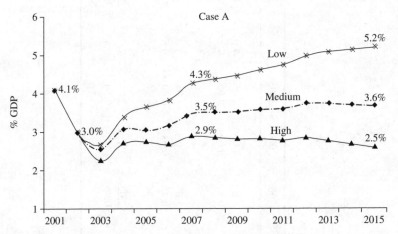

*Figure 6.10    Evolution of the interest payments/GDP ratio*

in the figures, showing the evolution of debt/GDP and interest pay-
ments/GDP ratios over time.[9]

In Figure 6.9, we can see that trends differ significantly according to the
scenario considered. For instance, while under the low scenario, debt sta-
bilizes at around 93 percent of GDP in the coming years, the ratio decreases
more sharply under the high macro scenario, reaching 45 percent of GDP
in 2015.

It becomes more meaningful to analyse differing levels of interest payments. Under the low scenario, interest payments rise to 5.2 percent of GDP in 2015, contrasting with 2.5 percent for the same year in the high one. Under the medium and high scenarios, interest payments are close or lower than the primary surplus we have assumed.

In sum, under the high and medium scenarios the debt situation seems to be 'manageable'. However, conditions assumed in the restructuring exercise do not seem sufficient if the low scenario prevails.

# STRUCTURING

## Debt Classes

It is necessary to specify a set of important factors related to the structure of the potential exchange offer. In order to do this, we begin by defining a cut-off date as well as recognizing different debt status.

The cut-off date is established with the objective of separating old debt from new issuances. Our original idea was that the cut-off date could have been 31 December 2001, concordant with the declaration of default, thus leaving out of the restructuring process all debt issued subsequent to that date. However, to the extent to which the amount of debt issued following that date continues to increase, it becomes more difficult to respect those commitments recently taken on. This in turn led us to consider the alternative of having to include this new debt in the restructuring process.

Looking ahead to the negotiation, another key element is to differentiate between privileged and non-privileged debt status. The international financial institutions, such as the International Monetary Fund (IMF) and the MDBs have always held a privileged status, by which the payment of their services has priority and should not suffer reductions in their value. They extend financings at terms and in circumstances in accordance with their status.

We can now proceed to identify various debt classes, following the types of debt instrument and according to assumptions stated previously (see Table 6.7).

Combining the cut-off date definition and the different status – privileged or non-privileged – of the public debt we can develop a matrix. In order to identify the amount to be restructured, we fill the cells with the debt classes mentioned (see Figure 6.11). In the upper row is the superior debt, which mainly includes multilateral institutions. Emerging from the crisis, and with a strong program, some support from the IFIs would be expected, implying signaling effects and financial relief. Extended fund facilities from the IMF

*Table 6.7    Debt classes*

| Instrument | Amount* (US$ bn) |
|---|---|
| 1   *IFIs + special parallel financing* | 33,597 |
|      IFIs | 31,065 |
|      Parallel financing | 2,532 |
| 2   *Paris Club* | 1,811 |
|      Paris Club | 1,811 |
| 3   *Commercial banks* | 1,463 |
|      Commercial banks + | |
|      Others | 1,463 |
| 4   *Bonds* | 98,925 |
|      Foreign currency bonds | 45,353 |
|      AR$ old bonds | 537 |
|      PDI | 2,536 |
|      Compensation bonds | 13,470 |
|      Bonds to depositors | 5,874 |
|      Domestic applicable law bonds | 31,154 |
|          *Redollarized bonds (revision of GLs + other bonds)* | *21,129* |
|          *Pesoified bonds* | *10,025* |
| 5   *Other liabilities* | 19,440 |
|      Originated in provinces | 10,611 |
|          *Commercial banks* | *4,533* |
|          *Bonds* | *4,704* |
|          *FFDP* | *1,374* |
|      Net bank recapitalization & related | 4,000 |
|      Arrears* | 4,829 |
| Total | 155,236 |

*Note:*    *Estimated values as of September 2002. Need to be adjusted at the time of exchange.

*Source:*    Own analysis based on Mecon.

as well as structural adjustment loans from the MDBs could eventually become available as long-term financing, accompanying structural reforms.

In addition to the direct loans that Argentina has with the multilateral institutions, the country has debts which were structured under the 'umbrella' of these same organizations, that is, co-financing or parallel multilateral financing. Such is the case of countries which lent money under agreement programs with the IMF, that is, Spain and Japan. We assign them similar treatment as IFIs, including these liabilities in the same category.

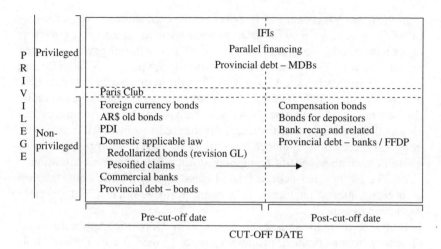

*Figure 6.11   Defining debt categories*

Debt with the Paris Club is often considered a special case. Even though to some extent it must be negotiated separately, the general impression is that this debt ought to be restructured under terms that are comparable to the corresponding category/ies.

Another particular case is the recently assumed provincial debt, with the intention of implementing the Fiscal Agreements (*Acuerdos Fiscales*) and the Program of Orderly Provincial Financing (*Programa de Financiamiento Provincial Ordenado*). In exchange for taking on their debt, the Republic retains the right to withhold up to 15 percent in tax-sharing revenues from the provinces. These liabilities include the following components:

1.  *Debt with commercial banks:* this debt was pesoified and then transferred to the Republic under similar terms. It is classified as a post-cut-off date for similar reasons as other pesoified debts.
2.  *Bonded debt:* issued before the cut-off date. It will be part of the debt to be restructured.
3.  *Debt with the so-called FFDP* (Provincial Development Fiduciary Fund), in turn divided into:

    ● funded by MDBs: gets preferred treatment;
    ● funded by commercial banks: already restructured due to pesoification;
    ● funded with FFDP own resources: already restructured due to pesoification.

In the lower left corner in Figure 6.11 is the debt category 'to be restructured'. This category is by far the most heterogeneous and complex in terms of its handling and comprises mainly securities, without privilege, issued prior to the cut-off date and which are currently not paid. It includes foreign and local currency bonds. Also in this cell of the matrix we include debt held directly by commercial banks and some of the provincial debt taken on by the Federal Republic. These should also be part of the restructuring exercise. Defining an equitable treatment for the creditors included in this category will represent a challenge, given the existence of a large quantity of instruments with widely different interest rates, maturities and valuation.

Besides the bonded debt, a related class is given by the consolidation of overdue interest payments. In general, past due interest had a certain particular treatment.

Guaranteed loans and other bonds with Domestic Applicable Law (Treasury bonds (*Bontes*), promissory notes (*Pagarés*) and Treasury bills (*Letes*)), which were unilaterally pesoified can be divided into two categories:

1.  The first one comprises those GLs whose holders have accepted pesoification. They already had a reduction in their claims as measured in US dollars. This would normally be considered as the acceptance of an exchange offer containing a reduction in NPV terms. Because of this reduced value of the claim, it becomes part of the new/restructured debt.
2.  The second group is formed by holders of bonds that would be re-dollarized, either through legal action or because they can request the delivery of the underlying assets swapped for GLs.

In the current world state of affairs, which is characterized by high capital mobility and cross-holdings of debt claims between residents and non-residents, re-dollarization of claims, unless accepted by the parties involved, is desirable and also consistent with a legal system that respects credit rights. A different topic is then how to fulfill those obligations. A practical way of doing it is by making the same offer to the other pre-cut-off date securities. However, as we noted above, for those debts that remain denominated in pesos, it would not then be appropriate to include them in the restructuring process, given the fact that they have already suffered a reduction in their due value. Although these liabilities were issued before December 2001, we assumed that their status was changed so as to assimilate them to the post-cut-off date debt when converted into local currency due to pesoification.

The lower right corner in Figure 6.11 includes non-privileged debt issued after the cut-off date. Should 31 December 2001 be chosen as the said date, then within this category would be included the bonds already issued to compensate banks for the asymmetric pesoification (Boden 2007 and 2012, Promissory Notes 2007 and 2012 (*Pagarés*) and the Coverage bond (*Cobertura*)), bonds granted to bank depositors due to the pesoification of their deposits (Boden 2005, 2007 and 2012) and all new debt structured in 2002 and in the current year (that is, new bonds to compensate banks for judicial injunctions and for the difference between CER and CVS indexation, and new bonds to capitalize the financial system). Also included in this category is the part of the provincial debt assumed by the Federal Republic and already restructured through the *Canje de Deuda Provincial* scheme.

Consequently, from the preceding analysis it is seen that, of a total debt of US$155 billion, the restructuring exercise would cover US$82 billion (sum of debts included in the lower left corner in Figure 6.11 plus the Paris Club debt), which represents 52 percent of total debt and assuming 50 percent revision of GLs. If this does not materialize, then the amount to be restructured would be US$61 billion, out of a total of US$146 billion at the prevailing exchange rate of US$1 = AR$3.64 (September 2002), which represents 41 percent of total debt. Although the total debt initially seems lower in this scenario, it is likely to be a much more complicated one for the following reasons:

1. the amounts stated are considered before reductions derived from restructuring of US dollar-denominated debt, which is higher in the previous scenario;
2. indexed debt, measured in US dollar terms, is likely to appreciate; and
3. AR peso-denominated debt instruments are likely to have shorter maturities and to be more onerous than the alternative.

The continuous issuance of post-cut-off date debt could potentially undermine the expected outcome. There is an additional risk posed by future liability build-up stemming from litigation over actions of a different origin, for example, disputes from foreign direct investment agreements, differences of pension payments and so on. The combined effects of these elements would result in higher cuts in the relative size of debt to be restructured. To honor the privileged debt, the one already restructured debt and the post-cut-off date debt with a given amount of resources, it would be necessary to produce a highly significant reduction in the remainder. This reduction could become materially impossible to enforce because of the particular dynamics. As a consequence, it may become necessary to redefine the cut-off date and/or categories.

**Incentives**

Involved parties are multiple and diverse. Their objectives, preferences and associated responsibilities differ significantly. Because of this, it would help if we could initially define what would be a 'fair' negotiation as one that gives the same treatment to every holder of a similar instrument or instruments with common characteristics. A practical way out is to use clusters that group together holders of a similar nature, particularly those with original maturities, as will be discussed below.

In order to have a fair approach to different debt clusters, it will be necessary to define a uniform valuation mechanism to be applied to different claims. There are three ways to perform this valuation exercise:

1.  The first approach likely to be implemented is to accelerate to the par claim, without considering existing differences among instruments. The outstanding values of each instrument the holder has would be considered at the time of the exchange.
2.  The second alternative is to offer a uniform maturity extension of capital payments for a predetermined number of years, maintaining the original contractual conditions of each claim.
3.  The third approach, in the case that original conditions are modified, would be to recognize claims in terms of NPV equivalencies. That is, to discount future committed cash flows. This framework takes into consideration, in addition to the par claim, the different interest rate and maturity structure. A practical shortcoming to applying this methodology arises in the determination of the discount factor. The objective should be that the obtained values be comparable with those which creditors had prior to the exchange.

Creditors and debtors that are current, or have been current up to an exchange offer, use the second or third approach. In the other extreme, in cases of long-standing default the first approach is more customary. In the Argentine case some consideration could be given to original maturities through grouping them in clusters and each cluster has some priority when the time comes to choose within a given option that would be part of the general exchange offer.

The importance of clearly defining the expected objective of a restructuring exercise and setting up a consistent timetable of actions to accomplish it has already been discussed. In order to develop an efficient process, it would be constructive to maintain a dialogue and negotiations with creditors while avoiding protracted discussions, thus limiting further value destruction. This means that negotiating with highly fragmented parties could become very time-consuming and would not necessarily yield results in a timely fashion. Making unilateral exchange offers without previous consultation also raises the significant risk of being rejected.[10] Therefore, equilibrium between protracted negotiations and material advances oriented towards regularizing the payment situation must be explored. To this end, a timetable with specific feasible goals could help. Efforts should focus on minimizing the time lag between the different steps of the process, for example:

- inaugurating the new administration;
- putting an economic program in place;
- negotiating with the IMF;
- communicating with all creditors;
- outlining offers to different types of creditors;
- marketing;
- proceeding with the offer; and
- closing.

In the meantime, there are some specific tasks that could be undertaken, such as:

- developing a database;
- creating proper information channels;
- clarifying the claim situation;
- defining the cut-off date; and
- arranging consultative committee/s.

To minimize misunderstandings it is important to have fluid, transparent and permanent communication between parties, generally avoiding privileged information. Sensitive information has to be treated confidentially. The debtor must take advantage of all technological capabilities available – including a dedicated website – in order to disseminate all the information related to the process. Another task is to develop a database capable of identifying the largest number of creditors.

Options like creating consultative committees, developing fora with the participation of distinguished members of the international financial community, or specific meetings with certain creditors should be considered.

Initially, several consultative committees could be set up according to geographical distribution and the nature of the holders (institutional, retail, and so on) and integrated by the most representative creditors of each class. The formation of various subcommittees with responsibilities for different subjects, such as economic and financial projections, the design of new securities' financial structure and the analysis of legal issues is also recommended.

It is desirable that these communication mechanisms facilitate the generation of a framework of trust among parties, based on adherence to rules and fulfillment of commitments made at the beginning of the process. Such a methodology would avoid litigation, which would hamper the country's economic perspectives, the likelihood of successful restructuring and relations among creditors.

Another issue that should be clear at the outset is the role that multilaterals will play. Given their characteristics, they have information that the rest of the creditors do not have, and in many instances, they have the capacity to influence the evolution of the process. As such, it becomes important to avoid a conflict of interests. In a workout context, a sequence that would begin with clarifying their involvement prior to proceeding with the final exchange offer is recommended.

An important obstacle to carrying out the negotiation process efficiently is the presence of certain minority creditors – holdouts – which may perceive that full repayment of their claims is a matter of perseverance, and that non-participation in the process is a good strategy. Often, they take legal action in order to achieve full repayment of their claims or as a pressure mechanism oriented towards persuading the debtor to buy back their claims. Court precedents reinforce this position. The mentioned behavior alters the process seriously threatening its chance of success.

Even though these court decisions have no practical effects while the debtor is in default, they become more relevant when the regularization of payments starts. This is because potential holdouts would want to exert their increased bargaining power when circumstances are normal. In this case, creditors would reconsider their participation in the exchange offer because committed future payments can become ineffective or less attractive due to legal actions or attachments placed by holdouts.

Because of this, it is important to design incentives in order to achieve the highest participation of creditors and minimize the presence of holdouts. It is important to note that there are legal and financial incentive schemes the debtor can consider with the objective of maximizing acceptance:

1. Consider the possibility of making up-front payments to those creditors participating in the exchange in order to make the proposal more attractive. Here, the system must be oriented to work as a *participation fee*, favoring only those who accept the exchange offer. Payments could be considered part of the exchange terms and partially deducted from interest or principal owed (that is, if the participation fee is 4 percent, consider exchanging 100 percent of the old bonds for 98 percent of the new bonds, thus resulting in a net fee of 2 percent).

2.  Apart from the participation fee, it is important to be able to clearly communicate from the beginning that eligible debt will be entitled to get similar treatment after the exchange is executed, regardless of formal initial acceptance. Creditors not participating in the exchange would not have their claims paid or purchased as per their original terms and conditions.
3.  Set a high participation rate so as to validate the exchange. This framework is widely utilized in restructuring exercises and is intended to generate collective incentives favoring the acceptance of the proposal.
4.  Analyse the introduction of exit consents in the old bonds so as to make them less attractive. A qualified majority would modify certain non-economic conditions of the old bonds. This modification would be done at the time of the exchange, when holders not only accept the proposal but vote positively for some non-essential (monetary) condition amendments. Examples of the changes to be introduced on the old bonds would be:

    - sovereign immunity waiver: generally, bonds include a clause through which the debtor abandons sovereign immunity associated with attachments or litigation. This clause could become inoperative while the exchange is being made;
    - jurisdiction: the applicable jurisdiction could be changed in the event of controversies, favoring the debtor's address;
    - covenants: exempt the debtor from the fulfillment of financial (that is, ratios) and/or legal (that is, negative pledge) covenants;
    - cross default: limit the possibility of declaring a cross-default event; and
    - listing: exempt the debtor from the obligation of keeping the old bonds listed on stock exchanges, thus reducing their liquidity.

5.  Design payment schemes on the new bonds that are immune to attachments from *holdouts*. An example could be channeling funds through an agent for the holders of new debt or the creation of trusts or a special purpose vehicle (SPV). For instance, through some arrangement like this, the debtor should pay in domestic currency to a trustee with a local address; then the agent would be responsible for converting pesos into foreign currency and paying creditors abroad. In principle, payments made by a sovereign debtor should not be attachable, because they come under local jurisdiction. Then, as the payments would be made by the trustee, those funds cannot be affected by legal actions.

It is also important to note, as mentioned before, that Argentine public sector debt creditors are very heterogeneous, meaning that they have very different preferences. An Italian holder may not be willing to accept a 'haircut' while an American institutional investor, influenced by regulation, would prefer to receive coupon payments similar to the old bonds and accept principal reductions. These different preferences must be addressed at the time of structuring the exchange proposal.

An offer can be structured designing a menu of options to be presented to creditors, developing at the same time a priority scheme to be applied in new bond allocations, seeking to give relevance to certain aspects or distinguishing characteristics of the instruments or of the creditors themselves (that is, maturity dates of old bonds, residence and so on).

Other issues to be analysed in the framework of the design of the restructuring proposals are:

1. Convenience of issuing bonds with upside schemes for creditors (value recovery rights, GDP indexed bonds). Even though this represents an additional incentive, generally creditors do not attribute meaningful value to them since they are difficult to price and, in the case that the economic situation improves beyond perspectives agreed with creditors in the restructuring, it could become very onerous for the debtor. Nevertheless, it could be argued as a compensation for holders of securities that become impaired.
2. Convenience of issuing bonds having some sort of *seniority* or collateral. The difficulty with this scheme is that it becomes a precedent for future issuances. On the other hand, it does not seem that the financial community is prone to granting funds to back restructuring operations, and that, with good reasons, investors do not value debt country tax collection collateral.
3. Convenience of issuing a limited number of bonds with relative higher liquidity, as opposed to a large number of liabilities but with less liquidity.

Introduction of *collective action clauses* (CACs) could facilitate some aspects of the process in the future. CACs allow amendments that become binding to all holders, but are made effective when certain majorities are obtained, which could affect monetary terms (dates and amount of payments, interest coupons, currency and place of payment, percentages needed to modify instruments) and non-monetary ones (immunity waiver, covenants and so on).

# CONCLUDING REMARKS

Crises like the one Argentina is facing should be useful in learning how to avoid making the same mistakes in the future. Throughout the chapter, we have stressed the importance of having a comprehensive program with coordinated actions on several fronts aiming to reach a sustainable growth path. Public sector debt and its adequate administration is an important component within this framework, but not the only one. As derived from own and third parties' experiences, not much can be achieved without mature and responsible policymakers. It is misleading to assume that through a financial debt restructuring, existing fundamental problems of the economy could be overcome. Solid institutions are also a key point in the construction of this program, in order to escape from unilateral decisions that alter the basic functioning of a democracy.

The resolution of the Argentine sovereign debt problem is both cause and effect of the normalization process of the economy. Lack of credit for the public and private sectors, deferral of consumption and investment decisions deeply harm the country's economic performance, thus generating massive value destruction.

The complexity of the problem increases as time elapses and a solution to the debt problem is delayed. What was originally a sovereign debt difficulty has become a wider problem. Private sector debtors that were originally perceived as good ones have been affected by capital controls and other limitations that increase risks originally taken by creditors. Possible court actions by creditors is another risk that increases as solutions are postponed.

The current international interest rate environment is historically very favorable for settling on terms that take advantage of it. This would benefit all parties involved.

To start the process of debt resolution, it would help to lay out a set of principles that is intended to govern the process. Specific parameters would then reduce uncertainties and improve economic performance. Otherwise, moving targets would only increase the risk of further capital outflows. Administrative steps can also be taken to expedite the process.

Rationale for the agreement is given by a beneficial solution for both creditors and the debtor. As a result of an adequate policy framework accompanied by a debt restructuring exercise, the debtor would improve its solvency and creditors would also benefit from a discount rate reduction on their assets. In order to arrive expeditiously at such a solution, it would be helpful if involved parties acted in a coordinated and cooperative fashion.

Therefore, the public sector ought to take the initiative and get the process going. This approach must include some dialogue, information dissemination, and the definition of some clear rules for the future based on some rationality within internationally accepted standards. A solution will emerge as an equilibrium between unilateral offers and protracted negotiations.

Given associated costs with the current situation, it is key to look for an agreement that minimizes the chance that these problems will recur. Thus, payment commitments must be realistic.

One of the most important points in structuring the proposal is the definition of different debt categories to be used in the restructuring. In order to ensure fairness, different debt categories must have differential treatment, while creditors within a category ought to be treated similarly.

Incentive schemes must be designed in order to prompt creditors' participation in the exchange, thus minimizing holdouts. The predetermination of high participation rates, the possibility of up-front payments, introduction of exit clauses in original bonds and the 'shielding' of new debt payments are useful mechanisms to foster the process.

Potential risk arises from hidden contingent liabilities due to legal disputes and the acknowledgment of debts. If unchecked they could increase the size of the debt to be restructured, potentially threatening to redefine the cut-off date and/or categories.

# APPENDIX 6A1 FURTHER DETAILS ON DEBT FIGURES

We shall summarize some of the main assumptions applied in the construction of our estimates of the public sector debt. To this end, we include a set of tables reflecting several effects that influence the evolution of public sector debt between December 2001 and September 2002.[11]

1.  Pesoification of GLs and subsequent devaluation of AR$ reduces debt by US$19.5 billion:

| Pesoification effect on GLs (estim.) | | Amount |
|---|---|---|
| 1 GLs subject to pesoification in US$ (original amount) | US$ bn | 42.258 |
| 2 Pesoified GLs (US$1 = AR$14 * CER 1.4) | AR$ bn | 82.826 |
| 3 Pesoified GLs (US$1 = AR$3.64) | US$ bn | 22.754 |
| Difference (1–3) – Debt decrease | US$ bn | (19.504) |

2.  However, we assume that 50 percent of the stock of GLs – existing in December 2001 – is redenominated in US dollars. As a result, the stock of debt increases by US$ 9.7 billion, between December 2001 and September 2002:

| Revision of GLs (prel. estim.) | | Amount |
|---|---|---|
| 1 50% of revision of GLs to US$ (original amount) | US$ bn | 21.129 |
| 2 50% of revision of GLs (US$1 = AR$1.4 * CER 1.4) | AR$ bn | 41.413 |
| 3 50% of revision of GLs (US$1 = AR$3.64) | US$ bn | 11.377 |
| Difference (1–3) – Debt increase | US$ bn | 9.752 |

3.  Bonds to compensate banks due to asymmetric pesoification, judicial injunctions and the difference between the evolution of CER and CVS increase the stock of debt by US$13.4 billion:

| Compensation bonds to banks (estim.) | Amount US$ bn equivalent |
|---|---|
| Issued | |
| 1 Boden y Pagaré 2007 in AR$ | 1.635 |
| 2 Boden y Pagaré 2012 in US$ | 6.156 |

| Compensation bonds to banks (estim.) | Amount US$ bn equivalent |
|---|---|
| 3  Cobertura | 3.234 |
| Total (1+2+3) – Debt increase | 11.025 |
| New Debt | |
| 4  CER | 1.044 |
| 5  Judicial injunctions | 1.401 |
| Total (4+5) – Debt increase | 2.445 |
| Total (1+2+3+4+5) – Debt increase | 13.470 |

4.  Bonds delivered to depositors which took the option of receiving public sector debt (Bodens) for their time deposits in the local banking system, as opposed to accepting pesoification (CEDROS). It is assumed that bank deposit exchange Phase II – already open – is accepted by only 5 percent of current holders of CEDROS. As a result, debt increases by US$5.8 billion:

| Bonds to depositors (estim.) | Amount US$ bn equivalent |
|---|---|
| 1  Boden 2005 in US$ | 886 |
| 2  Boden 2007 in AR$ | 134 |
| 3  Boden 2012 in US$ | 4.394 |
| 4  Boden 2013 in US$ | 461 |
| Total (1+2+3) – Debt increase | 5.874 |

5.  We assume that at some point, banks will compensate the government with the delivery of GLs in exchange for the reduction in their liabilities with depositors stemming from previous actions. The exchange factor is US$1 (of Bodens received by banks from the government) to AR$1.4 (plus CER) (of GLs delivered to the government). This leads to a reduction in the stock of debt equivalent to US$3.1 billion:

| Effect of bank deposits exchange (prel. estim.) | | Amount |
|---|---|---|
| 1  Bodens delivered to depositors in US$ | US$ bn | 5.874 |
| 2  GLs given by banks to the government (US$1 = AR$1.4 * CER 1.4) | AR$ bn | 11.513 |
| 3  GLs given by banks to the government (US$1 = AR$3.64) | US$ bn | 3.163 |
| Debt decrease | US$ bn | (3.163) |

6. The Federal government takes on provincial debt of a total amount of US$10.6 billion, as part of the implementation of the *Acuerdos Fiscales* (Fiscal Agreements) and the *Programa de Financiamiento Provincial Ordenado* (Program of Orderly Provincial Financing). Although the operation does not increase net consolidated debt, this is not the case when we look at the Republic's level of debt:

| Provincial debt transferred to the Republic (prel. estim.) | Amount US$ bn equivalent |
|---|---|
| 1 Debt with commercial banks | 4.533 |
| 2 Provincial securities | 4.704 |
| 3 Debt with FFDP | 1.374 |
| Total (1+2+3) – Debt increase | 10.611 |

7. We estimate that the cost of recapitalizing the banking system would increase debt by US$4 billion:

| Banking system recapitalization provinces (prel. estim.) | | Amount |
|---|---|---|
| Total – Debt increase | US$ bn | 4.000 |

8. Between December 2001 and September 2002 there was a reduction in the stock of debt due to the payments to multilaterals, pesoification of Letes, devaluation effect over local currency-denominated bonds, devaluation effect over other currency-denominated bonds and other effects. The amount, net of arrears, is equivalent to US$11.8 billion:

| Principal reduction (net of arrears) | | Amount |
|---|---|---|
| (–) T-Bills* | US$ bn | (6.739) |
| (–) Multilateral loans | US$ bn | (1.297) |
| (–) Official agency loans | US$ bn | (134) |
| (–) Commercial bank loans | US$ bn | (2.043) |
| (–) Securities* | US$ bn | (6.457) |
| (+) Principal arrears | US$ bn | 4.829 |
| Total | | (11.841) |

*Note:* *Includes pesoification/devaluation effect.

9. As a consequence of all these combined effects, the stock of debt, as of September 2002, exceeds US$155 billion:

| Debt | Amount |
|---|---|
| Debt as of December 2001 | 144.406 |
| (a) (–) Pesoification effect | (19.504) |
| (b) (+) Revision of GLs | 9.752 |
| (c) (+) Compensation bonds – asymmetric pesoification | 13.470 |
| (d) (+) Bonds to depositors | 5.874 |
| (e) (–) Reduction of GLs (deposits exchange) | (3.163) |
| (f) (+) Provincial debt | 10.611 |
| (g) (+) Banking system recapitalization | 4.000 |
| (h) (–) Principal reduction (net of arrears)* | (11.841) |
| (i) (+) Interest arrears | 2.535 |
| (j) (–) Others | (903) |
| Debt as of September 2002 R | 155.236 |

*Note:* *Includes payments made to MDBs and official agencies and the devaluation effect over local currency bonds (others than GLs) and Letes and the devaluation effect of other currencies.

# APPENDIX 6A2   IMPACT OF DIFFERENT DEBT RESTRUCTURING EXERCISES

Although in the debt restructuring exercise there will be several options derived from different combinations of interest rates, tenors and principal values, we developed two additional cases based upon some assumptions presented on pages 105–8. For simplicity, we developed a case B with a lower reduction than presented previously. The reduction is 17.5 points lower up front than the case presented earlier. The upper graphs in Figure 6A2.1 plot the evolution of both debt/GDP and interest payments/GDP ratios simulated under the different macro scenarios described in Table 6.6. A similar exercise was performed with an up-front reduction higher by 17.5 than case A. This exercise is plotted under case C.

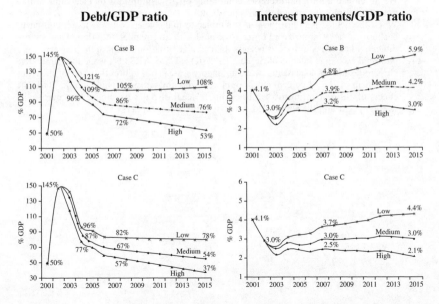

*Figure 6A2.1   Evolution of ratios simulated under different macro scenarios*

# NOTES

\*    This chapter was written at the end of 2002/early 2003.
1.    In a widely known case (Peru), a holdout attached the payments originally earmarked to pay the Brady bonds.
2.    For further details as to the estimates made, see Appendix 6A1.
3.    *Coeficiente de Estabilización de Referencia* (consumer price index) reflects variations in the consumer price index, and was applied to *pesoified* bank deposits.
4.    *Coeficiente de Variación Salarial* (wage index) reflects variations on average wages and was applied to a significant portion of bank assets.
5.    A portion of this debt – that owed to commercial banks through the FFDP – has also been restructured under the same terms as the *Canje de Deuda Provincial* (Provincial Debt Exchange).
6.    Overshooting could be even more pronounced in Argentina's case where associated risks were perceived as higher than in other cases.
7.    Details regarding the amount of debt to be restructured are explained in the next section.
8.    These restructuring conditions are the average of the new debt issuances.
9.    We developed additional exercises combining other assumptions of face-value reduction. The results are presented in Appendix 6A2.
10.    When the debtor is performing, it is simpler to make offers without much consensus because parties wish to avoid costs associated with an irregular situation. This is more difficult when the country has been in an irregular situation for more than a year.
11.    Nominal exchange rate (as of September 2002) is US$1:AR$3.64, while the cumulative CER indexation is 40 percent. We do not incorporate in our figures the effect of the reimbursement of the 13 percent cut in public salaries and pensions made in mid-2001, the effects of future contingent liabilities due to legal disputes or similar that eventually would appear and the acknowledgment of debts with suppliers.

131 - 32

(Argentina)

F 34

019

Pg 90 Title:

# Comment

## Allen Frankel*

The strong performance of emerging market credits (EMCs) in recent months has signaled the arrival of another financial spring. EMCs and other high-yield investments have performed well in an environment marked by short-term interest rates near the zero bound for several currencies.

Daniel Marx has outlined a case in which an Argentine debt exchange could create value for investors. He knowingly attributes this possibility to good responses to appropriate incentives rather than any financial alchemy. In my short comments, I seek briefly to shed some light on a few of the lessons learned in recent years concerning financing choices made in periods when countries regain access to foreign capital.

Argentina has just experienced an extraordinary period of crisis, during which most Argentine domestic cross-border financing transactions were severely affected. This included cross-border creditors with collateralized dollar-denominated loans to private firms. Some loans were backed by (collateralized by) domestic Argentine assets, such as home mortgages. Such collateralized credit arrangements were covered by the government's required redenomination (pesoification) of credit contracts. In these cases, losses could be attributed to the actions of the sovereign, since they occurred even in cases when the borrower was willing and able to service its debt. Other private contracts emerged unscathed. One example of this type of contract is a so-called future flow transaction.

The above discussion sets out a particularly cumbersome mechanism for countries to deal with post-crisis financing difficulties. Alternative mechanisms have been proposed that would deploy structured finance techniques to slice and dice risk exposures into several elegantly prepared debt tranches. Such tranches could contain default risk and explicit contingencies (for example, relating to movements in the price of oil). An attractive feature of these latter tranche types is that they involve exposure to shocks independent of a sovereign's actions.

Indeed, emerging market collateralized debt obligations (CDOs) have been organized to implement the tranching of a pool of underlying credit default swaps. The poor acceptance of these instruments in the market highlights the significance of the sovereign risk element. Securitization investors gain from the strict channeling of the more valuable cash flow streams, the firm's other claimants, including sovereign losses. The sovereign is still looking for revenue, and the cash flow streams assumed by foreign investors are no longer sources of revenue. Holders of remaining assets would bear more risk of sovereign asset 'grabs'. They would assume more political risk but would not receive compensation *ex post*. Securitization allows some emerging market firms to access foreign capital markets. Discussions of the organization of transfer payments among domestic firms are not a standard feature of discussions of international financial architecture. This short comment raises the question as to whether they should. Finally, I am fully aware that all I have done is to resurface the issues embodied in the Coase theorem, which states that when the parties affected by externalities can negotiate costlessly with one another, an efficient outcome results no matter how the law assigns responsibility for damages.

There may be instances where this is not true. In those instances, creditors should incorporate a moral hazard premium into their pricing.

In Chapter 13, Zettelmeyer expresses an appreciation for the issue in his discussion of the exclusivity problem. He raises concerns about the employment of collateralized financing techniques by borrowers in financially distressed countries.

## NOTE

* The views expressed are the author's own and do not necessarily reflect those of the Bank for International Settlements. For a discussion of the Argentine case and an overview description of financing technique see Moody's Investor Service, *The Impact of the Argentine Sovereign Default on Cross-Border Securitizations*, Special Report, 17 September 2002.

PART III


The Evolving Debate on Capital Account
Liberalization

# 7. Should capital controls have a place in the future international monetary system?

## Stephany Griffith-Jones, John Williamson and Ricardo Gottschalk

## INTRODUCTION

Capital account convertibility – the complete elimination of all capital con-trols – was often treated in the 1990s as an integral element of the market liberalization that was being urged on emerging markets. In the middle of the decade there was even talk of making it an objective of international policy that would be embodied (as a long-term target) in the IMF Articles. The Asian crisis brought sharp disillusionment, and since then opinion has tended to swing back to acceptance that emerging markets may be ill advised to seek the rapid elimination of capital controls. But that has not brought with it any consensus as to the future role of capital controls in the international monetary system.

This chapter aims to take stock of this debate. The next section (which is elaborated in Appendix 7A) reviews the main trends in the use of capital controls over the last decade. The third section discusses whether there is still a role for controls, and considers which forms of controls seem most apt under current world conditions of relatively free markets. The next section explores the possibility of developing measures aimed at promot-ing inflows to emerging markets in times of drought like the present. The chapter concludes by sketching a set of proposals for international policy in this area in the coming years.

## RECENT TRENDS IN CAPITAL ACCOUNT POLICY

Despite the loss of enthusiasm for propagating capital account liberaliza-tion, the trend has remained very much in the direction of liberalization over the past decade. Table 7.1 provides a summary description of the

*Table 7.1   Degree of capital account liberalization, 1990 and 2001*

|  | 1990 | 2001 |
|---|---|---|
| Latin America |  |  |
| Argentina* | PR | LL |
| Brazil | PR | LL |
| Chile | LL | LL |
| Colombia | PR | LL |
| Mexico | LL | LL |
| Peru | PR | L |
| Venezuela | LL | LL |
| Sub-Saharan Africa |  |  |
| Côte d'Ivoire | PR | LL |
| Kenya | LL | LL |
| Nigeria | PR | LL |
| South Africa | LL | LL |
| Tanzania | R | PR |
| Uganda | LL | L |
| North Africa & Middle East |  |  |
| Morocco | PR | LL |
| Tunisia | PR | LL |
| Egypt | PR | L |
| Turkey | LL | LL |
| South Asia |  |  |
| Bangladesh | PR | PR |
| India | PR | LL |
| Pakistan | PR | LL |
| Sri Lanka | PR | PR |
| East Asia |  |  |
| China | R | PR |
| Hong Kong | L | L |
| Indonesia | LL | LL |
| Korea | PR | LL |
| Malaysia | LL | LL |
| Singapore | L | L |
| Thailand | LL | LL |

*Note:*   R (repressed); PR (partly repressed); LL (largely liberalized); and L (liberalized).
\*   The score for Argentina in 2001 does not capture the restrictions the country adopted at the end of the year.

*Source:*   Authors' elaboration, based on information from the IMF *Annual Report on Exchange Arrangements and Exchange Restrictions*, 1991 and 2002, and country reports, when available.

extent to which each of 28 developing countries[1] had liberalized its capital account as of 1990 and as of 2001, the most recent year for which exchange restrictions have been reported by the IMF. For each country, a country's capital account regulations were classified as implying capital flows that were either repressed (R), partly repressed (PR), largely liberalized (LL) or liberalized (L) in the years 1990 and 2001. Details of how this classification was undertaken are provided in Appendix 7A. It can be seen that 15 of the 28 countries had a more liberalized capital account in 2001 than they had in 1990, while no country had moved in the opposite direction.

Of course, there were a number of cases of countries imposing or intensifying controls within that period, although in every case they had liberalized again before the survey was made in 2001. The most famous is doubtless Malaysia, which took drastic action to ban capital outflows on 1 September 1998. These restrictions were eased within a few months and largely lifted in less than the promised year. But there were also efforts to curtail capital inflows by imposing new regulations on the part of Chile, Colombia, Brazil, Malaysia (in 1994) and Thailand (which also imposed outflow controls in the early months of the Asian crisis in 1997). And Argentina imposed exchange controls on outflows in late 2001, after the information reflected in Table 7.1 was collected.

Malaysia is a country that has had a relatively open capital account for a long time, but that undertook important policy adjustments during the decade. In 1994, like many other emerging markets, it recognized that it was suffering from a surfeit of inflows. The authorities therefore implemented a number of regulations intended to curb short-term inflows: they prohibited the sale by residents to non-residents of money market securities; they forbade commercial banks engaging in swap and forward contracts with non-residents; they imposed ceilings on banks' net foreign exchange open positions; and they decreed reserve requirements for foreign exchange liabilities of commercial banks. Apart from the prudential regulations, these controls were lifted when the inflow pressures subsided. By 1998 Malaysia was suffering the opposite problem, of excessive capital outflows in the context of the Asian crisis. The authorities therefore closed down the offshore ringitt market, prohibited lending by residents to non-residents, and blocked the repatriation of non-resident portfolio capital for 12 months. The announcement of these measures was met by fervent denunciations and declarations that Malaysia had excommunicated itself from the international capital market and would fail to make its measures work, but in the event the measures proved eminently enforceable, were relaxed ahead of schedule, and by now are widely regarded as having been an intelligent response to the pressures that confronted the country.

The Chilean controls became something of a *cause célèbre* in the debate about capital account liberalization. In 1991 the new democratic government found to its surprise that it was being embarrassed by large capital inflows to Chile, which were threatening to undermine the highly competitive exchange rate that had enabled Chile in the 1980s to recover from the collapse of 1982 that had been provoked by a reversal of the excessive capital inflows of the preceding years. Determined to avoid the errors that had been perpetrated in 1978–81, the government maintained a minimum period of residence for equity inflows and imposed an unremunerated reserve requirement (an *encaje*) on all loans contracted abroad, whether by banks or by corporations, so as to reduce the profitability of capital inflows and thus diminish their volume (for a given interest differential). Since the period for which the reserves had to be held was a year no matter what the duration of the loan, the requirement was disproportionately costly for short-term loans, and thus had a second effect of biasing the term composition of loans toward the longer term, helping to curb the instability inherent in owing a mass of short-term debt. There evolved late in the 1990s a significant literature on whether the *encaje* had been effective in its first intended role of increasing monetary independence (everyone agreed that it had been effective in skewing the composition of capital inflows toward the longer term). Our view is that it was effective (see the analysis in Williamson 2000, pp. 37–45).

Brazil, Colombia and Thailand also made efforts in the course of the decade to curb capital inflows. Brazil's efforts are not generally rated as having been very effective, because of the complexity of the regulations and the frequent changes in them. Colombia adopted controls much more similar to those of Chile, although with an explicit increase in the reserve requirement for shorter-term loans. As in the case of Chile, there is agreement that the regulations were effective in lengthening the maturity of the loans but controversy about whether they also reduced the size of inflows. (Those who argue that these regulations were ineffective in curbing the volume of inflows seem strangely reluctant to acknowledge that if they are right then the *encaje* is an ideal – because completely non-distortionary – tax!) Thailand introduced restrictions intended to reduce short-term inflows in 1995, but these were not enormously effective because they were at variance with the policies intended to encourage the Bangkok International Banking Facility, an attempt to establish Bangkok as an offshore banking center that ended up by providing a conduit for short-term loans from the rest of the world to Thailand.

There are also some interesting instances of controls that have been maintained even in a liberal environment, such as the vestigial controls maintained by Singapore. Singapore has maintained regulations designed to prevent the emergence of an offshore market in Singapore dollars, notably by prohibiting residents from holding Singapore dollars in foreign bank accounts and by requiring foreigners who borrow Singapore dollars either to spend them in Singapore or else to convert them immediately into foreign exchange. It also prohibits financial institutions lending more than S\$5 million to any non-resident financial entity for speculation in the foreign exchange market, which is enforced by a requirement that the Monetary Authority of Singapore approve any loan by a Singapore financial institution to a foreign financial institution of more than S\$5 million.

Finally, it should be mentioned that some countries have still not gone very far in liberalizing their capital accounts. This is true in particular of the South Asian countries (though India and Pakistan have gone further than Bangladesh and Sri Lanka), and China. Many observers have argued that this caution served these countries well in avoiding contagion from the East Asian crisis in 1997. India is particularly interesting, for shortly before the crisis broke out the Tarapore Committee had recommended a ('gradual') three-year program for moving toward full capital account convertibility. In the event India has made only modest further moves in the subsequent six years, although the committee did lay down three preconditions (the establishment of fiscal discipline, an inflation target and bank solvency) and it is clear that the first and last of these remain unfulfilled. It could therefore be that it is not exclusively the change in the intellectual atmosphere produced by the East Asian crisis that has delayed the process of capital account liberalization in India, though one may suspect that this was the dominant factor.

## THE ROLE AND FORM OF CONTROLS

As observed above, the trend toward liberalization of capital flows is unambiguous. We do not challenge the view that complete liberalization is the natural end point for a developed country. When a country is trusted by the market, it is able to borrow more even in a difficult situation; it is most unlikely to find itself the victim of a 'sudden stop'. In the phrase of Reinhart et al. (2003), such a country has a high level of 'debt tolerance'; that is, it can be relied on to maintain debt service even when debt service payments are large. Because the market can rely on it to do that, lenders will be prepared to buy more of its paper without demanding a prohibitive increase in interest payments even when debt is high, so the phenomenon of the sudden stop is unknown. In that situation there is really only one motivation for maintaining capital controls that makes any sense (defense of the ability to tax interest from capital, see below), and so it is not surprising that countries eliminate the hassle of policing capital controls and take advantage of whatever efficiency advantages of free capital mobility there may be.

However, by no means all countries are in this happy situation. Most emerging markets are only too familiar with the phenomenon of the sudden stop, where they are unable to borrow more on any terms. Reinhart et al. (2003) try to divide emerging markets into two groups, those with a history of default where the capital market limits severely what they can borrow, and those without a history of default, where the capital market is more trusting. But even the group that has never defaulted includes countries like Korea, Malaysia and Thailand that were subjected to sudden stops in 1997. It is therefore the emerging market countries, particularly those with a history of default, about which one needs to worry, and ask whether it is wise for them to dispense with capital controls.

Should one really hold capital account liberalization responsible for the series of crises that have dogged emerging markets in recent years? After all, there have been many other candidates proposed: the macroeconomic fundamentals (such as the fiscal balance and the rate of inflation), the exchange rate regime, the effectiveness of prudential supervision of the financial system, and crony capitalism. We would not wish to argue that any of these are irrelevant, and yet none of them seems to be as systematically associated with whether countries have succumbed to crisis as the question of whether they have abolished capital controls.

**The Macroeconomic Fundamentals**

The 1980s' debt crisis was widely held to be the result primarily of fiscal weakness, which was reflected *inter alia* in a high rate of inflation. Yet these were conspicuously not issues in some of the more recent crises, most notably the Mexican crisis of 1994 and the East Asian crisis of 1997. Some writers have argued that these countries had latent fiscal problems, in that if the banks went bust and had to be bailed out, the result would be a jump in public sector debt that would make their fiscal position much weaker than appeared on the surface prior to the crisis. That is true, but it will also be true of any country that suffers a crisis that engulfs its banks, and decides to bail out the banks. The question is whether there was any reason for believing these countries to have been particularly susceptible to those dangers prior to their crises. We are not aware of those who have advanced this argument having given *ex ante* warnings of these countries' vulnerability.

## The Exchange Rate Regime

The proximate cause of many emerging market crises has been a run on a pegged currency. For a time there was a common view that this implied that every country should adopt a 'corner solution' for its exchange rate regime, either a floating rate or a fixed rate that was firmly pinned down by a currency board arrangement. We agree that allowing the currency to float serves to avoid one important source of vulnerability and provides an extra shock absorber. It is difficult, for example, to believe that the Brazilian authorities would have succeeded in riding out the 2002 panic without a full-scale crisis had the real still been pegged, even within a wide band. On the other hand, it is not true that whether a country had a pegged exchange rate serves to distinguish those Asian countries that succumbed to crisis in 1997 from those that did not. Bangladesh, China, Indonesia, Hong Kong, Sri Lanka and Vietnam all had pegged rates, and it can be argued that India, Korea, Malaysia, Pakistan, the Philippines, Taiwan and Thailand had de facto pegged rates, yet some of both groups had crises while others did not. Singapore, which avoided succumbing, had a formal but unannounced band that was allowed to depreciate in response to the crisis. And Brazil came perilously close to a full-scale crisis in 2002 despite having floated in 1999.

The idea that a currency board serves to avoid the risk of crisis looks pretty silly after the Argentine tragedy and the prolonged recession in Hong Kong. And the success of Singapore in riding out the crisis with an intermediate regime intact ought to be the last nail in the coffin of the two-corners doctrine.

## Prudential Supervision of the Financial System

This is once again a factor that one can reasonably expect to reduce crisis vulnerability. Had Thailand not had such weak banks in 1997, it would doubtless have found it possible to raise interest rates sooner, and that might conceivably have headed off the crisis that broke at the beginning of July. But this again seems an awfully poor discriminator of which countries succumbed to crisis in Asia in 1997. Prudential supervision in China and South Asia was surely weaker than in Malaysia and Hong Kong, yet it was the latter and not the former countries that suffered crises.

## Crony Capitalism

Much the same can be said about crony capitalism. Surely this was part of the problem in Indonesia, Korea and Thailand. But is there any reason for believing that crony capitalism was worse in those countries than in China or South Asia?

**Capital Controls**

Now apply the same test as was done above to the issue of whether the capital account had been liberalized. Using the same categories as in Table 7.1, Table 7.2 shows the status of capital account liberalization in all of the Asian countries that have been mentioned above as of 1997, the year the East Asian crisis started. It can be seen that there is an almost-perfect fit, with countries that had liberalized (scored LL or L) being exactly the ones that succumbed to the crisis, with one exception. That is Singapore, a country with quite unusually strong fundamentals and a large international creditor position, and also – as pointed out in the previous section – with a vestigial capital control designed specifically to ward off speculative attacks. The Latin American countries that suffered speculative attacks were also ones that had liberalized capital flows. There is of course nothing surprising in this: a liberalized capital account means that money can flood in freely when the herd takes a fancy to emerging markets in general or a specific country in particular, and is then free to bolt again when some negative shock leads to a change of opinion. And because

*Table 7.2   Degree of capital account liberalization in Asia, 1997\**

|  | 1997 |
| --- | --- |
| Bangladesh | PR |
| India | PR |
| Pakistan | PR |
| Sri Lanka | PR |
| China | PR |
| Hong Kong | L |
| Indonesia | LL |
| Korea | LL |
| Malaysia | LL |
| Singapore | L |
| Thailand | LL |

*Note:*   PR (partly repressed); LL (largely liberalized); L (liberalized).
\*   Corresponds to the first half of 1997.

*Source*:   Authors' elaboration, based on information from the IMF *Annual Report on Exchange Arrangements and Exchange Restrictions*, 1991 and 1998, and country reports, when available.

investors prefer holding short- to long-term assets, a country without capital controls can expect to have a mass of short-term debt which is vulnerable to rapid withdrawal when market sentiment does change.

Two other potential functions of capital controls are worth acknowledging. One is to increase the scope for a country to pursue a monetary policy dedicated to domestic needs even if it is not prepared to treat its exchange rate with 'benign neglect'. It is a well-known theorem of international monetary economics that a country cannot simultaneously have a fixed exchange rate, an independent monetary policy and perfect capital mobility. The usual conclusion is that countries should allow their exchange rates to float, with a minority view that it would be better to subjugate monetary policy to that in some center country. But it is also possible to hold the view that a better way of squaring the triangle would be to keep some capital controls.

The other function is to preserve the domestic tax base, and specifically to avoid inordinate hemorrhaging of capital in response to an attempt to tax the income from capital. If some countries (like the United States) did not exempt foreigners from the obligation of paying taxes on the interest earned on assets held there, then it would only be countries that wished to tax interest more heavily than the others that would need to worry about preventing erosion of their tax base. But the anti-social US action in 1984 of exempting foreign interest income from tax means that every other country now has to worry about the loss of its tax base. Many developed countries have bilateral tax information-sharing agreements with the United States, which means that they can gain the information that will enable them to police whether their residents are in fact reporting their income on assets held in the United States. Organization for Economic Cooperation and Development countries also have the option of joining the OECD multilateral tax information-sharing agreement, which gives them the same benefit of being able to police the payment of taxes on US income earned by their residents. But few emerging markets qualify on either ground. Hence if they want to continue to be able to collect tax on income from capital they do not have much option but to control capital outflows.

What about the arguments against capital controls?[2] Yes, some forms at least impinge very much on personal freedom, and some of us at least will take that to be an argument against those forms of controls (specifically, controls on the movement of personal capital). Yes, there is some evidence that capital mobility acts as a discipline on macroeconomic policy; just think of the experience of Luis Ignacio Lula da Silva's new government in Brazil. At the same time, capital inflows seem always to be either flood or drought, with none of that gradual build-up of pressure as policy deteriorates that one would look for in an efficient disciplinary mechanism. Another classic argument is that capital flows play a stabilizing role that helps to attenuate the impact of shocks. In developed countries, that is persuasive; but sudden stops tend to magnify shocks, not offset them, in emerging markets. Of course, the basic argument for capital mobility is that it allows savings and investment to be de-linked, thus permitting emerging markets to invest more than they save and grow faster as a result. But capital controls do not preclude a country borrowing on the international capital market and thus achieving this benefit. The question is whether *free* capital mobility yields benefits additional to those that can be reaped by controlled access to the international capital market. The empirical evidence has not so far been very favorable to the hypothesis that free capital mobility enhances growth; Quinn's (1997) finding of a positive relationship between liberalization and growth is adequately explained by the far more plausible hypothesis that *partial* liberalization (for example of foreign direct investment (FDI) and long-term capital) is beneficial to growth.[3]

We conclude that there is a case for maintaining some forms of capital controls in emerging market countries for a long time yet. We doubt whether this will amount to a case for keeping them permanently. Admittedly the Reinhart et al. (2003) paper does argue that once a country has blotted its copybook by defaulting it is permanently condemned to the sudden stops that make free capital mobility such a dubious proposition. But we find it more plausible to hypothesize that countries can in time change their image in the market; after all, Chile and Mexico, two of the classic defaulters, are now rated investment grade. Similarly, one would hope that in due course the tax case for capital controls will be eroded, either by the spread of tax information-sharing agreements, or by an international tax organization taking on the provision of tax information as one of its major tasks, or possibly by a withdrawal of the US tax concession that largely created the problem.

If some forms of control should persist, what form should these take? What criteria should guide one in selecting between different forms of control?

An obvious first criterion is *effectiveness*: whether a control measure will actually influence the flow that is being regulated, or whether it would be so easy to evade as to leave flows largely unaffected, for example, by re-labeling a flow. One should not doubt that some evasion will always occur; Nazi Germany did not succeed in eliminating all capital flight, even when it instituted the death penalty as punishment (Kindleberger 1987). The question is whether so much evasion will occur as to leave flows largely unaffected.

But capital controls have costs, in thwarting transactions that may be expected to improve welfare. A second criterion is that a control should minimize this cost for a given level of effectiveness. This means that one should ask whether a control is *market friendly*, in the sense that it would allow investors to judge for themselves how much they value allowing a particular transaction to go forward. Some flows are inevitably more important than others, and a bureaucrat who has to judge between them has no way of knowing which are the more important ones. A price-based measure leaves investors to decide for themselves whether they attach sufficient importance to a particular transaction for it to be consummated despite an alteration of incentives designed to influence the size of the total flow.

Third, there is the question of the *cost* of administering a system of capital controls. This means the cost to both the government and investors of complying with, or evading, regulations.

What sort of controls do these three criteria suggest? They suggest avoiding the imposition of different regulations on different forms of flow[4] that cannot be readily distinguished from one another or that can be readily substituted for one another. They suggest either covering a wide variety of different types of flow in the same way, or else focusing on those flows that are likely to have a particularly important effect, for example, in contributing to speculative pressures. Controls should be limited and strategic rather than complex and widespread.

Consider how those principles apply to the principal forms of control that were initiated during the past decade, as revealed above. These are:

- prohibition of withdrawal of foreign-owned assets (as in Malaysia in 1998);
- prohibition of asset sales between residents and non-residents, or lending by one group to another;
- alternatively, a requirement to seek a license for such transactions;
- ceilings on banks' foreign exchange positions;
- imposition of an additional reserve requirement on banks' foreign exchange liabilities;
- closure or prevention of an offshore market in a currency; and
- imposition of a reserve requirement on foreign borrowing (an *encaje*).

The first of these is almost inevitably a temporary measure, since foreign investors would object strenuously to an attempt to lock them in permanently and could surely organize retaliatory action. As a temporary measure, the Malaysian experience suggests it can be effective, but it would certainly have to be judged as market unfriendly.

The prohibition (or subjection to a licensing requirement) of all asset sales between residents and non-residents would appear difficult to police, since it involves an attempt to control a wide range of activities of individuals and small firms as well as large actors. It again scores badly on the criterion of market friendliness. More limited prohibitions (or requirements to seek permission) that are directed at specific visible actors, as in Singapore, are less vulnerable to the critique of ineffectiveness.

Ceilings on banks' foreign exchange positions are easy to police, and are regarded by many advocates of a liberal capital account as acceptable since they can be presented as a form of prudential control. However, loans to domestic banks are easily substituted by loans to domestic corporations from foreign banks, meaning that this form of control is likely to be of limited effectiveness. Additional reserve requirements on banks' foreign currency liabilities are a more market-friendly version of the same type of control, and are therefore subject to a similar critique of limited effectiveness.

A central bank is unable to police what goes on in an offshore market, which is why a country that is unhappy with the prospect of its currency being used in ways it cannot control is obliged to prevent an offshore market entirely. The experience of Malaysia and Singapore shows that this is feasible; the potential primary depositors in such a market have to be prevented from depositing the currency in an offshore account, by prohibitions on residents holding offshore deposits and a requirement that foreigners have to convert their acquisitions of domestic currency into foreign exchange.

Although the financial markets periodically found new ways of evading the Chilean *encaje*, which the central bank had to combat by periodic additions to the regulations, the surprise is that it proved sufficiently durable that the financial market people still complained about it after seven years. This would seem to point to the advantage of having a regulation that is relatively broad (treating all loans in the same way) but does not attempt to cover all the less-important asset transactions as well. The *encaje* was a price-related measure that allowed investors to go forward with a loan to which they attached particularly high importance.

This brief review suggests that the most suitable measures for imitation would be the Chilean *encaje* and the Singaporean prohibition of foreign borrowing for purposes of speculating against the currency. Ironically, those are exactly the two controls that have been targeted for emasculation by the United States in the two bilateral free trade agreements that it has signed, with Chile and Singapore, respectively.

## MEASURES TO ENCOURAGE FOREIGN BORROWING IN TIMES OF DROUGHT

The agenda discussed above focuses on thwarting flows, either in or out, that private actors would wish to make out of consideration exclusively of their commercial interest. However, in the current situation it is not clear that this is the most urgent issue. Since the Asian crisis, net capital flows to emerging market economies have fallen very sharply, as can be seen in Figure 7.1; since 2000, net flows to emerging markets have been very close to zero or even negative. Net debt flows, in particular, have turned strongly negative, leading the World Bank (2003) to conclude that 'the developing world has become a net capital *exporter* to the developed world'. In the case of Latin America, one of the regions worst hit by sharp declines in capital flows, net private flows to the region are estimated by the Inter-American Development Bank (IADB) to have declined from around 5 percent of the region's GDP in 1996 to zero in 2002. Furthermore, net transfers to Latin America in 2002 (net flows minus interest payments and profit remittances), reached a large negative amount of US$39 billion!

There are reasons to fear that at least in part this sharp decline is due to structural changes that may not be reversed easily. For example, international banks have crossed the border by establishing subsidiaries or branches in developing countries, and therefore replaced foreign lending by domestic intermediation. And some portfolio equity investors feel that there are not many 'sufficiently large' companies left for equity investors to

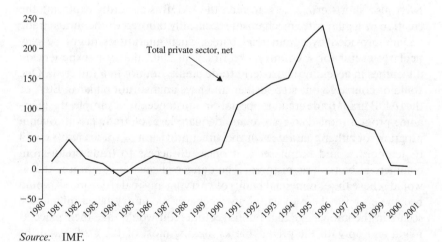

*Source:*  IMF.

*Figure 7.1    Private capital flows to emerging economies (in US$ bn)*

buy in developing countries (Griffith-Jones 2002). To the extent that these flows are determined by cyclical factors (linked for example, to general levels of risk aversion and more specifically, memories of recent crises in emerging markets), an important question is: how long is the relevant cycle? The sharp decline of capital flows to developing countries has already lasted for five years.

To the extent that the new trend towards a drought of capital flows to emerging markets is likely to last longer yet, the policy agenda needs to shift, both at the national and the international levels. The immediate problem is how to encourage sufficient private flows to developing countries. Here we shall focus on measures to be taken internationally, and/or in source countries, though measures in developing countries are also important.

One of the novel problems that has arisen during and in the aftermath of recent crises is that *trade credit* has dried up. This is particularly problematic, as it inhibits the impact of the large depreciations that have typically accompanied crises on the expansion of exports, which is usually the key to post-crisis recovery. Argentina and Indonesia illustrate this problem; Brazil, even though it avoided a full-scale crisis, also saw a significant drying up of trade credit during the panic of 2002. This is a relatively new phenomenon; lines of trade credit were mostly maintained during the debt crisis.

At present, government institutions such as export credit guarantee agencies (ECAs) and multilateral development banks (MDBs) limit their activities (providing guarantees and credits) to longer-term assets. An important policy question is whether they should extend their activities to cover also short-term assets. In fact, the IADB is currently exploring the creation of a guarantee mechanism specifically tailored to encourage trade finance provided by commercial banks. Such guarantees might be particularly useful for a country like Brazil in 2002 that was experiencing difficulties in accessing short-term trade credit, but not in a full crisis. One could of course go one step further, and have an institution like an ECA or the IADB grant trade credit in special circumstances, for example, if a guarantee program failed to restore an adequate level of trade credit. Such a program for either guarantees or the direct provision of trade credits could be temporary, and be phased out once full access to trade credit from commercial banks was restored. The danger of such a solution is that it would relieve the commercial banks of carrying any real risk, since it would become easy for them to withdraw whenever a country faced difficulties, secure in the knowledge that public sector credit would take their place. It might end up with the private banks making most of the profits and the public sector banks carrying most of the risk; but this danger is inherent in any proposal for countercyclical lending by the public sector.

In the case of *long-term trade credit*, ECAs already play a large, even if declining, role in guaranteeing credits. An important issue is the extent to which ECAs and development banks should be willing to be countercyclical in the guarantees they grant. We hold the view that international financial markets tend to overestimate risk in difficult times and underestimate it in good times,[5] which implies that there is a strong case for introducing an explicit countercyclical element into risk evaluations made by export credit agencies. In times when banks and other creditors lowered their exposure, export credit agencies would increase or at least maintain their levels of guarantees. When matters were seen to improve by the markets, so that banks increased their willingness to lend, then ECAs could decrease their exposure, for example by selling export credit guarantees in the secondary market. This would avoid a greater countercyclicality of guarantees resulting in an increased average level of guarantees.

To the extent that ECAs are increasingly using models to estimate risks (as is the case of the UK Export Credits Guarantee Department (ECGD)), it is important that these models 'see through the cycle'. Such models should utilize measures of risk that are less affected by short-term variations than market-sensitive measures of risk typically are.

One possible way to increase the effectiveness of MDB guarantees in inducing private flows would be to guarantee only those risks that the markets are not prepared to cover (for example, possibly covering only country risk and not commercial risk). It would also be possible to cover only initial maturities, and then roll over the guarantee once these initial payments have been made. Other mechanisms include reinsurance of guaranteed risk, whenever feasible, and introducing guarantees in local currency instruments. Alternatively, in some cases private actors may be willing to lend for early maturities and institutions like the IADB or the World Bank may need to guarantee later maturities or provide co-financing for later maturities. This is particularly appropriate for infrastructure investments, which have high initial sunk costs and very long gestation periods before the project becomes profitable (see Griffith-Jones 1993; Gurria and Volcker 2001). Because of this, infrastructure projects often need financing for periods of up to 25–30 years, while the private market normally will only provide loans with significantly shorter maturities. This mismatch between financing needs, as well as the complexity of infrastructure projects and the shorter-term loans on offer from banks, make infrastructure projects a good candidate for partial public guarantees.

One suggestion is therefore to have public sector institutions play a much more consciously anti-cyclical role than has been customary. Our other suggestion is to urge a more proactive role for *socially responsible investment* (SRI). Traditionally, SRI has tended to have a negative slant, focusing on restrictions on investing in undesirable activities, such as those that employ child labor, do not meet environmental or labor standards, or indulge 'sins' like smoking, drinking and gambling. These restrictions can discourage investment in developing countries,[6] since a feature of underdevelopment is the existence of low wages and lower environmental standards than in rich countries (that is what it means to be poor, and it is precisely low wages that send the market a signal to make the investments that will allow a country to develop).

A new definition of SRI should specify that one of its central aims would be a *positive one*, to support *long-term* private flows to developing countries that *help fund pro-poor growth*. This would over time help to improve labor standards, both because incomes and especially wages would grow faster and because SRI foreign investors by being present and engaged in developing countries could have a positive influence on wages.

A change in the concept of what amounts to SRI, both by institutional and retail investors (where SRI has an important and growing presence), from a negative 'anti-bad things' to an emphasis on pro-poor growth in developing countries, could potentially have a positive impact on both the level and stability of private flows to developing countries. In particular, pension funds could potentially provide more stable flows as their liabilities are on average very long term. In the UK, legislation introduced in 1999 required that all pension funds set out in their annual report the way that social and environmental factors were taken into account in their investment decisions. This facilitates the ability of pension fund trustees and members to examine the practice of their fund, and lobby for change if they wish. The change in the UK regulation was soon replicated in a variety of other European countries. Also in the United States there are large institutions, both pension funds and religious foundations, that have a tradition of SRI, whose investments could be in part channeled to emerging markets if they were intellectually convinced that this would help to improve the world.

An important challenge is therefore to influence SRI investors to expand their horizons and recognize their responsibility for helping to promote development. Note that this need not imply an inferior long-run investment performance, for there is evidence that the return/risk ratio of a portfolio that has a part of its assets invested in developing-country equities will be higher in the long term than if it invests purely in developed countries. (See for example, Armendariz et al. 2002.) The potential is large, given the rapidly growing scale of SRI assets. For example, in the UK, Sparkes (2002) reports that the scale of these funds has increased tenfold in ten years to stand at US$326 billion in 2001. An estimate of global SRI assets (in Table 7.3), shows the very large scale, as well as the dominance of the United States and the UK.

*Table 7.3    Global SRI universe (2001)*

|                | (US$ billion) |
| -------------- | ------------- |
| United States  | 2332          |
| United Kingdom | 326           |
| Canada         | 31            |
| Rest of Europe | 18            |
| Total          | 2710          |

*Source:*   Persaud (2003), based on Sparkes (2002).

It is not fanciful to hope that such a switch in the objectives of SRI investors could be achieved in coming years. In a recent survey of UK SRI investors' attitude, which questioned these investors about what they considered the most important issues to be, 97.7 percent cited 'Third World people' as an issue of concern. This is not reflected in the current investment patterns of SRI funds: only a very small part of their money is at present invested in companies whose activities would promote growth and development in developing countries.

A natural complement to a policy of encouraging inflows is to avoid the introduction of measures that inappropriately discourage lending. A serious concern here is the current Basle Capital Accord proposals.

The Basle Committee of G10 banking regulators has proposed a new Capital Accord, with the expressed aim of more accurately aligning regulatory capital with the risks that international banks face. Recent research shows clearly that the current Basle proposal would significantly overestimate the risk involved in international bank lending to developing countries, and would therefore result in an excessive increase in the capital requirements on such lending. This would be likely to lead to a sharp increase in the cost of bank borrowing by developing countries, and thus a significant fall in the supply of bank loans.[7]

This is particularly serious as in the last five years bank lending to the developing world has already fallen sharply. The current proposals are thus doubly problematic, both in terms of the Basle Committee's own aims (more accurate measurement of risk for determining capital adequacy) and due to their further discouragement of already insufficient bank lending to emerging markets.

The inconsistency with the Basle Committee's own aims arises because one of the major benefits of lending to – and investing in – developing countries is their relatively low correlation with mature markets. This hypothesis has been carefully tested empirically, and very strong evidence has been

found – for a variety of variables, and over a range of time periods – that correlation between developed and developing countries is significantly lower
than correlation only among developed countries. For example, spreads on
syndicated loans – which reflect risks and probability of default – tend to rise
and fall together within developed regions more than between developed
and developing countries; similar results are obtained for the correlation of
profitability of banks. Furthermore, broader macroeconomic variables
(such as growth of GDP, interest rates, evolution of bond prices and stock
market indexes) show far more correlation within developed economies
than between developed and developing ones.

   These empirical findings imply that a bank that has a loan portfolio that
is diversified between developed and developing countries will have a lower
level of risk than one that is focused exclusively on lending to developed
economies.

   The current Basle proposals do not incorporate the benefits of international diversification, even though the capital requirements that Basle
regulators determine are supposed to help banks cope with risk. This will
incorrectly and unfairly penalize lending to developing countries unless the
Basle Committee in its next (and almost final) revision of the proposed
standards incorporates the benefits of international diversification. There
are no practical, empirical or theoretical obstacles to such a change, which
could potentially benefit the developing world at the same time as securing
more accurate measurement of risk and capital adequacy requirements. It
would be technically wrong, economically unwise and politically insensitive
not to make this change.

## CONCLUDING REMARKS

This chapter has shown that the trend toward liberalization of capital flows
has continued in recent years, despite the loss of intellectual enthusiasm for
rapid establishment of capital account convertibility in emerging markets
following the Asian crisis. It is of course true that the issue of the moment
is hardly preventing excessive capital inflows to these countries; on the contrary, they are currently suffering a prolonged drought of inflows. We have
made several suggestions as to what might be done to alleviate this. One
proposal is to have the MDBs accept a novel role in guaranteeing, or if
necessary providing, short-term trade credits where a shortage is provoked
by cyclical pressures leading to a withdrawal of commercial banks from
that role. Another is to persuade ECAs to incorporate a consciously countercyclical element into their policy stance toward medium-term trade
credits, so that they would be more willing to increase their exposure in

times of drought but might sell off some of their export credit guarantees in the secondary market when the markets are anxious to hold this type of paper. A third idea is to convince 'socially responsible investors' that promoting development is an objective that they should embrace. In addition, it is important that the Basle Committee amend its proposals to avoid a technically incorrect penalty on bank lending to developing countries that is embedded in its current proposal.

However, there will be occasions when prudence will demand controls aimed at reducing the danger of new crises in emerging markets. We have argued that these controls should be limited and strategic rather than complex and widespread, focused very clearly on the main justification for maintaining capital controls in emerging markets, which is minimizing the danger of speculative crises. We argued that two of the various types of control that have been utilized in recent years meet this criterion exceptionally well, namely the Chilean *encaje* and the Singaporean restriction on borrowing local currency for speculative purposes. Ironically, and tragically for the prospect of emerging markets becoming high-income economies without more unnecessary crises along the way, these are the very two controls that have been targeted for emasculation by the United States Treasury in US negotiations for its first two bilateral free trade areas with non-neighboring countries.

## APPENDIX 7A    REVIEW OF EXPERIENCE SINCE 1990

We have seen in Table 7.1 that most countries took measures to liberalize their capital accounts during the 1990s.[8] This was the case even among those countries that were relatively liberalized at the beginning of the decade, such as Mexico and Turkey. Typically, countries moved from a situation in which they were partly repressed to one in which they were largely liberalized.

**Degree of Liberalization by Region**

There are clear differences, however, by region (see Table 7A.1).

In the year 1990, capital accounts were, on average, partly repressed in all regions with the exception of East Asia, where the capital accounts were already largely liberalized. During the 1990s, all regions showed some liberalization, but the extent differed. According to our scores (which, of course, should be treated with caution), Latin America went the furthest towards full capital account convertibility. Sub-Saharan Africa and North Africa & Middle East also undertook major liberalization steps. The smallest change was observed in South Asia, a region that in 2001 was still classified as partly repressed. East Asia, while already fairly liberalized by the early 1990s, undertook modest additional liberalization.

*Table 7A.1    Degree of capital account liberalization, by region*

|  | Averages | | | | Standard deviation | |
|---|---|---|---|---|---|---|
|  | 1990 | 2001 | 1990 | 2001 | 1990 | 2001 |
| Latin America | 2.43 | 3.60 | PR | LL | 0.57 | 0.19 |
| Sub-Saharan Africa | 2.62 | 3.31 | PR | LL | 0.50 | 0.65 |
| North Africa & Middle East | 2.63 | 3.34 | PR | LL | 0.58 | 0.49 |
| South Asia | 2.03 | 2.50 | PR | PR | 0.24 | 0.45 |
| East Asia | 3.01 | 3.25 | LL | LL | 0.80 | 0.68 |
| Total | 2.59 | 3.26 | PR | LL | 0.64 | 0.60 |

*Note:*   PR (partly repressed): 1.76–2.75; LL (largely liberalized): 2.76–3.75.

*Source:*   Authors' elaboration, based on information from the IMF *Annual Report on Exchange Arrangements and Exchange Restrictions*, 1991 and 2002, and country reports, when available.

It should be noted that these regional patterns are based on our sample of countries; although we believe these countries are fairly good representatives of their regional neighbors, they may not necessarily reflect what happened in other countries of the regions. Still, the patterns observed are consistent with the view that the regions that liberalized most are those that have become most vulnerable to currency and financial crises. In contrast, South Asian countries, which by 2001 exhibited the lowest degree of capital account liberalization, escaped unscathed from the financial crises that occurred in the last few years.

The degree of homogeneity concerning capital account liberalization varies across regions. The highest degree of homogeneity (measured by the standard deviation of the score numbers assigned to the regions' countries – see Table 7A.1) can be found in South Asia in the 1990s, when all countries were fairly repressed, and in Latin America in 2001, when all countries were largely liberalized. By contrast, East Asian countries witnessed a relatively high degree of heterogeneity, both in the early 1990s and in 2001. This reflects the coexistence of contrasting economic models in the region.

Looking more closely within each region, a number of facts and trends are worth highlighting, regarding the types of capital account restrictions these countries used to reduce the volume of capital inflows in times of surges, and to limit capital outflows. Some of these, reported below, are not fully reflected in the scores above, as the latter are assigned for just two points in time, failing to fully capture what happened between 1990 and 2001.

**Latin American Countries**

In Latin America, Chile, Mexico and Venezuela were already largely liberalized at the beginning of the 1990s, but that contrasted strongly with all the other countries, which were partly repressed, with Argentina and Peru being the most heavily repressed. This reflected the historical tradition of closed capital accounts and the debt crisis of the 1980s.

As the first country to reach a debt restructuring agreement under the Brady plan, Mexico took the first, and already by then very large, liberalization steps at the end of the 1980s, almost a big-bang approach. At that time, the Mexican government allowed non-residents to invest in the stock markets, hold domestic bonds, including public ones, and acquire money market instruments (Griffith-Jones 1996). The country then undertook further liberalization steps as it entered the OECD in 1994 (Griffith-Jones et al. 2003a).

Argentina adopted a similar liberalization strategy in 1991, liberalizing its capital account quite rapidly and intensively. The country's degree of liberalization is not fully reflected in its scores for 2001, however. This is because since it began suffering from the crises of the late 1990s, and particularly from the Brazilian devaluation of early 1999, it started reimposing restrictions, which were intensified in late 2001 and early 2002 when it imposed major capital controls on outflows to stem massive capital flight. The country's score for 2001 does not capture these latest, more stringent, controls. After Mexico, Argentina had the most liberalized capital account in Latin America for most of the 1990s.

Like Mexico and Argentina, Peru adopted deep and fast liberalization of the capital account, from an initial position of very restrictive controls. The exchange rate was unified and a free-floating regime adopted, FDI received equivalent treatment to domestic investment, capital could be freely repatriated, non-residents could acquire domestic securities, and residents and non-residents could open foreign currency-denominated accounts, although with high reserve requirements against such accounts (Ariyoshi et al. 2000).

Most of the other countries also started liberalizing their capital account in the early 1990s. However, their policies had important elements of gradualism. Some of these elements took the form of restrictions to avoid excessive capital inflows during times of capital surges.

Chile (which had already largely liberalized by 1990) has been a paradigmatic case in the use of restrictions to reduce the volume of capital inflows and to influence their composition. In the early 1990s, the country experienced excessive capital inflows. To avoid excessive currency appreciation and other undesirable macroeconomic imbalances, in June 1991 the country's authorities adopted an unremunerated reserve requirement (URR) (the Chilean *encaje*), to reduce the volume of capital inflows and change their composition towards flows with longer maturity. This created a simple, non-discretionary and prudential mechanism, which penalized short-term foreign currency liabilities more heavily.

Initially, the URR was of 20 percent on foreign debts with maturity of more than one year, to be deposited at the central bank for one year, and for flows with maturity of less than one year, to be deposited during the whole stay period (or at least for 90 days, see Ffrench-Davis and Tapia 2001). FDI was subject to a minimum period of stay of three years. As pressures on the exchange rate continued, in May 1992 the URR was raised to 30 percent, and the minimum period of a one-year deposit was applied to all maturities. The stay requirement for FDI was reduced to one year.

In July 1995, the URR was extended to cover funds remitted from the sale of secondary American Depositary Receipts (ADRs), which were being extensively traded and putting pressure on the exchange rate (Ffrench-Davis and Tapia 2001). In October 1996, foreign investment wanting to enter the country under Decree Law 600 (DL 600) started to be screened. Until then, speculative forms of investment were entering the country through the DL 600 door disguised as capital increases, investments in financial services and 'associated loans', and the purpose of the newly implemented screening system was to subject such investments to the deposit requirements (Griffith-Jones et al. 1998). In June 1998 the deposit requirement was lowered to 10 percent, and in September 1998 it was further lowered to 0 percent. This was a response to the change in the international scenario, in which capital flows to developing countries had dried up. Chile's restrictions were aimed at affecting both the volume and maturity of flows, and they could be modified in response to changes in circumstances, and in order to reduce loopholes. It should be noted that, in parallel to the restrictions on inflows, Chile liberalized capital outflows by residents gradually during the 1990s, although a few restrictions remain even today.

Restrictions on capital inflows in Chile achieved several goals, as has been widely recognized, even by the IMF. First, there is widespread consensus that the URR helped change the maturity structure of capital inflows towards longer-term flows (Edwards 1999; Gallego et al. 1999; Ariyoshi et al. 2000 and de Gregorio et al. 2000). Second, due to this debt structure biased towards the long term, Chile survived better the effects of the Asian crisis, having experienced relatively mild volatility in the exchange and interest rates, and only a small loss of international reserves (Massad 1998). Finally, there is some evidence that capital restrictions also contributed to reducing the overall level of net inflows (Gallego et al. 1999; Williamson 2000), which in turn helped control the overheating of the economy that would have led to higher inflation and bigger current account deficits (Le Fort and Lehman 2000).

Other Latin American countries that were facing similar macroeconomic management problems as those in Chile due to large capital inflows – Brazil and Colombia – also adopted market-based restrictions to reduce the volume of capital flows and influence their composition.

Colombia adopted a Chilean-type deposit requirement. These deposits were applied for the first time in 1993 for foreign loans with maturity of less than 18 months, at a 47 percent level over one year. A particular feature of the Colombian measures was that they differentiated between maturities, having higher reserve requirements for shorter loans. Between 1993 and 1996, the maturity coverage expanded and the deposit rates increased. Rates were reduced after 1996 and totally removed in 1998 (Ariyoshi et al. 2000).

In Brazil, market-based controls took the form of an entrance tax on certain capital transactions, together with other restrictions. Restrictions were adopted mostly on short-term fixed income securities, with the government exercising varying degrees of control over time (Prates 1998; Gottschalk 2000). In times of surges, they restricted the entry of flows by raising tax and non-tax barriers, while at times of reversal, generally caused by crisis contagion, they reduced such barriers so as to encourage inflows. The decision to tax investment in fixed income and not stocks reflected the desire to influence the composition of capital flows and to reduce the monetary/public finance impact of flows channeled to government debt instruments (Garcia and Valpassos 1998). Reportedly, the complexity of Brazil's regulations (and their frequent changes) undermined their effectiveness.

**East Asian Countries**

As mentioned earlier, East Asian countries experienced some further liberalization in the 1990s. However, the standard deviation in the region – our indicator of the degree of heterogeneity, or dispersion – both for 1990 and 2001 is the largest among all regions (see Table 7A.1). This means that the regional average conceals sharp differences among the countries of the region. Four types of country can be found in East Asia. First, China, a very restricted country in 1990 which undertook little liberalization during the 1990s. Second is Korea, a country with a starting position of partly repressed but that liberalized quite vigorously. Third is a group of countries that had already largely liberalized in the early 1990s (Indonesia, Malaysia and Thailand) that undertook some further liberalization steps. Fourth are two city-states (Hong Kong and Singapore) that were already liberalized in the early 1990s.

The Chinese policy towards capital account liberalization is closer to South Asian countries than to its subregional neighbors, in that it liberalized FDI first and kept strong restrictions on all other forms of capital flows, and then started to relax such restrictions only very gradually. By 2001, China was the most restrictive of all the Asian countries in our sample, according to our classification. Many transactions, such as the acquisition of domestic bonds by non-residents, are not permitted, while others (such as the issue of bonds abroad by residents) require prior approval. Transactions involving money market instruments and derivatives are mostly prohibited, and external borrowing is restricted, with a need for prior approval that is granted only under certain conditions.

Korea is the country that, starting from an initial fairly restrictive position, undertook the largest capital account liberalization during the decade, to reach a fairly open stance by 2001. The country started out gradually, with residents being permitted to issue securities abroad and foreigners being allowed to invest directly in the Korean stock market (though limits existed on the latter). From 1993 until 1997, the process was accelerated with the lifting of barriers on short-term borrowing to different sorts of domestic activities previously restricted, investment by non-residents in public bonds, and permission to issue equity-linked bonds and non-guaranteed bonds by small and medium-sized firms, and non-guaranteed long-term bonds by large firms (Chang et al. 1998).

Some restrictions were maintained, however, particularly on some forms of capital inflows, due to concerns about surge of capital inflows, caused by interest rate differentials. These were mainly in the form of ceilings on foreign investment in domestic equity securities and borrowing from abroad by non-banks (Wang 2000). However, the exceptions to these, which proved harmful, included the liberalization of trade-related short-term financing to domestic firms and short-term foreign currency borrowing by domestic banks (Shin and Wang 1999).

Thailand, Malaysia and Indonesia, in turn, belong to a category of countries that had already had many years of experience with a fairly open capital account.

Thailand's liberalization was the most aggressive of these during the 1990s, particularly in the early 1990s with the creation of the Bangkok International Banking Facility (BIBF), which through tax privileges greatly encouraged external flows, especially short-term ones (Johnston et al. 1997). In 1995, restrictions were imposed to reduce the volume of (mainly short-term) capital inflows, which became excessive in the first half of the 1990s. These restrictions included a 7 percent reserve requirement on non-resident baht accounts with a maturity of less than one year and on short-term borrowing of finance companies; limits for open short and long foreign currency positions (with lower limits for short positions); and reporting requirements by banks on risk control measures regarding foreign exchange and derivatives (Ariyoshi et al. 2000). However, capital continued to flow in large amounts by taking different forms (Siamwalla et al. 2003). In response to that, in 1996 the reserve requirements were extended to short-term borrowing by commercial and BIBF banks.

According to Ariyoshi et al. (2000), such controls on capital inflows succeeded in reducing the volume of inflows, lengthening their maturity, reducing the short-term debt to total debt ratio, and reducing the growth of non-resident baht accounts. However, these developments were not sufficient to avoid the reversal of capital flows the country experienced in 1997.

Like Thailand, Malaysia has been relatively open for years, and experienced a massive surge of capital inflows in the early 1990s. Until then, the limits on capital inflows consisted mainly of ceilings on foreign currency borrowing, beyond which approval was required. To further limit such flows, especially short-term ones, in 1994 the authorities prohibited the selling by residents to non-residents of money market securities, and commercial banks were forbidden to engage in swap and forward contracts with non-residents. Ceilings were imposed on banks' net foreign exchange open positions, and reserve requirements were decreed for foreign currency liabilities of commercial banks. Most of these controls were subsequently lifted, with only the prudential ones remaining in place. The assessment of Ariyoshi et al. is that such controls were effective both in reducing the volume and changing the maturity of flows.

During 1997 and early 1998 Malaysia suffered massive capital outflows. In response to that, in September 1998 the country's authorities adopted a number of restrictions on capital outflows. These included: prohibition of using domestic currency in trade payments and offshore trading, prohibition of credit facilities between residents and non-residents, and repatriation of non-resident portfolio capital, which was blocked for 12 months (Ariyoshi et al.). Controls were later relaxed and then totally eliminated.

Indonesia greatly encouraged capital flows, especially FDI, from the start of the decade. Bank lending to the domestic corporate sector also became prominent in the 1990s. In the mid-1990s, there was an effort to prioritize FDI over other types of flows, with ceilings on foreign lending being used as an instrument, but with poor effectiveness (Gottschalk and Griffith-Jones 2003).

Finally, Hong Kong and Singapore are among the few developing countries with almost totally liberalized capital accounts as early as 1990. Both countries remained open, though a few restrictions are in place. For example, in Hong Kong, the disclosure and position limits on derivative products are required, in addition to prudential limits on open foreign exchange positions and on certain forms of capital outflows. In the case of Singapore, there are upper limits for foreign lending from residents to non-residents in Singapore dollars, and an obligation for non-residents to convert proceeds in Singapore dollars into foreign currency. These measures are aimed at discouraging the international use of the domestic currency. Also, there are certain prudential limits and restrictions on capital outflows.

**South Asian Countries**

As mentioned earlier, South Asian countries have adopted a cautious approach to capital account liberalization. FDI was liberalized first. In India, portfolio equity flows were selectively liberalized during the 1990s, and the liberalization of external borrowing was very limited. The country relied extensively on quantitative and other controls. These included overall quantitative ceilings, approvals on a case-by-case basis, different degrees of restriction according to the maturity of foreign liabilities, and end-use restrictions. Strong limits were imposed on short-term debt. In June 1997 – thus just before the East Asian crisis broke out – the Tarapore Committee recommended a timetable for further capital account liberalization in India (Reserve Bank of India 2000). The proposed liberalization included both capital inflows and outflows; liberalization was to be progressive, in three phases, over three years. However, these liberalization steps were conditional on the country meeting certain preconditions. By 2001, India's capital account was still only partially liberalized, with strong restrictions remaining in place, particularly on capital outflows by residents.

Apparently due to this more cautious approach, and to its high level of foreign reserves, the country managed to escape the financial crises of the 1990s and even to avoid contagion effects during the East Asian crisis. In addition, it managed to maintain relatively strong economic growth during the 1990s, even during periods of major recessions in the crisis countries of the region (Ariyoshi et al. 2000).

Alongside India, Pakistan is the other South Asian country that pursued significant liberalization steps during the 1990s. In fact it went further than India, with most types of capital inflow liberalized. Most of the remaining restrictions are on capital outflows by residents, though lately some initial steps have been taken to liberalize outflows.

Although having undertaken some liberalization steps, the capital account in both Bangladesh and Sri Lanka remains quite repressed. These two countries have maintained capital restrictions in the form of outright prohibitions (for example, in the case of money market instruments and derivatives) and central bank approval (for example, for commercial borrowing in the case of Bangladesh and long-term borrowing in the case of Sri Lanka). Capital outflows by residents are still strongly restricted, especially in Bangladesh.

**North African and Middle-Eastern Countries**

In North Africa, Morocco and Tunisia moved from an initial position of partially repressed to largely liberalized capital accounts by 2001, although they were still more restricted than many other countries of the sample that reached the status of largely liberalized. These were due to remaining restrictions mainly on inflows, related to the acquisition of money market instruments and derivatives, and capital outflows by residents, particularly portfolio flows.

Egypt and Turkey, in turn, liberalized fully all forms of portfolio inflows, leaving a few restrictions on some forms of capital outflows by residents (mainly lending to non-residents and outflows by institutional investors).

**Sub-Saharan African Countries**

Sub-Saharan African (SSA) countries face a somewhat different set of issues as compared to the so-called emerging market economies. Most of them are poor, and tend to have large current account deficits, funded mainly by aid. If they liberalize the capital account, and private flows were to come in, then they would become very vulnerable to reversals of private flows on account of an external shock. Large outflows by residents, if permitted, might be an even more important source of vulnerability for SSA countries than reversals of private capital inflows, as the inflows are unlikely to be so large.

Yet, despite such considerations that would seem to advise the adoption of a cautious approach, most SSA countries covered in this study took major steps to liberalize their capital accounts in the 1990s. The exception was Tanzania, which proceeded very cautiously throughout the 1990s, though recently it too has initiated a bolder liberalization strategy (see Griffith-Jones and Gottschalk 2002).

Uganda is the Sub-Saharan country that liberalized its capital account most during the 1990s. It started to liberalize the current account in the late 1980s, and by 1992 had removed exchange control restrictions. In 1997, it achieved full capital account liberalization, maintaining in place only a few prudential regulations in the financial system. The main purposes of the liberalization reforms were to reduce the savings–investment gap, attract FDI and finance privatization. Restrictions on the capital account that were until then in place were seen as ineffective in stemming capital flight (Kasekende 2002). The main positive results associated with the reforms during the 1990s were an increase in FDI, and an increase in domestic private sector investment as well. On the negative side, Uganda experienced high exchange rate volatility, which has generated greater uncertainty.

Kenya was another fast liberalizing country in the region. In a context of shortage of foreign reserves and large fiscal deficit, in 1991 the country embarked on a program of reforms that included rapid current and capital account liberalization. The latter included permission to hold foreign currency certificates of deposit, which could be traded by residents and non-residents, used for any foreign exchange transaction, and reclaimed at the central bank at face value. In addition, some companies could hold foreign currency-denominated bank accounts abroad and domestically (Ariyoshi et al. 2000). In 1994, the domestic currency became fully convertible, and in 1995 most of the remaining controls on foreign exchange transactions were removed (including access by foreigners to shares and government securities). Among the few exceptions, foreigners could hold portfolio equities up to 5 percent individually and 40 percent in aggregate. The overall result of capital account liberalization in Kenya in the context of broader reforms was macroeconomic volatility and increased capital flight (Ariyoshi et al.).

South Africa is the only emerging market economy in the region. Since 1994, when the South African economy was reintegrated with the world economy, the country's authorities have taken two broad steps to liberalize the capital account. First, they liberalized capital flows for non-residents in March 1995, and from July 1995 started a liberalization process concerning capital flows by residents (Gottschalk 2002). The liberalization of capital flows by non-residents was implemented very rapidly in March 1995, when foreign exchange restrictions on non-residents were removed and the exchange rate was unified (Wesso 2001); liberalization covered all forms of flow, including short-term capital. The liberalization of capital flows by residents, in contrast, has been gradual and sequenced. Starting in mid-1995, institutional investors were initially permitted to invest abroad through an asset-swap mechanism. The objective of this mechanism was to ensure balance of payments neutrality (National Treasury 2001). This mechanism was removed in 2001, however, and replaced with certain limits. Nowadays, institutional investors are allowed to make foreign transfers of up to 10 percent of their net inflow of funds during the previous year. In addition, they are subject to overall limits of 15 percent of the total assets for pension funds, fund managers and insurers, and 20 percent for unit trusts (IMF 2001; National Treasury 2001). Corporations and individuals are also permitted to hold financial assets abroad, although the limits they face are more restrictive, especially for individuals.

The attention the South African authorities devoted to capital outflows by residents, and their lesser concern regarding capital inflows, probably reflected the fact that, in spite of being an emerging economy, they perceived the major threat to be capital outflows by residents, given the initial lack of confidence in the country's prospects by the monied minority. South Africa in fact witnessed less of a capital inflow surge during the decade than many other emerging economies, though the cycles of inflows and their reversal were much shorter and, therefore, in many ways very damaging to the country's macro economy.

Côte d'Ivoire is the only Francophone country in our sample, but certainly very representative of the countries that are members of the West African Economic and Monetary Union (WAEMU[9]). Capital inflows to Côte d'Ivoire are quite unrestricted, and this applies equally to all countries of the Union (IMF 2002). A few restrictions still remain, mainly on capital outflows by residents.

## NOTES

1. The countries are: Argentina, Brazil, Chile, Colombia, Mexico, Peru and Venezuela (Latin America); Côte d'Ivoire, Kenya, Nigeria, South Africa, Tanzania and Uganda (Sub-Saharan Africa); Morocco, Tunisia, Egypt and Turkey (North Africa and the Middle East); Bangladesh, India, Pakistan and Sri Lanka (South Asia); China, Hong Kong, Indonesia, Korea, Malaysia, Singapore and Thailand (East Asia).
2. The argument here is based on the arguments against capital controls considered by Cooper (1999).
3. See Williamson (1999, p. 132) for a fuller discussion.
4. A recent study (Begg et al. 2003, Table 1) distinguishes nine types of flow: direct investment; investment in real estate; stock market operations (inter alia portfolio equity); security and money-market operations; accounts with financial intermediaries; credits related to commercial transactions; financial loans; transfers in performance of insurance contracts; and personal capital movements.
5. Banks and other market participants' assessments of risk are often importantly determined by the state of global preferences for risk and by contagion between developing countries, and not much influenced by countries' fundamentals (for econometric evidence, see FitzGerald and Krolzig 2003).
6. A recent example of this is when the large US pension fund, Calpers, introduced a number of restrictions on their investment (for example, minimum labor standards). This led to the withdrawal of their investments from several major developing countries.
7. See a full analysis in Griffith-Jones et al. (2003b).
8. To classify each country's capital account regulations as either repressed (R), partly repressed (PR), largely liberalized (LL), or liberalized (L), scores were assigned from 1 (R) to 4 (L) to the following items and sub-items of the countries' balance of payments: 1. FDI: direct investment and the liquidation of investment; 2. Portfolio flows: shares, bonds and collective investment securities; 3. Money market and derivatives: money market instruments, and derivatives and other instruments; 4. Credit operations: commercial credits, financial credits, and guarantees, sureties and financial facilities; 5. Capital outflows by residents: FDI, lending, portfolio flows (shares, bonds and other securities), institutional investors, money market instruments and derivatives. The items' scores and the total scores are the simple average of the sub-items' and items' scores, respectively. The regional scores, in turn, are the simple average of the scores assigned to the region's countries. Since decimal values were obtained for the total scores, the following score ranges were established: repressed (R): 1.00–1.75; partly repressed (PR): 1.76–2.75; largely liberalized (LL): 2.76–3.75; and liberalized (L): 3.76–4.00. An item considered repressed usually means outright prohibition, and partly repressed, when authorization is required. A largely liberalized item usually is subjected to market-based restrictions, such as unremunerated reserve requirements, or ceiling limits and other quantitative/administrative restrictions.
9. The WAEMU comprises the following countries: Benin, Burkina Faso, Côte d'Ivoire, Guinea-Bissau, Mali, Niger, Senegal and Togo.

## REFERENCES

Ariyoshi, A., K. Habermeier, B. Laurens, I. Otker-Robe, J.I. Canales-Kriljenko and A. Kirilenko (2000), 'Capital controls: country experiences with their use and liberalization', IMF Occasional Paper no. 190, International Monetary Fund, Washington, DC, 17 May.

Armendariz, E., R. Gottschalk, S. Griffith-Jones and J. Kimmis (2002), 'Making the case for UK pension fund investment in development country assets', mimeo, Institute of Development Studies, University of Sussex, Brighton, July.

Begg, David, Barry Eichengreen, Lásló Halpern, Jürgen von Hagen and Charles Wyplosz (2003), 'Sustainable regimes of capital movements in accession countries', CEPR Policy Paper no. 10, Center for Economic Policy Research, London.

Chang, H., H. Park and C. Yoo (1998), 'Interpreting the Korean crisis: financial liberalisation, industrial policy and corporate governance', *Cambridge Journal of Economics*, **22**, 735–46.

Cooper, Richard N. (1999), 'Should capital controls be banished?', *Brookings Papers on Economic Activity*, 1, Washington, DC.

de Gregorio, J., S. Edwards and R.O. Valdes (2000), 'Controls on capital flows: do they work?', *Journal of Development Economics*, **63** (1), October, 59–83.

Edwards, S. (1999), 'How effective are capital controls?', NBER Working Paper 7413, National Bureau of Economic Research, Cambridge, MA, November.

Ffrench-Davis, R. and H. Tapia (2001), 'Three policy varieties to face capital surges in Chile', in R. Ffrench-Davis (ed.), *Financial Crises in 'Successful' Emerging Economics*, Santiago: McGraw-Hill and Washington, DC: Brookings Institution.

FitzGerald, V. and D. Krolzig (2003), 'Modelling the demand for emerging markets assets', mimeo, Oxford University, January.

Gallego, F., L. Hernandez and K. Schmidt-Hebbel (1999), 'Capital controls in Chile: Effective? Efficient?', Working Paper of Central Bank of Chile no. 59, December.

Garcia, M. and M. Valpassos (1998), 'Capital flows, capital controls and currency crisis: the case of Brazil in the nineties', discussion paper, Department of Economics, Rio de Janeiro, November.

Gottschalk, R. (2000), 'Sequencing trade and capital account liberalization: the experience of Brazil in the 1990s', Occasional Paper, UNCTAD/UNDP, UNCTAD/EDM/Misc, 132, September.

Gottschalk, R. (2002), 'Capital account liberalization: the international experience and lessons for South Africa', report prepared for the South African National Treasury, December.

Gottschalk, R. and S. Griffith-Jones (2003), 'The financial crises of the late 1990s: summary and policy lessons', in S. Griffith-Jones, R. Gottschalk and J. Cailloux (eds), *International Capital Flows in Calm and Turbulent Times: The Need for a New Financial Architecture*, Ann Arbor, MI: University of Michigan Press.

Griffith-Jones, S. (1993), *Loan Guarantees for Large Infrastructure Projects: the Issues and Possible Lessons for a European Facility*, Luxembourg: Commission of the European Communities.

Griffith-Jones, S. (1996), 'The Mexican peso crisis', IDS Discussion Paper 354, Institute of Development Studies, University of Sussex, Brighton, July.

Griffith-Jones, S. (2002), 'Capital flows to developing countries: does the emperor have clothes?', mimeo, Institute of Development Studies, University of Sussex, Brighton.

Griffith-Jones, S., R. Wood and J. Cailloux (1998), 'EU/Chile capital flows', study prepared for DG-1 of the European Commission.

Griffith-Jones, S. and R. Gottschalk (2002), 'Capital account liberalization in Tanzania', report prepared for the Bank of Tanzania, October.

Griffith-Jones, S., R. Gottschalk and X. Cirera (2003a), 'The OECD experience with capital account liberalization', in UNCTAD, *Management of Capital Flows: Comparative Experiences and Implications for Africa*, New York and Geneva: United Nations.

Griffith-Jones, Stephany, Miguel Segoviano and Stephan Spratt (2003b), 'Basel II and developing countries: diversification and portfolio effects', Institute of Development Studies, University of Sussex, Brighton, www.ids.ac.uk/ids/global/finance/intfin.html.

Gurria, J.A. and P. Volcker (2001), 'The role of the multilateral development banks in emerging market economies: new policies for a changing global environment', report commissioned by Carnegie Endowment, Emerging Markets Partners and the Inter-American Dialogue, Washington, DC, April.

IMF (2001), *Annual Report on Exchange Arrangements and Exchange Restrictions*, Washington, DC: International Monetary Fund.

IMF (2002), *Annual Report on Exchange Arrangements and Exchange Restrictions*, Washington, DC: International Monetary Fund.

Johnston, B., S. Darbar and C. Echeverria (1997), 'Sequencing capital account liberalization: lessons from the experiences in Chile, Indonesia, Korea and Thailand',

IMF Working Paper, WP/97/157, International Monetary Fund, Washington, DC, November.

Kasekende, L. (2002), 'Capital account liberalisation: the Ugandan experience', paper presented at the Overseas Development Institute, 21 June.

Kindleberger, Charles P. (1987), 'A historical perspective', in D.R. Lessard and J. Williamson (eds), *Capital Flight and Third World Debt,* Washington, DC: Institute for International Economics.

Le Fort, G. and S. Lehmann (2000), 'El Encaje, los Flujos de Capitales y el Gasto: una Evaluacion empirica', Working paper of Central Bank of Chile no. 64, Santiago, February.

Massad, C. (1998), 'The liberalization of the capital account: Chile in the 1990s', in S. Fischer (ed.), *Should the IMF Pursue Capital-Account Convertibility?*, Essays in International Finance, no. 207, Princeton, NJ: Princeton University Press, May.

National Treasury (2001), 'The role of the National Treasury in the economy', mimeo, South Africa National Treasury.

Persaud, A. (2003), 'Global responsible investment', Lecture note, Mercers', School Memorial Professor of Commerce, Gresham College, London, 20 March.

Prates, D.M. (1998), 'Investimentos de Portfolio no Mercado Financeiro Domestico', in Fundap. Abertura Externa e Sistema Financeiro, Final report, ch.1, Sao Paulo, May.

Quinn, Dennis (1997), 'The correlates of change in international financial regulation', *American Political Science Review*, **91** (3), September, 531–51.

Reinhart, Carmen M., Kenneth S. Rogoff and Miguel A. Savastano (2003), 'Debt intolerance', paper presented to the Brookings Panel on Economic Activity, Washington, DC, March.

Reserve Bank of India (2000), 'Recommendations of Tarapore Committee on capital account convertibility', www.rbi.org.in/index/dl . . . 001&secid=21/0/0&archivemode=0, accessed 26 June 2000.

Shin, I. and Y. Wang (1999), 'How to sequence capital market liberalization: lessons from the Korean experience', KIEP Working Paper 99–30, Korea Institute for International Economic Policy, Seoul.

Siamwalla, A., Y. Vajragupta and P. Vichyanond (2003), 'Foreign capital flows to Thailand: determinants and impact', in S. Griffith-Jones, R. Gottschalk and J. Cailloux (eds), *International Capital Flows In Calm and Turbulent Times: The*

*Need for a New Financial Architecture*, Ann Arbor, MI: University of Michigan Press.

Sparkes, R. (2002), *Socially Responsible Investment: a Global Revolution*, Chichester: John Wiley & Son.

Wang, Y. (2000), 'Getting the sequencing right: the Korean experience in the capital market liberalization', mimeo, Korea Institute for International Economic Policy, Seoul.

Wesso, G.R. (2001), 'The dynamics of capital flows in South Africa: an empirical investigation', *Quarterly Bulletin*, SA Reserve Bank, June, 59–77.

Williamson, John (1999), 'Implications of the East Asian crisis for debt management', in A. Vasudevan (ed.), *External Debt Management: Issues, Lessons and Preventive Measures*, Mumbai: Reserve Bank of India.

Williamson, John (2000), *Exchange Rate Regimes for Emerging Markets: Reviving the Intermediate Option*, Washington, DC: Institute for International Economics.

World Bank (2003), 'Striving for stability in development finance', *Global Development Finance*, April.

168- 98

F32  024
F33  019

(Deleted Countries)

# 8. Is democracy incompatible with international economic stability?

## David Leblang*

---

## INTRODUCTION

One of the enduring triumphs of the Bretton Woods system is the recognition by its founders that policymakers in industrial democracies are answerable to both domestic and international constituencies. The founders purposely built a flexible system to allow democracies to work, to provide elected politicians room to balance domestic monetary autonomy and exchange rate stability. Consequently, and at least for a time, the Bretton Woods system allowed both democracy and international economic stability to flourish. With the 60th anniversary of the agreement approaching in 2004 we observe democracy spreading to an ever-larger number of countries; yet we also see a growing number of international financial crises. As discussions about the future international financial architecture intensify it is timely to re-examine the relationship between domestic policy autonomy and international economic stability.

One of the key differences in the international economic environment when the Bretton Woods era is compared to the present day concerns the degree of capital mobility. During Bretton Woods, capital markets were relatively segmented and policymakers could meet constituent demands without being overly concerned about the consequences of policy on exchange rate stability. With the growing integration of capital markets, policymakers do not have as much flexibility; expansionary monetary policy used for redistribution, for example, often places downward pressure on the exchange rate. This does not mean, however, that democratic politics are incompatible with international economic stability. The relative transparency and predictability of the policy process in democracies may provide markets with confidence in macroeconomic affairs. Democracy is thus a double-edged sword, providing international capital markets with opportunities for both increased stability and volatility. These considerations are of obvious importance when building the foundations of a new international financial system.

Giving domestic politics a central place in a discussion of exchange rate regimes, capital controls and economic crises is not without precedent and is certainly appropriate as the 60th anniversary of the Bretton Woods Accords approaches. The Bretton Woods system differed from prior monetary regimes in three fundamental ways. First, the gold-exchange standard of the inter-war years was replaced by an adjustable peg exchange rate system whereby countries could alter their parities in the event of 'fundamental disequilibrium'. Second, adjustable pegs were feasible (if not sustainable) as capital controls were permitted to insulate domestic economies from the ravages of international capital flows. Third, the International Monetary Fund (IMF) was established to assist countries experiencing balance of payments difficulties.

The establishment of similar institutions and rules was unnecessary prior to the First World War, though not because capital mobility was limited. In fact, confronted with high capital mobility during the late 19th and early 20th centuries, policymakers fixed the value of their currency to gold and could credibly commit to defending the parity. This commitment was viewed as credible by international financial markets because policymakers were insulated from the demands of their constituents: suffrage was limited, labor unions had limited representation in government and electoral rules favored established status quo political parties. The expansion of suffrage, the rise of labor unions, and the growth of parliamentary democracy between the wars and especially after the Second World War made policymakers more accountable and, as a result, called policymakers' commitment to maintain the peg to gold into question.

The Bretton Woods system, through adjustable pegs and capital controls, allowed policymakers to shift monetary policy away from exchange rate management and focus it on domestic priorities such as full employment.[1] This shift of emphasis reflected an explicit recognition that a balance between domestic monetary autonomy and exchange rate stability requires significant restrictions on capital mobility.

Adjustable pegs and capital controls were not sufficient, however, to guarantee international economic stability, as the deepening of the welfare state and the growth of global capital markets put domestic monetary policy autonomy in conflict with exchange rate stability. Part of the demise of the Bretton Woods system can certainly be traced to these domestic political changes. The adjustable peg was replaced by a system of floating exchange rates for the majority of the industrialized world. Once integrated into global capital markets, floating exchange rates did provide policymakers with the ability to implement policies – expansionary and otherwise – demanded by their constituencies. This policy flexibility, however, comes at the expense of exchange rate stability.

While political considerations were critical factors in the creation of institutions to manage the post-war global economy, they are rarely given pride of place in contemporary discussions of international economic policy. This focus is especially timely as a 'third wave' of democratization reaches new shores and as scores of national currencies are toppled by flows of speculative capital. Is democracy to blame for the rash of economic instability that has struck developing economies? Does democratization lead policymakers to adopt policies that are inconsistent with the exchange rate peg leading, subsequently, to speculative attacks? What role do capital controls play in insulating a policymaker from the ravages of the global capital market as larger electorates demand increasingly redistributive policies?

This chapter sheds light on these questions. I examine the relationship between political democracy at the domestic level – suffrage, electoral rules and leftist government partisanship – and international economic policy outcomes – exchange rate regime choice, capital market openness, and currency crises – in developing countries during the post-Bretton Woods era. I find that the expansion of democracy since 1970 does not have the same consequences for international economic stability that it did during the interwar period. In fact, I find that democracy increases economic stability directly and indirectly. Because democracies are more transparent there is less economic uncertainty about the future course of government policies as compared to authoritarian governments. Consequently, countries with larger electorates experience fewer speculative attacks. Policymakers in democracies also influence the likelihood of speculative attacks indirectly, by choosing exchange rate regimes and capital controls policies that are compatible with exchange rate stability and by stockpiling foreign exchange reserves to be used to defend the exchange rate parity.

Following this introduction, the next section provides a brief overview of the theoretical and empirical issues and provides a first cut at understanding the trends in domestic politics, international economic policy and speculative attacks. The third section goes beyond global trends and uses panel data for between 110 and 130 developing countries to examine the political and economic causes of speculative attacks. The findings suggest that there is an incompatibility between democracy and the maintenance of fixed exchange rate regimes. The fourth section examines two possible explanations for these results: the relationship between democracy and international economic policy choice and holdings of international reserves. The fifth section discusses possible problems of endogeneity and shows how a focus on democratization can shed some light on the recently observed phenomena referred to as 'fear of floating'. The final section concludes.

# DEMOCRACY, INTERNATIONAL ECONOMIC POLICY CHOICE AND SPECULATIVE ATTACKS

What are the consequences of expanding democracy for economic policy choice and currency crises in the developing world? If democratization and the associated expansion of suffrage create pressure for redistributive policies, does the implementation of these policies come at the expense of exchange rate stability? A useful framework for examining these questions is based on the seminal work of Mundell (1961, 1963) and has been referred to interchangeably as the 'impossible trio' or the 'unholy trinity'. As suggested by these phrases the idea is that three desired policies – exchange rate stability, capital market integration, an independent monetary policy – are incompatible. A useful illustration of the unholy trinity, adapted from Frankel (1999) in Figure 8.1, shows that policymakers can achieve two but not all three policy outputs: an independent monetary policy with capital controls allows for exchange rate stability while the use of (expansionary)

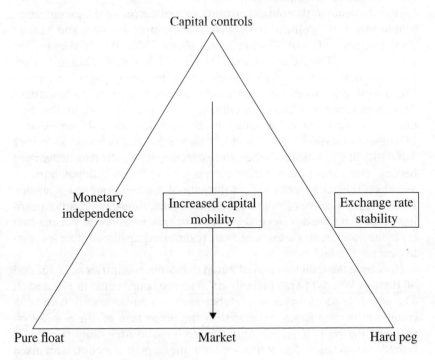

*Source:* Adapted from Frankel (1999).

*Figure 8.1    International economic policy choices*

monetary policy in an economy without capital controls puts downward pressure on the exchange rate. The downward arrow in Figure 8.1 is meant to indicate that increasingly integrated capital markets – through technological and institutional innovations – places monetary policy autonomy and exchange rate stability in conflict. This may be too strong a statement, as Frankel's message is that nothing in theory says that a proportion of pressure on the exchange rate cannot be taken by monetary policy while the rest is taken on the exchange rate.

From a political perspective, however, making exchange rate and monetary policy in concert may be problematic as policy tends to reflect compromise between various constituencies.[2] If these policy compromises push the government's holdings of reserves downwards, the consequence may be a currency crisis as speculators attempt to sell the domestic currency short (Krugman 1979). Even if fundamentals are strong, policymakers in expanding democracies may run into difficulties as crises can occur if speculators even anticipate a policy change that is incompatible with the exchange rate peg (for example, Obstfeld 1994).

How do democratic political institutions and the rise of democratization fit into this story? Political economists (for example, Bussiere and Mulder 2000; Frieden et al. 2001; Poirson 2001; Leblang 2002, 2003) have examined two avenues leading from democratic politics – a mobilized electorate, elections, political fractionalization, electoral institutions, changes in partisanship and so on – to exchange rate vulnerability in developing countries.[3] First, democratic processes can influence the expectations of market participants directly by contributing to policy uncertainty. If an election outcome is uncertain – if it is unclear which individual or party will garner a majority of votes or seats – then domestic currency holders can hedge their bets by selling short the domestic currency. Second, institutional, partisan and electoral incentives can affect the path of macroeconomic aggregates. From the perspective of political business cycles, for example, an impending election may lead policymakers to pursue macroeconomic policies that are inconsistent with the exchange rate regime leading directly to a speculative currency attack.

How have these factors played out in developing countries since the end of Bretton Woods? Some preliminary evidence is presented in Figure 8.2. The figure shows global trends (global averages) for between 110 and 138 countries[4] in democracy, measured as the percentage of the population that has the right to vote; capital controls, measured using the IMF's binary classification for restrictions on the capital account; and fixed and intermediate exchange rate regimes, again measured using the IMF's *de jure* classification of exchange arrangements.[5] The annual number of speculative attacks is also represented in the figure by the vertical

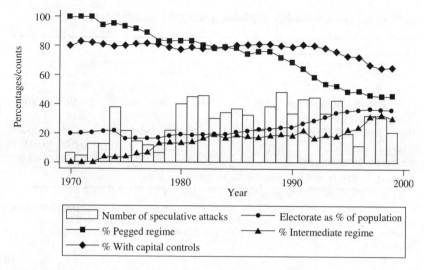

*Figure 8.2    Trends in the developing world, 1970–1999*

bars. Information on data sources and variable codings is contained in Appendix 8A.

Figure 8.2 confirms well-known trends: pegged exchange rate regimes and capital controls have been on the decline since 1970. Pegged exchange rate arrangements have been replaced by both intermediate and floating (the omitted category in this figure) regimes. The average size of the electorate has also increased steadily since 1975, increasing more rapidly since 1990. What is a bit more interesting, however, is that while we may think that speculative attacks are relative newcomers to the international financial system, they are, in fact, far from new phenomena for countries in the developing world. The frequency of attacks also seems to be associated with an increase in the size of the global electorate and the existence of capital controls.

A first attempt to sort out these relationships from a systemic point of view is presented in Table 8.1. The table contains Poisson regressions modeling the yearly number of global speculative attacks as a function of the yearly percentage of countries with capital controls, the average size of the electorate in the developing world, and a number of control variables.[6] Those control variables – all measured in terms of global averages for the developing world – include inflation, government consumption as a percentage of GDP, year-on-year growth, and the state of the business cycle measured as the deviation of GDP per capita from a trend. To minimize

*Table 8.1   Poisson models of global speculative attack frequency*

| Variable (all variables measured at $t-1$) | (1) | (2) |
|---|---|---|
| Constant | −0.61  (1.98) | −2.82  (3.17) |
| Inflation | −0.001 (0.07) | 0.02  (0.07) |
| Government Consumption/GDP | 0.04  (0.07) | 0.10  (0.10) |
| Year-on-Year Growth | −7.83* (3.82) | −6.46  (4.12) |
| Per Capita GDP Deviation from Trend | 0.16* (0.004) | 0.01*  (0.004) |
| Capital Controls | 0.03* (0.015) | 0.03*  (0.015) |
| Electorate/Population | 0.04* (0.01) | 0.056* (0.023) |
| Fixed or Intermediate Exchange Rate Regime | | 0.012  (0.013) |

*Note:* *$p < 0.10$; $N = 29$; coefficients are maximum likelihood estimates from a Poisson regression model with standard errors in parentheses. The dependent variable is the number of speculative attacks per year in 110−138 developing countries from 1971 to 1999.

the possibility of reverse causality, the independent variables are lagged by one year.

The results in Table 8.1 are somewhat consistent with those obtained by Eichengreen (2001) for a wider, albeit much shorter sample. Inflation and government consumption as a percentage of GDP has no statistically significant impact on the likelihood of global crises, while higher rates of economic growth decrease and fluctuations in the business cycle increase the occurrence of speculative attacks. Column 1 also includes the capital controls and size of electoral enfranchisement variables. Rather than providing policymakers with insulation from international economic pressures, the existence of capital controls in larger portions of the developing world is associated with an increasing number of speculative attacks. This positive coefficient squares with panel data studies (for example, Glick and Hutchison 2001; Bordo et al. 2001; and Leblang 2003) that find speculative attacks and/or currency crises more likely during a given year in countries that have capital controls. The results in Table 8.1 provide additional evidence to support theoretical models showing that the existence of capital controls sends a negative signal to markets; policymakers that employ controls are more likely to use inconsistent policies and may be unwilling to defend the exchange rate parity (for example, Bertolini and Drazen 1997a, b).

The coefficient on size of the electorate as a proportion of the total population is also positive and statistically significant, suggesting that the broadening and deepening democracy in the developing world is related to a greater frequency of speculative attacks. This finding is consistent with stories about the rise of democracy and breakdown of fixed exchange rates during the interwar years: in an effort to provide public and private goods to expanding constituencies, policymakers instituted policies that reduced their ability to focus monetary policy on the exchange rate (Eichengreen 1992; Simmons 1994).

Column 2 in Table 8.1 includes the proportion of countries that reported to the IMF that they had a fixed or intermediate exchange rate regime as an explanatory variable in the regression.[7] A larger proportion of fixed and intermediate regimes have a positive but statistically insignificant effect on the number of speculative attacks. The direction of this coefficient implies that with even a small degree of capital mobility it is increasingly difficult for policymakers to sustain anything other than floating exchange rate regimes. Including this variable does not change conclusions regarding the influence of capital controls and the electorate: those variables are still statistically significant and positive, meaning that higher levels of either variable lead to a greater number of speculative attacks.

As compelling as these results appear, it is important to recognize that they are based on (a) global averages that do not necessarily reflect within-country experiences and (b) a sample of 29 observations and a set of variables that are highly collinear (for example, the correlation between the proportion of countries with fixed and intermediate exchange arrangements and the size of the electorate is –0.92). It is necessary to turn to a more fully developed multivariate analysis in order to trace out the relationships between the spread of democracy, international economic policy choice and speculative attacks. This task is the subject of the next section.

## DEMOCRACY, INTERNATIONAL POLICY CHOICE AND SPECULATIVE ATTACKS

While the Poisson model provides a broad picture of global trends it does not allow inferences to be made about the relationship among democracy, exchange rate regimes, capital controls and speculative attacks across countries. In this section I draw on extant economic and political studies of the correlates of speculative attacks and currency crises to ascertain whether the same results obtained from the Poisson model are replicable using cross-sectional and time-series data.

Studies of the economic and political correlates of speculative currency attacks abound.[8] Economic factors thought to affect speculative attacks include measures of domestic economic aggregates (holdings of foreign exchange rate reserves, the monetary base, the growth of domestic credit, and overall GDP per capital growth) as well as indicators of external vulnerability (the current account balance, stocks of foreign debt, the behavior of foreign interest rates, and the (over) valuation of the exchange rate). Scholars have also realized that speculative attacks are contagious, spreading from country to country via various investment and trading channels (for example, Eichengreen et al. 1995; Masson 1998). Political factors such as government fractionalization, electoral uncertainty, the electoral cycle, partisan identification of policymakers, and institutional transparency have also been found to play a significant role in leading to speculative attacks.

This study deviates from standard practice in two ways. First, rather than relying solely on institutional measures of democracy I attempt to ascertain the extent to which policymakers are pressured to respond to the needs of diverse constituencies. Given the existence of democratic institutions, a larger electorate (as a percentage of the total population) should be able to demand larger packages of private and public goods, and consequently, larger public spending from their elected officials. Policymakers, therefore, will have to redirect instruments such as monetary policy from exchange rate maintenance towards constituent service.

I measure democracy as the proportion of the population that has the right to vote in competitive elections. By competitive elections I mean that two or more parties win seats in the parliament/legislature. If the franchise exists and elections are not competitive then this variable is coded as 'zero'. Limiting the effect of electoral size to those periods when competitive elections exist captures some of the institutional notions of democratic practice found to be important determinants of international economic policy choice (for example, Simmons 1994; Leblang 1999).

While prior scholarship has not examined an explicit link between the expansion of suffrage and speculative currency attacks, the idea that political democracy influences the international economic decisions of policymakers is not new.[9] The experiences of Western European nations during the 1920s and 1930s illustrates the relationship between democratization, the expansion of suffrage and pressure felt by policymakers to use expansionary policies for redistributive purposes (Eichengreen 1992; Simmons 1994). Expanding the right to vote beyond propertied males undermined the credibility of policymakers to use monetary policy solely for exchange rate management. From the perspective of Obstfeld-type currency, a larger electorate may call into question a policymaker's commitment to defend the exchange rate peg even if the economy has strong economic fundamentals.[10]

The rise of democratic institutions may also lead currency speculators to evaluate the ideology and institutions that influence the preferences of policymakers. On the one hand, drawing on traditional political business cycles models, one could posit that left (that is, from a leftist party) governments prefer monetary policy autonomy to exchange rate stability; consequence markets may anticipate expansionary monetary policy that is incompatible with the maintenance of the exchange rate parity.[11] The degree to which institutional rules influence the configuration of governing coalitions may also lead speculators to bet against a nation's currency. Proportional representation (PR) institutions often lead to fragmented party systems and shifting governing coalitions. Confronted with these conditions, policymakers may increasingly pursue particularistic policies as a means of securing political support; these policies may be – in either real or perceived terms – incompatible with the exchange rate parity (Leblang 1999).

Second, unlike most studies that only focus on countries that have stated policies of pegging their exchange rate peg, I look across all *de jure* exchange rate arrangements. While it may not make sense to think about a speculative currency attack on a flexible or floating exchange rate regime, there is at present sufficient evidence to suggest that the actual exchange rate regime behavior of countries does not always conform to official statements. Calvo and Reinhart (2000) have colorfully referred to this situation as 'fear of floating' to draw attention to the idea that policymakers often declare that they have adopted a floating exchange rate regime but behave as if they want to maintain an exchange rate peg. Similar conclusions have been reached by Levy-Yeyati and Sturzenegger (2000) Bubula and Otker-Robe (2002), and Reinhart and Rogoff (2002).

The idea that policymakers may systematically behave in a manner inconsistent with their stated exchange rate policy makes sense if one compares *de jure* exchange rate regimes – as reported by national authorities – with capital account policies – as classified by staff at the International Monetary Fund. I report this combination of policies for pegged, intermediate and floating exchange rate arrangements in Table 8.2.[12] The patterns of policy combinations reported in the final column confirm the global trends described earlier: pegged exchange rates are the most prevalent, followed by intermediate and then floating exchange rate regimes. What is interesting, however, is that 78 percent of those countries reporting a floating exchange rate regime also have controls on the capital market. This lends credence to the 'fear of floating' school as it looks as if some policymakers who say that they are floating do so with the aid of an inner tube.[13] The mismatch between *de jure* and *de facto* exchange rate regimes is interesting in its own right; I return to this issue in the penultimate section.

The first two columns in Table 8.2 indicate the occurrences of speculative attacks across this combination of exchange arrangements and capital market policies. Ignoring capital controls policy for a moment, it is interesting that speculative attacks are fairly evenly distributed across all

*Table 8.2   International economic policy and speculative attacks in
            developing countries: 1970–1999*

|  | Speculative attack$_{t+1}$ | | |
| --- | --- | --- | --- |
|  | No | Yes | Total |
| Peg yes, controls no | 390 | 50 | 440 |
|  | (88.64) | (11.36) | (100.00) |
| Peg yes, controls yes | 1614 | 360 | 1974 |
|  | (81.76) | (18.24) | (100.00) |
| Intermediate yes, controls no | 93 | 15 | 108 |
|  | (86.11) | (13.89) | (100.00) |
| Intermediate yes, controls yes | 310 | 80 | 390 |
|  | (79.49) | (20.51) | (100.00) |
| Float yes, controls no | 73 | 9 | 82 |
|  | (89.02) | (10.98) | (100.00) |
| Float yes, controls yes | 222 | 64 | 286 |
|  | (77.62) | (22.38) | (100.00) |
| Total | 2702 | 578 | 3280 |
|  | (82.38) | (17.62) | (100.00) |

*Note:*   Cell entries are unweighted counts with row frequencies in parentheses. Exchange rate
regime and capital control classification are based on the IMF's *Annual Report on Exchange
Arrangements and Exchange Restrictions*. Speculative attack coding is based on a measure of
exchange market pressure. Definitions and sources are contained in Appendix 8A.

three exchange rate regimes; we cannot reject the null of independence if we
ignore capital controls ($p = 0.234$). Consistent with the 'hollowing out'
hypothesis that suggests the intermediate area between a hard peg and a
pure float (see Figure 8.1) is increasingly vulnerable in a world of mobile
capital, fixed and intermediate exchange rate regimes are more attack prone
than floating regimes. The consequence, according to this perspective, is that
countries will be pushed to hard pegs (for example, dollarization) or free
floats.[14] Turning to capital controls, comparisons across capital control policies are consistent with the findings from the Poisson model. Holding constant the exchange rate regime, there is a statistically significant difference in
attack frequency depending on the implementation of capital controls with
attacks more likely when controls in place ($p = 0.000$).

### A Multivariate Model of Speculative Attacks

I examine the role of democracy – measured in terms of electorate size –
using a logit model and a panel of between 110 and 130 developing countries
observed annually from 1976 to 1999. Problems of data availability limited

the sample to 2090 observations. Precise descriptions of the variables are contained in Appendix 8A.

In what follows I rely on a twofold classification that differentiates between pegged/intermediate and floating regimes. Theoretically, the difference across these exchange rate regimes is one of degree – the degree to which policymakers say that they will allow the exchange rate to fluctuate *vis-à-vis* a reference currency, currencies or indicator. Empirically I am unable to reject the null hypothesis of no difference between *de jure* pegged and *de jure* intermediate exchange rate regimes in any of the empirical testing that follows.

Table 8.3 contains three logit models of attack likelihood. The first column contains a variable measuring size of the electorate, dummy variables for the exchange rate regime (pegged/intermediate with floating being the omitted category) and the existence of capital controls together with a number of economic and political factors found to be important in prior

*Table 8.3    Democracy, international economic policy and speculative attacks*

| Variable (all variables measured at $t-1$) | (1) | (2) |
| --- | --- | --- |
| Time Since Last Crisis | −0.03* (0.01) | −0.03* (0.01) |
| M2/Reserves | 0.003* (0.001) | 0.003* (0.001) |
| Log (Reserves) | −0.05* (0.03) | −0.05* (0.03) |
| Domestic Credit Growth | −0.78* (0.31) | −0.78* (0.31) |
| Real GDP Growth | −4.71* (1.34) | −4.66* (1.36) |
| Current Account/GDP | 0.88 (0.76) | 1.04 (0.73) |
| Foreign Debt/GNP | 0.001 (0.001) | 0.001 (0.001) |
| Exchange Rate Overvaluation | 0.23* (0.08) | 0.22* (0.08) |
| US Interest Rate | 0.03 (0.03) | 0.03 (0.02) |
| Change in Electorate Size | 0.06 (0.53) | 0.08 (0.53) |
| Electorate Size | −0.58* (0.31) | −0.61* (0.32) |
| Left | 0.31* (0.11) | 0.31* (0.12) |
| PR Institutions | 0.17 (0.18) | 0.17 (0.18) |
| Election | 0.23 (0.17) | 0.24 (0.16) |
| Election (time $t$) | 0.02 (0.20) | 0.03 (0.20) |
| Contagion | 0.03* (0.01) | 0.03* (0.01) |
| Pegged/intermediate regime, No controls | 0.88 (0.67) | |
| Pegged/intermediate regime, No controls | 1.10* (0.63) | |
| Float, controls | 1.15* (0.65) | |
| Pegged/intermediate exchange regime | | 0.05 (0.23) |
| Capital controls | | 0.35 (0.24) |

*Note:*  *$p < 0.10$; $N = 2090$; cell entries are logit coefficients with robust standard errors in parentheses.

studies. To minimize potential problems of reverse causality, all independent variables are lagged one year. I also report robust standard errors to account for unequal error variances across countries.

The first variable in column 1 of Table 8.3 measures the number of years that elapsed since country $i$ last experienced a speculative attack. Not only does inclusion of this variable control for time dependence, it can also be interpreted as a country-specific baseline hazard rate. This variable is negative and statistically significant, indicating that there are country-specific, and unmeasured, factors that make countries less vulnerable to speculative attacks.

The results in column 1 of the table show that there is statistical support for the argument that country-specific – and unmeasured – factors make countries vulnerable to speculative attacks as the coefficient on the variable measuring the number of years since the last speculative attack is negative and statistically significant at conventional levels. The same cannot be said for the set of variables measuring the performance of domestic economic aggregates whose results are mixed. Two measures of domestic monetary policy – the ratio of base money to foreign exchange reserves and the growth of domestic credit – are both statistically significant but have opposite signs. Two other measures of domestic economic performance, however, do square with expectations: countries with higher levels of foreign exchange reserves (entered as a log) and higher rates of per capita GDP growth are less likely to experience speculative attacks.

Measures of external vulnerability are also a mixed bag. Only the variable measuring the overvaluation of the real exchange rate is statistically significant. The current account balance, the ratio of foreign debt to gross national product, and the level of foreign interest rates (in this case the US rate) fail to attain conventional levels of statistical significance.[15] The contagion variable that is, the number of other countries that experience a speculative attack at time $t$, is statistically significant and positive. This suggests that trade and/or investment channels help contribute to the spread of speculative attacks across countries.

I include three variables to measure international economic policy choice: a pegged or intermediate exchange rate regime with capital controls, a pegged or intermediate exchange rate regime without capital controls, and a floating exchange rate regime with capital controls. A situation where a country has a floating exchange rate regime without capital controls is the comparison group. The coefficients on these economic policy choice variables are all positive, indicating that speculative attacks are least likely when a policymaker states adherence to a floating exchange rate and does not place controls on the capital account. This finding is not surprising and is consistent with both expectations and the tabular data contained in Table 8.2. It is also not surprising that both sets of policy choices that include capital controls are more likely to be vulnerable to speculative attack. What is surprising is that these two coefficients are nearly identical to each other, meaning that a stated policy of pegging (or intermediate) is no different from a statement about floating so long as both are accompanied by capital controls. It is also surprising that the coefficient on policy combination for pegged without capital controls is not statistically different from the omitted category – floating without controls.

It would be tempting to argue that this suggests the relevance of capital controls and the irrelevance of the exchange rate regime when it comes to institutional determinants of capital controls. To test this conjecture I include in column 2 separate variables for controls and the *de jure* pegged/intermediate exchange rate. If all of institutional action in column 1 comes through capital controls then this variable by itself should be statistically significant. The results in column 2 come as a surprise as both variables are statistically insignificant, though in the expected direction. The combination of exchange rate and capital controls policy influences the decisions of currency speculators.

Other correlates of speculative attacks do not perform well here. To measure the potential impact of political business cycles I include dummy variables coded for the year before and year of an election. Neither of these variables is statistically significant, although both are in the expected direction.[16] Likewise, the measure of the existence of proportional representation institutions is statistically insignificant, suggesting that within democracies electoral rules to not play a role in precipitating a speculative attack. The finding that left governments are more likely to experience a speculative attack is also at odds with prior research though it does square with the implications of traditional political business cycle models.[17]

Democracy and democratization is measured, respectively, by the size of the electorate and the change in the size of the electorate. While increasing the size of the electorate increases the likelihood of a speculative attack, the coefficient is far from statistically significant. This is surprising as the expectation from accounts describing the relationship between democracy and speculative attacks suggests a robust and positive relationship. What is even more counterintuitive is that the coefficient on the variable measuring the size of the electorate is well defined and is negatively signed. In contrast to the results from the global Poisson regression in the second section above, policymakers with larger electorates, all other things being equal, are less likely to face speculative attacks.[18] This result suggests at least a preliminary answer to the question posed in the title: democracy, at least in terms of the size of the electorate, is associated with international economic stability not instability.

There are two plausible explanations for this finding. The first has to do with the nature of democracy and democratic institutions. Democracies, as

compared with other forms of government, place a premium on transparency and have relatively clear lines of responsibility and accountability.
These characteristics influence the behavior of speculative markets in two
ways. First, transparency of policy decreases the uncertainty associated
with the policy process. A reduction in uncertainty in turn leads markets to
have more accurate expectations (in terms of smaller forecast errors)
regarding the future course of government policy. Second, policymakers in
democracies are accountable to various constituencies who have power to
remove them from office. In presidential systems this can happen as a result
of an election while in parliamentary systems this may occur as the consequence of a vote of no confidence. If reneging on an easily recognizable and
verifiable commitment – that to maintain the exchange rate parity – places
them in a vulnerable position, then the policymaker will work hard to
defend the parity. A commitment to defend the exchange rate may be
sufficient to deter an attack in the first place (for example, Leblang 2003).

A second explanation for the finding that larger electorates are associated with a lower likelihood of speculative attack is based on the idea that
policymakers in democracies may make better institutional and policy
choices. That is, knowing that markets react to real or anticipated incon-
sistencies between macroeconomic policy and the exchange rate parity, policymakers in democracies may choose exchange rate regimes that provide
them with more domestic policy flexibility or they may stockpile reserves
to serve as a buffer against speculative attacks.

Certainly these two sets of explanations are not mutually exclusive. The
first explanation suggests a direct effect leading from democracy to a reduction in the likelihood of speculative attacks. The negative and statistically
significant coefficient on the size of the electorate variable provides evidence
in support of this proposition. An indirect link between democracy and
speculative attacks is suggested by the second explanation: democracies
choose better international economic institutions and have higher levels of
reserves, both of which decrease the likelihood of speculative attacks. An
examination of these indirect effects is taken up in the next section.

## DO POLICYMAKERS IN DEMOCRACIES ACT DIFFERENTLY? POLICY CHOICE AND RESERVE HOLDINGS

### International Economic Policy Choice

Do policymakers who are answerable to larger electorates select international economic policies that decrease the probability of a speculative

attack? Put in context of the results of the previous section, the question can be put more succinctly: does a larger electorate make policymakers more likely to float the exchange rate and eschew capital controls? Studies of the correlates of exchange rate regimes and capital controls are plentiful.[19] Most studies, however, while recognizing the mutual interdependence of exchange rate and capital market policy, do not examine them simultaneously. They tend to treat one of these choices as exogenous; that is, given capital controls, what sort of exchange rate regime do policymakers select? Or, given a pegged exchange rate regime, is a country more or less likely to have capital controls?[20] The empirical manifestation of this research strategy is that an exchange rate regime variable, for example, is used as the dependent variable to be 'explained' by a set of economic and/or political variables with a (usually lagged) capital controls variable included on the right-hand side.[21] This modeling choice has consequences for our understanding of speculative attacks.

To evaluate whether democracy influences the likelihood of speculative attacks through the choice of international economic policies, I estimate a multinomial logit model of these choices and include the same political variables from the speculative attack model. A set of control variables, drawn from the extant literature and described below, are also included.

Table 8.4 contains the results of a multinomial logit model of exchange rate regime and capital control policy. The coefficients in the three columns represent comparisons between the relevant policy combination (described in the top row) and a regime floating without controls (the omitted category).[22] I again utilize robust standard errors to deal with possible heteroscedasticity and use lagged values for pegged/intermediate regimes as well as for capital controls to account for persistence over time. Some of the interpretation below is based on the calculation of marginal effects; those results, omitted for the sake of space, are available on request.

Due to the large number of results I highlight the most interesting findings:

- Lagged variables for the exchange rate regime and capital controls show that these institutional policies have a high degree of persistence; policymakers with pegged/intermediate exchange rates and with capital controls are likely to keep those policies in place. The same can be said for policymakers that have floating exchange rate regimes at time $t-1$; they are unlikely to switch to more rigid regimes.
- Countries with greater dependence on international trade (as measured by trade openness) are less likely to have capital controls, regardless of the exchange rate regime. Trade concentration (the percentage

*Table 8.4    Multinomial logit model of international economic policy choice*

| Variable (variables measured at $t-1$) | Peg/intermediate controls no | Peg/intermediate controls yes | Float yes, controls yes |
|---|---|---|---|
| Peg/intermediate | 5.54* | 7.73* | 2.41* |
|  | (0.67) | (0.75) | (0.72) |
| Capital Controls | 1.02 | 7.19* | 7.56* |
|  | (0.79) | (0.93) | (1.06) |
| Trade Concentration | −9.46* | −1.81 | −0.81 |
|  | (4.90) | (2.20) | (2.48) |
| Trade Openness | −0.007 | −0.01 | −0.02 |
|  | (0.01) | (0.01) | (0.02) |
| Relative Economic Size | −0.76 | 2.09 | 2.61 |
|  | (1.74) | (1.80) | (1.82) |
| Real GDP Growth | −5.40* | −8.20* | −10.73* |
|  | (3.20) | (3.06) | (3.34) |
| Inflation | −0.07 | −0.02 | −0.004 |
|  | (0.08) | (0.03) | (0.02) |
| Savings/GDP | 0.05* | 0.05* | 0.03 |
|  | (0.02) | (0.02) | (0.02) |
| Government Consumption/GDP | 0.10* | 0.11* | 0.06 |
|  | (0.05) | (0.05) | (0.05) |
| Change in Electorate Size | −4.41* | −6.38* | −5.25* |
|  | (2.16) | (2.28) | (2.23) |
| Electorate Size | −4.53* | −3.76* | −2.43* |
|  | (0.95) | (0.86) | (0.91) |
| Left | −0.02 | 0.46 | 0.56 |
|  | (0.56) | (0.57) | (0.64) |
| Size of Agricultural Sector | −0.02* | −0.00 | −0.004 |
|  | (0.01) | (0.01) | (0.010) |
| PR Institutions | 0.04 | −0.34 | −0.51 |
|  | (0.53) | (0.54) | (0.54) |

*Note:*  *$p < 0.10$; $N=1709$; cell entries are multinomial logit coefficients with robust standard errors in parentheses.

of country $i$'s trade with its three largest trading partners) does not appear to have a systematic effect on the combination of international economic policies. Policymakers in countries with larger economies (measured GDP relative to the United States) are less likely to have pegged exchange rate regimes with or without capital controls; distinctions across other sets of choices are not statistically significant.

- The economic variables drawn from the capital controls literature suggest that countries with higher savings ratios (public savings as a percentage of GDP) and larger governments (government consumption as a percentage of GDP) are more likely to peg or choose intermediate arrangements than to float. Within these regimes there is no clear preference so far as the capital account is concerned.
- The existence of PR institutions make floating with capital controls more likely than pegging, although there is no difference regarding capital controls. The same can be said about left governments. These findings square with prior research suggesting that policymakers with PR institutions and with leftist orientation have a greater preference for monetary policy autonomy than other policymakers (for example, Eichengreen and Leblang 2003b).
- I also include a variable that measures the proportion of the population employed in the agricultural sector to capture the influence of interest group politics on exchange rate and capital controls policy (for example, Frieden 1991; Frieden et al. 2001). The results in Table 8.4 support this notion as all policy combinations are less preferred compared with floating without controls.

The consequences of variables measuring the electorate are perhaps the most compelling. Holding constant the size of the electorate, an increase in the size of the electorate decreases the probability of having any regime other than a float without capital controls. The same can be said about this variable in level terms. Policymakers in countries with larger electorates are more likely to adopt floating exchange rate regimes without capital controls. Both of these variables are statistically significant across all comparisons of policy combinations.

This model of international economic policy supports the conjecture that policymakers in increasingly democratic countries that have to answer to a larger electorate are more likely to select increasingly flexible exchange arrangements. These policymakers are also more likely to abandon capital controls as a means of either exchange rate insulation or generating revenue via the inflation tax. This is consistent with prior findings regarding the linkage between democracy and capital liberalization: democracies tend to respect property (investor) rights and are reluctant to expropriate the holdings of foreign investors (for example, Dailami 2000; Quinn 2000).

Democracies, then, are likely to experience fewer speculative attacks because they choose international economic policy institutions – a *de jure* floating exchange rate regime without capital controls – that are not crisis prone. Is the same true about the stockpiling of foreign exchange reserves?

**Democracy and Holdings of Foreign Exchange Reserves**

The findings in the third section support the notion that speculative attacks are less probable when countries have large stocks of foreign exchange reserves. Reserves can serve as a 'war chest' that governments can turn to in order to fend off a speculative attack. The idea that a deepening of democracy would be associated with larger holdings of foreign exchange reserves is consistent with the models and empirical analysis of Aizenman and Marion (2002a, b), who find that more corrupt governments have smaller reserves.

I examine the relationship between foreign reserve holdings and the electorate in Table 8.5. Here the dependent variable, a government's holdings of foreign exchange reserves minus gold, is differenced to induce stationarity. Along with the level and size of the electorate, I include variables for the exchange rate and capital controls regime, the partisan orientation of government and, as suggested by Aizenman and Marion (2002a), the log of total population, the log of total GDP, and a measure of trade openness. I also include the lagged level of reserves to control for changes in the dependent variable that may be associated with an initial level of reserve holdings. The model includes an autoregressive term as well as a full set of country dummy variables to capture unmeasured, country-specific factors that may lead countries to hold foreign exchange reserves.

The results in Table 8.5 largely support prior research as well as the conjecture that democratization leads to larger holdings of foreign exchange.

*Table 8.5    Democracy and foreign exchange reserves*

| Variable (all variables measured at $t-1$) | | |
|---|---|---|
| Log(Reserves) | −0.30* | (0.015) |
| Log(Total Population) | 0.41* | (0.08) |
| Log(Current GDP) | 0.015* | (0.005) |
| Trade Openness | 0.004* | (0.0007) |
| Electorate Size | 0.17* | (0.08) |
| Change in Electorate Size | 0.19* | (0.10) |
| Left | −0.001 | (0.040) |
| Peg, no controls | −0.03 | (0.10) |
| Peg, controls | −0.10 | (0.09) |
| Floating, controls | −0.007 | (0.09) |

*Note:*  *$p < 0.10$; $N = 2241$; dependent variable is the change in (logged) foreign exchange reserves minus gold in US dollars; cell entries are ordinary least square estimates; model is estimated with a common AR(1) disturbance and a set of 124 country dummy variables.

The coefficient on the lagged level of reserves indicates that larger levels of reserves are associated with smaller changes. Reserve holdings also increase as a function of a larger population, larger economy and larger exposure to international trade. Democratization – both in terms of levels and rates of change – has the anticipated positive and statistically significant effect as larger and growing electorates lead policymakers to acquire a buffer to stave off speculative attacks. Interestingly, none of the exchange rate and capital controls regime variables is statistically significant, indicating that holdings of reserves do not necessarily respond to the stated policies of governments.

## DISCUSSION

The statistical results of the two previous sections provide evidence in support of the argument that democracies with larger electorates are less likely to experience speculative attacks. The negative and statistically significant coefficient on electorate size in Table 8.3 shows that there is a direct effect and the models in the last section show an indirect effect. The movement to floating exchange rates and the holding of larger stocks of reserves, both associated with increases in the size of the electorate, decrease the likelihood of speculative attacks.

This conclusion is not completely satisfactory as it may be the arrangement of international economic institutions and the holdings of foreign exchange reserves that reduce crises, and these factors may not be unique to democracies. Put differently, can policymakers in authoritarian regimes adopt floating exchange rates without capital controls and stockpile reserves in an attempt to decrease the frequency of speculative attacks? A simple answer to this question can be gleaned from Table 8.3, where the exchange rate and capital control regimes and foreign exchange reserve variables are included along with the size of the electorate. If the effect of electorate size operated only through these other variables then it should not have a significant independent effect as it does in columns 2 and 3 of Table 8.3. I re-estimated the model in column 2 of Table 8.3 using predicted values of the exchange rate regime–capital controls combination from Table 8.4 and the predicted level of foreign exchange reserves from Table 8.5. While not reported here for the sake of space, substituting these predicted variables for the actual values does not change the findings of Table 8.3 substantively or significantly. This lends additional support to the argument that electorate size has an independent effect on the likelihood of speculative currency attacks.

One final puzzle that deserves attention concerns the finding that policymakers in countries prefer to either peg or float with capital controls as their

188 The evolving debate on capital account liberalization

electorates increase in size. Given that both of these regimes are more crisis prone than floating without controls, why is this decision made? Is this finding a result of a disjuncture between what policymakers say they do and how they actually behave? As mentioned above, there has been a growing body of scholarship concluding that policymakers often proclaim to have floating exchange rate regimes while in fact they act as if they are maintaining a fixed or intermediate (that is, a more stable) regime (for example, Calvo and Reinhart 2000; Levy-Yeyati and Sturzenegger 2000; Bubula and Otker-Robe 2002; and Reinhart and Rogoff 2002). Calvo and Reinhart (2000) use the phrase 'fear of floating' to describe a situation where policymakers announce that the *de jure* exchange rate is a floating (or more flexible) regime while behavioral measures suggest that the exchange rate is fixed. What role, if any, does democracy play in the decision by policymakers to have a fear of floating?

An attempt to address this question is contained in Table 8.6, where the dichotomous dependent variable is coded as 1 if a country declares that its *de jure* exchange rate is more flexible than its *de facto* rate. Along with a set of economic controls I also include the measures of electorate size as well as the length of time since the last currency crisis. The coefficient on

*Table 8.6    Fear of floating*

|  | Logit coefficient |
| --- | --- |
| Fear of Floating $(t-1)$ | 2.50*  (0.26) |
| Debt/GNP | 0.000  (0.001) |
| US Interest Rate | −0.09*  (0.04) |
| Exchange Rate Overvaluation | 0.27*  (0.13) |
| Capital Controls | −0.13  (0.37) |
| Trade Concentration | 1.49  (1.71) |
| Trade Openness | 0.000  (0.004) |
| Relative Economic Size | 1.12  (0.86) |
| Change in Electorate Size | 1.17  (0.75) |
| Electorate Size | 1.17*  (0.57) |
| Left | −0.10  (0.22) |
| Size of Agricultural Sector | 0.003  (0.005) |
| PR Institutions | −0.31  (0.27) |
| Time Since Last Crisis | −0.05*  (0.02) |

*Note:*    *$p < 0.10$; $N = 1039$; dependent variable is coded 1 where *de jure* regime (Fix = 1, Intermediate = 2, Floating = 3) is greater than the *de facto* regime (Fix = 1, Intermediate = 2, Floating = 3) based on the Levy-Yeyati and Sturzenegger (2000) classification.

electorate size is positive and statistically significant, indicating that policymakers with larger electorates do have a 'fear of floating'.

Why would policymakers with large electorates claim to have a floating
exchange rate regime and behave as if they were managing a peg? As capital
is increasingly mobile and information can flow instantly from one market
to another, a devaluation can have ramifications with both domestic constituents and international investors. For both, devaluing a pegged or intermediate exchange rate may signal a lack of commitment on the part of the
government, the consequences of which are likely not limited to a decrease
in investment and may lead to the loss of political office. As elected officials
are held more and more accountable for the management of macroeconomic policy, it is in their political best interests to remove exchange rate
policy from the public eye. Publicly proclaiming that the currency is being
allowed to float is a step in that direction.

Behaving as if the currency is pegged allows the policymaker to reap
some of the benefits of exchange rate stability. It allows internationally oriented domestic actors – traders and investors – to engage in longer-term
transactions in the event that forward markets do not exist. Exchange rate
stability may also be seen by international markets as a signal that the government is maintaining a policy of sound macroeconomic management. Of
course, the government does not gain the benefit of using the exchange rate
as a nominal anchor. It may be the case that countries with a fear of floating have other domestic monetary rules (for example, inflation targeting)
that provides a degree of anti-inflationary credibility.

## CONCLUSION

The question posed in the title of this chapter – is democracy incompatible
with international economic stability? – is one that is difficult to answer and
one with tremendous normative implications. It is also one that is timely as
discussions intensify about the appropriate role of institutions such as the
International Monetary Fund and as a growing number of countries contemplate subordinating their own currency to the euro or US dollar. Given
the approaching 60th anniversary of the Bretton Woods agreement it is
important to (re) consider if and how international economic policies conflict with the process of democratization.

I approach the question of the relationship between democracy and
international economic stability by focusing on the linkage between the size
of the electorate and the likelihood of speculative attacks. I find that policymakers with larger (and growing) electorates are more likely to adopt
floating exchange rate regimes, dismantle capital controls and hoard larger

foreign exchange reserves. These policies, in turn, decrease the likelihood of a speculative attack. Democracy and democratic politics, however, also have a direct negative impact on the likelihood of speculative attacks. This effect may be due to an increase in policy transparency or a decrease in policy uncertainty that is associated with democracies. It may also be due to the fact that policymakers in democracies are able to demonstrate their policy resolve and, as a consequence, are able to deter speculative attacks.

The association between democracy and *de jure* floating exchange arrangements is also interesting in that there is a discrepancy between what policymakers say they do and how they actually behave. It is likely that policymakers in democracies say that they are floating in an effort to depoliticize exchange rate policy; to decrease the likelihood that they will be blamed for appearing weak in the event that the exchange rate loses a significant percentage of its value. What is interesting about this is that it appears that the exchange rate peg has lost some of its attraction as a nominal anchor. This may be because alternative monetary policy tools – inflating targeting rules, currency boards or independent central banks – are becoming increasingly available and attractive. These considerations will play a central role as the international monetary system continues to evolve.

# APPENDIX 8A   SAMPLE AND VARIABLE DESCRIPTIONS

*Exchange Rate Regime Classification*   The IMF's *Annual Report on Exchange Arrangements and Exchange Restrictions* provides 15 categories of classification: (1) dollarized, (2) currency board, (3) monetary union to outside (CFA) or inside (European Monetary Union) set of countries, (4) single currency peg, (5) published basket peg (SDR (special drawing right) or non-SDR), (6) secret basket peg, (7) cooperative system (European Monetary System or predecessor), (8) crawling peg, (9) target zone, (10) unclassified rule-based intervention, (11) managed float with heavy interventions, (12) unclassified managed float, (13) other floats, (14) float with light intervention, and (15) float with no intervention. Three *de jure* regimes were created: pegged (categories 2–6), intermediate (categories 7–13) and float (categories 14–15). For the four-category multinomial logit, I grouped together the pegged and intermediate cases; for the six-category model all three categories are used separately.

*Capital Controls*   The IMF's *Annual Report on Exchange Arrangements and Exchange Restrictions* provides a dummy variable coded 1 when there are restrictions on the capital account. Updated data come from Ghosh et al. (2002).

*Trade Concentration*   Data from the IMF's *Direction of Trade Statistics* were used to calculate the share of country $i$'s trade with its three largest trading partners.

*Trade Openness*   Measured as imports plus exports as a share of GDP was provided by the World Bank's *World Development Indicators*.

*Relative Economic Size*   Measured as country $i$'s real GDP relative to the real GDP of the United States. The data come from Ghosh et al. (2002) and were corrected for transcription errors.

*Real GDP Growth*   Measured as the change in total GDP. The data come from Ghosh et al. (2002) and were corrected for transcription errors.

*Inflation*   The period average of CPI index growth. The data come from Ghosh et al. (2002) and were corrected for transcription errors.

*Savings/GDP*   The World Bank's *World Development Indicators* provides a measure of public savings as a share of GDP.

*Government Consumption/GDP*   The World Bank's *World Development Indicators* provides a measure of government consumption expenditures as a share of GDP.

*Electorate Size*   The International Institute for Democracy and Electoral Assistance's, *Voter Turnout in the World Since 1945*, contains information on the size of the voting age population (VAP) for every election since 1945. The value for VAP was assumed to be constant for years between elections and was assumed to be zero for the period before free elections were held. The value for VAP was recoded as zero for periods when competitive elections did not occur. Competitive elections are coded as occurring based on the coding rules for electoral competitiveness from the Database of Political Indicators (DPI); those rules state that a competitive election occurs when multiple parties exist and more then one party wins seats in the legislature/parliament.

*Left*   Coded as 1 if the government is from a leftist party. The data are from the DPI.

*Size of Agricultural Sector*   This is the share of the economically active population employed in the agricultural sector. The variable comes from the World Bank's *World Development Indicators*.

*PR Institutions*   Coded 1 if the country has proportional representative electoral rules *and* also has competitive elections as identified by the DPI. Data are from the DPI.

*Herfindahl Index of Government*   The sum of squared seat shares of all parties in government. The data are from the DPI.

*Speculative Attack*   Coded 1 if a speculative attack occurred during any month in a given year. The monthly occurrence of a speculative attack is based on a measure of exchange market pressure that looks at changes in exchange rates and reserves each weighted by the inverse of their respective variances. The monthly data come from Leblang (2003).

*M2/Reserves*   The data come from the World Bank's *World Development Indicators*.

*Domestic Credit Growth*   The change in private lending to the banking sector is from the World Bank's *World Development Indicators*.

*US Interest Rate*  The year-end deposit rate in the United States. The variable is from the IMF's *International Financial Statistics*.

*Time Since Last Crisis*  Measures the number of years since country *i* experienced its last currency crisis. Counting begins in 1970.

*Contagion*  Measures the number of countries (less country *i*) that experienced a speculative attack during the year in question.

*Sample*  Afghanistan, Islamic State of, Albania, Algeria, Antigua and Barbuda, Argentina, Armenia, Azerbaijan, Bahamas, The, Bahrain, Bangladesh, Barbados, Belarus, Belize, Benin, Bolivia, Botswana, Brazil, Bulgaria, Burkina Faso, Burundi, Cameroon, Cape Verde, Central African Republic, Chad, Chile, China, Colombia, Comoros, Congo, Costa Rica, Côte d'Ivoire, Cyprus, Czech Republic, Djibouti, Dominica, Dominican Republic, Ecuador, Egypt, El Salvador, Equatorial Guinea, Estonia, Ethiopia, Fiji, Gabon, Gambia, The, Ghana, Grenada, Guatemala, Guinea, Guinea-Bissau, Guyana, Haiti, Honduras, Hong Kong, Hungary, India, Indonesia, Iran, Islamic Rep. of, Iraq, Israel, Jamaica, Jordan, Kazakhstan, Kenya, Korea, Republic of, Kuwait, Latvia, Lebanon, Lesotho, Liberia, Libyan Arab Jamahiriya, Lithuania, Madagascar, Malawi, Malaysia, Maldives, Mali, Mauritania, Mauritius, Mexico, Moldova, Morocco, Mozambique, Myanmar, Nepal, Netherlands Antilles, Nicaragua, Niger, Nigeria, Oman, Pakistan, Panama, Papua New Guinea, Paraguay, Peru, Philippines, Poland, Qatar, Romania, Russian Federation, Rwanda, São Tomé and Príncipe, Senegal, Seychelles, Sierra Leone, Singapore, Slovak Republic, Slovenia, Solomon Islands, South Africa, Sri Lanka, St. Lucia, St. Vincent and Grenadines, Sudan, Suriname, Swaziland, Syrian Arab Republic, Tajikistan, Tanzania, Thailand, Togo, Tonga, Trinidad and Tobago, Tunisia, Turkmenistan, Uganda, Ukraine, United Arab Emirates, Uruguay, Vanuatu, Venezuela, Vietnam, Zambia, Zimbabwe.

## NOTES

\*   I am grateful to William Bernhard, Barry Eichengreen and Tom Willett for allowing me to draw on our joint research and to William Bernhard and Jude Hayes for their constructive comments. Support from National Science Foundation grants SES-0096295 and SES-0136866 are gratefully acknowledged.

1.   See Eichengreen (1992 and 1996) for a discussion.

2.   While important from a theoretical point of view, I ignore the role of central banks in both the discussion and empirical work that follows. The reasoning is that there are few central banks in developing countries that are comparable to the independent banks that exist in OECD countries.

3.   These arguments are detailed in Leblang and Willett (2003).

4.   Throughout this chapter the sample of countries classified as 'developing' was determined by a simple decision rule: those countries with IMF country codes greater than 199. While this coding may be controversial in that it includes South Africa, Israel, Mexico and so on as developing, it is a straightforward coding rule. A list of countries is included in Appendix 8A.

5.   A note about the use of these measures is appropriate here. While others (for example, Quinn 2000) have constructed more nuanced measures of capital market liberalization those data are not available for the countries and time periods analysed in this chapter. It is worth noting that the sample of data he has provided is correlated with the dichotomous IMF measure at 0.83. Scholars have also assembled codings of exchange rate regimes based on behavioral rather than institutional measures (for example, Levy-Yeyati and Sturzenegger 2000; Reinhart and Rogoff 2002). While these measures are useful in examining the ways in which exchange rate regimes influence economic performance, they are based on retrospective assessments of the movement of exchange rates, reserves, interest rates and so on. My focus here is not only on the political determinants of what governments say they do but also on the way markets evaluate those statements; as a result, the use of *de jure* regimes is more appropriate. I do compare *de jure* and *de facto* regimes in the conclusion.

6.   This approach – the Poisson regression and operationalization of control variables – is based on Eichengreen (2001) who examines the number of financial crises from 1880 to 1997 in a sample of 21 countries. I should mention that including a variable for the average size of the electorate in Eichengreen's 117-year sample produces the same result – a higher average size of the electorate is associated with a greater frequency of currency crises. Those results are available from the author upon request.

7.   Including the percentage of countries with pegged and intermediate exchange rate regimes as separate variables, while certainly feasible, is not informative as these two variables are highly correlated by construction.

8.   Examples of studies focusing on economic variables include Frankel and Rose (1996), Sachs et al. (1996), Corsetti et al. (1998), Kaminsky et al. (1998) and Berg and Pattillo (1999), to name but a few. Studies by Bussiere and Mulder (2000), Haggard (2000), Leblang and Bernhard (2001), Frieden et al. (2001) and Leblang (2002, 2003) focus explicitly on political variables as factors leading to currency crises.

9.   The following arguments are developed in greater detail in Bernhard and Leblang (1999), Leblang (1999) and Eichengreen and Leblang (2003b).

10.  Empirical work on the post-Bretton Woods era by Leblang (1999) and Broz (2002) builds on these arguments in examinations of the rise of democracy and the shift from fixed to floating exchange rate regimes in the developing world.

11.  Extant empirical evidence, however, shows the reverse. Garrett (1995) finds that left governments in post-1970 Europe had lower exchange rate variability compared with right governments. Simmons (1994) and Leblang (2003) find for the interwar and modern periods, respectively, that governments of the left are more likely to successfully defend their exchange rate peg and, consequently, may be able to deter attacks from occurring.

A plausible explanation for this is that left governments may be more reliant upon fixed exchange rates to bolster claims that they are committed to price stability.

12. For the discussion and statistical analysis of speculative attacks I drop Panama from the sample as it constitutes the only country that reports adhering to a dollarized regime for the period under investigation.

13. Calvo and Reinhart (2000) refer to a situation where a policymaker says that they follow a floating exchange rate regime yet have a larger than normal holding of foreign exchange reserves as 'floating with a life-jacket'. I return to this issue in the penultimate section.

14. The inherent vulnerability of intermediate regimes was illustrated nicely by Eichengreen (2001, p. 267) 'Intermediate regimes are fragile. Operating them is tantamount to painting a bull's eye on the forehead of the central bank governor and telling speculators to "shoot here." '

15. In alternative specifications I experimented with weighted averages of foreign interest rates weighted by the percentage of foreign debt denominated in the currencies of the United States, Britain, France, Germany, Japan and Switzerland. I also worked with various ratios of foreign debt – short-term debt and total external debt – to aggregates such as reserves, GNP and exports. Using any of these specifications did not change the basic results I present in this section.

16. This is probably due to the level of the measurement. Studies by Frieden et al. (2001) and Leblang (2002, 2003) use monthly data and do find that there are electoral effects on speculative attacks.

17. Using monthly data Leblang (2002) finds that left governments are more vulnerable to speculative attacks than center and right governments. Leblang and Bernhard (2001) find that right governments in OECD countries are more likely to experience speculative attacks in the run up to an election as markets anticipate a shift to the left.

18. To minimize the chance that this relationship is not spurious I added two variables highly correlated with the size of the electorate: a time trend as we have seen that the world's electorate has increased over time and the level of GDP per capita because democracy is highly correlated with wealth. Including either or both of these variables in the logit model does not change the statistical significance of the electorate size variable; in fact, both the year and GDP per capita variables end up being insignificant at the 90 percent level.

19. Recent surveys of the literature include Poirson (2001), Corden (2002), Juhn and Mauro (2002) on exchange rate regime choice; Johnston and Tamirisa (1998) and Eichengreen (2002) on capital controls; and Bernhard et al. (2002) on the politics of monetary institutions. Empirical studies have found that economic characteristics such as economic size, economic openness, a preference for monetary expansion (inflation), and concentration of trade play a role in explaining the exchange rate choices of developed and developing countries. Studies of capital controls have found trade openness, economic growth, GDP per capita, a ratio of gross domestic private savings and the percentage of GDP consumed by the government sector to be statistically significant variables.

20. This critique is not original. In his review of capital account liberalization, Eichengreen (2002 p. 352) writes: 'But it is not clear what should be regarded as endogenous and exogenous in this analysis. Does their willingness to adopt a more flexible exchange rate determine the readiness of some countries to remove controls? Or do increases in capital mobility, associated perhaps with the removal of capital controls, lead to the adoption of a more flexible exchange rate, either voluntarily or as the result of a crisis? One suspects that the causality runs both ways'. In their study of the determinants of capital controls and pegged exchange rate for a 21-country sample over the 1880–1997 period, Eichengreen and Leblang (2003b) use a bivariate probit model to examine the simultaneity of these choices.

21. In the interests of fairness I have followed this strategy myself in studies of capital controls (Leblang 1997) and exchange rate regime choice (Leblang 1999: Bernhard and Leblang 1999).

22.   As noted above I also estimated this model using the threefold exchange rate regime classification, resulting in a six category dependent variable. After estimating the multinomial
logit model using the sixfold classification tests of the IIA (independence of irrelevant
alternatives) assumption confirmed the necessity of collapsing pegged and intermediate
exchange arrangements.

# REFERENCES

Aizenman, Joshua and Nancy Marion (2002a), 'The high demand for reserves in
the Far East: what's going on?,' manuscript, University of California, Santa Cruz,
CA and Dartmouth College, Hanover, NH.

Aizenman, Joshua and Nancy Marion (2002b), 'International reserve holdings with
sovereign risk and costly tax collection,' NBER Working Paper 9154, National
Bureau of Economic Research, Cambridge, MA.

Berg, Andrew and Catherine Pattillo (1999), 'Are currency crises predictable?
A test,' *IMF Staff Papers*, **46**, 107–38.

Bernhard, William, J. Lawrence Broz and William Roberts Clark (2002), 'The political economy of monetary institutions,' *International Organization*, **56**, 693–724.

Bernhard, William and David Leblang (1999), 'Democratic institutions and
exchange rate commitments,' *International Organization*, **53**, 71–97.

Bertolini, Leonardo and Allan Drazen (1997a), 'Capital account liberalization as a
signal,' *American Economic Review*, **87**, 138–54.

Bertolini, Lenardo and Allan Drazen (1997b), 'When liberal policies reflect shocks,
what do we learn?', *Journal of International Economics*, **42**, 249–73.

Bordo, Michael, Barry Eichengreen, Daniela Klingebiel and Soledad Maria
Martinez-Peria (2001), 'Is the crisis problem growing more severe?', *Economic
Policy*, **32**, 51–82.

Broz, J. Lawrence (2002), 'Political system transparency and monetary commitment
regimes,' *International Organization*, **56**, 861–88.

Bubula, Andrea and Inci Otker-Robe (2002), 'The evolution of exchange rate
regimes since 1990: evidence from de facto policies,' IMF Working Paper
WP/02/155, International Monetary Fund, Washington, DC.

Bussiere, Matthieu and Christain Mulder (2000), 'Political instability and economic
vulnerability,' *International Journal of Finance and Economics*, **5**, 309–30.

Calvo, Guillermo and Carmen Reinhart (2000), 'Fear of floating,' *Quarterly Journal
of Economics*, **117**, 379–408.

Corden, W. Max (2002), *Too Sensational: On the Choice of Exchange Rate Regimes*,
Cambridge, MA: MIT Press.

Corsetti, G., P. Pesenti and N. Roubini (1998), 'Paper tigers? A model of the Asian
crisis,' Manuscript, Department of Economics, New York University.

Dailami, Mansoor (2000), 'Managing risks of global financial market integration,' in
Charles Adams, Robert Litan and Michael Pomerleano (eds), *Managing Financial
and Corporate Distress*, Washington, DC: Brookings Institution, pp. 447–80.

Eichengreen, Barry (1992), *Golden Fetters: The Gold Standard and the Great
Depression, 1919–1939*, New York: Oxford University Press.

Eichengreen, Barry (1996), *Globalizing Capital: A History of the International
Monetary System*, Princeton, NJ: Princeton University Press.

Eichengreen, Barry (2001a), 'International financial crises: is the problem
growing?', manuscript, University of California, Berkeley, CA.

Eichengreen, Barry (2001b), 'What problems can dollarization solve?', *Journal of Policy Modeling*, **23**, 267–77.

Eichengreen, Barry (2002), 'Capital account liberalization: what do the cross country studies show us?', *World Bank Economic Review*, **15**, 341–66.

Eichengreen, Barry and David Leblang (2003b), 'Exchange rates and cohesion: historical perspectives and political-economy considerations,' *Journal of Common Market Studies*, **41**, 797–822.

Eichengreen, Barry, Andrew Rose and Charles Wyplosz (1995), 'Exchange market mayhem: the antecedents and aftermath of speculative attacks,' *Economic Policy*, **21**, 45–61.

Frankel, Jeffrey (1999), *No Single Currency Regime Is Right for All Countries at All Times*, Essays in International Finance, No. 215, Princeton, NJ: Princeton University Press.

Frankel, Jeffrey and Andrew Rose (1996), 'Currency crashes in emerging markets: an empirical treatment,' *Journal of International Economics*, **41**, 351–66.

Frieden, Jeffry (1991), 'Invested interests: the politics of national economic policies in a world of global capital,' *International Organization*, **45**, 425–61.

Frieden, Jeffry, Piero Ghezzi and Ernesto Stein (2001), 'Politics and exchange rates: a cross-country approach,' in Jeffry Frieden and Ernesto Stein (eds), *The Currency Game*, Washington, DC: Inter-American Development Bank.

Garrett, Geoffrey (1995), 'Capital mobility, trade, and the domestic politics of economic policy,' *International Organization*, **49**, 657–87.

Ghosh, Atish, Anne-Marie Gulde and Holger Wolf (2002), *Exchange Rate Regimes: Choices and Consequences*, Cambridge, MA: MIT Press.

Glick, Reuven and Michael Hutchison (2001), 'Capital controls and exchange rate instability in developing economies,' Center for Pacific Basin Monetary and Economic Studies, Economic Research Department, Federal Reserve Bank of San Francisco, Pacific Basin Working Paper PB00–05.

Haggard, S. (2000), *The Political Economy of the Asian Financial Crisis*, Washington, DC: Institute for International Economics.

Johnston, Barry and Natalia Tamirisa (1998), 'Why do countries use capital controls?', IMF Working Paper WP/98/181, International Monetary Funds, Washington, DC.

Juhn, Grace and Paolo Mauro (2002), 'Long-run determinants of exchange rate regimes: a simple sensitivity analysis,' IMF Working Paper WP/02/104, International Monetary Fund, Washington, DC.

Kaminsky, Graciela, Saul Lizondo and Carmen Reinhart (1998), 'Leading indicators of currency crises,' *IMF Staff Papers*, **45**, 1–48.

Krugman, Paul (1979), 'A model of balance of payments crises,' *Journal of Money, Credit and Banking*, **11**, 311–25.

Leblang, David (1997), 'Domestic and systemic determinants of capital controls in the developed and developing world,' *International Studies Quarterly*, **41**, 435–54.

Leblang, David (1999), 'Domestic political institutions and exchange rate commitments in the developing world,' *International Studies Quarterly*, **43**, 599–620.

Leblang, David (2002), 'The political economy of speculative attacks in the developing world', *International Studies Quarterly*, **46**, 69–91.

Leblang, David (2003), 'To defend or to devalue: The political economy of exchange rate policy, *International Studies Quarterly*, **47**, 533–59.

Leblang, David and William Bernhard (2001), 'The politics of speculative attacks in industrial democracies,' *International Organization*, **54**, 291–324.

Leblang, David and Tom Willett (2003), 'Managing the middle in an era of global capital,' paper presented at the 2003 meetings of the International Studies Association, Portland, OR, 17 March.

Levy-Yeyati, Eduardo and Federico Sturzenegger (2000), 'Classifying exchange rate regimes: deeds vs. words,' manuscript, Universidad Torcuato Di Tella, Buenos Aires.

Masson, Paul (1998), 'Contagion: monsoonal effects, spillovers and jumps between multiple equilibria,' IMF Working Paper 98/142, International Monetary Fund, Washington, DC.

Mundell, Robert A. (1961), 'A theory of optimum currency areas', *American Economic Review*, **51**, 657–65.

Mundell, Robert A. (1963), 'Capital mobility and stabilization policy under fixed and flexible exchange rates,' *Canadian Journal of Economics and Political Science*, **29**, 475–85.

Obstfeld, Maurice (1994), 'The logic of currency crises', NBER Working Paper no. 4640, National Bureau of Economic Research, Cambridge, MA.

Poirson, Helene (2001), 'How do countries choose their exchange rate regime?,' IMF Working Paper WP/01/46, International Monetary Fund, Washington, DC.

Quinn, Dennis P. (2000), 'Democracy and international financial liberalization,' unpublished manuscript, Georgetown University, Washington, DC, June.

Reinhart, Carmen and Kenneth Rogoff (2002), 'The modern history of exchange rate arrangements: a reinterpretation', NBER Working Paper no. 8963, National Bureau of Economic Research, Cambridge, MA.

Sachs, Jeffrey, Aaron Tornell and Andres Velasco (1996), 'Financial crises in emerging markets: the lessons from 1995,' *Brookings Papers on Economic Activity*, **1**, Washington, DC: Brookings Institution, 147–215.

Simmons, Beth (1994), *Who Adjusts? Domestic Sources of Foreign Economic Policy During the Interwar Years*, Princeton, NJ: Princeton University Press.

F 3 2

# 9.   Capital flows and capital controls

## Harold James

No debate in international economics has been as prolonged, sustained and intense, or – for that matter – as inconclusive, as that over the benefit or harm of capital flows and therefore implicitly about the desirability of capital controls. This chapter discusses some of the circumstances why individual countries and the system as a whole may prove more restrictive of capital flows in the future than was the case in the 1990s: a discussion which is actually in large part quite independent of the debate about the economic repercussions of capital movements.

There were, historically, two periods in which the discussions about capital movements and capital controls were especially intense: in the 1930s and 1940s, in the wake of the Great Depression; and again in the 1990s. In the first, capital flows were widely seen as the major culprit for the Great Depression. An influential account by Ragnar Nurkse explained that irrational movements had been prompted by the instability of the international monetary system, and of an inadequate mechanism for setting exchange rates. The argument expounded by Nurkse relies heavily on the idea that hot money flows, which had in particular been a concomitant of political crises in the 1930s and which were thus thought to undermine democracy and international peace as well as international economic relations, were triggered primarily by expectations of exchange rate movements. J.M. Keynes's great plea of the 1930s was to 'let finance be national'. An alternative tradition, in which Gottfried Haberler explained that the fixed exchange rate regime was the source of the problem, was largely derided at the time, though it is accepted by almost all economic historians who deal with the period today.

In the 1990s, capital account liberalization, which had been applied since the later 1970s, largely successfully, by many industrial countries, was seen as a part of a more general liberalization and reform process in developing countries; also in the 'Washington Consensus' as identified by John Williamson. The IMF debated amending Article VI (concerning capital movements) in its Articles of Agreement: in the old version (which still remains in effect today), it permits the application of capital controls (excluding current transactions).

This part of the 'Washington Consensus' was the most hotly contested. Pronounced advocates of trade liberalization, such as Jagdish Bhagwati, were almost equally firm in warning about the dangers of capital market liberalization. From inside and then from outside the World Bank, Joseph Stiglitz launched polemics against the harm done by (and the self-interestedness of the advocates of) capital market liberalization. In the wake of the 1997–98 Asian crisis, the IMF began to concede that it had previously neglected to emphasize the importance of building a strong and robust financial sector prior to capital market opening.

The theoretical case for capital liberalization rests on the idea that a free movement of capital allows its allocation for investments which produce the highest return, and that these are frequently in emerging markets which can use the international availability of technology to move up the developmental scale. This is not just a question of foreign direct investment (FDI), which is often linked with important technology transfers (and most analysts as a result conclude that FDI is a 'better' and less destabilizing form of capital movement). Portfolio flows can also increase liquidity in the domestic markets of capital-importing countries, and should also increase the extent of development of domestic financial markets (which traditionally have been a substantial brake on development). The availability of foreign capital inflows may also be a spur to improve government policies, and to reduce harmfully high levels of taxation. On the other hand, portfolio and banking flows are vulnerable to herd behavior on the markets (as of course are domestic stock markets in big and rich industrial countries). In emerging markets, they have produced contagious epidemics of twin currency and banking crises.

Empirical studies suggest that the record of success is very patchy, and that – unlike trade opening – there is no overwhelming correlation between capital market liberalization and stronger economic growth. In particular, two of the most important rapidly growing economies (whose success has been central in reducing worldwide poverty) – China and India – have quite extensive capital controls, and many poor African countries have few capital controls but only trivial capital inflows. A great deal of discussion has focused around the capital controls applied by Chile and Malaysia, although Chile dismantled its controls (on inward flows) in the wake of the 1997 Asian crisis, and Malaysia relaxed its controversial controls on outflows in September 1999 and dismantled them entirely in May 2001.

There has been surprisingly little discussion of why countries decide to impose and reduce capital controls. Of course, it is possible to come to the conclusion that these decisions are made on the basis of a sober discussion of the economic case, but that is quite implausible. There are two ways of thinking about the politics of the imposition of capital controls.

One approach looks at domestic politics. Who benefits from capital controls? If their effect is to make it harder for capital to move, and thus to make the price of capital higher, the demand for such controls is likely to come from elites looking for a higher return on assets. It is thus part of a rent-seeking behavior that is always easier when there are reduced or restricted flows of the factors of production. One recent study (Johnson and Mitton) has made this point very clearly about the Mahathir regime and its rescue of crony capitalism in Malaysia.

In addition, many controlled systems have imposed a financial repression, in which low interest credits are allocated through a political mechanism to favored sectors. This is also a system-supporting kind of controls, in which existing elites have a strong interest in the maintenance of the status quo, even if it reduces long-term prospects for economic growth.

The demand for capital market protection is thus not a matter of economics alone. Another approach looks at the external environment in which the debate about capital controls is conducted, and especially at the connection between capital controls and security considerations. This sort of analysis almost never occurred in the 1990s, although it was commonplace in the other decade when capital mobility formed a topic of intense debate, in the 1930s.

In the 1930s, in the aftermath of the big currency crises of 1931, there was an apparently quite simple link between capital flows and weakened security. That link consisted in the budgetary response generated by large capital outflows. In order to restore confidence in the wake of capital losses, a fiscal correction was needed. But most budgetary items were not discretionary, and the part of the budget that could most easily be reduced without causing major domestic civil unrest was military expenditure. Attacks on the currency thus led in a pretty straightforward way to a reduction in military capacity, and an increase in vulnerability. In some of the most famous incidents of volatile capital movements in the 1930s, there is evidence of the formulation of such strategies: in French financial attacks on Austria and Germany in 1931 in order to prevent a proposed Austro-German customs union; and in secret attempts of the Nazi regime after 1933 to set off speculative attacks on France, which were intended to weaken France's military preparedness. The mixing of security and finance increased the general aura of paranoia that was characteristic of the 1930s.

Governments at that time responded to capital movements with the imposition of capital controls (mostly on outflows). Since – as the history of the last 25 years in Latin America has also shown – these controls are not very watertight, the usual response was to try to make them effective with ever more draconian penalties.

Regimes also tried to identify which social groups might be most likely to move money across frontiers: in France, attention focused mostly on the financial and business elites; while in Germany, and in many other Central European countries with officially anti-Semitic policies, the repression associated with capital controls focused on Jews. The identification of specific ethnic groups as being more likely to move capital (in part obviously because of the fact of persecution) resurfaced in the wake of 1997, when in ethnically mixed states, notably Malaysia and above all Indonesia, the ethnic Chinese population was accused of perpetrating capital flight. In early 2002, Malaysia introduced a dramatically tightened new immigration regime, which resulted immediately in the departure of some 300,000 foreigners.

But the 1990s, in the aftermath of the end of the Cold War, generally presented a diametrically opposed picture to the 1930s. Security considerations played a greatly reduced role in decisions about monetary policy. An interesting illustration of the way in which a better security environment affected monetary policy is that the Czech Republic sold its entire gold reserves (an obviously costly asset) immediately that NATO (North Atlantic Treaty Organization) membership came into effect.

The 21st century is quickly becoming much less secure than the closing years of the 20th century. After September 11, 2001, we live in a world in which security considerations again have a strong priority. Some increased surveillance of international capital movements is already recognized as a necessity in order to obstruct the movement of funds for terrorist activity. There will also be more discussion about what countries (especially the large industrial countries) can do to limit capital movements that they consider to be a risk (in political terms).

Some of the literature on capital flows has suggested one sort of influence in the 1990s: that capital flowed to risky countries because of expectations that there was some sort of political guarantee. Russia had big inflows until 1998, because it was assumed that it was 'too nuclear to fail': that the extent to which its nuclear weapons stocks (and atomic reactors) posed a security challenge of such dimensions that the G7 and the international financial institutions (IFIs) could never abandon it. Such an argument is obviously an extreme and more politicized version of the general moral hazard case made about emerging markets post-1994 Mexico, by figures as politically diverse as Milton Friedman, George Soros and Joseph Stiglitz. The argument about moral hazard as a result of expectations of bailouts by international institutions, and especially in regard to the 1997 Asian crisis, is usually grossly overstated: many of the loans made were to private sector borrowers, who would not be protected by rescue packages of the IFIs. But the nuclear argument had a broader resonance than just former members of the Soviet Union. Indeed the attention given to Russia's nuclear problems was one (of a larger number) of considerations that convinced the Indian and Pakistani governments that it would be desirable to develop nuclear weapons quickly. It may have been a part, too, of the calculations about nuclear black-mail for a crisis-stricken economy that the North Korean leadership has regularly applied since 1994.

The prevailing sentiment of the 1990s was to buy off security threats, and in some countries it created incentives to nuclearize. After 2001–02, the mood has changed.

The Iraq war has brought a quite different side of this issue to the fore-front of debate: whether there is a case for penalizing lenders to states which are aggressive or threatening or even undemocratic. In the past this issue has often been in the background of some of the debate around the debt of very poor states, in which it is argued that the expensive debt service of the debt of bad regimes should not be a perpetual burden on the people of a country, if the regime changes: but in these cases, the debt is almost all owed to countries or to IFIs. The debate about the financial legacy of the Iraq war has the potential to place a fundamental new uncertainty in the inter-national financial system. The cost of the war for the United States is rela-tively trivial. But conflicts will arise about the priority attached to different claims on Iraq: Kuwaiti claims for reparations for the 1990 invasion (some $200 billion), the need to rebuild and reconstitute Iraqi society after the damages done by dictatorship and sanctions, and the claims of Iraq's foreign (non-reparations) creditors.

The Iraqi debt is not large compared to total international indebted-ness. But as with German reparations in the 1920s, a comparatively small sum can blow up the system because it produces unbearable international tensions.

The new debate about debt will be conducted in a world polarized by the political conflicts which led up to the war, and continued while it was being fought. The largest creditors of Iraq are France and Russia (with at least $8 billion each), as well as the Gulf states against which the United States may also want to exert political pressure. France and Russia were the main sources of obstruction and frustration on the UN Security Council. The debt also arises in large part from the sale of weapons to Iraq, which in the case of Russia continued until days before the outbreak of war. Russian equipment designed to frustrate the precision guidance of the Global Positioning System used by US missiles almost certainly directly led to deaths of US soldiers in 'friendly fire' incidents (where targeting was dis-oriented by Russian equipment), as well as of Iraqi civilians. On the other hand, there is little Iraqi debt owed to the United States.

Consequently, it will be very tempting for the global superpower to demand the cancellation of Iraqi debt. There would be considerable

American *Schadenfreude* at the scale of French and Russian losses, which will be seen as a quite legitimate penalty for supporting a deeply immoral regime in Iraq. Americans can make a strong moral case. If those who lend money to dictators or authoritarian leaders were threatened systematically by debt repudiation, the whole worldwide democratization and pacification effort would be much quicker. The same logic could easily be applied to Iran. This is a case that has long been made by many critics of the burden of debt service on developing countries. The argument is a financial version of Wilsonianism: the application of morality to lending in order to build a better world.

The world's fastest growing developing economy, China, also has a considerable external debt ($170 billion at the end of 2001). It is also, very obviously, not a democracy. Nor are its interests those of the United States. Supposing the principle of 'wicked debt' is applied to China?

Applying financial Wilsonianism would introduce high risk premia and make much of international lending significantly more precarious. Like reparations and war debts in the 1920s, which also had a basis in morality, Wilsonianism applied to the debt of dictators would produce new uncertainties and a new threat to the entire international financial system.

The new security concerns, and a new consensus about the desirability of focusing on national issues, is likely to focus attention on the negative sides (rather than the benefits) of capital market liberalization. Such a move is already evident in the background to much of the contemporary discussion. This more negative focus is characteristic of a period in which the momentum of financial globalization is slowing appreciably, and the likelihood of a backlash against it simultaneously increasing. At this point it is important to give a historically-based warning, that the costs of such backlashes have been very considerable.

# REFERENCES

Bhagwati, Jagdish (2000), 'Free trade, yes; free capital flows, maybe', in Jagdish Bhagwati, *The Wind of the Hundred Days: How Washington Mismanaged Globalization*, Cambridge and London: MIT Press, pp. 21–4.
Friedman, Milton (1998), 'Clear lessons to be learnt from the East Asian episode', *The Times*, 12 October.
Haberler, Gottfried von (1937), *Prosperity and Depression: a Theoretical Analysis of Cyclical Movements*, Geneva: League of Nations.
Johnson, Simon, T. Mitton (2003), 'Cronyism and capital controls: evidence from Malaysia', *Journal of Financial Economics*, February, **67**, pp. 351–82.
Keynes, John M. (1933), 'National self-sufficiency', *Yale Review*, June.
Nurkse, Ragnar (1944), *International Currency Experience: lessons of the Inter-war Period*, Geneva: League of Nations.

Soros, George (c2002), *George Soros on Globalization*, New York: Public Affairs.
Stiglitz, Joseph E. (2002), *Globalization and Its Discontents*, New York: W.W. Norton.
Williamson, John (1996), 'Lowest common denominator or neoliberal manifesto? The polemics of the Washington consensus', in John Williamson, *Challenging the Orthodoxies*, New York: St. Martin's Press and London: Macmillan, pp. 13–22.

206-24

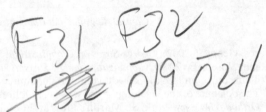

# 10. Exchange rates and capital controls in developing countries[*]

**Vijay Joshi**

What are the implications of financial globalization for exchange rate regimes in developing countries? It is to this question that this chapter is addressed.

## THE IMPOSSIBLE TRINITY AND THE BIPOLAR VIEW

I begin with the well-known trilemma, sometimes referred to as the 'Impossible Trinity', to which policymakers in any open economy must respond. A crucial insight of the Impossible Trinity is that the choice of exchange rate regime cannot be considered separately from the choice of policy stance towards capital flows.

The standard formulation of the Impossible Trinity says that it is impossible to achieve the following three desirable goals simultaneously: exchange rate stability, capital market integration and monetary autonomy. Any pair of goals is achievable by choosing a suitable payments regime but requires abandoning the third. Specifically:

1. Exchange stability and capital market integration can be combined by adopting a fixed exchange rate but requires giving up monetary autonomy. The authorities lose the power to vary the home interest rate independently of the foreign interest rate.
2. Monetary autonomy and capital market integration can be combined by floating the exchange rate but requires giving up exchange stability. The authorities have the freedom to choose the home interest rate but they must in consequence accept any exchange rate that the market dictates.
3. Exchange stability can be combined with monetary autonomy but requires giving up capital market integration. In the presence of capital controls, the interest rate–exchange rate link is broken.

The Impossible Trinity needs careful interpretation on two counts. First, it is a theorem only if 'capital market integration' is understood to mean *perfect capital mobility*. Capital account convertibility (hereafter CAC), meaning the absence of *policy* barriers to capital flows, is consistent with imperfect capital mobility. There can be *natural* barriers to mobility (for example, due to risk) that make domestic and foreign assets imperfect substitutes. This creates some scope for (short-run) sterilized intervention and hence for some monetary autonomy even with a fixed exchange rate. Second, the Impossible Trinity, strictly speaking, has nothing to say about intermediate regimes between fixed and floating exchange rates.[1] This raises the question: why should a country not enjoy *partial* exchange stability and *partial* monetary autonomy consistently with CAC?

Financial globalization has sharply increased the mobility of capital flows, reducing both the natural and the policy barriers to capital flows. According to the Trinity, this reduces the policy menu to a simple choice between fixed and floating exchange rates. But, as stated above, this ignores the option of choosing an intermediate regime.

The 'bipolar view', an important extension of the Impossible Trinity, specifically addresses this point. It postulates that no intermediate regime is sustainable in the presence of high capital mobility. The strong version of the view says further that high capital mobility is inevitable because capital controls are not feasible. In this view, the policy choice does indeed reduce to fixed versus floating rates since all intermediate regimes are unsustainable.[2] The bipolar view predicts that all countries will move to the 'fixed' and 'floating' corners of the spectrum of exchange rate regimes.

We need to be clear what the terms 'fixed', 'floating' and 'intermediate' exchange rates mean. The following definitions are implicit in the bipolar view and will be used in the rest of this chapter. A *fixed* exchange rate is defined as one which is irrevocably fixed, that is, a super-hard peg. An *intermediate* regime is one in which the authorities have an exchange rate target. The target does not have to be fixed or explicit. It could be informal, unannounced or shifting. Thus an intermediate regime covers adjustable pegs, bands, crawling pegs and crawling bands. It also includes 'managed floating' if the float is managed to attain a target level or path of the exchange rate. A *floating* exchange rate is one in which the authorities do not have an exchange rate target, formal or informal. This obviously includes a clean float. It also includes a managed float so long as the management does not attempt to target the exchange rate.

The problem created by financial globalization can now be stated as follows: both fixed and floating exchange rates have their disadvantages. Governments therefore strongly prefer an intermediate regime where they retain some control over both the interest rate and the exchange rate. But if the bipolar view is correct, intermediate regimes are not feasible with financial globalization. So governments have perforce to fix or float.

The above discussion raises the following questions. Are the alternatives facing the authorities as restricted as the bipolar view implies? If not, what is the menu of regime options? And finally, which of the feasible regimes is *optimal* (that is, the best or the least bad)? These questions are analysed below from a developing-country standpoint.

If exchange rate arrangements are of three types (fixed, floating and intermediate), and if each could be combined with CAC or capital controls, there are, in principle, six possible alternatives:

1. fixed exchange rate + CAC;
2. floating exchange rate + CAC;
3. intermediate exchange rate + CAC;
4. fixed exchange rate + capital controls;
5. floating exchange rate + capital controls; and
6. intermediate exchange rate + capital controls.

I rule out (4) because it is surely dominated by (6). The latter permits the authorities to deploy monetary and exchange rate policy as separate instruments. It would be foolish to reject this freedom and opt for a fixed exchange rate with capital controls. For similar reasons, (5) is also dominated by (6) unless the capital controls have, for good reasons, been almost fully but not fully relaxed. I have some comments on such an option in my discussion of (6). Thus, the alternatives in play are (1), (2), (3) and (6). The strong version of the bipolar view says that the effective choice is between (1) and (2) because (3) and (6) are not feasible. But the bipolar view is only a hypothesis, so (3) and (6) must also be examined. The contention of this chapter is that the bipolar view is, broadly speaking, right about the non-sustainability of (3). But (6) is a feasible option in some developing countries and may even be optimal.

When it comes to judging optimality, there have to be criteria of judgment. A consensus list of criteria would run as follows. A payments regime should be judged by whether it can:

- act as a nominal anchor against inflation;
- facilitate macroeconomic real adjustment;
- promote microeconomic efficiency; and
- reduce vulnerability to crises (this refers back to the feasibility issue).

As a background to the rest of the chapter, the evidence regarding the evolution of exchange rate regimes is summarized in this paragraph

*Table 10.1   Exchange rate regimes (% at 'corners')*

|  | 1990 | 2001 |
|---|---|---|
| All countries | 31 | 61 |
| Developed | 26 | 96 |
| Developing | 31 | 57 |
| Emerging | 23 | 78 |
| Non-emerging | 34 | 53 |

*Note:*   32 countries are classified as 'emerging', namely, Argentina, Brazil, Bulgaria, Chile, China, Colombia, Czech Republic, Egypt, Ecuador, Hong Kong, Hungary, India, Indonesia, Israel, Jordan, Korea, Malaysia, Mexico, Morocco, Nigeria, Pakistan, Panama, Peru, Philippines, Poland, Russia, Singapore, South Africa, Sri Lanka, Thailand, Turkey and Venezuela.

*Source:*   Bubula and Otker-Robe (2002).

(see Table 10.1). The picture for the developed countries seems to correspond well with the bipolar hypothesis: the overwhelming majority of them are now at the 'corners' of the spectrum of exchange rate regimes. As of 2001, the United States, Japan, the eurozone, the UK, Australia and Canada are floating. Within the *eurozone*, the constituent countries have abandoned their national currencies. In developing countries, the move towards the 'corners' is less sharp. In 2001, roughly three-quarters of the 'emerging' and one-half of 'non-emerging' developing countries were at the 'corners'. That still leaves a substantial number of countries (72 out of 186 IMF members) not at the corners, that is, in the 'intermediate exchange rate' category. Two further points should be borne in mind. First, although Table 10.1 does not bring this out, almost all the movement in developing countries has been towards the floating corner, not the fixed. And as one would expect, the movement is greater in 'emerging' countries than in 'non-emerging' countries. Second, although the table claims to be based on a *de facto* rather than *de jure* classification of regimes, it is likely that it underestimates the number of developing countries with intermediate regimes.

## FIXED EXCHANGE RATE PLUS CAC

In this regime, the central bank commits itself irrevocably to defending a fixed exchange rate. Since governments can break their promises, the commitment has to be backed up by exceptionally strong legislative/constitutional safeguards. Recent experience in Argentina suggests that even currency boards can break up, so perhaps only the adoption of a foreign currency as legal tender ('dollarization') qualifies as a 'fixed exchange rate'.

The strength of this regime is that it provides a firm anchor against inflation, provided of course that the peg currency is stable in value. This is a vitally important consideration for small, open economies and for countries with a propensity to hyperinflation.

The outstanding weakness of this regime follows from the complete surrender of monetary sovereignty that it entails. Seigniorage is either fully lost (dollarization) or highly circumscribed (currency board). So is the ability to use monetary policy to adjust to asymmetric shocks, a safety-valve of major value when money wages and prices are sticky downwards (provided that real wages are flexible). This is particularly germane for large, relatively closed economies (for example, Argentina, India). 'Pure' fiscal policy may be an available macro instrument, but only if it is used strictly in line with the dictates of functional finance.

Microeconomic efficiency considerations favor this regime. Exchange risk disappears, which should encourage trade and investment and reduce the cost of capital. But this is subject to the caveat that other types of risk (arising from variation in interest rates and profitability of investment) may increase. The cost of capital may not fall if default risk and country risk rise.

In this regime, the instability of the *effective* exchange rate can be a major problem. A fixed exchange rate normally means a rigid link to a single major currency such as the dollar. But if the dollar floats against the euro and the yen, and the economy is diversified in trade, the home currency is effectively floating. This reduces the microeconomic advantage of exchange rate certainty, and can also be a source of exogenous macroeconomic shocks. In the mid-1990s, this problem was experienced by both Argentina and East Asia, when the dollar appreciated strongly. The macroeconomic problem can be attenuated by pegging to a basket of currencies, thus stabilizing the effective exchange rate. But the microeconomic problem remains since the home currency now floats against *all* major currencies though the weighted average is constant. Transparency and therefore credibility are also adversely affected by a basket peg.

Proponents of dollarization have emphasized its crisis-insulation properties. Since the currency peg is unalterably fixed, speculators do not have a target to shoot at. But this is only strictly true if the country 'goes all the way' to dollarization. Even a currency board is fragile: if credibility is lost, speculation returns with a vengeance. Moreover, even if this regime is proof against a *currency* crisis, it is arguably as or more vulnerable to a crisis of the real economy, especially in the form of a prolonged recession.

Does a fixed exchange rate make sense from a national standpoint? The conditions for its success are very demanding. Without downward flexibility of wages and prices, it can be a recipe for disaster. Some developing countries may need to adopt it for the negative reason that they are too small and too open to benefit from exchange rate variation. Some others may have to adopt it to burn out inflation if domestic nominal anchors have been irretrievably compromised. Even so, there is no guarantee that inflation will be brought down *speedily*. So cumulative overvaluation and consequent recession and crisis remain a danger, as the many sorry examples of Latin American stabilizations indicate. The political connotations of dollarization are also significant. A national currency is a potent symbol. Dollarization smacks of foreign domination. For all these reasons, although dollarization is fashionable in some quarters, it is very doubtful whether it would suit most developing countries, other than a few micro states and possibly some countries where this is the only solution to hyperinflation.

It is not surprising therefore that very few developing countries have moved to the fixed end of the exchange rate spectrum in the last decade. Only two countries have dollarized, namely, Ecuador and Guatemala, both in 2000. The success of these experiments is distinctly uncertain. Three Baltic countries adopted currency boards in 1991 but they were not moving from flexible rates; they were in fact breaking away from a monetary union, namely, the erstwhile USSR. Argentina, Bulgaria and Bosnia were the only other countries to move to a currency board in the last decade. Argentina's broke up spectacularly in 2002.

## FLOATING EXCHANGE RATE PLUS CAC

With a floating exchange rate, the authorities do not have an exchange rate target. Monetary policy is governed by domestic output and inflation objectives and the exchange rate finds its level in the market.

The strength of this regime is that it facilitates real adjustment. Exchange rate movements provide a natural cushion against real shocks. In addition and in contrast to a fixed exchange rate, monetary policy can also be freely deployed to adjust to cyclical and other disturbances.

A floating exchange rate avoids currency crises by definition, if a crisis is defined as the failure of an exchange rate defense by the authorities. But the relevant question is whether it results in *excessive* volatility of the exchange rate (that is, more than justified by fundamentals). If so, it can be crisis prone though not exchange rate crisis prone.

Despite intensive efforts, economists have failed to explain exchange rate movements on the basis of fundamentals. There is evidence that foreign exchange traders have extrapolative expectations at short horizons and that short horizons dominate currency trading. As a result, exchange rate blips can get magnified beyond a reasonable limit before they collapse. Floating exchange rates thus exhibit both short-run volatility and medium-run misalignments. These fluctuations can impose severe costs. (But it has to be said that there is not much econometric support for this proposition as far as the developed countries are concerned.)

A floating exchange rate can be inflationary unless it is supported by a firm domestic nominal anchor. The latter could take the form of a money supply target. However, the current fashion is for inflation targeting, conducted by an independent central bank. But if the inflation target is rigid, monetary policy cannot be freely varied to counter fluctuations in *output*. (Even if one believes in a 'natural rate of unemployment' that is not amenable to monetary policy, only a now-discredited rational expectations view would claim that monetary policy should not be deployed to counter cyclical fluctuations.) In practice, therefore, central banks practice 'constrained discretion': the speed of attainment of the inflation target is left to the discretion of the central bank. Walking this particular tightrope requires a high degree of competence and credibility. The preconditions of successful inflation targeting are not easy to meet.

A floating exchange rate is not suitable for small, highly open economies in which traded goods constitute a high proportion of output. In these circumstances, most transactions and prices are strongly affected by exchange rate variations. This description covers many small developing countries but also many developed ones. The desire to escape exchange rate uncertainty and the perceived propensity of floating exchanges to cause inflation were important motives in the drive to form the European Monetary Union (EMU).

There are good reasons to think that developing countries, whether open or relatively closed, face *special* difficulties with floating exchange rates:

- Floating rates cry out for an inflation anchor. Inflation targeting is problematic in developing countries given fiscal dominance, the frequency of supply shocks, and the lack of requisite technical expertise.
- Developing countries lack the financial infrastructure that is appropriate for floating exchange rates. Their financial and foreign exchange markets lack depth, which is likely to increase the amplitude of exchange rate fluctuations. Moreover these thin markets are potentially subject to manipulation by hedge funds.[3]
- The financial credibility of developing countries is weak or fragile. Even a soundly-based monetary expansion may arouse market fears

of future irresponsibility. This imposes severe limits on the flexibility of monetary policy, which is the main advantage claimed for a floating exchange rate.[4]

- Forward cover is unavailable, except at short maturities. This is partly because the appropriate market infrastructure does not exist but mainly because of the lack of financial credibility. Another way of putting this point is that developing countries cannot undertake local-currency-denominated foreign borrowing. Since domestic bond markets are also undeveloped, a bias is created towards a debt structure that is overdependent on unhedged external borrowing. This makes the national balance sheet vulnerable to large exchange rate changes. It can be argued in response that a floating exchange rate is a necessary condition for the development of a forward market. Even if true, it may not be a sufficient condition since financial credibility does not automatically follow from floating the exchange rate.[5]

The upshot of the above is that developing countries' 'fear of floating' is not irrational. Developed countries are better suited to floating exchange rates, which do give them a measure of monetary autonomy. Even so, it is significant that European countries have chosen to abolish intra-Europe exchange rate fluctuations by adopting a common currency.

## INTERMEDIATE EXCHANGE RATE REGIME PLUS CAC

The case for an intermediate regime is that a compromise between exchange rate stability and monetary autonomy is better than giving up one of these goals altogether. Some ability to vary interest rates is essential in responding to shocks but some exchange rate targeting may also be required for anti-inflationary purposes or to prevent unnecessary fluctuations of the exchange rate away from its equilibrium level (for example, to deal with capital inflows that are judged to be temporary). Of course, an intermediate regime involves giving governments discretion. One of the drawbacks of a Bretton Woods type 'adjustable peg' was that exchange rates were altered infrequently. But an intermediate regime does not have to be so inflexible. It can take the form of a crawling peg, a target zone with bands, or even a crawling band with a basket peg. These regimes seek to achieve a balance between rules that bind the government and focus market expectations on the one hand and discretion for the government to act flexibly within the rules on the other hand. (It should not be thought that in the polar regimes, the issue of government discretion is wholly absent. The operation of inflation targeting in a flexible rate regime requires complex decisions about the stance of monetary policy. In a fixed rate regime, decisions have to be made about fiscal policy.)

The outstanding problem with intermediate regimes is vulnerability to currency and banking crises. The theoretical explanation of this phenomenon relies on two basic ideas:

1. An exchange rate target for the authorities also provides a target for speculators. Speculative attacks can take place even if the fundamentals are sound (or at least not manifestly unsound). This is the notion of 'second-generation' self-fulfilling crises. A speculative attack can succeed by raising the political and economic cost to the authorities of maintaining the exchange rate at the target level, even if the fundamentals are in good order.
2. An exchange rate target lulls economic agents into complacency about exchange risk and leads them into heavy, unhedged foreign currency borrowing. This distorts the debt structure of the economy and vastly increases the potential damage of a successful speculative attack.

The theoretical underpinning of the above ideas is not fully coherent and has loose ends. But empirically, the succession of currency crises that have afflicted intermediate regimes in the last decade does constitute strong prima facie evidence in favor of the crisis-vulnerability hypothesis. The crises include those that occurred in Exchange Rate Mechanism (ERM) countries (1992), Mexico (1994), Thailand, Korea, Malaysia and Indonesia (1997/98), Brazil and Russia (1999), and Argentina and Turkey (2001). Note also that at least four of these crises occurred in countries with *flexible* intermediate regimes (crawling bands), namely Mexico, Indonesia, Russia and Turkey. This suggests that *all* intermediate regimes are vulnerable, not only old-style adjustable pegs. It would still be possible to insist that all the crises in the 1990s were rooted in fundamentals and that the intermediate regimes would have been sustainable if only fiscal and financial policies had been sound enough. But this line of thinking no longer carries conviction.

Vulnerability to capital account crises may not be a major issue in those developing countries that are not yet linked into the world capital market and thus have 'natural' barriers to capital mobility. No doubt, this accounts for the prevalence of intermediate regimes in such countries. But as the countries 'emerge', one can expect these regimes to be progressively more subject to instability.

# INTERMEDIATE EXCHANGE RATE REGIME PLUS CAPITAL CONTROLS

Intermediate regimes in the presence of capital mobility are vulnerable to currency crises. But, as seen above, polar regimes are also crisis vulnerable in a broader sense. In addition, they lead to loss of control over either the interest rate or the exchange rate, both of which alternatives impose significant costs and constrain macroeconomic policy.

This naturally leads to the question of whether the least bad regime may not be an intermediate regime with some capital controls. Of course, capital controls impose costs but the issue is whether the cost–benefit calculus favors this regime over the others.[6] The crux of the matter can be briefly put: free capital movements can be hugely beneficial if they are well behaved but in the real world they can be perverse. There is therefore a case for government action to counter this perversity.

The costs of capital controls arise from the reduction in the scope for intertemporal trade and risk diversification. In addition, free capital movements are good for improving financial sector efficiency. Arguably, they also impose a desirable discipline on policymakers.

The underlying reason for the perversity of capital flows is the deep informational failures in capital markets. One manifestation of these is 'herd behavior' and the tendency to 'panics, manias and crashes'. Some but by no means all capital market perversity can be explained by the moral hazard that lender-of-last-resort facilities generate. But these facilities cannot be wholly abolished, and for good reason. Prudential regulation can reduce (but not entirely eliminate) the perversity of capital flows. The need to guard against the perversity of capital movements applies with particular force to 'emerging' countries. First, they are small in relation to capital flows. For example, during the East Asian crisis, several countries had a one-year swing in capital flows that exceeded 10 percent of GDP. It is doubtful if even the United States or Europe could easily manage an avalanche of this size. Second, the prudential and supervisory structures in developing countries are inadequate if not rudimentary. Realistically, they will take a long time to reach a satisfactory level.

The costs of capital controls can be reduced by limiting their scope. Capital controls need not and should not have a wide sweep. Foreign direct investment (FDI) brings large benefits and it is generally stable and 'bolted down'. Portfolio equity investment is also reasonably stable. The unstable elements are predominantly debt and credit flows, especially bank loans, in particular those that are short term and have to be rolled over frequently. It is to these volatile flows that capital controls have to be directed. In what follows, we assume that capital controls are of this focused variety.

In the context of exchange rate regimes, the advantage of capital controls is that they significantly reduce the crisis vulnerability of intermediate regimes. This is a major gain. In addition, the authorities can retain some control over both the interest rate and the exchange rate. They can have some exchange rate targeting and retain some monetary autonomy. Governments have good reasons to prefer such a regime over the polar extremes of fixed and floating exchanges. What *kind* of intermediate regime to have is a further decision that the authorities have to take.

A clear role for capital controls would be to prevent a build-up of excessive debt, particularly of the short-term, foreign exchange-denominated, unhedged variety. This suggests the need to control the open foreign exchange positions of banks. But the net may have to be cast wider since such loans could also be contracted by the corporate sector directly. Other desirable controls include those which 'throw sand in the wheels of speculation', for example, restrictions on non-resident financial institutions borrowing on the local market to short-sell the domestic currency.

Ironically, the case for 'prudential regulation' of the financial system is now generally accepted, but capital controls are regarded as suspect. But focused capital controls are best viewed as a sub-category of prudential controls.

The following trajectory may well be optimal for a 'typical' developing country. In the process of emerging, the country has an intermediate exchange rate regime sheltered by capital controls on short-term debt inflows and outflows by residents. As it matures, it moves progressively towards making the intermediate regime more flexible while at the same time, diluting its capital controls. In the penultimate stage it floats and institutes an inflation target with only a few key capital controls in place (rather like Singapore). Finally, it arrives at full maturity and floats like the G3 countries with full CAC.

Are focused capital controls feasible? The strong bipolar view says 'No' because the market would always find a way round them. But it is notable that most developed countries had capital controls for a prolonged period after the Second World War. Some developing countries have run capital controls successfully, for example Chile, China, India and Malaysia. Even Singapore, which has a very open capital market, has restrictions designed to prevent speculation. Chilean capital controls, which were equivalent to a tax on inflows that varied positively with loan maturity, have been extensively studied. The consensus view is that they did lengthen the maturity of the debt.

Capital controls can be porous but that is not necessarily a sign of failure if they can prevent large and sudden movements of hot money. Of course a precondition of their effectiveness is the presence of a minimum level of administrative competence and honesty and the absence of gross macro-economic incompetence or irresponsibility. But these conditions are no harder to meet than the ability to run prudential and supervisory systems which nowadays seems to be taken for granted as the answer to the perversity of capital flows.

India's successful experience with capital controls is not generally known. The controls gave macroeconomic policy an extra degree of freedom and insulated the country from the East Asian and other currency crises. The Indian experience is analysed in some detail in Appendix 10A.[7]

## DEVELOPING-COUNTRY EXCHANGE RATE REGIMES AND THE ROLE OF THE IMF

I have argued above that:

- A fixed exchange rate with CAC would not be suitable for a large majority of developing countries.
- These countries also lack the market sophistication, regulatory infra-structure and policy credibility to combine CAC with a floating exchange rate.
- Policymakers in developing countries therefore have good reasons to avoid both fixed and floating rates and to opt for an intermediate regime in which they retain some control over both the interest rate and the exchange rate. But such a regime would be highly crisis vulnerable in the presence of CAC. Some developing countries that are not yet linked to the world capital market may have sufficient natural insulation from capital flows to make such a regime sustainable but this insulation will vanish as they 'emerge'.
- The least bad arrangement for many emerging and potentially emerging countries during their transition to financial maturity, is an intermediate regime at the flexible end buttressed by some well-targeted capital controls.

If the above view is accepted, it has some implications for the IMF's policy stance towards developing countries. Until 1997, the IMF was a strong advocate of CAC and also of the bipolar view. Recently, its attitude has been more cautious but its overall stance remains negative. The above arguments suggest that there is a strong positive case for regarding intermediate exchange rates with well-targeted capital controls as the norm for a majority of developing countries during the long lead-time to financial maturity. If so, two points follow.

First, the IMF should strongly discourage developing countries from combining intermediate exchange rates with CAC. Whether and how this should be reflected in its lending policies is admittedly a tricky question and needs further consideration.

Second, the IMF must go beyond general admonition against controls or unwilling acceptance of them. It must adopt a more supportive stance towards such restrictions and, more importantly, provide technical assistance to developing countries in designing 'best practice' capital controls, drawing on the extensive experience of countries that have successfully operated them (and that includes developed countries) and countries that have been unsuccessful in doing so. Many developing countries sorely need detailed guidance in taking a view on inflow and outflow controls, controls on residents and non-residents, controls on different varieties of capital flow (FDI, portfolio equity, bonds, bank borrowing) and of different maturity (short term, long term), different entities to be controlled (banks, other financial institutions, non-financial companies), different methods of control (taxes, quantitative restrictions), and the duration of controls (permanent, temporary). They need special advice on ways of preventing speculation against their currencies, for example, restrictions on forward and swap markets, on non-resident financial operations in domestic markets and on offshore markets in domestic currency. The object should be to devise systems suited to country circumstances which maximize the net benefit from capital flows. None of this is incompatible with the IMF continuing its insistence on fiscal rectitude and general prudential regulation.

The IMF has avoided the above issues because of a general attitude that a simple rule (freedom of capital movement) is best (like freedom of trade). But free trade and free capital movements are different kinds of animal. The time has come for the IMF's policy stance to reflect the ambiguity of theory and evidence with respect to the desirability of free capital movements.

# APPENDIX 10A

## India's Response to the Impossible Trinity, 1991–2001 and Beyond

India is a rather successful example of an intermediate exchange rate buttressed by focused capital controls. Since the 1991 reforms, the country has grown at a satisfactory rate of 6 percent per annum (4 percent per capita) and has avoided the crises and contagion that have bedeviled the performance of many emerging countries.[8]

### India's External Payments Regime

India's payments regime is firmly in the 'intermediate exchange rate plus capital controls' category. The exchange rate is classified as 'market determined' by the Indian government and as 'floating' by the IMF. In fact, it is heavily managed and best described as a 'dirty crawl'. The rupee–dollar rate has exhibited longish periods of stability, punctuated by crawling depreciations in order to keep the real effective exchange rate roughly constant (at the 1994/95 level).

An intermediate exchange rate fits India's circumstances. A fixed exchange rate would be unsuitable. It is a low-inflation country, with a conservative financial tradition, so it does not need the exchange rate as a nominal anchor. The country is subject to plenty of asymmetric shocks relative to possible peg countries such as the United States. Since India is a large, relatively closed economy, it would be very costly to respond to these shocks by demand management alone, in the absence of exchange rate adjustment. Nominal wage and price inflexibility combined with real wage and price flexibility is a fair characterization of India's labor and product markets. Consequently, changes in the nominal exchange rate are necessary and effective in producing changes in the real exchange rate. Another important consideration is that India needs flexible monetary policy because the flexibility of fiscal policy is severely constrained by high budget deficits. This too rules out a fixed exchange rate.

But floating the exchange rate is also not a viable option. The country is not yet ready to adopt inflation targeting. The authorities wish to target the exchange rate, though not rigidly, for various reasons: to keep the exchange rate mildly undervalued to promote the growth of exports, to build up foreign exchange reserves in periods of strength, and to prevent a self-fulfilling collapse of the exchange rate in times of weakness.

The considerations above constitute the rationale for India's adoption of an intermediate exchange rate. But such a regime would be highly vulnerable to volatile capital flows. India's capital controls should be seen as a device to counter this problem.

India has had capital controls since the late 1950s. There was *selective* liberalization of these controls in the 1990s when the reform process began. The regime can be summed up as liberal for foreign direct and portfolio equity investment but restrictive for debt-creating inflows, particularly of the short-term variety. All permitted inflows are freely repatriable. Capital outflows by residents are tightly controlled.

A crucial aspect of the system is controls on banks. This is important because bank borrowing has been strongly associated with crisis. Banks' foreign asset and liability positions are monitored and subject to set limits. Offshore trading of the rupee is not permitted (though a thin offshore market does exist). There are restrictions on domestic currency lending to non-residents, so opportunities for short-selling the currency are very circumscribed. The swap and forward markets are also controlled since these markets could be used to speculate against the rupee by circumventing the restrictions on direct short-selling. Thus, the overall policy thrust has been to limit forward trading to hedging current account transactions. Of course, there is a price to pay: the forward market lacks adequate liquidity and depth.

**Regime Performance**

The above regime enabled India to moderate a capital-inflow surge from 1993 to 1995, avoid contagion from the East Asian and other currency crises, and offset an industrial slowdown towards the end of the decade. These shocks were handled by a mixture of monetary policy (including sterilized and unsterilized intervention), and moderate exchange rate changes. But this tightrope walk would not have been possible without capital controls. They prevented excessive short-term inflows and outflows and enabled the authorities to pursue a flexible monetary policy without losing control of the exchange rate.

A comparison of India and the East Asian countries in 1996 (that is, just before the East Asian crisis of 1997) is highly instructive and indicates why India escaped crisis and contagion (see Table 10A.1). It is clear from the first six columns of the table that in most respects, India's fundamentals (fiscal balance, inflation, current account balance, non-performing assets, debt–exports ratio and debt–service ratio) were worse or no better than those of the crisis countries. Exchange rate policy too is not a distinguishing feature. All these countries were on a loose dollar peg, though the precise mechanism – band, crawl or crawling band – varied. India's exchange rate was no more volatile than the exchange rates of the crisis countries, so the incentive for unhedged borrowing was very similar.[9]

The critical difference between India and the crisis countries can be seen in the last two columns of Table 10A.1. India managed to keep short-term

*Table 10A.1   Indicators of crisis vulnerability, 1996 (%)*

|  | FB/ GNP | ΔP/P | CAB/ XGS | NPA | NCEDT/ XGS | TDS/ XGS | SDT/ EDT | SDT/ RES |
|---|---|---|---|---|---|---|---|---|
| India | −9.0 | 9.0 | −11.7 | 17.3 | 103.6 | 21.2 | 5.3 | 27.1 |
| Indonesia | −1.0 | 8.0 | −13.0 | 8.8 | 180.5 | 36.6 | 25.0 | 166.7 |
| Korea | 0.0 | 4.9 | −14.6 | 4.1 | 82.0 | 9.4 | 49.4 | 192.7 |
| Malaysia | 0.7 | 3.5 | −6.4 | 3.9 | 40.4 | 9.0 | 27.9 | 39.7 |
| Philippines | 0.3 | 8.4 | −9.9 | n.a. | 80.1 | 13.4 | 19.9 | 67.9 |
| Thailand | 0.7 | 5.8 | −19.5 | 7.7 | 110.9 | 12.6 | 41.5 | 97.4 |

*Notes:*
FB/GNP: Fiscal balance as a proportion of GNP.
ΔP/P: Rate of consumer price inflation.
CAB/XGS: Current account balance as a proportion of exports of goods and services.
NPA: Non-performing assets of commercial banks as a proportion of total advances.
NCEDT/XGS: Non-concessional external debt as a proportion of exports of goods and services.
TDS/XGS: Debt service as a proportion of exports of goods and services.
SDT/EDT: Short-term external debt as a proportion of total external debt.
SDT/RES: Short-term external debt as a proportion of foreign exchange reserves.

*Sources:*
FB/GNP, NPA: Bank of International Settlements, *Annual Report*, 1997/98 and 1999/00.
CAB/XGS, NCEDT/XGS, TDS/XGS, SDT/EDT, SDT/RES: World Bank, *Global Development Finance*, 1999.
ΔP/P: IMF, *International Financial Statistics*.

debt under control, both in relation to total debt and in relation to foreign exchange reserves. Thus, India avoided the crisis by avoiding an unstable debt structure, an outcome that was the direct result of controls on debt-creating short-term inflows.

A relevant political economy question is why India was able to resist the concerted pressure in favor of CAC exerted by the IMF and the US Treasury in the early and mid-1990s (until 1997). Extreme free-market ideology did not have a constituency in India and economic reform was quite explicitly of the gradualist variety. Foreign banks, which are normally a strong pressure group in favor of CAC, had a very small presence in India. Most important, India was 'too big to be bullied' by Wall Street, the IMF and the US government.

**The Future**

Should India move rapidly to CAC in the near future? I do not think so, because:

- The prerequisites of CAC are not present. The fiscal deficit is in the region of 10 percent of GDP. The financial sector is not robust. The incidence of non-performing assets (NPAs) is still high (an average of about 12 percent of advances) on official figures. True NPAs are even higher due to 'evergreening'. Prudential supervision of the financial sector is still highly imperfect as evidenced by several recent scandals involving major financial institutions. In this situation, CAC would make the macro economy highly vulnerable.
- The flexibility of macroeconomic policy would be significantly curtailed in the presence of CAC. India's capital controls enable policymakers to combine monetary autonomy and exchange rate targeting.
- CAC would erode the tax base, an important consideration in a country where fewer than 10 million people out of a population of 1 billion pay income tax.
- The main downside of capital controls is that they slow down the improvement in financial sector efficiency, the lack of which is itself an impediment in moving to CAC. But an early move to CAC would not help financial sector reform if it precipitated a financial crisis.
- It could be argued that abolishing capital controls would serve to discipline policymakers and, in particular, bring about a reduction in India's high fiscal deficits. But experience shows that capital market discipline can be capricious. Moreover, India is a country where sensitivities about foreign domination are very strong. If CAC is followed by crisis, a reversal of reform, including of CAC itself, is possible in the Indian context. The solution to India's fiscal problem has to be internal and cannot be imposed by external financial discipline.

India's wish to integrate into the world economy is not in the long run compatible with the severity of its capital controls. The issue is one of timing and sequencing. When fiscal consolidation has taken place and the financial system has been strengthened, India's capital controls should be significantly relaxed. Even so, it is an open question whether the *total* elimination of capital controls is a good idea. It may be sensible to retain indefinitely some controls on banks' net open positions in foreign currency. With capital controls significantly liberalized, India's present intermediate exchange rate system will become less tenable and India will have to move towards floating and inflation targeting.

The long run is a long way away. Currently, an intermediate regime with targeted capital controls is the appropriate regime for India's circumstances. A rapid move to CAC could disrupt the country's large and unfinished reform agenda.

# NOTES

\*     I have previously published a journal article which is substantially similar to this chapter; see Joshi (2003c). Copyright permission is gratefully acknowledged.
1.     See Frankel (1999).
2.     For the strong and weak versions of the bipolar view, see, respectively, Eichengreen (1994) and Fischer (2001).
3.     See Cooper (1999).
4.     See Calvo and Reinhardt (2000).
5.     See Eichengreen and Hausmann (1999).
6.     See Williamson (1993), Bhagwati (1998) and Cooper (1999).
7.     For a fuller analysis of the Indian experience, see Joshi (2003a, 2003b).
8.     This appendix is based on the more detailed treatment in Joshi (2003a, 2003b). For a critical analysis of India's reforms, see Joshi and Little (1996).
9.     India's exchange rate policy was, however, better in one respect. When the dollar began to appreciate in 1995, the Indian authorities allowed the rupee to depreciate against the dollar. So, unlike the crisis countries, India's real effective exchange rate did not appreciate much in 1996.

# REFERENCES

Bhagwati, J. (1998), 'The capital myth: the difference between trade in widgets and in dollars', *Foreign Affairs*, **77** (3), 7–12.

Bubula, A. and I. Otker-Robe (2002), 'The evolution of exchange rate regimes since 1990: evidence from de facto policies', IMF Working Paper WP/02/155, International Monetary Fund, Washington, DC.

Calvo, G.A. and C.M. Reinhardt (2000), 'Fear of floating' NBER Working Paper no. 7993, National Bureau of Economic Research, Cambridge, MA.

Cooper, R. (1999), 'Should capital controls be banished?', *Brookings Papers in Economic Activity*, I, 89–125.

Eichengreen, B. (1994), *International Monetary Arrangements for the 21st Century*, Washington, DC: Brookings Institute.

Eichengreen, B. and R. Hausmann (1999), 'Exchange rates and financial fragility', NBER Working Paper no. 7418, National Bureau of Economic Research, Cambridge, MA.

Fischer, S. (2001), 'Exchange rates: is the bipolar view correct?', *Journal of Economic Perspectives*, **15**, 3–24.

Frankel, J. (1999), *No Single Currency Regime Is Right for All Countries or All Times*, Essays in International Finance, No. 215, Princeton, NJ: Princeton University Press.

Joshi, Vijay (2003a), 'Capital controls and the national advantage: has India got it right?', in G. Underhill and X. Zhang (eds), *International Finance Governance under Stress*, Cambridge: Cambridge University Press, pp. 182–202.

Joshi, Vijay (2003b), 'India and the Impossible Trinity' *The World Economy*, **26** (4), 555–83.

Joshi, Vijay (2003c), 'Exchange rate regimes: is there a third way?', *World Economics Journal*, **4** (4), October–December, 15–36.

Joshi, Vijay and I.M.D. Little (1996), *India's Economic Reforms 1991–2001*, Oxford: Oxford University Press.

Williamson, J. (1993), 'A cost-benefit account of capital account liberalization', in B. Fischer and S. Reisen (eds), *Financial Opening: Policy Issues and Experiences in Developing Countries*, Paris: Organization for Economic Cooperation and Development.

PART IV

Exchange Rate Regime and
Future Monetary Arrangements

# 11. Exchange rate system for 'mature' economies in a global economy

**Lord Skidelsky**

F33

## INTRODUCTION

The main purpose of this chapter is to take issue with Bordo's claim that targeting inflation represents a 'major technical improvement' over targeting the exchange rate. It argues that the Bretton Woods system of fixed, but adjustable, exchange rates gave the best all-round performance of all the exchange-rate regimes we have had, and that this constitutes a prima facie case for trying to recreate something like it. It further argues that the causes of the collapse of the fixed exchange rate systems of the last century have been misinterpreted to support the current near consensus in favor of floating. It claims that the advocates of 'autonomous' monetary policy which floating supposedly makes possible make exaggerated claims on its behalf. Indeed, I believe that the theoretical arguments in favour of floating would never have achieved wide political acceptance had they not chimed in with US unilateralism. The thrust of the chapter is that a fixed-exchange rate regime is more in tune with global economic integration than is a system of floating exchange rates, which comes out of the stable of nationalist economics and carries the seeds of currency wars and protectionism.

Most contemporary writers on exchange rates subscribe to what Obstfeld and Taylor (1998) have called the 'open-economy trilemma'. A country cannot simultaneously maintain fixed exchange rates and an open capital market while pursuing a monetary policy oriented toward domestic goals. Specifically, fixed-exchange rates combined with freedom of capital movement leave inflation and employment goals at the mercy of international finance. Since choices concerning these objects should be made by a country's own authorities, the choice of exchange rate regime resolves itself into floating with free capital movements or fixing with capital controls. Since most economists and policy-makers today regard control of capital movements as unfeasible or undesirable, floating emerges as the only choice for the mature economies (pending the utopian arrival of a single global currency backed by a world government). Subscribers to the trilemma doctrine tend to be highly skeptical about the currency union established in the European Union (EU), mainly on the ground that it abolishes the monetary freedom of the individual country members, without providing any effective substitutes (for example, fiscal transfers from the center to deal with asymmetric shocks). Some opponents of the single currency are against such transfers in any case, since they presuppose a European government which they oppose.

It is widely agreed that economies which need to import foreign capital to develop may have neither the capacity nor the ability to have independent monetary policies, with either fixed or flexible exchange rates. But the question of exchange-rate choice for developing countries has been addressed by Vijay Joshi (see Chapter 10 in this volume).

Bordo follows this general line of argument. He contends that the choice of exchange-rate regime should be governed by degree of financial maturity. Mature economies should float; immature ones should give up (or limit) their quest for monetary independence. But as they develop maturity they too can look forward to floating. Further, he regards inflation-targeting as marking a technical advance over exchange-rate targeting, because it can deliver macroeconomic stability without the deflationary and other costs associated with fixed-exchange rate systems (Bordo 2003).

He thus reverses the view taken in the past that with financial maturity countries should move from floating to fixing. In the late 19th century, joining the gold standard signalled the commitment to maintaining sound monetary and fiscal policies. But, argues Bordo, it was not the gold standard which made sound monetary and fiscal policies credible; it was the prior achievement of a sound monetary and fiscal constitution (degree of financial maturity) which made commitment to the gold standard credible.

The implication of this argument is that, provided a country has 'mature' financial institutions, the commitment to low inflation can be detached from commitment to defend a particular exchange rate. Indeed, Bordo argues that 'a domestic fiat nominal anchor' represents a 'major technical improvement' over an exchange-rate anchor, because it achieves credibility of commitment without the high resource costs of the classical gold standard (ibid., pp. 17, 24–5). 'A consequence of this analysis', Bordo writes, 'is that logically, the pre-1914 core countries that had developed strong money and financial markets and institutions before World War I ought to have floated – something which they did not' (ibid., p. 17); and so should the core countries today (ibid., p. 24).

This argument is far from convincing. Bordo admits that low inflation-targeting is 'consistent' with floating, not compelled by it. Indeed, the argument has traditionally gone the other way; floating enables a country, or its government, to choose its own rate of inflation. By contrast, under a fixed exchange rate regime, inflation rates are necessarily equalised throughout the system; a country inflating faster than its trade competitors will run out of reserves, compelling it to take corrective measures.

What this implies is that commitment to maintaining a fixed peg is not an unnecessary add-on to low inflation policies but an essential part of the commitment to them. The same degree of credibility does not attach to low inflation targeting. A fixed exchange rate provides an external constraint on the policies of governments. Under floating they are subject to a purely self-denying ordinance. Floating is consistent with a variety of national policies in respect of inflation or unemployment; it does not constrain any of them. This is not to deny that low inflation and floating can go together. But it is the performance of a monetary regime under stress that is the main test of its robustness. As I shall argue, the present system of 'inflation targeting' has not been subject to any real inflationary pressure. This has enabled it to claim the credit for outcomes which it did not produce.

A further point is that floating is, in intention, a purely national policy, which may easily develop nationalist overtones. The most determined floater – the United States – is also the country least willing to be tied down to international obligations – 'rules of the game' – either in the financial or political sphere. Although floating lessens the disruptive effects of individual country adjustment to shocks, it does so by transferring these effects to the general system of trade and finance. It is therefore in contradiction to the logic of economic and political integration.

For these reasons, I doubt whether monetary evolution points to universal floating. Historically, episodes of floating have been intervals between longer periods of fixing – interludes of unusual turbulence in economic or political life. As the turbulence dies down people's thoughts will return to fixing. It is highly unlikely that the economic and political integration of the West can proceed much further without stabilizing the exchange rate between the dollar and the euro. In particular, as a lower inflation environment takes hold in the two areas, the integrationist argument for fixing will start to seem more compelling than the credibility argument for floating. There is a strong case for making the former an explicit aim of currency policy. The next section tries to shed some light on the reasons for the collapse of the two major fixed exchange rate systems of modern times: the gold standard and the Bretton Woods gold exchange (or dollar) standard which succeeded it. The subsequent section raises questions about the extent of the benefits in terms of domestic policy independence which floating is supposed to bring. The final section concludes.

# EXCHANGE RATE SYSTEMS AND THE TRILEMMA

The theory of the trilemma may be seen as an attempt to summarize our historical understanding of why it proved so difficult to maintain a fixed exchange rate system in the 20th century. Two main conclusions have emerged: the gold standard was wrecked by the rise of democracy and the demand for political control over the business cycle; the Bretton Woods system was destroyed by the breakdown of barriers to the free movement of capital. Both can be questioned. But first a brief history.

The 'classical' gold standard finally broke down in 1931. Interwar experience of floating currencies created a consensus for 'fixed but adjustable' rates after the Second World War, Nurkse arguing in an influential paper (1944) that floating rates added major sources of uncertainty to trade and capital formation. The 'fear of floating' gave rise to the Bretton Woods system of fixed but adjustable rates, supported by the International Monetary Fund. After the collapse of the Bretton Woods system in the early 1970s 'fear of floating' gave way to 'fear of fixing' in the Anglo-American world (and among Anglo-American economists and policymakers) but not in the EU, where a 'mini-Bretton Woods system' was created as a step towards a single European currency.

Historically, periods when exchange rates were fixed are associated with better macro performance than when floating is dominant. The best performance in overall results – growth, employment, prices, stability – was achieved under the Bretton Woods system of fixed but adjustable exchange rates (c.1950–1971/73). The years from 1950 to 1973 have been called a 'golden age of economic development: an era of unprecedented sustained economic growth in developed and developing countries' (Davidson 1999, pp. 56–7). The average annual growth rate of OECD real GDP per capita from 1950 to 1973 was double that of the peak performance before, and also of the 20 years since (Adelman 1999). There are sound logical reasons for this. Provided that certain preconditions are met – that the system is credibly supported, and that not too much is expected of its adjustment mechanisms – then it will, on balance reduce uncertainty and the waste associated with uncertainty. This provides the best background for the growth of trade and investment.

According to currently received wisdom, the credibility of the gold standard rested on the 'incompletely understood' connection between monetary policy and the domestic economy, and the restricted nature of the franchise; it broke down in face of better economic understanding and the political demands for full employment from newly empowered voters (Eichengreen 1994, pp. 43, 47–9).

What wrecked Bretton Woods was the emergence of capital mobility (Obstfeld and Taylor 1998, cited in Bordo 2003, p. 5). There is much dubious history in all this, which leads to wrong conclusions for policy.

In fact, the gold standard was doomed by the First World War, not by a full employment commitment which only came after the Second World War; in Britain and Germany, working-class parties were the most robust defenders of the gold standard. What the First World War did was to destroy the system of international politics and finance on which the adjustment mechanisms of the pre-war gold standard had depended (including migration and the pivotal role of the City of London). The partly restored gold standard of the 1920s not only started off with severely misaligned currencies, but was subject to shocks which no system of fixed exchange rates could have survived (see Skidelsky 1999).

The collapse of the Bretton Woods system has been attributed to growing mobility of capital. Hence the birth of the dogma that a fixed exchange rate system can only be maintained with capital controls. In fact, growth of capital mobility had little to do with the breakdown of the Bretton Woods (gold exchange) system. The collapse of the central relationship among the major currencies – the dollar, the franc, the Deutschmark, sterling – was brought about by the inflationary financing of the Vietnam war by the United States in the late 1960s, which took priority over the defense of the $35 gold price. This deprived the system of its anti-inflationary anchor; its disintegration was an inevitable response to American political decisions – which under different administrations might have gone a different way.

The thrust of this argument is that, contrary to received wisdom, there was nothing ineluctable about the demise of fixed exchange rate systems in the last century. Without the two world wars and the intervening Great Depression, it is perfectly conceivable that the world would have evolved a modified version of the gold standard system to which Keynes looked forward before the First World War: one in which gold occupied much the same position as the monarch does in the British constitution. As time erodes the effects of these disturbances on the world's political and economic structures, re-fixing of major currencies may well be seen as part of the evolving process of reconnecting our own world with the world which existed before 1914.

## THE THEORY AND PRACTICE OF MONETARY INDEPENDENCE

A monetary authority is said to be independent if it can fix the rate of inflation or level of unemployment at whatever it wants it to be. This is said to require either a floating currency or control over capital movements. Friedman put the case for floating (1953, p. 210): 'Flexible rates would allow each country to pursue the mixture of unemployment and price trend object-ives it prefers'. Keynes stated the case for fixing with capital controls: 'In my view the whole management of the domestic economy depends on being free to have the appropriate rate of interest without reference to rates prevailing elsewhere in the world. Capital control is the corollary of this' (1942).

In the history of economic thought, the doctrine of monetary indepen-dence first emerged, in the writings of Fisher (1911), Wicksell ([1898] 1936) and Keynes (1923), as the 'modern' method of achieving price stability. It was put forward as an alternative to, or modification of, the gold standard, under which the internal price level was pushed around by the vagaries of gold production. The monetary reformers of that day were so keen on price stability because they understood that there was a connection – though how this worked was less clear – between price fluctuations and fluctuations in the real economy; it was the latter which it was their real object to prevent. But in order to establish the possibility of deliberate inflation targeting they had to rely on some version of the quantity theory of money (QTM). They also had to argue that monetary policy could be made 'politician proof'. Both sets of arguments have been taken over by modern advocates of inflation-targeting.

The feasibility of inflation targeting presupposes exogenous money; the credibility of inflation targeting presupposes exogenous politicians. Belief by agents in both is a necessary condition for full credibility of inflation tar-geting. Since the management of expectations is now a key part of the man-agement of money, any failure of credibility arising from one or other of these sources undermines the value of the commitment.

The model of the macro economy underlying all nominal targeting (whether the target is the inflation rate or the exchange rate) is the QTM. If the central bank can control the rate of growth of some monetary aggre-gate it can control the price level. In the early days of monetarist enthusi-asm, it was thought that the best policy for low inflation was to combine 'a money supply rule with floating exchange rates' (Congdon 1992, p. 20). Today, central banks attempt to control the price level by using interest rates to regulate the volume of bank credit (deposits). The Bank of England's current inflation target is 2.5 percent a year. To achieve this the Bank (more exactly, its Monetary Policy Committee) raises the interest rate when inflation is expected to go above target, and lowers it when it is expected to go below. The Bank thus enjoys a 'constrained discretion', allowing monetary policy to be expansionary in response to an anticipated output decline. In its attention to both prices and output, and its rejection of a simple link between money and prices, monetary policy today is

broadly Keynesian (Skidelsky, 2001). Inflation targeting is based on fore-
casts of money growth, prices and output, as well as of inflation and output
gaps. All these are subject to a high level of uncertainty. (By contrast, the
only indicator for monetary policy under a fixed exchange rate system is
trends in the movement of reserves.)

Current arrangements for the conduct of monetary policy have sought to
insulate it from political interference – from what Keynes called the 'wicked
Chancellor problem'. Central banks have been given varying degrees of
independence from political control. But the problem of the endogenous
politician remains. Typically, the inflation targets themselves are decided by
governments, and are subject to change in the light of circumstances. For
example, the Reserve Bank of New Zealand Act of 1989 specifies that price
stability is to be defined by agreement between the government and the governor of the central bank and is subject to revision. The view that politicians
are thus 'exogenous' to the conduct of monetary policy is illusory – probably even in the case of the European Central Bank (ECB) which is mandated to price stability by the Maastricht Treaty. G3 countries are reluctant
to commit themselves to long-term inflation targets: 'Everyone knows that
the Federal Reserve operates some form of inflation targeting regime, but
the exact policy objective is vague' (Financial Times, 24 April 2003, p. 22)
In all countries with flexible currencies, governments retain unfettered discretion to adjust the inflation rate in the light of unilaterally determined circumstances. Contrast this with the commitment under Bretton Woods to
alter exchange rates only with IMF agreement.

The achievement of low rates of inflation throughout the OECD world
since the mid-1980s has been hailed as an example of what monetary independence can achieve under floating. But is this true?

The era of floating has coincided with the reduction of inflation to very
low rates throughout the OECD world. This has been hailed as a success for
inflation targeting by independent central banks. But it is inherently unlikely
that a uniformly low inflation rate should have emerged from a large number
of independent choices of inflation target. Rather, the OECD experience
suggests that low inflation is at least partly the result of structural changes
in the world economy. It is not so much inflation targeting which has produced a uniformly low inflation rate; it is reduced inflationary pressure
which has enabled monetary authorities to achieve low inflation targets.

This issue goes back to the currency versus banking school debate of the
1840s. In essence, the banking school contended that there could never be
any over-issue of notes: the supply of money was always exactly propor-
tioned to the demand for money (loosely, the needs of trade). One of the most
prominent modern exponents of the banking view was the late Nicholas
Kaldor: 'an excess in the supply of money cannot come into existence; and

if it did, it would be automatically extinguished through the repayment of bank indebtedness (or its equivalent)' (Kaldor 1985, p. 8). According to this view, a monetary authority which has regard for either the unemployment rate or the solvency of the banking system is bound to accommodate the supply of money to any demand for it.

Kaldor did not claim that monetary policy was impotent. But it works on prices indirectly through its impact on the level of output and employment. A deflationary policy hits output and employment; the reduction in activity brings down prices in its train. According to this view, it was the reduction in the 'demand for money' (deposits) in the 1980s that drove inflation to low levels.

The heretical view that real structural forces influence nominal variables ignores the fact that what needs to be explained is the persistence of low inflation as output and employment recovered in the 1990s. This issue has been addressed by Roger Bootle (1997). According to Bootle, the reason for inflationary pressures in the 'golden age' of the 1950s and 1960s lay in the institutional structures of the economy of that period which diminished price competition and inhibited market forces: managerial capitalism and producer power, at the root of which lay economies of large-scale production. Bootle argues that globalization has led to a systematic decline in inflationary pressure. Since the 1980s, changes in technology, weakened unions, a more competitive climate, both domestically and internationally, and the changing composition of the labor force, have eased the pressure on central bankers.

The Keynesian defense of floating is that it enables a country to pursue a full employment policy. The argument is that, with a floating rate, a monetary authority can set interest rates with sole regard to domestic conditions. In a fixed exchange regime, monetary policy is powerless, if capital is mobile. The home interest rate cannot differ from the foreign interest rate because any difference would be eliminated by capital movements. As a result, the country loses one of its principal weapons in fighting unemployment. Given the current taboo on deliberately budgeting for a deficit, interest rate policy has become pre-eminent in the fight against unemployment. This is the basis of the charge that the euro has locked the main European economies into a suboptimal level of activity.

Prima facie, this argument is compelling. Few economists doubt that Germany would have benefited from a lower interest and exchange rate than those produced by the policy of the ECB. However, the prolonged stagnation of Japan, which has enjoyed monetary independence, casts some doubt on the validity of this view. Despite pushing nominal interest rates to near zero, the Bank of Japan has been unable to prevent prices from falling and thus the *appreciation* of the real interest rate. A positive real rate

of return on money can make holding it more attractive than buying investments, or goods and services. In this case, monetary policy – the expansion
of some monetary aggregate – is ineffective in stimulating the economy.
Tim Congdon (2003) calls this the 'narrow liquidity trap' – all that massive
bond purchases by the central bank do is to swell the commercial banks'
cash ratios. This situation arises when loans to the private sector are
expected to be relatively less profitable than holding cash or when yields on
bonds have fallen so low that the most probable next move is an upward
yield movement which will reduce their capital value. Congdon (ibid., p. 8)
cites figures which show that in 2001–02, massive bond purchases by the
Bank of Japan resulted in a trebling of banks' cash reserves. But their loan
portfolios declined by almost 10 percent.

Economists have proposed various unorthodox measures to stimulate
the Japanese economy. Krugman (1999, p. 73) argued for a straightforward
policy of inflation to force down real interest rates. But he did not explain
how monetary policy could inflate the economy in face of consumer reluctance to spend. Martin Feldstein (2001) proposed that the authorities
should cut the sales tax to zero and at the same time announce that it would
be raised to 10 percent at a definite date in the future. This idea dates back
to the stamped money plan of the German-Swiss economist Silvio Gesell.
His aim was to create the definite expectation that money would lose its
value if it was not spent immediately. The Japanese economy has at last
begun to recover without the aid of these stimulants.

In summary, the adoption by governments and central banks of OECD
countries of a 'domestic precommitment strategy' to low inflation has
played relatively little role in producing persistently low inflation rates
(it may well have played a part in limiting price volatility); while the
Japanese experience suggests that the ability of monetary independence to
stimulate a depressed economy is exaggerated. On the other hand, the
volatility associated with floating increases the uncertainty of international
trade and investment.

In the course of the most recent episode of floating the argument has
shifted from saying that floating is the means by which a country could
choose its own inflation rate to one saying that it is the regime which best
enables the system of inflation control to be credible. There is something so
counter-intuitive about this that perhaps only an economist would put it
forward.

The doctrine that floating is inherently superior to fixing – as opposed to
being something one might be driven to in a crisis – is of predominantly
Anglo-American provenance; it is not shared in Continental Europe or in
most of the rest of the world. Its logic lies in politics, not in economics. It
has provided a theoretical cover for liberating US policy from the constraint

of internationally agreed rules, freeing it to pursue an economic national-
ism, which is the counterpart of its political unilateralism.

## CONCLUSION

The issue posed by Bordo's paper is whether stable macroeconomic conditions are best achieved by low inflation targeting or by targeting exchange-
rates. Most of the arguments in favor of the first emphasize the lack of
credibility of the second. I have argued that there are credibility problems
with both, but that the credibility problems of fixed-exchange rate systems
have been exaggerated, while the benefits of floating have been exaggerated
and its disadvantages ignored. I agree, therefore, with Robert Cooper that,
in today's world, 'a cost–benefit calculation for flexible versus fixed
exchange rates will gradually alter the balance against flexibility, even for
large countries' (Cooper 2001, p. 117). However, it will probably take a
financial or geopolitical crisis to persuade the United States to abandon its
commitment to financial unilateralism.

## REFERENCES

Adelman, I. (1999), 'Long-term economic development', Working Paper no. 589,
    California Agricultural Experiment Station, Berkeley, CA.
Bootle, R. (1997), *The Death of Inflation: Surviving and Thriving in the Zero Era*,
    London: Nicholas Brealey.
Bordo, M.D. (2003), 'Exchange rate regime choice in historical perspective', Henry
    Thornton Lecture at the Cass Business School, City University, London, mimeo,
    26 March.
Congdon, Tim (1992), *Reflections on Monetarism*, Aldeshot, UK and Brookfield,
    USA: Edward Elgar.
Congdon, Tim (2003), 'Debt management and deflation', Lombard Street Research
    Limited, London, 4 April.
Cooper, Richard N. (2001), 'Exchange rate choices', in Jane Sneddon Little and
    Giovanni P. Olivei (eds), '*Rethinking the International Monetary System*, USA:
    University Press of the Pacific.
Davidson, Paul (1999), 'The case for capital regulation', in R. Skidelsky (1999).
Eichengreen, B. (1994), *International Monetary Arrangements for the 21st Century*,
    Washington, DC: Brookings Institution.
Feldstein, M. (2001), 'Japan needs to stimulate spending', *The Wall Street Journal*,
    16 July.
Fisher, Irving (1911), *The Purchasing Power of Money*, New York: Macmillan.
Friedman, M. (1953) 'The case for flexible exchange rates', in *Essays in Positive
    Economics*, Chicago: University of Chicago Press.
Kaldor, N. (1985), 'How monetarism failed', *Challenge*, May–June.

Keynes, J.M. (1923), *A Tract on Monetary Reform*, Vol. IV, *Collected writings of John Maynard Keynes*, London: Macmillan.
Krugman, P. (1999), *The Return of Depression Economics*, New York: W.W. Nanton.
Nurkse, R. (1944), *International Currency Experience*, Geneva: League of Nations.
Obstfeld, M. and Alan M. Taylor (1998), 'The Great Depression as a watershed: international capital mobility over the long-run', in M.D. Bordo, Claudio Goldin and Eugene N. White (eds), *The Defining Moment: The Great Depression and the American Economy in the Twentieth Century*, Chicago, IL: University of Chicago Press for NBER.
Skidelsky, R. (1999), 'Historical; reflections on capital movements', in *Capital Regulation: For and Against*, London: Social Market Foundation.
Skidelsky, R. (2001), 'Personal view', *Financial Times*, 16 August.
Wicksell, K. (1936), *Interest and Prices: A Study of the Causes Regulating the Value of Money* (published in German, 1898), London: Macmillan, on behalf of the Royal Economic Society.

238-57

E31

F33 E52

023

019 024

# 12. The exchange rate regime and monetary arrangements in South Africa

**E.J. van der Merwe**

## INTRODUCTION

The Bretton Woods system of fixed exchange rates served the world well for more than two decades after the Second World War. Under this system, members of the International Monetary Fund were required to address temporary balance of payments disequilibrium by means of macroeconomic policy measures and not by exchange rate changes. Only in the case of 'fundamental balance of payments disequilibrium' could countries adjust the par values of their currencies. This system succeeded in providing the world with relative exchange rate stability for a long time.

In the 1960s, pressures began to build up sharply against the Bretton Woods system because of the large deficits in the balance of payments of the United States and the reluctance of member states to adjust their exchange rates even when they encountered serious structural balance of payments disequilibrium. As a result, the system of stable exchange rates was finally abandoned at the beginning of 1973. Countries were then forced to restructure their exchange rate regimes and monetary arrangements.

This chapter will discuss the changes that were made to South Africa's exchange rate regime and monetary arrangements after the end of the Bretton Woods system, which finally led to the adoption of an inflation targeting monetary policy framework with a freely floating currency in the year 2000. Although we have only applied this framework for three years, it is also interesting to review how well it has worked over this short period.

# THE FOUR PHASES OF EXCHANGE RATE REGIMES AND MONETARY ARRANGEMENTS

Four distinct phases of exchange rate regimes and monetary arrangements can be distinguished in South Africa following the termination of the Bretton Woods system, namely:

1.  a phase of direct monetary controls and the desire to maintain some stability in the exchange rate of the rand during the 1970s;
2.  the transition to more market-oriented measures and the adoption of money supply targets in the 1980s;
3.  a period of informal inflation targeting and managed floating of the rand during the 1990s; and
4.  the adoption of a formal inflation-targeting monetary policy framework and a floating exchange rate regime from the year 2000.

## The Phase of Direct Monetary Controls

The disintegration of the Bretton Woods system of fixed exchange rates forced the authorities to adjust the country's exchange rate regime. At first, the Reserve Bank decided to devalue the rand and peg it to the dollar because the relatively undeveloped domestic market in foreign exchange did not allow a floating exchange rate and most of the country's foreign transactions were denominated in dollars. In June 1972 the pound sterling started to float downwards against other major currencies, and to maintain a recovery in the balance of payments South Africa linked the rand to sterling. After four months the rand was again pegged to the US dollar because the continued depreciation of sterling did not suit domestic economic objectives.

In order to reflect more closely the changes in South Africa's underlying balance of payments and domestic economic conditions, a policy of 'independent managed floating' was adopted in June 1974. In accordance with this policy, smaller but more frequent adjustments were made to the middle market rate of exchange with the dollar. Speculative attacks on the rand caused the authorities to again change their exchange rate policy as from 27 June 1975. They announced on this date that the rand–dollar rate would be kept constant for long periods and only be adjusted when it was regarded as essential in the light of basic changes in the domestic or international situation.

All these exchange rate regimes were applied under fairly restrictive exchange control measures. Restrictions were applicable to transactions by residents and the repatriation of foreign investments. Moreover, from 1968 a limit was applicable on the local borrowing facilities of South African subsidiaries of foreign companies because it was argued that domestic-owned enterprises should have first claim on the limited domestic financial resources. These measures were made more restrictive or liberal during the 1970s, depending on domestic and international economic conditions at the time. However, they generally remained relatively restrictive during most of this decade.

In addition to exchange control, other direct monetary controls were also applied because of the perceived need to maintain the parity of the rand and to maintain low interest rates for mortgage bonds and agricultural loans. These direct control measures included ceilings on bank credit to the private sector, deposit rate controls, import deposits and hire-purchase controls. At times, banks were also asked to extend credit on a selective basis.

It soon became apparent that this system of direct monetary controls led to an inadequate attainment of the objectives of price stability, balance of payments equilibrium and optimal and stable economic and employment growth. The Commission of Inquiry into the Monetary System and Monetary Policy in South Africa (1984) found that certain deficiencies in the monetary system were responsible for this, namely:

1.  the rates of increase of monetary aggregates were not adequately controlled by the system;
2.  the system led to disintermediation and reintermediation practices being applied which caused marked fluctuations in the velocity of circulation of money;
3.  interest rates were not always allowed to rise to levels that would have been appropriate to achieve more moderate and stable growth in bank credit extension and money supply;
4.  spot and forward rates of the rand were not always allowed to adjust to levels that would have contributed to the appropriate level of monetary demand;
5.  the rand moved with the dollar for long periods at a time without taking domestic economic conditions into consideration because the rand–dollar peg was changed only infrequently. This often gave rise to speculative capital outflows; and
6.  a heavy reliance was placed on exchange control, which was an economically inefficient way of rationing the available foreign exchange among the various domestic uses and deterred the inflow of foreign capital.

**The Phase of Market-oriented Measures and Monetary Targeting**

In view of these deficiencies, the government decided to adopt more market-oriented measures in conducting monetary and exchange rate arrangements.

This phase started in 1980 when first deposit rate controls and then bank credit ceilings were abolished. Following these steps, the monetary authorities began to permit interest rates to become more flexible and to rise more readily and to a greater extent in response to market forces than had previously been the case. This transition from direct controls to market-oriented measures from the beginning of the 1980s was also accompanied by a relaxation and simplification of exchange control, but unfortunately financial sanctions against the country forced the authorities to reinstate strict exchange control measures from the beginning of 1985 and to declare a standstill on the repayment of foreign debt from September 1985.

In accordance with the recommendations of the Commission of Inquiry into the Monetary System and Monetary Policy in South Africa, a major reform of the foreign exchange practices was initiated in this period. The objective was to establish a unitary exchange rate system over the long term

> under which an independent and flexible rand [would] find its own level in well-developed and competitive spot and forward foreign exchange markets in South Africa, subject to Reserve Bank 'intervention' or 'management' by means of purchases and sales of foreign exchange (mainly US dollars), but with no exchange control over non-residents and only limited control over residents (p. 121).

Because of the continued application of exchange control over non-residents, the system up to the beginning of 1983 was one of dual exchange rates, with a managed, market-determined exchange rate for a 'commercial rand' and a more freely floating rate for a 'financial rand'. Following the abolition of exchange control over non-residents in February 1983, the financial rand disappeared. For a brief period, South Africa then had a unitary exchange rate system. After the introduction of the debt standstill in September 1985, the financial rand was reintroduced and a dual exchange rate system was operated throughout the rest of the 1980s.

In this dual exchange rate system the spot exchange rate for the commercial rand was essentially determined by market forces, but the Reserve Bank regularly intervened in the market by buying or selling spot or forward dollars to smooth out undue fluctuations in the exchange rate of the commercial rand. In addition, the Reserve Bank was responsible for the determination of forward rates, which were based on spot rates and the interest rate differential between the rand and the dollar. The forward rates were therefore only simulated market rates and could be completely inconsistent with expected exchange rate or interest rate movements, such as would have governed their determination under free conditions.

The exchange rate of the financial rand was determined under relatively free conditions. The financial-rand rate depended mainly on the supply of and demand for financial-rand deposits in the books of authorized banks in South Africa. These deposits were created when a non-resident sold an asset to a resident or when funds of a capital nature became payable to a non-resident, such as inheritances from estates or distributions from trusts. Obviously because the financial-rand system was based on exchange control rulings, the Reserve Bank could interfere in the market by changing these rulings. At times the Reserve Bank also intervened directly in the financial-rand market by selling or purchasing financial rand to influence the financial-rand rate. The largest part of the transactions in the financial-rand market, however, took place without Reserve Bank interference.

The flexibility created in the determination of interest rates and the exchange rate of the rand allowed the authorities to introduce formal monetary targets in South Africa in March 1986. This flexibility was necessary because interest rates and exchange rates cannot be determined independently of the money supply or of each other. The introduction of these targets only took place at a time when the rest of the world was starting to question their value because the usefulness of monetary targeting largely depends on the stability of the demand for money. The process of rapid financial innovation and changes in the financial system as well as in the monetary policy stance to a more market-related approach during the early 1980s weakened the case for imposing monetary targets during these years.

The international debate at the time regarding monetary targeting was not so much about the usefulness of monetary targeting, but rather on the way that it should be applied. The issue was whether these targets should be applied in the form of a rigid and overriding money rule or more flexibly with some scope for discretionary judgment in deciding what combination of money supply growth and the level of interest rates and exchange rates to aim at in any given set of circumstances.

With the benefit of experience in other countries, South Africa opted for targets with a fair measure of flexibility and a 'low profile'. This meant that interest rates and exchange rates were not left completely free to be determined by supply and demand conditions in the market. Instead, the Reserve Bank continued to exercise discretionary judgment in deciding on the most appropriate combination of money supply, interest rates and exchange rates taking the underlying economic conditions into consideration. At the same time the Bank realized that if the monetary targets were breached or changed too often, the exercise would become a mockery.

### The Phase of Informal Inflation Targeting

Monetary targeting was introduced in South Africa during a difficult period characterized by a decline in the gold price and in the prices of other commodities, serious droughts in the country and social unrest and strikes. On top of this came international actions aimed at bringing about political changes by constraining economic development by means of trade boy-cotts, a disinvestment campaign and the withdrawal of foreign loans from the country.

In these circumstances, South Africa's economic growth rate declined to low levels, the balance of payments came under severe strain, the foreign reserves were reduced to low levels, the demands on the budget increased, the deficit before borrowing widened to record proportions and unemploy-ment rose sharply. Monetary and other policy measures were forced to concentrate on short-term demand management to ensure that obligations on foreign debt were met without defaulting, to underpin domestic expend-iture even if it meant that interest rates had to be kept at low levels, to support employment and to provide for the protection of internal and external security. As a result, the objective of price stability was relegated downwards in the priority scale of the authorities.

This situation changed dramatically in the 1990s. The successful com-pletion of socio-political reforms paved the way for the normalization of South Africa's position in the world. The international punitive actions against South Africa were repealed especially after the Government of National Unity came into power in April 1994. South Africa became reinte-grated in the world economy and in international financial markets. However, the world financial system was vastly different from the one the country had left in the 1970s and 1980s. A revolution in electronics and communications had led to a strong movement of globalization in finan-cial markets. This process forced the liberalization of domestic financial markets in many countries, led to the abolition of exchange controls and exposed countries directly to the disciplines of international markets.

In the early 1990s, the South African authorities accordingly embarked on a policy of gradually relaxing exchange control. The first step in this regard was the final debt rescheduling agreement which was concluded with foreign creditors on 27 September 1993. This was followed by the abolition of the financial-rand mechanism or dual exchange rate system as from 13 March 1995, which removed nearly all the exchange control restrictions on non-residents. In the last half of the 1990s the exchange control restric-tions on residents were progressively relaxed. However, limits are still applicable on many transactions that residents can undertake.

The normalization of South Africa's relations in the world allowed the Reserve Bank to focus monetary policy to a more longer-term perspective than the 1980s, with the intention of creating a financial environment that would be conducive to higher economic growth. The objectives of mon-etary policy became:

- to reduce the rate of inflation to the average rate of inflation in trading partner and competitive countries;
- to manage the money creation process in such a way that an adequate, but not an excessive, amount of new money would be supplied to the system;
- to maintain positive real interest rates;
- to increase the gold and foreign exchange reserves to a more comfortable level; and
- to develop a sound financial infrastructure consisting of healthy financial institutions and efficient working financial markets that could facilitate the implementation of policy and provide the financial services needed by a developing and vigorous economy.

In a sense, the monetary policy framework of the 1990s can be described as an informal inflation targeting framework because of the emphasis it placed on the reduction of inflation. Other economic goals became subordinated to this institutional commitment and a target was set for inflation but without specifying the time period over which it would be attained. The primary objective was to bring the domestic inflation rate gradually in line with the average rate of inflation in the country's major trading partners and major international competitors. This was regarded as essential to protect South African producers against competition from the rest of the world and to avoid periodic disruptive adjustments in the exchange rate of the rand.

This 'informal inflation target' did not increase the transparency and accountability of monetary policy and also differed from formal inflation targeting in that an intermediate target, the growth in money supply, anchored monetary policy decisions. It was, however, soon realized that in the changed domestic and international environment, it was unwise to rely too much on money supply to steer monetary policy. The term 'money supply guidelines' accordingly began to be used in preference to 'money supply targets'.

The operations of foreign banks and the easier access of domestic banks to financial resources in the rest of the world made it difficult to control money supply. The fact that the guidelines were mostly missed was also an indication that control was either not possible or would have required an undesirable monetary policy stance.

In the process of liberalizing and reintegrating South Africa into the international financial markets, large increases in the money supply occurred that were not directly or indirectly related to the spending on real goods and services. The income velocity of circulation of the money supply continued to decline. More money became available for every unit of goods and services produced in the country, but this rise in money did not affect inflation. By contrast, inflation started to move downwards. The relationship between money supply growth and inflation therefore became unstable, which reduced the usefulness of money targets for monetary policy purposes.

Consequently, towards the end of the 1990s the Reserve Bank moved to an eclectic or pragmatic monetary policy framework. The growth in money supply and bank credit extension were still regarded as a vital element in the process of inflation creation and were monitored closely. The Bank, however, also closely monitored other financial and real indicators in making decisions on the appropriate level of short-term interest rates. These indicators included production prices, the gross domestic product deflator, the exchange rate of the rand, the shape of the yield curve, nominal salaries and wages, nominal unit labor cost, the gap between potential and actual national output, money market conditions, the overall balance of payments position, the gross gold and other foreign reserves, and the public sector borrowing requirement.

In the 1990s, the Reserve Bank intervened heavily on its own initiative in the spot and forward market to influence supply and demand conditions in the domestic market in foreign exchange. With these operations the aim was to smooth out undue short-term fluctuations in the exchange rate, but it was explicitly stated by the Bank that it did not target the exchange rate. Instead, it preferred to rely primarily on market forces, within the framework of the existing exchange control and tariff protection, to determine the general level of the exchange rate of the rand.

The extent to which the Bank intervened in the foreign exchange market was clearly reflected in the changes in the net open position in foreign reserves of the Bank, that is, the net gold and other foreign reserves of the Bank less the balance on its net oversold forward book. For example, the net oversold position in foreign reserves increased from US$14.0 billion at the end of 1995 to US$22.2 billion at the end of 1996, that is, during a period in which the exchange rate of the rand was under pressure. After having declined to US$16.3 billion at the end of December 1997, the net open position in foreign reserves rose again to a peak of US$23.2 billion on 30 September 1998.

Despite this active intervention, large fluctuations were discernible in the weighted average value of the rand, particularly during the second half of the 1990s in an environment of more liberalized exchange controls. For instance, the nominal effective exchange rate of the rand declined by 19.0 percent in 1996, rose by 7.8 percent in 1997, declined again by 18.5 percent in 1998 and rose by 0.6 percent in 1999. The weighted value of the rand, however, tended downwards in the 1990s and this downward movement was larger than the inflation rate differential between South Africa and its main trading partners and international competitors.

The monetary policy framework of informal inflation targeting also had certain other important disadvantages. But it was implemented in such a way that it achieved considerable success in bringing down the rate of inflation. After inflation in the consumer price index had generally fluctuated around a level of about 15 percent in the late 1980s and the beginning of the 1990s it moved below double digits in 1993 and declined to 5.2 percent in 1999.

**The Phase of Formal Inflation Targeting**

In February 2000, the government announced that South Africa had formally adopted an inflation-targeting monetary policy framework. This framework was applied because:

1. it provides an anchor or ultimate objective to monetary policy decision-making;
2. it promotes a more coordinated approach between monetary and other policy measures;
3. it makes monetary policy more transparent which increases its effectiveness; and
4. it helps to focus monetary policy and the clear rules and procedures of this system strengthens the accountability and governance of the central bank.

The inflation target was specified as an average rate of increase of 3 to 6 percent in the overall consumer price index excluding mortgage interest cost in metropolitan and other urban areas, that is, a variant of the headline inflation rate. The headline inflation rate was not used as it is affected directly, with a short lag, by changes in the Reserve Bank's repurchase rate. By including price changes in metropolitan as well as other urban areas, the most comprehensive price index available in South Africa was used in setting the target. The inflation target was specified as a range since it leaves some discretion to the central bank in taking decisions on the monetary policy stance.

The adoption of inflation targeting in South Africa does not mean that the central bank is not concerned with the attainment of sustained high economic growth and employment. It does, however, clearly state what the overriding or primary objective of the central bank is, and implies that monetary policy cannot contribute directly to economic growth and employment creation. By creating a stable financial environment monetary policy fulfills an important precondition for the attainment of economic development.

In the application of inflation targeting in South Africa, allowance is made for supply shocks in taking policy decisions. An escape clause has been incorporated in the inflation-targeting framework which allows the central bank under certain conditions to deviate from the stated inflation targets provided that it indicates how the targets will again be reached in future. Such discretion in the case of extraordinary events beyond the control of the central bank is regarded as essential to avoid costly losses in output and employment. The objective of the exercise nevertheless continues to be the achievement of the target, and the inherent discipline of inflation targeting is not thrown overboard by applying discretion when the need arises.

The application of an inflation-targeting monetary policy framework improves the credibility of monetary policy by making the public more aware of the forward-looking approach of monetary policy. In view of the long lags of between 12 and 24 months for changes in interest rates to fully impact on inflation, monetary policy decisions are made to affect future price movements. The pre-emptive character of inflation targeting should prevent wide fluctuations in prices, output and interest rates.

The financial stability can, however, be disturbed at times by sharp adjustments in the exchange rate. The destabilizing effects of flexible exchange rates have caused some countries to adopt inflation targeting combined with a rigid or heavily managed exchange rate regime. If such an approach is adopted, it raises the question what will the authorities do in the case of conflict between the objectives of price and exchange rate stability? For example, how will the authorities react if there is upward pressure on the country's currency while the inflation rate is above target?

In view of such possible conflicts and to create greater credibility to monetary policy, South Africa opted for inflation targeting combined with exchange rate flexibility. This does not mean that the Reserve Bank is not concerned about the exchange rate of the rand, because exchange rate changes impact on inflation. But it does mean that the central bank has no specific target for the exchange rate of the rand and that the value of the currency is basically determined by supply and demand in the domestic market for foreign currency. The Reserve Bank does not buy and sell foreign currencies in the market with the objective of keeping the exchange rate of the rand at a specific level or within a specific band.

In view of the large net open position in foreign reserves of the Reserve Bank at the end of the 1990s and the negative effect that this has had on foreign investments and the evaluation made by international rating agencies, it has been a stated objective of the authorities to close down this exchange risk of the central bank. With spot and forward transactions, this position was relatively quickly reduced from US$23.2 billion at the end of September 1998 to US$13.0 billion at the end of 1999 and US$9.5 billion at the end of 2000. This created expectations that the exchange rate of the rand would generally depreciate and led to speculative transactions. As a consequence, the government indicated that from October 2000 this position would only be reduced further by means of proceeds arising from privatization or from government loans obtained abroad. By using these proceeds, the net open position in foreign exchange of the Reserve Bank was reduced to US$1.8 billion at the end of November 2002.

With the strong recovery of the rand at the end of 2002 and during the first four months of 2003, the Reserve Bank has on occasions taken the opportunity to purchase dollars in the market on a moderate scale to strengthen its foreign exchange holdings. These operations helped further to reduce the Bank's net open position in foreign currency to US$1.2 billion on 31 March 2003. Such operations purely represent prudent management of the Reserve Bank's balance sheet and have not been undertaken to influence the level of the exchange rate of the rand.

## THE EFFECTIVENESS OF THE MONETARY AND EXCHANGE RATE REGIME

This section is concerned with how effectively the inflation-targeting monetary policy regime combined with a floating exchange rate of the rand has worked in South Africa in an environment wherein exchange control was gradually liberalized. Unfortunately, we have a history of only three years in which this regime has been applied. Some preliminary conclusions can nevertheless be made regarding the following pertinent questions:

1.  Was it wise for South Africa to liberalize exchange controls?
2.  Was the decision to gradually reduce exchange controls correct?
3.  Is inflation targeting an appropriate monetary policy model for South Africa as an emerging-market economy?
4.  How effective has inflation targeting been in the past three years?
5.  How effective has the floating exchange rate regime operated?
6.  Should South Africa not rather apply a fixed exchange rate system?

### The Liberalization of Exchange Controls

With the normalization of socio-political conditions and the reintegration of South Africa in the world economy, the authorities probably had no other choice but to liberalize the relatively restrictive exchange controls of the country. Serious doubts in any case also existed about the effectiveness of exchange control.

The rationale for applying exchange control is based on the assumption that it can effectively regulate capital flows. Empirical evidence clearly pointed to the fact that ingenious ways were used to circumvent these controls. One of the channels most frequently used was underinvoicing of exports and overinvoicing of imports. In addition, multinational companies used transfer-pricing policies to evade controls, while leads and lags in foreign payments and receipts made it difficult for capital controls to shield current account transactions from exchange rate fluctuations. Remittances of saving by foreign workers in the domestic economy and by residents working abroad as well as tourist expenditures, were also used as vehicles for the acquisition of foreign assets.

It can therefore be concluded that capital controls in South Africa, as in most other countries, were definitely not foolproof. On the other hand, exchange controls must have had some success in regulating capital flows. This one can clearly deduce from the considerable lobbying that took place to have these controls removed.

Although exchange control was therefore relatively successful in keeping domestic savings within the country, it had a number of disadvantages, such as:

1. There was a conflict between controlling capital flows and the effective application of monetary policy. Monetary policy can only operate effectively if account is taken of the close relationship that exists between money supply, interest rates and exchange rates. Experience has shown that it is difficult to get the most desirable combination of these aggregates under exchange controls.
2. At times the exchange control measures in South Africa distorted domestic interest rate levels. For instance, a substantial rise in the gold price in the early 1980s led to a large increase in liquidity which, in turn, contributed to low levels of nominal and real levels of interest rates.
3. Exchange control deterred inward foreign investment in South Africa. It is inherently difficult to quantify to what extent South Africa did not receive new foreign investment on account of the existence of exchange control, but the mere fact that the country made use of capital controls probably constrained inward foreign investments significantly.
4. Exchange control is an economically inefficient way of rationing the available foreign exchange among the various domestic users. When not only the size but also the composition of the demand for foreign exchange is determined by administrative discretion, the chances are good that such a distribution of foreign exchange may by suboptimal.

5.   Exchange control has significant direct costs for the central bank
     and the private sector. The Reserve Bank and all authorized foreign
     exchange dealers have to employ a large number of people at a consid-
     erable cost to administer exchange control. In addition, other enter-
     prises in the private sector incur costs in dealing with exchange control
     matters and, in some instances, by employing outside professionals to
     assist them.

## A Gradual Removal of Exchange Control

In view of these disadvantages and as it became increasingly difficult to
apply exchange control effectively in an integrated globalized world, the
authorities decided to liberalize capital controls in South Africa. After
reaching this decision, they had to decide further whether to withdraw
exchange control immediately or to do it in a gradual manner. In the end a
gradual rather than abrupt approach of withdrawal was followed.

In retrospect this was probably a wise decision. After having applied one
or other form of restrictions on capital flows for more than 30 years, a 'big-
bang' approach could have led to a large outflow of capital. The risk of
applying such an approach was just too big, particularly in view of the
uncertainties regarding capital flows at the time. A phased approach allowed
the consequences of certain relaxations to be absorbed before further steps
were taken. Furthermore it enabled the economy to adjust slowly to the
shocks created by the removal of capital controls. Admittedly it at times also
led to speculation when the public expected relaxations to be announced.
However, an abrupt withdrawal would probably have exerted an excessive
downward pressure on the foreign reserves and the exchange rate of the
country, while it would also have caused interest rates to rise sharply.

The policy of gradually withdrawing exchange control allowed the
country some flexibility in managing large and volatile international capital
flows. During periods of large speculative capital outflows, the authorities
could be cautious in announcing exchange control relaxations, and vice
versa. However, once a control is relaxed it is difficult to reinstate it. With
the policy followed by the government, it would accordingly be difficult to
reimpose such restrictions in future without losing some credibility.

Taking recent crises in some emerging markets into consideration, the
question arises whether capital restrictions could not under certain circumstances play a useful role in reducing some of the volatility that seems
to be recurring all the time. In particular, restrictions that could change the
composition of capital flows could be useful in this regard. Such restrictions
must then of course only be applied as a temporary measure. Experience
has taught South Africa that this could be a dangerous approach to pursue,

because direct controls have a tendency to remain in place even long after the problem leading to their introduction has been solved. South Africa has therefore opted for the removal of all direct capital controls over time, which imply that other measures will have to be used to temper the effect of volatile capital flows on the domestic economy.

**The Appropriateness of Inflation Targeting as a Framework**

A further question regarding South Africa's monetary and exchange rate regime that could be asked is whether inflation targeting is the appropriate framework for the country to apply? Inflation targeting is sometimes regarded as less appropriate for emerging-market economies for a number of reasons, namely:

1. These economies are normally relatively open and are more exposed to external shocks than industrialized economies, which complicates the implementation of inflation targeting.
2. Most of the emerging-market countries are commodity-based economies where changes in international commodity prices have a large impact on prices and domestic economic activity.
3. Emerging-market economies are generally more dependent on international capital flows and their financial infrastructure is less developed than in advanced countries. Fluctuations in these flows therefore have a marked impact on emerging-market economies.
4. A large part of the obligations of banks, corporations and governments of emerging-market economies is denominated in foreign currencies, while domestic assets are generally mainly denominated in the local currency. These currency mismatches can be costly with large exchange rate changes which may make emerging-market countries less willing to apply a flexible exchange rate regime than industrialized countries.
5. Central banks in emerging-market economies do not have the autonomy to apply an inflation-targeting framework in a credible manner.

Although most of these characteristics are to a lesser or greater degree applicable in South Africa, the government has been able to introduce and apply an inflation-targeting framework with some success. South Africa is a relatively open economy with the value of exports and imports in total amounting to nearly 50 percent of gross domestic product. A large part of South African exports consist of agricultural and mining products such as gold, platinum, diamonds and wool, dependent on international commodity prices, while the low savings ratio at a level of 16 percent of gross domestic product makes the country heavily dependent on international capital flows. The exchange rate of the rand and the domestic inflation rate are therefore affected considerably by external shocks such as changes in international commodity prices or fluctuations in capital flows, and the overall balance of payments position of the country has always been an important constraining factor to sustainable high economic growth. When inflation targeting was introduced it was important to allow for the occurrence of such shocks by means of an escape clause and by specifying the inflation target in the form of a band. These measures allow for some flexibility in the determination of the monetary policy stance without loss of credibility.

Although South Africa's foreign currency-denominated liabilities exceed its foreign currency-denominated assets, this is not an important consideration in the determination of exchange rate policy. Well-developed money, capital and foreign exchange markets exist in the country which make it possible to hedge such open-risk positions. The financial markets in South Africa also react quickly to the monetary instruments that are applied, which reduces the delay in impacting on inflation and increases the effectiveness of monetary policy. Moreover, the country has sophisticated information and communication systems, which favor the application of an inflation-targeting monetary policy framework.

The South African Reserve Bank has a good record in South Africa and operates in an autonomous manner with minimum interference from government. In fact, the independence of the Reserve Bank is guaranteed and entrenched by the Constitution of South Africa which provides that in the pursuit of its primary objective, the Bank 'must perform its functions independently and without fear, favor or prejudice'. Although the inflation target is jointly set by government and the central bank to obtain coordination between policy measures, once the target has been determined the central bank is free to use any market-related instrument to achieve its ultimate objective.

## The Effectiveness of Inflation Targeting

South Africa therefore generally fulfills the preconditions that are necessary for the successful implementation of inflation targeting, and the relative openness of the economy has been taken into account in determining the framework within which decisions are made. The question then is how well has this system worked?

Unfortunately, a formal inflation-targeting framework was only introduced in South Africa in February 2000. This relatively short period over which it has been applied includes only one year, 2002, for which a target was specified. In 2002 the rate of increase in the overall consumer price index for metropolitan and other urban areas excluding mortgage interest costs (the CPIX) averaged 10 percent, or 4 percentage points above the upper limit of the target range. In a Statement of the Monetary Policy Committee on 20 March 2003 it was indicated that the target was not met, largely due to extraordinary events that could not be foreseen and which were beyond the control or influence of monetary policy.

Four factors were mainly responsible for the high rate of increase in the general price level in 2002, namely:

1. a sharp depreciation in the external value of the rand related to the contagion effects of the political situation in Zimbabwe, financial stability problems experienced in emerging-market economies such as Argentina and Turkey, increased risk-aversion of international investors and leads and lags in payments for imports and exports;
2. an increase in food prices of 16.7 percent in 2002 because of the depreciation of the currency and a drought experienced by some countries in Southern Africa;
3. an increase in international oil prices due to concerns about a possible US-led attack on Iraq and disruptions in the supply of oil resulting from general strikes in Venezuela; and
4. large increases in administered prices which have a weight of almost 25 percent in the CPIX.

When it became apparent that the inflation rate was starting to accelerate and that the inflation target would not be met, corrective measures were immediately taken to bring the rate of increase in CPIX within the target as soon as possible. The official lending rate of the Reserve Bank, the repo rate, was increased by 400 basis points in 2002 to slow down inflation. However, these measures probably would have been taken in an informal inflation-targeting framework or even under the targeting of monetary aggregates and therefore does not necessarily indicate that formal inflation targeting is a more efficient framework than these other monetary policy regimes. It is nevertheless interesting to consider whether these corrective measures would have been taken so soon under these other monetary policy frameworks. Inflation targeting provides a discipline which probably results in decisions being taken sooner than under the other monetary policy regimes.

More importantly, the application of inflation targeting in South Africa has increased the transparency of monetary policy. Considerable efforts have been made to explain to the public why certain monetary policy decisions were taken. This has been done by means of monetary policy statements released immediately after each meeting of the Monetary Policy Committee and Monetary Policy Reviews published twice a year. A number of Monetary Policy Forums have also been arranged in the major cities in South Africa; they take place every six months and monetary policy is discussed with interested persons. In addition, a presentation is made to the Portfolio Committee of Finance, a government committee concerned with financial matters, at the end of every quarter.

As a result of the introduction of inflation targeting, the forecasting models of the Reserve Bank have been improved considerably. With the help of central bank officials of the United Kingdom, Canada, Australia and Sweden, the Reserve Bank's econometric techniques and model structure were revised to facilitate decisionmaking. The prediction of inflation is of the utmost importance in the implementation of monetary policy as policy measures must be forward looking to be effective.

**The Effectiveness of Floating Exchange Rates**

The adoption of a freely floating exchange rate regime together with the inflation-targeting monetary policy framework have led to substantial swings in the exchange rate of the rand. The nominal effective exchange rate of the rand decreased by 12.5 percent in 2000 and 34.5 percent in 2001, but then increased again by 26 percent in 2002 and by 19 percent in the first four months of 2003.

The depreciation in the exchange rate of the rand during 2000 and 2001 mainly reflected the low level of foreign exchange reserves of the country and investors' concerns about developments in other emerging-market economies rather than weaknesses in fundamental economic factors in South Africa. It is further interesting to note that the exchange rate of the rand also depreciated substantially in the period of managed floating during the 1990s. For instance, in 1996 the weighted average exchange rate of the rand declined by 19 percent and in 1998 with the crisis in East Asia it decreased by 18.5 percent. Even when a relatively fixed exchange rate system was applied, the rand at times depreciated sharply. These recent changes in the exchange rate are therefore not necessarily related to the exchange rate regime that has been adopted, but probably rather reflect the liberalization of capital controls.

Perhaps even more interesting is the fact that the rand appreciated substantially during 2002 and the first four months of 2003. This was the first time in the past 30 years that such a sharp reversal in the exchange rate of the rand had occurred. In the past, the external value of the rand normally had a distinctly downward tendency. This recovery of the rand was probably related to sound macroeconomic policies pursued consistently by the authorities, relatively high interest rates in South Africa, uncertainties about economic conditions in most of the advanced economies and a general flow of funds to emerging-market economies.

**Floating versus Greater Exchange Rate Stability**

The wide fluctuations in the exchange rate of the rand obviously complicates monetary policy decisionmaking and the planning of enterprises involved in international trade. Why does South Africa then not rather opt for a more stable rather than a flexible exchange rate regime?

A number of reasons can be given for South Africa's preference for a flexible exchange rate regime. First, it has already attempted to maintain a more fixed exchange rate system by pegging the rand to the dollar, sterling and a basket of currency without any success. This caused the authorities to change to a flexible exchange rate approach.

Second, South Africa does not comply with the characteristics normally regarded as essential for the success of maintaining a more fixed exchange rate regime such as being a small country relatively open to foreign trade, with a high labor mobility, the availability of fiscal measures to cushion fluctuations in the business cycle, an adequate level of foreign exchange reserves, a well-supervised and regulated financial system, a business cycle correlating closely with that of the country to which the currency will be linked and the desire to integrate with a larger trading partner or currency area. With the exceptions of being highly dependent on foreign trade and having a sophisticated and efficiently regulated financial system, none of the other characteristics for a fixed exchange rate regime seems to apply in the case of South Africa.

Third, in a world of floating exchange rates it is impossible to obtain complete exchange rate stability. At most the rand can be pegged to one foreign currency, such as the US dollar, to which some other currencies may also be linked. But even then the rand would be floating with the dollar against all the other currencies not linked to it. The rand could also be pegged to a basket of currencies, but would then, of course, float against all of them. Floating in one form or another is therefore unavoidable under the present circumstances.

Finally, monetary policy flexibility is lost with dollarization, a currency board or fixed pegging. Interest rate levels are basically determined by the authorities of the country to which the domestic currency is pegged. Changes in interest rates will therefore be based on developments in another country without necessarily taking domestic economic conditions into consideration. This may lead to unstable conditions in the domestic economy and the attainment of low economic growth and employment creation.

Although South Africa has opted for a freely floating exchange rate regime, it would of course prefer to have greater exchange rate stability. As the Commission of Inquiry into the Monetary System and Monetary Policy has pointed out:

> Other things remaining equal, a more stable exchange rate would be preferable to a less stable one. But if the choice for South Africa lies, as it does under the present international exchange rate regime, between general economic stability and exchange rate stability, the former is clearly preferable to the latter (p. 123).

In these circumstances, South Africa is therefore striving to obtain greater exchange rate stability by applying healthy macro- and microeconomic policy measures in a country with a high growth potential. Unfortunately, large swings in international capital flows are making it difficult to obtain this objective, and in many instances these fluctuations in capital flows are caused by developments in other countries.

## CONCLUSION

From this brief discussion regarding the exchange rate regime and monetary arrangements, the following conclusions can be drawn:

1.  Although South Africa is a relatively open commodity-based economy dependent on international capital flows which can fluctuate considerably, it nevertheless generally fulfills the preconditions that are necessary for the successful implementation of inflation targeting. Largely owing to extraordinary events that could not be foreseen and which were beyond the control of monetary policy, the target was not met in the first year for which it was specified.
2.  Inflation targeting has probably provided a greater discipline to monetary policy than that which would have applied with other monetary policy frameworks.
3.  With the integrated globalized financial markets it was essential to remove exchange control restrictions in a gradual manner, because these rulings were in conflict with the effective application of monetary policy, distorted domestic interest rate levels, deterred inward foreign investments and have significant direct and indirect costs.
4.  In view of the wide fluctuations in international capital flows, exchange controls that could change the composition of capital flows could be a useful measure to create stability, provided that it is applied on a

temporary basis. The problem is that such restrictions have a tendency to remain in place for a long period of time.

5. The liberalization of exchange controls has led to sharp fluctuations in the exchange rate of the rand. Such fluctuations must be accepted in a world of floating exchange rates because it is impossible to obtain exchange rate stability under present circumstances. Even in the case of pegging the rand to another currency or to a basket of currencies, dollarization or a currency board, the rand would still float against most currencies. Exchange rate stability can only be achieved with a major revision of the international exchange rate regime.

6. The recent wide fluctuations in the exchange rate of the rand have, however, considerably complicated the task of the monetary authorities. This was at times made even more difficult because some of the fluctuations in the capital flows were not related to domestic economic developments or policies, but were due to circumstances in other countries. Under present international arrangements it therefore seems even more important that monetary policy be aimed consistently at the achievement of financial stability.

## REFERENCE

Commission of Inquiry into the Monetary System and Monetary Policy in South Africa (1984), 'The monetary system and monetary policy in South Africa', RP 70/1984, Government Printer, Pretoria.

PART V


The Aftermath of the SDRM Debate: CACs
in Practice, Access Limits and the Concept of
a Code of Good Conduct

# 13. How can the cost of debt crises be reduced?

**Jeromin Zettelmeyer**[1]

## INTRODUCTION

There is a consensus that sovereign debt restructuring is difficult and costly for both creditors and debtors, and that the international financial architecture should be reformed in ways that reduce these costs. There is less consensus on what such reforms consist of. Reform initiatives since the early 1980s have included: creating a statutory regime for resolving sovereign debt crises, promoting the use of collective action clauses and other bond clauses that stipulate what to do in the event of a crisis, improving collective creditor representation, temporary standstills in connection with official lending into arrears, creating a code of conduct, and directly stabilizing debt prices through official lending or some kind of centralized fund (see Rogoff and Zettelmeyer 2002, for references and a survey). Not all of these initiatives are mutually exclusive. But they differ greatly, and reflect different understandings of the nature of the problem.

This chapter makes the point that how one thinks about reducing the costs of debt crises should depend on why one thinks they are so costly in the first place. It briefly sketches two schools of thought, and interprets some recent reform proposals in that context. It then turns to a particular way of thinking about the costs of debt restructuring that has received less attention so far, but has some interesting implications for the reform program. This focuses on the idea that high restructuring costs are a substitute for explicit legal seniority, and that they could be reduced if legal seniority in sovereign debt markets is allowed to develop through either statutory or contractual means.

## HISTORICAL ACCIDENT AND INERTIA

The most widespread view of debt restructuring costs is that they reflect the shortcomings of the present 'international financial architecture' – in other words, the collection of existing institutions, contractual arrangements and policy practices at the international level. This 'architecture' in turn is taken as a given, that is, its components are viewed as either exogenous or as policy parameters that can be changed, though perhaps at a cost. The debate then focuses on how to draw the line between truly exogenous aspects of the architecture and the policy parameters, and on how the latter should be changed (if at all). What is common to this way of thinking is a willingness to set aside the question of *why* contractual arrangements, institutions and policies at the international level are as they are. The endogenous variables in this school are the behavior of market participants (including national policymakers) that operate *within* this architecture. The architecture itself is not endogenous.

The 'architecture' analogy is quite suggestive. The analogy is one of a house, or perhaps a city, that was inherited from history. It exists in its present form because it was built in a particular way in the past, in response to incentives or needs that may have little to do with those of its present inhabitants. Things that are considered part of the 'architecture' do not generally change by themselves: they must be changed through a policy or institutional reform effort. But the good news is that with such an effort, most structures can be torn down and rebuilt, or at least renovated and cleaned up. Unlike in Oscar Wilde's *Canterville Ghost*, an attempt to clean the carpets will not lead to the stain mysteriously reappearing the next morning.

While not explicitly asked, the question of why the present architecture exists is thus implicitly answered by pointing to a combination of history and inertia. Institutions are set up in ways that may be ill-suited to today's problems. Contracts follow models that are inherited or copied from other markets. For example, sovereign bonds issued in a particular jurisdiction may not generally contain collective action clauses because *corporate* bonds in the same jurisdiction are barred from having them, and sovereign bonds simply follow that template. Changes to the status quo are difficult because they require coordination. In the international institutions, majorities must be found that support amendments or policy reforms. Even at the level of individual contracts, it is hard to go against market practice. First-mover problems abound.

From the perspective of the policy debate, the implication is that there is little in the present architecture that one would assume to be efficient, or even that would reflect optimizing behavior in the absence of inertia and status quo bias. Consequently, the argumentative threshold for making a case for architecture reform is not that high. One merely needs to argue that the architecture gives rise to costly and inefficient *outcomes*. For example, if the practice of issuing sovereign bonds that are hard to restructure largely reflects history and inertia, it is very unlikely to be efficient in any broader sense. So the observation that this practice gives rise to collective action problems that create or prolong debt crises may be enough to justify a reform proposal, such as the more widespread use of collective action clauses, or a statutory insolvency regime. This is the way in which the architecture debate has traditionally been conducted, both in the official and in the academic community.

The traditional view is attractive for two reasons. First, one feels that the 'history and inertia' paradigm contains a large dose of truth. Anyone working at a large international or national institution will tell you that. Second, even when the paradigm is wrong, ignoring the 'why' behind the present architecture may be an acceptable short cut. Policy prescriptions based on observed outcomes alone may well be robust to possible stories that rationalize the status quo.

But there is a risk that this might not be the case. Then, reform prescriptions may be counterproductive or simply wasted. As in Wilde's tale, efforts to clean the carpet would simply lead to the stain reappearing the following morning, although perhaps in a different color. To get rid of the stain, we would have to exorcise the ghost. At a minimum, we would have to take account of the actions that the ghost might come up with after we have left the room.

## ENDOGENOUS DEFAULT COSTS

At the opposite end of the spectrum is the view that the costs of debt crises result from the optimal response of creditors and debtors to fundamental distortions and enforcement problems. Because of these problems, market participants purposely pick debt forms that are hard to restructure – for example, widely dispersed bonds without collective action clauses. This is inefficient *ex post* – after a default has occurred – but it may be efficient *ex ante*. In any case, it is an equilibrium outcome. Default costs cannot be reduced unless the fundamental reasons that give rise to equilibrium default costs are somehow addressed or at least mitigated.

The most popular variant of the endogenous default cost story is the idea that default costs are a consequence of a willingness-to-pay problem on the side of the debtor. The notion that default costs are the reason why sovereign debtors repay is quite established – it practically started the literature on sovereign debt in the early 1980s (see Eaton and Fernandez 1995 for a survey). From there, it requires a relatively small step to conclude that observed default costs should be viewed as endogenous. Debtors and creditors have some control over default costs through the way in which they write their contracts. Consequently, they will choose contracts that trade off the benefits of high default costs – deterring debt repudiation – with the deadweight costs that arise if defaults occur through no fault of the debtor. This idea was first worked out in the corporate debt context by Bolton and Scharfstein (1996), and in the sovereign context by Dooley (2000) and Dooley and Verma (2003).

The consequences of this view for the debate on reforming the international financial architecture are quite profound. First, it knocks down the presumption that if debt structures lead to inefficient outcomes, they will probably also be inefficient in any meaningful broader sense. If debt structures are chosen for a purpose, then they could quite possibly be efficient *ex ante* although they are inefficient *ex post*, and messing with them might make things worse overall. Second, to the extent that debt structures are endogenous, attempts to change them by reforming the international financial architecture might be an illusion unless the deep enforcement problems to which they respond are also affected by the reform. This is the argument expressed in the carpet stain analogy.

Collective action clauses are the most obvious application of this pessimism, as Dooley himself observes in his 2000 paper. According to his view, attempts to reform the international financial architecture by encouraging more widespread use of collective action clauses cannot possibly be successful, because these clauses were available to market participants before and yet were purposely not chosen. In this view, arm-twisting market participants into adopting such clauses will result either in increased borrowing costs, which may be inefficient *ex ante*, or in no change at all, if market participants find ways to recreate default costs that offset the impact of these clauses (or if the clauses did not have an appreciable impact on default costs to begin with).

Statutory approaches such as the Sovereign Debt Restructuring Mechanism (SDRM, see International Monetary Fund 2003) also become harder to justify under the endogenous default cost view, but fare a bit better than collective action clauses. The traditional argument that creating institutions that reduce the cost and time of debt restructuring is a good thing no longer applies automatically. However, statutory proposals could be welfare improving for two reasons. First, they may actually address a deep distortion, which is the inability of contracts to condition default costs on the reasons why the country defaulted. For example, some statutory proposals have argued that orderly insolvency procedures should only be accessible to countries that demonstrate unsustainable debt burdens by some objective criterion. This criterion roughly maps into the distinction between 'strategic defaults', that is, debt repudiations, and 'bad luck defaults'. If it could be implemented, it would eliminate the deadweight loss arising from the fact that participants are stuck with contracts that are hard to renegotiate even when defaults arise through no fault of the debtor.

Second, even if the statutory mechanism does not make the distinction between bad luck defaults and repudiations, it could be welfare improving if default costs under the status quo are excessive not just in an *ex post* sense but also *ex ante*. As will become clearer below, the fact that default costs are endogenous does not mean that they are necessarily at *ex ante* efficient levels. In the presence of incomplete contracts or additional distortions, default costs might be too high even from the perspective of deterring default *ex ante*.

In sum, the endogenous default cost view provides a theory of how costly debt crises could arise as a consequence of optimizing behavior. As such, it holds the debate on reforming the international financial architecture to a higher standard: a particular proposal must be shown to lead to an improvement not just *ex post* but also *ex ante*. Its main limitation is that it underemphasizes contractual and institutional inertia, by assuming that contractual structures are chosen optimally each time, and ignoring coordination problems that may limit those choices. Consequently, some of its conclusions – in particular, on collective action clauses – are too strong.

Another limitation – although this arises mainly from faulty interpretation of the endogenous default cost view rather than the approach itself – is that it invites a Panglossian view of the world. From the idea that contracts reflect optimal choices, it is easy to conclude that they are also efficient, and that because of that, any attempt to reform the international financial architecture is pointless. As illustrated in the next section, this is not necessarily the case.

## DEFAULT COSTS AND THE EXCLUSIVITY PROBLEM

We now turn to a variant of the endogenous default cost approach which focuses on an incomplete contracts problem in debt markets which has been recognized for some time – starting with seminal papers by Sachs and Cohen (1982) and Kletzer (1984) – but has until recently received relatively little attention. This is sometimes referred to as the 'exclusivity problem'. In a nutshell, the exclusivity problem is that debtors cannot commit not to issue additional debt in the future. If they do, this will have the effect of diluting the claims of existing debt holders. There are several channels through which this can happen. The most obvious one is that if the extra borrowing is used for consumption, there will be the same fixed amount of recoverable assets to go around in a default, which will have to be divided by more creditors. (More generally, dilution through a pure quantity effect will occur if the extra borrowing does not generate proportionally higher assets that could be distributed in the event of a default.) Other channels include issuance of new short-term debt, or debt that is harder to restructure, so new debt holders have effective seniority in the sense that they will be the last to experience default.

Since the initial debt holders realize the possibility that their claims may be diluted, they will reflect this in the original borrowing terms, so the exclusivity problem ultimately backfires on the debtor country. Assuming that default costs are fixed, there are two possible consequences: interest rates are higher than if the country could commit not to borrow further (see Kletzer, or a simpler sketch of Kletzer's model by Eaton 2004), or the country may be excluded from debt markets altogether (Bolton and Jeanne 2004). However, if the country has some control over the costs it faces in the event of a default, it can mitigate the consequences of the exclusivity problem by locking in higher default costs (ibid). For example, it can issue the initial debt in a form that is very hard to restructure, and thus less prone to dilution. But this gives rise to deadweight losses if a default occurs out of bad luck. As shown by Bolton and Jeanne, this is not just inefficient *ex post*, but also inefficient *ex ante*. In the face of an exclusivity problem, equilibrium default costs are *higher* than the (constrained efficient) default costs that would arise in response to the standard willingness-to-pay problem.

Because the exclusivity problem gives rise to debt contracts that are inefficient *ex ante*, changes in the financial architecture can make a positive difference. There are several avenues through which reforms might work. First, to the extent that dilution is achieved by making new debt harder to restructure than old debt, a statutory insolvency mechanism such as the SDRM – under which the cost of restructuring is effectively equalized for all unsecured debt – would remove the problem. Since the *ex post* restructuring cost is lower under an SDRM, the country would *ex post* always be better off by invoking it. Thus, the presence of an SDRM would effectively shut down one channel through which dilution can occur, namely issuing new debt with high restructuring costs. However, the SDRM as it is designed at present would not deal with dilution via a pure quantity effect – the main channel described above – since under the SDRM earlier debt holders would not have priority, but would be treated just the same as subsequent debt holders.

The one reform that could deal with the exclusivity problem in all its incarnations is a mechanism that would allow old debt to achieve *explicit* seniority over new debt. This has the same effect as removing the distortion directly by allowing debtors to commit to a particular debt level, that is, making future debt issues impossible. With explicit seniority, the debtor could still issue debt in the future, but this would be subordinated to the old debt. For this reason, the possibility of future debt issues are not a concern for the initial debt holders, and will not be reflected in the initial borrowing terms. In turn, this implies that the country has no incentives to contract in debt structures that are excessively hard to restructure and result in excessively costly debt crises if things do not evolve as planned.

## TOWARD EXPLICIT SENIORITY IN SOVEREIGN DEBT

Currently, there is only one mechanism through which countries can issue debt that is explicitly senior, namely collateralization by existing assets or future receivables. Collateralized borrowing is unlikely to be a solution to the exclusivity problem for two reasons. First, with few exceptions (mainly, some oil or gas exporting countries), it is small as a share of public external debt in emerging markets and developing countries (about 6.5 percent of total bonds and loans outstanding in 2002, according to a recent IMF study). This is presumably a consequence of the sovereign nature of the debtor. Second, to the extent that governments do not fully take into account future taxpayer interests in their borrowing decisions, one would not want to push a form of borrowing which eliminates default as a last-resort recourse after irresponsible borrowing behavior in the past. Since governments sometimes face significant incentives to overborrow (see Bolton 2003 for a summary of arguments) collateralized debt may be *too* senior from a domestic welfare perspective.

Other than through collateralization, the main form of creating legal seniority at the corporate level is through subordination (see Wood 1990). Specifically, a creditor could establish seniority through a covenant in his/her debt contract that prohibits the debtor from issuing any subsequent debt unless it is subordinated to the initial creditor's claims. The form of subordination could be flexible. Without undermining its basic purpose, certain forms of credit, such as trade credit, might be exempted and regular scheduled principal and interest payments to the junior debtor outside a default situation could be allowed.

At present, seniority through contractual subordination is not observed in sovereign debt markets for at least two reasons. First, it requires constant monitoring of the debtor by the initial creditor. As Bolton and Skeel (2003) observe, if the debtor manages to issue future debt that is not subordinated, then the initial creditor may not be able to enforce his/her priority claim in the event of default. Second, it requires a legal regime that enforces the priority implicit in contracts in the event of default.

Creating an institutional and legal environment that would allow these conditions to be met for sovereign debt is difficult, but feasible. It could be attempted in the context of a new statutory regime, as proposed in a recent paper by Bolton and Skeel. However, embedding explicit legal seniority in a new statutory regime may not be necessary. Many of the features of that regime follow from objectives that go beyond the enforcement of priority, namely, eliminating collective action problems before, during and after the debt restructuring and ensuring interim financing. Both the IMF's SDRM proposal and the Bolton and Skeel proposal focus on these objectives as a way of lowering the costs of debt restructuring *ex post*, that is, regardless of how contracts were written. But if excessive debt restructuring costs are in part a reflection of the lack of priority, then enforcing priority alone would reduce the costs of restructuring *indirectly*, by encouraging debt forms that are easier to restructure. Since statutory proposals such as the SDRM (and by extension, the more ambitious Bolton–Skeel proposal) do not currently have the requisite support in the international financial community, reforms that allow the enforcement of contractual priority should be pursued separately if they can be achieved with a more modest legal apparatus.

Indications are that this might indeed be the case. Crucially, enforcing priority *across creditors* does not require any action that would conflict with the sovereignty of the *debtor*. Nor does it require shielding the debtor from legal action either during or after the debt restructuring, in a way that would require changes to national laws. All that is required is that the junior creditor be forced to surrender any payments received in contravention of the subordination stipulated in his/her (and the initial creditor's) debt contract. This could be enforced by the courts in the jurisdiction in which the subordinated debt was issued. Doing this would not require an amendment of the IMF's Articles of Agreement. In fact, it might not require any statutory changes at all. In particular, if the senior creditor is a party to subsequent debt contracts between the country and the junior creditor, then priority could be established on a purely contractual basis. Inclusion of the senior creditor as a party in future debt contracts – or an inter creditor agreement in additon to the debt contract – could be required by the initial debt contract. These subsequent contracts would then require that any payments received by the junior creditor (perhaps excepting regular scheduled payments that take place while the senior creditor is also being paid, or prior to some trigger that reflects the solvency of the country, such as its overall level of indebtedness) be held on trust for the senior creditor. This structure of contracts would allow the senior creditor to sue the junior creditor in the event that priority is not respected.

As stated above, a critical requirement for this form of subordination to work – and presumably one reason why we have not observed it in the past – is the difficulty of monitoring debtor behavior. This is where the main institutional change is required. Dealing with the exclusivity problem in sovereign debt, through explicit seniority or otherwise, requires transparency in debtor behavior – ideally, through a global registry of sovereign debt, as has been periodically proposed since the 1980s debt crisis (for example, Eaton 2004; Kaeser 1990). This would have to capture not only bond issues, which are generally well publicized, but also loans. A statutory change that makes debt registration compulsory might be contemplated. But it is possible that the credit markets themselves might create sufficient incentives for countries to register their debts, since countries that are suspected of hiding debts from the registry would face higher borrowing costs.

## SUMMARY

Reform proposals that attempt to reduce the costs of debt crises tend to assume (implicitly) that the contracts and institutions that influence debt restructuring costs largely result from historical accident and inertia. While there is some truth to this view, it ignores the fact that debt contracts are written by the market participants in a way that may be a response to deep distortions in the sovereign debt market. One of these deep distortions is the 'exclusivity problem': the problem that creditors can never be sure that their claims will not be diluted by future borrowing of the debtor country. To avoid the high borrowing costs (or exclusion from credit markets) that result from the exclusivity problem, debtors have an incentive to issue debt that give rise to inefficiently high default costs. This is one of the reasons why debt crises are so costly, and why it has been so difficult to persuade debtors and creditors to adopt more flexible debt contracts.

The most effective solution to the exclusivity problem is to foster the creation of an explicit legal seniority structure in sovereign debt. With explicit seniority, initial creditors will not have to worry about dilution, and the incentive to contract in debt forms that are hard to restructure is reduced. The creation of an explicit legal seniority structure will require reforms, but probably not a statutory change at the international level. This is because the objective of those reforms would not be to reduce debt restructuring costs *ex post* – that is, regardless of how contracts have been written – but merely to change incentives in a way that persuades market participants to adopt more flexible debt structures. The most significant piece of the reform would be an international debt registry which creates transparency about the indebtedness and debt contract terms of each debtor country. This would help creditors monitor the behavior of debtors in a way that allows debt contracts to restrict the contractual form (and perhaps quantity) of future borrowing.

## NOTE

1. The views expressed in this chapter are those of the author and do not necessarily represent the views or policies of the IMF.

## REFERENCES

Bolton, Patrick (2003), 'Toward a statutory approach to sovereign debt restructuring: lessons from corporate bankruptcy practice around the world', IMF Staff Paper no. 50 special issue, 41–71; International Monetary Fund, Washington, DC.

Bolton, Patrick and Olivier Jeanne (2004), 'Structuring and restructuring sovereign debt: the role of seniority', draft, February, available from the authors.

Bolton, Patrick and David S. Scharfstein (1996), 'Optimal debt structure and the number of creditors', *Journal of Political Economy*, **104** (1), 1–25.

Bolton, Patrick and David Skeel (2003), 'Inside the black box: how should a sovereign bankruptcy framework be structured', draft, April, available from the authors.

Dooley, Michael P. (2000), 'Can output losses following international financial crises be avoided?', NBER Working Paper no. 7531, National Bureau of Economic Research, Cambridge, MA.

Dooley, Michael P. and Sujata Verma (2003), 'Rescue packages and output losses following crises', in Michael P. Dooley and Jeffrey A. Frankel (eds), *Managing Currency Crises in Emerging Markets*, Chicago: University of Chicago Press, pp. 125–46.

Eaton, Jonathan (2004), 'Standstills and an international bankruptcy court', in Andrew G. Haldane (ed.), *Fixing Financial Crises in the Twenty-first Century*, Chapter 15, London and New York: Routledge, pp. 261–76. www.bankofengland. co.uk/conferences/conf0207/main.htm.

Eaton, Jonathan and Raquel Fernandez (1995), 'Sovereign debt', in Gene M. Grossman and Kenneth Rogoff (eds), *Handbook of International Economics*, Vol. 3, Amsterdam: North-Holland pp. 2031–77.

International Monetary Fund (2003), 'Report of the Managing Director to the International Monetary and Financial Committee on a Statutory Sovereign Debt Restructuring Mechanism', April, www.imf.org/external/np/omd/2003/040803.htm.

Kaeser, Daniel (1990), 'Pour un système équitable de désendettement' (proposal for an equitable debt reduction system), speech given at a Swissaid forum on solutions to the debt crisis, Lausanne, October, available from the author. Shorter versions of the speech were published in *Schweizerische Handelszeitung*, 5 April 1990, and *Domaine Public*, 1 November 1990.

Kletzer, Kenneth M. (1984), 'Asymmetries of information and LDC borrowing with sovereign risk', *Economic Journal*, **94** (374), 287–307.

Rogoff, Kenneth and Jeromin Zettelmeyer (2002), 'Bankruptcy procedures for sovereigns: a history of ideas, 1976–2001', *IMF Staff Papers*, **49** (3), 470–507.

Sachs, Jeffrey and Daniel Cohen (1982), 'LDC borrowing with default risk', NBER Working Paper no. 0925, July, National Bureau of Economic Research, Cambridge, MA.

Wood, Philip R. (1990), *The Law of Subordinated Debt*, London: Sweet & Maxwell.

271- 93

( LDC<sub>s</sub>)

# 14. Who is the cheapest-cost avoider in the sovereign debt market? Restating the case for the SDRM and greater restraint in IMF lending[1]

**Curzio Giannini**

## INTRODUCTION

The debate on the international financial architecture, if we take the Mexican crisis of 1994–95 as its starting point, has now been going on for almost a decade. While a sense of fatigue is inevitable in the circumstances, outright skepticism would be misplaced. Institutional reform is a complex process. At the international level, the process gets even more complex, due to both the greater number and diversity of actors, and the comparatively underdeveloped institutional environment.

Yet, successful institutional reform is not a novelty at the international level. The long-standing realist claim that international cooperation is but a cover for power struggle has long been disproved. Two prominent examples suffice to make the case. Before the Second World War no one predicted that the major countries would ever agree on a formal treaty enshrining fairly precise rules of the game for their monetary relations. Yet, not only was the Bretton Woods Treaty negotiated but it can *post factum* also be considered to have been an astounding success, since the post-war era has been the longest period of high growth and monetary stability that the West has ever known. In Europe, in the same vein, many predicted as late as the early 1990s that the project to decouple monetary union from political union would never take off. But fiat powers, we have learned, can also be shared, when countries perceive it is in their best interest to do so. As a result, we now have the euro, which is also proving instrumental in paving the way for ever-deeper political integration across the European Union (EU).

Admittedly, the present debate has been hindered by a failure to build a consensus view as to what are the features of the present environment that need to be fixed, and why. Too many conflicting claims still coexist in the literature, often reverberating on policy statements. If identification of a market failure is clearly not sufficient to trigger a policy response, as a result of collective action problems or governmental failures, we certainly cannot expect determined action when the market failure to be cured is itself in doubt.

In this chapter I shall not tackle all the issues raised in the debate on the international financial architecture. Rather, I shall focus on only one area, which, however, does seem to lie at the core of the discussion – the area of sovereign debt crises and their resolution. First, I shall try to clear the ground from those exaggerated claims I referred to above. Second, I shall restate the case for the new international financial architecture, relying on the notion of cheapest-cost avoider, drawn from the law and economics toolbox. Then, I shall assess the results so far achieved, arguing that they are far from negligible and that in the main they go in the right direction. Finally, I shall discuss the reasons why the present opposition of the private financial community to the reform of the international financial architecture may have been overstated. Historically, the financial community has often opposed institutional change, only to join the ranks of its advocates *post factum*. And indeed, views within the private sector have already changed considerably since the inception of the debate. Further experience, especially in connection with the resolution of the Argentine crisis, may convince private investors that in this case, too, institutional reform may also be in their interest.

## THREE EXAGGERATED CLAIMS

The debate on the international financial architecture has been hindered by a few recurrent claims that in my view are vastly exaggerated, and therefore unproductive. I think it useful to clear the ground from them before moving on.

*Proposition 1*  The IMF cannot and should not act as lender of last resort (LOLR) for countries.

This is the easiest proposition to dispose of. One could argue that the IMF was indeed conceived to be a special type of lender of last resort from the outset. Article I of the IMF Statute states that one of the fundamental purposes of the organization is 'to give confidence to members by making the general resources of the Fund temporarily available to them under adequate safeguards, thus providing them with opportunity to correct maladjustments in their balance of payments without resorting to measures destructive of national or international prosperity'. Of course, the framers of the statute envisaged a limited LOLR role, as testified by the prohibition to lend against 'a large or sustained outflow of capital' (Article VI), and the mechanism for adjusting exchange rate parities in the presence of a 'fundamental disequilibrium'. However, the environment in which the IMF operates has undergone considerable change since then, and the institution has adjusted to the new environment with the tacit (and sometimes explicit) consent of its membership. The prohibition of Article VI, formally still in place, has been the first to give – a reminder that statutory provisions are binding only to the extent that they are believed to be useful by at least some shareholders. With capital account convertibility, the IMF has gradually expanded its confidence-enhancing role, through not only its crisis packages, but also its precautionary programs and surveillance.

The legal argument being found wanting or at best ineffective, there are two more ways to rationalize proposition 1 on economic grounds. The first would be by pointing at the inability of the IMF (due to its credit union structure) to create money *ex nihilo* (Capie 2002). But the idea that the LOLR needs under all circumstances unlimited access to resources rests on a confusion between lending in support of market trades (which is now best portrayed as a form of monetary policy) and lending in support of individual institutions, which does not imply money creation powers. When referring to IMF dealings with borrowing countries, it is the latter concept that matters (Freixas et al. 2000). Hence, the key issue is not whether the IMF could or should be an international LOLR, but rather how LOLR activity could best be organized at the international level to allow for the greater complexity of the economic, legal and institutional environment. The second way would be by emphasizing the moral hazard generated by the IMF's LOLR operations. But this, argument, too, is hard to square with the fact that IMF lending, at least so far, has contained no clearly discernible subsidy element (Jeanne and Zettelmeyer 2001). To produce moral hazard, an LOLR has to socialize at least some of the costs from private risk taking. So far, this has not been the case. And the distinction between creditor moral hazard and debtor moral hazard *per se* is not helpful, because, in the absence of frictions, to avoid moral hazard it is sufficient that one of the sides in a creditor relation bears the cost of risk taking – a straightforward application of the Modigliani–Miller theorem. If there are frictions, of course, the way costs are allocated may impinge on the overall efficiency of the institutional set-up – a theme

I shall return to in the next section. But this has nothing to do with moral hazard as such.

*Proposition 2*    The main market failure to be corrected through changes in the international financial architecture relates to creditor coordination.

Coordinating creditors in case of default is always a problem, the more so in the typically highly fragmented bond markets. But is this the main problem we have? I would contend not. In the past, creditors did manage to coordinate themselves irrespective of collective action problems when they perceived a clear interest in doing so. Both in the second half of the nineteenth century and in the 1930s – two periods in which recourse to bond finance was widespread – creditors readily formed voluntary committees to foster their interests. And they were effective in the endeavor, since actual yields on average compensated investors for interruptions to debt service and write-downs of principal (Eichengreen 1991). Nor can one attribute this striking outcome to greater involvement on the part of creditor countries' governments in the negotiations, since authorities rarely resorted to aggressive trade policy to extract concessions in favor of their citizens from defaulting countries. The main reason behind such high *ex post* yields seems to be that, after defaulting, countries recognized that the sooner they settled old scores, the sooner they would be allowed to access the capital market again. Indeed, regarding the 1930s there is evidence that countries that interrupted debt service recovered more quickly from the Great Depression than did countries that resisted default (Eichengreen and Portes 1990).

If creditors managed to coordinate themselves so effectively in the past, why should they find it harder to do so today? One reason could be the existence of contract provisions, like acceleration clauses, which tend to trigger automatic responses in the face of a hostile act by the debtor, thereby making a considered reaction by creditors more difficult to achieve. Another possible reason is that the availability of large sums of IMF financing in the presence of a capital account crisis alters the incentives under which both debtors and creditors operate: the nastier the crisis, the more likely an IMF package will be forthcoming (Miller and Zhang 2000). Prima facie, this last reason is made plausible by the fact that the existence of the IMF is by far the most conspicuous difference between our present international financial environment and that of the 1930s.

Whatever the true reason, however, it is clear that creditor problems *per se* cannot explain why sovereign default is perceived to be a bigger problem now than it used to be. One must dig deeper to understand why the international financial architecture has become such a prominent issue in the authorities' agenda.

*Proposition 3*   Any attempt to establish an international analogue to domestic insolvency procedures would entail the disruption of the sovereign debt market.

This proposition is often heard, and has been made most forcefully by Dooley (2000) and Shleifer (2003). The underlying idea is that the inability of debtors and creditors to quickly renegotiate contracts is an endogenous response to one peculiarity of international financial dealings involving sovereign entities – the impossibility of seizing assets held by the sovereign within its jurisdiction. Any attempt to dilute creditor rights, by making renegotiation easier, would impede the functioning of the debt market.

Plausible as it may sound at first blush, the proposition does not stand closer scrutiny. The purpose of bankruptcy proceedings is not that of pre-judging the interests of one or the other of the parties involved in any specific instance. Rather, they have a twofold objective: to preserve the debtor's assets from unnecessary dissipation; and to reduce uncertainty as regards the process through which assets will be allocated after default, thereby hopefully reducing overall transaction costs. The existence of procedures to achieve these ends is more important than the substance of any specific procedure. And in fact there is considerable variety around the world concerning the mechanics of insolvency rules, as a result of differences in local legal traditions and societal preferences. Those who fear that the sovereign debt market might be disrupted by the establishment of explicit rules for dealing with international insolvency assume that such a proceeding would resemble the US Chapter 11, which is often cited as a very pro-debtor insolvency regime. But, as mentioned, all insolvency procedures are to some extent 'pro-debtor', since they must avert unnecessary asset dissipation. The real question then is: how much protection should debtors be afforded in order to improve social welfare? An answer to this question cannot be given in abstract terms, and I shall come back to it in the next section with reference to the sovereign debt market. But there are at least three reasons to find proposition 3 an unproductive oversimplification. First, Chapter 11 does not exhaust the range of possible insolvency regimes to be taken as a model. A recent report issued under the aegis of the G10 deputies, for example, distinguishes between stakeholder- and official-centered insolvency rules, based on the role courts actually play during a firm's reorganization (Contact Group 2002). In the light of the greater legal fragmentation of the international environment, there can be little doubt that any sovereign insolvency regime would have to be of the former variety, that is, it should give greater voice to creditors in the resolution process than is normally the case in official-centered regimes. Second, to assess the extent to which a particular insolvency regime is pro-debtor, one has to go beyond the surface. For instance, what are we to make of the fact that practitioners estimate that more than 50 percent of US corporate restructurings take place in the shadow of the law, that is, without invoking Chapter 11?[2] Does this make the US bankruptcy regime overall more pro-creditor or more pro-debtor? Finally, it sounds somewhat paradoxical that opponents of sovereign insolvency rules, like Shleifer (2003), should cite the US municipal bond market as a model, in terms of average spreads and default rates, for sovereign debt. US municipalities, in fact, are subject to a special chapter of the insolvency regime – Chapter 9 – which on paper looks even more pro-debtor than Chapter 11. If Chapter 9 has delivered such good results, why should it not be replicated, with all the necessary adaptations, internationally?[3] Surely, either there must be some missing link in the argument, or one must admit that the distinction between pro-creditor and pro-debtor systems is too vague to be of any use.

In sum, there seems to be ground to believe that a sovereign insolvency system would disrupt the sovereign debt market no more than the development of national bankruptcy rules has disrupted national financial markets. This does not mean that anything would be acceptable. The devil, as always, will reside in the detail. But, as Rogoff has recently remarked, a well-designed sovereign insolvency proceeding, 'is no more likely to encourage bad habits among responsible governments than a new lung cancer treatment would encourage non-smokers to start smoking' (Rogoff 2003). As to irresponsible governments, it is not clear why creditors should feel that their rights are better protected in the current institutional vacuum than in a world featuring predictable and dependable procedures for dealing with sovereign insolvency.

## WHAT IS THE PROBLEM?

The international environment has two features that distinguish it from the domestic environment. Both have to do with the notion of sovereignty. First, property rights at the international level are not backed by a universally agreed and predictable enforcement structure. This makes them fundamentally weaker than in a national context. Second, debtors' actions, either directly in the case of a sovereign borrower or indirectly in the case of a corporate borrower, are affected by the vagaries of domestic politics in the recipient country. This means that the 'debtor' is a form of collective action in disguise: its actions will be the outcome of a game between many principals (the various interest groups) with conflicting interests and an agent (the government) which may also have an agenda of its own. Treating the 'debtor' as an individual endowed with stable preferences and perfect rationality, as most of our analytical models do, is likely to have very little heuristic potential (Dixit 1998). Political economy considerations are an inevitable component of the debtor–creditor relationship at the international level.

These two features combined are a source of strain for international financial relations. Weak property rights tend to reduce the equilibrium level of international lending. 'Myopic' governments, that is, governments that do not seem to maximize any discernible social welfare function, by contrast, produce a tendency to overborrowing. Painful debt crises can be considered a consequence of this tension. Let us defer once more to Rogoff (2003) for a neat and concise description of the mechanism:

> [B]y making defaults extremely costly, risky forms of debt – particularly those that are prone to collective action problems – provide a measure of confidence to international investors . . . In other words default costs provide a punishment that in some sense substitutes for effective property rights at the international level.

But in what sense are defaults costly for the borrowing country? Even though waivers of sovereign immunity are now common practice, there are typically very few assets that dissatisfied creditors can attach when a sovereign defaults. If defaults are costly, it is because they entail in some sense a prohibition on future borrowing: unlike financial firms, and to some extent also unlike corporate borrowers, sovereign debtors after default incur a financing gap that, barring further external borrowing, needs to be eliminated through a current account reversal. Of course, the country may well find a lender willing to take the risk of providing money while debt service is suspended, since the prohibition on lending has no legal status. But such lending may itself be attached by other creditors through the legal system. Thus, without legal protection the debtor is for all practical purposes unable to raise additional finance, and has to undergo output costs in order to achieve the needed current account reversal.

Now, as Rogoff himself remarks, default costs of this type are a very poor substitute for stronger property rights. That is, they may be seen as an inefficient solution to the problem. To see why, a concept drawn from the law and economics toolkit can prove very helpful. When allocating the cost of accidents between the various parties involved, the law, and the judges that are asked to interpret it, have to make a judgment about who is the cheapest-cost avoider. This means identifying the party which, due to its means, skills or resources, is in a position to take least-cost action to minimize the chances that the accident will occur again in the future. The principle, which is due to Calabresi (1970), is intrinsically dynamic, and aims at reducing social costs by modifying the incentives rather than by static cost minimization.

One can make the case that relying on default costs only tends to pick the wrong cost avoider, because it does not duly allow for the second peculiarity of the international environment, namely, the intrinsically political nature of the debtor. The local taxpayer as a rule has in fact only a limited grip on its government's actions, which as mentioned above are the result of a game among many principals. Moreover, incumbent governments may have an incentive, to prolong their stay in office, to conceal relevant information or act against the interest of the majority of their citizens. This does not mean that countries will always be unreliable borrowers. Domestic political constraints can be changed, and there are indeed countries that manage to strengthen their policymaking and their institutions. But in the short run, domestic political constraints lead to delays in recognizing the existence of an external debt problem, and to gradualism in changing policy course when the need is finally recognized. Above all, as explained by Johnson (1997), they make the probability of success of a given policy change endogenous, namely, dependent on how consensus is built and preserved around the new policy regime. This gives incumbent governments an incentive to postpone recognizing the existence of a debt problem, to avoid unpopular action to stem it. All the while, by contrast, private investors, which consist in the main of financial institutions specializing in active portfolio management and information processing, are free to react in real time as they see fit. The result of this basic asymmetry is that most of the time there is a tendency, in the sovereign debt market, to 'overborrowing', or 'overlending', accompanied by episodes of what Guillermo Calvo has called 'sudden stops', with potential international spillovers.

Note that the very existence of the IMF is an implicit recognition of the inefficiency of the market solution to the tension. If we really thought that default costs were an optimal response to the peculiarities of the international environment, why care to have an institution mandated with the task indicated in the already quoted Article 1 of the IMF's statute?

The general move to capital account liberalization has scaled up the IMF's task in this respect considerably. Under the pressure of events, the IMF (indeed, the official community at large), has developed the notion of catalytic official finance (COF). However, this is not the place to review the theoretical underpinnings and historical evolution of this notion.[4] For our purposes, it suffices to say that COF is an attempt to avert outright default by applying a recipe comprising three ingredients: strong policy conditionality, large but nonetheless limited (in the sense of not covering the whole financing gap) financial support, and reliance on private finance to make up for the part of the financing gap not covered by official resources.

The problem with COF, however, is that it does not basically change the nature of the problem. Above all, COF does not make up for the lack of legal protection from which a country suffers in case of default: indeed, COF aims precisely at averting default. But this outcome cannot be taken for granted, and if default occurs then the IMF will be just another creditor in trouble – even more in trouble, given that COF implies by definition that large sums of money are lent. Thus, the IMF, like any other creditor, needs to protect itself from the risk of default. And this is done not only by imposing conditionality, but also through a careful rationing of disbursements, reliance on short-term lending and the application, when the SRF is used, of a penalty rate. As a whole, these practices amount to a recognition of the resilience of domestic political constraints and of the uncertainty surrounding the success of the agreed policy package. And a side-effect of their use is that of increasing the burden for the local taxpayer, whose grip on its government's policies remains limited. But why should private investors, whose actions remain equally 'sovereign', that is, voluntary, throughout, feel reassured by an LOLR that needs to protect itself from the very risk it is supposed to insure against, thereby possibly also increasing this risk? As a consequence, COF may even be counterproductive: while *ex post* it may fail to restore confidence, knowledge that it will be forthcoming if things go wrong may discourage careful monitoring on the part of lenders.

The argument may be given a theoretical twist. What many often fail to realize is that an LOLR policy, at both the national and international levels, is optimal only on the assumption that the LOLR itself has either superior information or superior enforcement powers with respect to private investors. In all other cases, a policy of debt service suspension can be shown to be socially preferable.[5] This fairly robust result of the theoretical literature on debt crises has been consistently ignored in the policy debate.

There is no reason to go to the other extreme, and argue that COF will always be ineffective. There will be cases where the time gained through an IMF catalytic package will be used to relax the domestic political constraints and set the country on the right policy course. Indeed, the recent crisis management history features a number of success stories, from Mexico (1994–95), to Brazil (1999), and possibly to Korea (1998). However, one could make the case that these success stories are better explained in terms of superior enforcement powers (Mexico) and reliance on moral suasion (Brazil and Korea) than on COF *per se*. Thus, it is fair to say that the record of COF is in general rather weak. Even when it appears to have finally functioned, it led, with the exception of Brazil in 1999, to a far higher amount of domestic adjustment than originally envisaged (Figure 14.1). Moreover, in some cases COF was clearly used, for lack of better alternatives, to handle unsustainable debt situations, with Argentina being the most prominent example, although probably not the only one. And, finally, the frequent use of COF (and the need to regularly 'augment' official resources in the process to make up for the disappointing contribution of

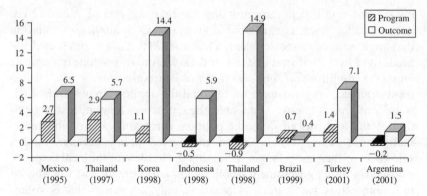

*Sources:* IMF, *World Economic Outlook* database; Ghosh et al. (2002).

*Figure 14.1   Current account adjustment in selected crisis countries (as a percentage of GDP)*

the private sector) has left the IMF with a concentration of risks in its portfolio never seen before (and probably very uncommon in central bank history, either), as shown in Figure 14.2. Jeanne and Zettelmeyer (2001) are probably right, as I have argued above, that IMF lending in the past has contained no subsidy element, since the repayment record of the IMF is so good that its loans can be considered significantly less risky than private loans, so that lower-than-market interest rates were justified. But does this apply to the present situation? One hopes so, of course. But the fact that Argentine authorities have used the threat of default on IMF loans as a bargaining chip should be taken as a further warning that COF is a two-edged sword, to be used more sparingly than has been the case.

Overall, I think these are good reasons not so much to disavow COF, but rather to complement it with tools that make it feasible for the debtor countries to take earlier action to counter a dangerous debt path. Such tools must allow the country to raise additional money while a debt restructuring is pending, along the lines of the 'debtor-in-possession financing' common to many domestic insolvency proceedings. To the extent that they do so, they will have the immediate impact of reducing default costs, and therefore of shifting part of the burden for crisis handling from the local taxpayer to the international investor. But this form of burden sharing has no punitive purposes, nor is it based on equity considerations. Rather, it is predicated on the assumption that the private investor is a better cost avoider, namely, that it is better placed to assess risks and take measures to discipline borrowers than the local taxpayer. The existence of the IMF

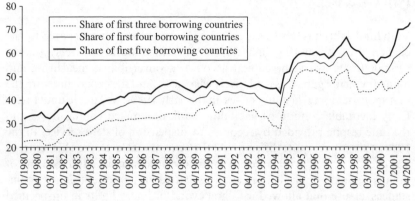

Source: Based on IMF data.

*Figure 14.2  Concentration in IMF lending* (percentages)

simply cannot substitute for responsible risk taking at the international level. At the end of the process, if the strategy is implemented consistently, there should be fewer crises, and the resolution costs of those that break out will be lower. But there can be no guarantee that this result will come about. All depends on achieving the right blend of determination and pragmatism on the three key components of the strategy: (a) action to reduce the immediate cost for the borrower of approaching its creditors to negotiate a debt settlement (so that the debtor will be encouraged to take early action); (b) action to make more rigorous the access policy of the IMF (so that IMF resources will not be used to postpone facing a problem of debt unsustainability); and (c) action to develop rules and procedures to keep the inevitable conflict of interests between debtors and creditors from turning into open hostility (to minimize negotiation costs).

## ARE WE MAKING PROGRESS?

Institutional reform simply cannot be expected to take place overnight, the more so since any genuine act of institution building is unprecedented. The future being unknown, contracts fundamentally incomplete and interests often conflicting, the pros and cons must be carefully identified and assessed at each step of the reform process. Theory will provide at best limited guidance. Bearing this statement in mind, the answer to the question in the title of this section is an unqualified 'yes', for the following reasons.

**IMF Access Policy**

With hindsight, it is fair to say that the IMF was caught unprepared by the challenge of promoting financial stability in a world of freely mobile capital. In the world of capital account inconvertibility, measuring and filling financing gaps was a relatively easy task. And the experience with the first spate of capital account crises, in the early 1980s, was made under relatively favorable conditions, including bank-dominated capital flows and the time respite provided by recourse to suspension of debt service. In the 1990s, things were quite different. At the operational level, the IMF entered the decade armed with a set of ordinary access limits (100 percent of quotas annually and 300 percent cumulatively), an 'exceptional circumstances' clause that allowed it to go beyond ordinary limits in unspecified circumstances, and a range of facilities optimized for dealing with standard macroeconomic and structural problems. Under the pressure of events, two new facilities, embodying considerable departures from previous practice, were set up. Of these, the contingent credit line (CCL) was on paper the most innovative, as it was meant to prevent crises through a form of *ex ante* conditionality, but it had no practical impact. As of today, in spite of a subsequent revision to make it more attractive to eligible borrowers, no country has yet applied for the CCL.

The story of the supplemental reserve facility (SRF) is somewhat more complex. Established in 1998 in the midst of the Asian crises, the SRF was built around Walter Bagehot's old idea that LOLR operations should be unlimited in size and based on penalty rates and a short-term lending horizon. Accordingly, the facility was subject to no access limit, so that it could be used for large loans without invoking the exceptional circumstances clause. However, from the standpoint of the debtor country borrowing large amounts of money short term and at penalty rates implied a heavy burden, difficult to meet under the stress conditions typical of a capital account crisis. Thus, over time the IMF developed the practice of blending the SRF with other facilities subject to ordinary limits. To achieve the required blend, in most cases the exceptional circumstances clause had to be invoked. The result of all this was a great confusion as to the rules being followed by the IMF in its access policy. Were ordinary limits meant to apply to all lending, or just to some facilities? Were capital account crises meant to be handled through SRF lending only, or through a varying mix of facilities according to circumstances? What were people to make of the exceptional circumstances clause, given its increasingly frequent use? What was the meaning of an exception recurring more often than the norm?

Against this background, it is no surprise that access policy should have figured so prominently in the reform effort. In early 2003, the IMF board reconsidered both the facilities to be used and the criteria to be followed in dealing with capital account crises. As regards the CCL, the review process is still underway, and will not be completed before November 2003, when the facility is due to expire. But there is now much skepticism within the official community as to the facility's real potential.[6] With relation to the overall access policy, the board has agreed on a set of criteria and procedures to be followed when exceptional access is invoked in connection with a capital account crisis.[7] Of the four substantive criteria, the most important is that the country should face a debt burden that appears sustainable under rather unfavorable circumstances. Procedural requirement include instead early board involvement in the decision process and an *ex post* evaluation of the decision eventually taken. Since criteria and procedures apply to IMF lending, irrespective of the facility used, it follows that they will have to be met also for SRF financing.

The new access policy represents a very important progress over past practice. Exceptional access in connection with capital account crises from now on cannot be taken as a matter of course. But what if a country faces a large current account crisis? The question is not trivial, since all countries hit by a capital account crisis since 1994 also ran a current account deficit, with figures ranging from 2 to 8 percent of GDP (Ghosh et al. 2002). And, after all, the exceptional circumstances clause has not been explicitly abrogated. Thus it is possible that the existence of a large current account deficit could be used to exert pressure on the IMF to grant exceptional access to a country whose external debt does not appear to be sustainable. Recognizing the loophole, at its 2003 Spring meetings the IMFC has clarified that the new procedural requirements will apply to all exceptional access proposals, irrespective of the underlying causes. But nothing was said of the relevant criteria – and it is criteria, rather than mere procedures, which matter when political pressure starts mounting. Probably, an explicit abrogation of the exceptional circumstances clause would have been preferable, but is hard to tell how important the loophole actually is. So, one cannot but concur with the managing director, who at the Spring meetings made the point that 'the ways in which these criteria and procedures are applied in practice in reaching judgments about access will be decisive, and an assessment is planned by the end of the year'.

**Collective Action Clauses**

When CACs were advocated for the first time, in the G10 Rey Report (Group of Ten 1996), it was made clear that their evolution should be 'a market-led process if it is to be successful', and that 'such effort should receive official support as appropriate'. In fact, the reverse is probably closer to what has actually happened. Given the lack of enthusiasm on the part of the private sector, the G10 deputies took the initiative of designing model clauses. The private sector followed suit, proposing its own set of model clauses. The main difference between the two sets lies with the required majority for changing the terms of the original claim, which is higher in the private sector's version. But on the whole the two sets are broadly consistent, and the fact that the official and the private sectors now find themselves in agreement on the need to promote CACs is an important achievement. Wisely, the IMF has acknowledged that it does not befit it to endorse model clauses, as it is for debtors and creditors to find which formulation suit them best, in keeping also with local legal traditions.

The growing consensus on the desirability of CACs in the private sector has also had the effect of mollifying the debtor countries' reluctance to adopt them, which was the most serious obstacle perceived within the official community. Thus, Egypt, Lebanon, Qatar and finally Mexico, have issued significant amounts of bonds governed by New York Law and including CACs. The EU, which had already announced that it would issue bonds with CACs in 2002, has also finally agreed to pass to the operational phase starting in June 2003. Since the reception of the new bonds has been very favorable in a number of countries, it seems likely that other important emerging market countries will adopt CACs in the near future. On its part, the IMF has committed itself to promoting CACs through its surveillance and outreach activities.

The main task now is that of embodying CACs within a code of good conduct regulating relations between debtors and creditors in the delicate phase of CACs' activation, to prevent the inevitable conflicts of interest from degenerating into hostile acts. Following an initiative by the Banque de France, the G7 is taking leadership on this front, in collaboration with eminent personalities of the private sector.

**Sovereign Debt Restructuring Mechanism**

When, in November 2001, Anne Krueger made her by now famous speech advocating an SDRM, many were taken aback, interpreting the new policy as a U-turn with respect to past practices. This interpretation, however, is inaccurate. Already at the time of the drafting of the Rey Report, in fact, the IMF had made the point that sovereign bankruptcy proceedings might facilitate orderly workouts, provided that the IMF's Articles of Agreement were modified to provide adequate legal backing. It was the Rey Group which, after prolonged discussions, concluded that 'the establishment of a formal international bankruptcy procedure would not be feasible or appropriate under present circumstances or in the foreseeable future' (Group of

Ten 1996, p. iii). In the following years, the IMF simply took stock of its main shareholders' view, and concentrated on making the most out of the existing tools. The main merit of Anne Krueger's speech lay in drawing everybody's attention to the need for reopening the discussion on the 'rules of the game'. It was in some sense a provocation, and a welcome one, for which she deserves full credit.

Krueger lamented that the lack of a sovereign bankruptcy mechanism had two undesirable consequences. First, 'it can lead a sovereign with unsustainable debts to delay seeking a restructuring, draining its reserves and leaving the debtor and the majority of its creditors worse off'. Second, 'it can complicate the process of working out an equitable debt restructuring that returns the country to sustainability' (Krueger 2002, p. 2). Taken together, these two features justified action aimed at 'preserving asset value', namely, at reducing the immediate cost for the country of approaching its creditors to seek a restructuring. This raised two practical problems, though. By how much should costs be reduced, and how? The original proposals made by Krueger appeared to many (the present writer included), as too intrusive, as they implied giving the IMF the authority to endorse a stay on creditor litigation, so that the sovereign debtor would have automatic protection from disruptive legal action while restructuring negotiations were underway, and also the power to adjudicate dispute at the end of the process. This expanded role of the IMF appeared inappropriate not only because the institution lacked the necessary competence (a gap that could easily be filled over time) but, more deeply, because the IMF, as a privileged lender, would have conflicting interests with the creditors it would be expected to rule. As discussions progressed, two further reasons for being more flexible on the matter of the stay emerged. On the one hand, legal experts pointed out that the risk of a 'grab race' on the part of dissatisfied creditors in the sovereign debt market appears rather remote. As a matter of fact, litigation is an extremely rare phenomenon in sovereign dealings, and tends to take place, if at all, after a restructuring has been agreed with the majority of creditors. An automatic stay would therefore be in some sense redundant, an unnecessary complication. On the other hand, since the key feature, from the debtor's standpoint, of a formalized work-out would be its ability to guarantee 'debtor-in-possession' financing, and given that the IMF's lending into arrears policy looked like the natural candidate for such financing, it seemed more sensible to find ways to make lending into arrears (LIA) acceptable to creditors and not too generous for sovereign debtors than unnecessarily depriving creditors of their rights.[8]

As a result of these considerations and of the ongoing dialogue between the IMF, the private sector, the legal community and policy circles, the original proposal has gradually been modified, becoming on the whole more flexible and at the same time more consensual than originally envisaged. The possibility of a stay on creditor rights has been preserved, but its enactment has been left to creditors themselves to stem free-riding behavior within their ranks. At the same time, the role envisaged for the IMF within the mechanism has been greatly reduced. Under the present scheme, the IMF would be given no new legal power, and it would continue signaling its stance through its willingness to support and provide assistance for a country's adjustment program. To this end, in the meantime (in September 2002) the board revisited LIA policy to clarify the 'good faith' criterion introduced back in 1999. This review, which aimed at making LIA more palatable to private investors in a context where creditor rights have not been suspended, resulted in the listing of a number of steps the debtor country's government should undertake when seeking a restructuring. These guidelines could and should usefully be integrated into the code of good conduct being drafted in relation to CACs, already mentioned above. The new formulation appears to place the SDRM, in terms of the costs it might entail for the debtor, somewhere between a purely voluntary restructuring and outright default, with a desirable incentive structure (Bossone and Sdralevich 2002). Implementation of the scheme, therefore, may well result, as is now the case in several national contexts, in most restructurings taking place 'in the shadow of the law'. Although there are still several open issues to be settled (among which the possible merits of including into the SDRM bilateral official finance and the structure and functioning of the dispute resolution forum) one can safely argue that much progress has been accomplished in the design of a reasonable and realistic sovereign bankruptcy mechanism. The time may not yet be ripe for its implementation, an issue I shall turn to in the next section. But the technical work is almost done, which is *per se* proof of the seriousness with which the IMF and the official community at large has gone about the task.

## WHAT ARE THE MAIN STUMBLING BLOCKS?

Even if CACs became standard practice for all new bond issues, there would remain two problems: retroactivity and aggregation. As regards retroactivity, how are we to make sure that CACs will gradually be extended to all outstanding bonds? Early on in the discussion on the two-track approach, the option of introducing into the legal system of the main financial centers so called meta-clauses was contemplated, but soon discarded on the ground that the move would be too intrusive and possibly difficult to implement. The next-best alternative would appear to be swapping old bonds for new ones featuring CACs. But these swaps would be difficult to organize unless the issuing country already had a debt problem and was willing to approach its creditors for a restructuring. An interesting experiment is going on in this respect in Uruguay. This country has recently launched a swap operation of about $5 billion, which, relying on the use of exit consents, aims at reducing the debt burden by lengthening the maturity of the relevant bonds, and introducing CACs in the new bonds accepted by its creditors. The main obstacle ahead lies in the very high participation rate (90 percent of principal) required for the operation to go through, which cannot be taken for granted given that exit consents were not originally conceived to alter pecuniary aspects of existing bonds. To increase the chances of success of the operation, the IMF has thrust its weight in support of Uruguay, by making it clear that the conclusion of the swap will be a precondition for a new IMF program. At the time of writing, however, there is yet no indication as to creditors' reactions.

However, the room for experimentation appears rather limited in the area of aggregation. Even if all bonds (new and outstanding) included CACs, a country seeking a restructuring would have to approach (and await a response from) as many groups of bondholders as there are issues. In the case of Argentina, for example, which has more than 100 different bond issues outstanding, accomplishing this part of the task would already have appeared nightmarish.

Aggregation is the one issue over which the SDRM has a clear comparative advantage over the contractual approach (of course, if we are willing to concede that voluntary swaps can take care of the retroactivity problem). But support in favor of the SDRM is at present so scant that it is hard to envisage that the scheme will come to fruition any time soon. How are we to explain the present lack of support? The temptation to blame the present stalemate on divergences within the official sector, with the Europeans keener on the SDRM and the Americans much cooler, is great, but should be resisted. The existence of differences on the two shores of the Atlantic cannot be denied, but it does not seem to be the key issue. The SDRM is supposed to change the framework within which debtors and creditors interact. It is to them, then, that one should turn to understand the present resistance to change.

As regards private creditors, there can be no mistake: they are at present strongly opposed to the SDRM. This is understandable. No one would like to be singled out as the cheapest-cost avoider in any given context. It takes much persuasion, and possibly some hard fact, to show that a short-term cost may be the necessary price on the road to a larger long-run gain. As Bolton (2002) remarks, bankruptcy reform at the national level has always been the subject of political strains and important ideological divisions, and it has often been enacted with very thin majorities, although post factum the usefulness of the reform has rapidly established itself. Why should the international discussion prove different? As he puts it: 'while similar ideological divisions on the necessity and orientation of a statutory sovereign debt restructuring exists today, the day may well come when such a procedure is seen as an essential building block of the international financial architecture' (p. 13).

Two precedents taken from post-war international financial history indicate that Bolton might indeed be right. People have long forgotten that the Bretton Woods scheme, and in particular the establishment of the International Monetary Fund, were strongly opposed by the two major financial establishments of the time, Wall Street and the City, on the ground that, if implemented, it would fuel moral hazard on the debtor side. In the words of the influential American Bankers Association (ABA) (1943):

> [A] system of quotas or shares in a pool which gives debtor countries the impression that they have a right to credits up to some amounts is unsound in principle, and raises hopes that cannot be realized. Such a system would encourage the impression that credits received may not have to be liquidated, and would invite abuses of the facilities.

The ABA fought strenuously against the Bretton Woods agreement, and was defeated only because the US administration was willing to stage an impressive campaign to convince public opinion that a resumption of growth worldwide and multilateralism would better serve American interests than a narrow defense of the creditor community.[9]

The second example is more recent, and perhaps even more telling. When CACs were first propounded, in combination with LIA and recourse to temporary standstills, in the G10 Rey Report (Group of Ten 1996), the reaction of the financial community was incredibly harsh. Even before the publication of the document, the Institute of International Finance (IIF 1996) issued a letter in which the Report's recommendations were called 'misguided', on the ground that they would run against the principle that contracts are to be honored and would therefore fuel (again!) moral hazard on the debtor's side. However, some further years of experience and reflection have apparently convinced the IIF that the Rey Report's recommendations had some merit after all, since CACs now figure prominently in the organization's list of recommended actions!

All in all, although the views of the various parties in the negotiations should all be respected and factored into the policy agenda, history instructs us not to overemphasize the financial sector's opposition to institutional reform, which is a long-standing feature of capitalist development (Arrighi 1994). Financial firms, like all other parties, act on the basis of the options they perceive. In this light, the true test of whether an SDRM is desirable, and feasible, will be the resolution of the Argentine crisis. Perceptions may rapidly change in its aftermath.

It is perhaps more striking that some debtor countries should oppose the SDRM. But here, too, there is ground for optimism. Many emerging market countries clearly perceive the SDRM as a progress. Misgivings still loom only in some Latin American countries, like Mexico and Brazil. But again this is understandable, since these are the two countries where COF seems to have functioned, namely, which managed to stem a crisis without resorting to debt restructuring. Why should they now support a reform that might result in the short run in higher risk premia, or in a reduction of capital flows to emerging markets as a whole? To the concerns of such countries, one might respond in two ways. First, by pointing out that the present level of capital flows to emerging market countries is already pretty low as compared to the early 1990s, and this clearly has nothing to do with the SDRM, which does not yet exist (Figure 14.3). More likely, it has to do with changes in perceptions as to the availability of official finance to make up for emerging markets' financing gaps, a feature that is bound to stay. Given this, the SDRM can only improve the outlook for emerging markets as a whole. Second, institutional reform can never be tailored to specific needs. If well conceived, it expands the range of options, not the opposite. As I have argued before, and in keeping with repeated official statements, COF will remain an option for countries whose external debt burden appears sustainable under alternative scenarios. Mexico and Brazil may well continue to fall in this category in the future. If so, they may voluntarily opt out from the SDRM, in the sense of committing themselves not to invoke the scheme. Their own not-too-distant past, however, should instruct them to question the wisdom of such an approach.

## CONCLUSION

I have argued that the main objective of the present effort to revise crisis management practices is to encourage countries to take early action to counter an unsustainable debt path.

To do so, creditors must be willing to take a greater share of the immediate burden of a country's suspension of debt service, on the assumption that they are better cost avoiders than sovereign debtors. At the end of the process, if the strategy is implemented consistently, there may be fewer crises, and the resolution costs of those that break out will be lower. Successful institution-building does not consist in choosing a point along a given trade-off. Rather, it is a conscious attempt to shift the curve so as to improve social welfare.

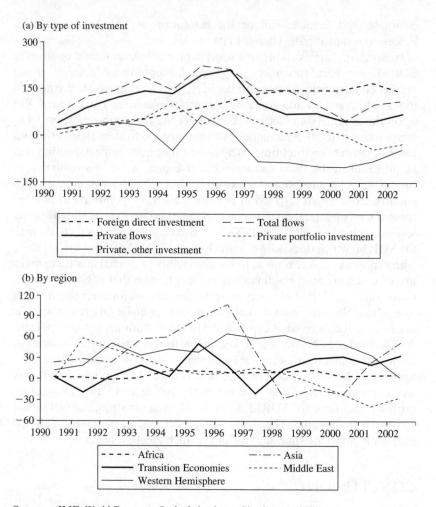

*Sources:*   IMF, *World Economic Outlook* database; Ghosh et al. (2002).

*Figure 14.3   Net private capital flows to emerging markets, 1990–2002* (in billions of US dollars)

I have also made the point that to look at the SDRM in isolation would be dangerous. More than the specific details of the scheme, what matters is that sovereign bankruptcy proceedings be cast within an overall 'vision' of the role of the IMF. Furthermore, a vision which places less emphasis on the role of lender and more emphasis on the role of certifier of sound economic policies and enforcer of an agreed code of good conduct. This twofold role of certifier and enforcer needs only to be acknowledged and refined, with determination and pragmatism; but it is already there. Recent developments in the area of access policy, CACs and the SDRM are only making it more visible, and cogent.

A notable omission in this chapter concerns whether and how to amend the IMF's Statute. I believe this issue to be of secondary importance, not because the task would be extremely complex – after all, we live in a challenging world, so we should not be deterred by a specific challenge, daunting as it might be. But much of value could probably be achieved through more modest moves, such as marginally changing national legislation in key financial centers, or reviving, if necessary through new interpretations, passages of the IMF Articles of Agreement that have lain dormant or simply been unexplored for decades. Legal experts tend to be wary of partial moves, fearing they would not stand the test of an unsympathetic court. But, courts, like everybody else in the 'market', respond to signals and incentives. The lack of a fully worked-out international legal system need not be seen only as a hindrance. Under certain circumstances, it could also prove a blessing, if sufficient political consensus were to be mustered on the desired innovations. And consensus grows out of persuasion and experience. On both fronts, time is working in favor of the reformers.

## NOTES

1. The views expressed in the chapter are the author's only, and do not necessarily reflect those of the Banca d'Italia. Comments by Biagio Bossone and Carlo Cottarelli on a previous draft are gratefully acknowledged.
2. See Gilson (1996).
3. The reason why Chapter 9 seems to work so effectively is related to the need of municipalities to raise additional money while in default. When the Orange County of California defaulted, in 1994, the County's government issued a leaflet to explain its negotiating behavior. To the question 'why can't we just forget about that debt?', the posted answer was 'if we don't pay, it will have a tremendous and negative impact on Orange County. We would find it very difficult to enter the bond markets, which is why we pay for building roads, flood control facilities, jails, freeways, etc., to support a growing economy'. This motivation helps explain why governments, be they local or national, resist default to the greatest possible extent, and often try voluntarily to negotiate debt settlement agreements. I shall develop this argument in the next section.
4. For a survey of COF's history and empirical record, see Cottarelli and Giannini (2002).
5. See Wallace (1988) and Rogoff (1999).
6. At the Spring Meetings, the IMF has been urged by the International Monetary and Financial Committee (IMFC) to explore other ways, including precautionary programs, to foster the CCL's objective, especially concerning crisis prevention.
7. The new policy has not changed the definition of normal access, which remains set at 100 percent of quota annually and at 300 percent cumulatively.
8. The problem of protecting LIA from legal dispute is often neglected in public discourse, but it has played an important role in the development of the IMF's legal thinking on

crisis management. That the issue is still unresolved can be gauged by the fact that the program agreed with Argentina in early 2003, which provided a limited cash relief to Argentina interpretable as LIA, was crafted in such a way as not to imply actual disbursements of new money from the IMF.
9.   Gardner's (1969) account of the Bretton Woods negotiations still makes illuminating reading.

# BIBLIOGRAPHY

American Bankers Association (1943), *The Place of the United States in the Post-War Economy*, New York: ABA, September.

Arrighi, Giovanni (1994), *The Long Twentieth Century. Money, Power, and the Origins of Our Time*, London: Verso.

Bolton, Patrick (2002), 'Towards a statutory approach to sovereign debt restructuring: lessons form corporate bankruptcy practice around the world', paper presented at the Annual Research Conference of the IMF, Washington, DC, 7–8, November.

Bossone, Biagio and Carlo Sdralevich (2002), 'The new approach to sovereign debt restructuring: setting the incentives right', IMF Policy Discussion Paper, PDP/02/4, International Monetary Fund, Washington, DC.

Calabresi, Guido (1970), *The Costs of Accidents: A Legal and Economic Analysis*, New Haven, CT: Yale University Press.

Calro, Guillermo, www.bsos.umd.edu/econ/ciecpp5.pdf.

Capie, Forrest (2002), 'Can there be an international lender-of-last-resort?', in Charles Goodhart and Gerhard Illing (eds), *Financial Crises, Contagion, and the Lender of Last Resort. A Reader*, Oxford: Oxford University Press.

Contact Group on the Legal and Institutional Underpinnings of the International Financial System (2002), 'Insolvency arrangements and contract enforceability', Basle, September, www.bis.org.

Cottarelli, Carlo and Curzio Giannini (2002), 'Bedfellows, hostages, or perfect strangers? Global capital markets and the catalytic effect of IMF crisis lending', IMF Working Paper, WP/02/193, International Monetary Fund, Washington, DC.

Dixit, Avinash (1998), *The Making Of Economic Policy. A Transaction-Cost Policy Perspective*, Cambridge, MA: MIT Press.

Dooley, Michael (2000), 'International financial architecture and strategic default: can financial crises be less painful?', Carnegie-Rochester Conference Series on Public Policy, 53.

Eichengreen, Barry (1991), 'Historical research on international lending and debt', *Journal of Economic Perspectives*, **2**, Spring.

Eichengreen, Barry and Richard Portes (1990), 'The interwar debt crisis and its aftermath', *World Bank Research Observer*, **5** (1), January.

Freixas, Xavier, Curzio Giannini, Glenn Hoggarth and Farouk Soussa (2000), 'Lender of last resort: what have we learned since Bagehot?', *Journal of Financial Services Research*, **18** (1).

Gardner, Richard (1969), *Sterling–Dollar Diplomacy. The Origins and the Prospects of Our International Economic Order*, New York: McGraw-Hill (expanded edn).

Ghosh, Atish, Timothy Lane, Marianne Schultze-Gattas, Aleš Bulir, Javier Hamann and Alex Mourmouras (2002), 'IMF-supported programs in capital account crises', Occasional Paper no. 210, International Monetary Fund, Washington, DC.

Giannini, Curzio (2002), 'Pitfalls in international crisis lending', in Charles Goodhart and Gerhard Illing (eds), *Financial Crises, Contagion, and the Lender of Last Resort. A Reader*, Oxford: Oxford University Press.

Gilson, Stuart C. (1996), 'Managing default: some evidence on how firms choose between workouts and Chapter 11', in J.S. Bandari and L.A. Weiss (eds), *Corporate Bankruptcy. Economic and Legal Perspectives*, Cambridge: Cambridge University Press.

Group of Ten (1996), *The Resolution of Sovereign Liquidity Crises* ('Rey Report'), Basle, May.

Haldane, Andy and Mark Kruger (2001), 'The resolution of international financial crises: private finance and public funds', Bank of Canada Working Paper, Ottawa, 2001–20, November.

Institute of International Finance (1996), *Resolving Sovereign Financial Arrears*, Washington, DC: Institute of International Finance.

Jeanne, Olivier and Jeromin Zettelmeyer (2001), 'International bailouts; moral hazard and conditionality', *Economic Policy*, **33**, October.

Johnson, Omotunde (1997), 'Policy reform as collective action', IMF Working Paper, WP/97/163, International Monetary Fund, Washington, DC.

Krueger, Anne O. (2002), *A New Approach to Sovereign Debt Restructuring*, Washington, DC: International Monetary Fund.

Miller, Marcus and Lei Zhang (2000), 'Sovereign liquidity crises: the strategic case for a payment standstill', *Economic Journal*, January.

Rogoff, Kenneth (1999), 'International institutions for reducing financial instability', *Journal of Economic Perspectives*, **4**, Fall.

Rogoff, Kenneth (2003), 'Emerging market debt. what is the problem?', paper presented at the Sovereign Debt Restructuring Mechanism Conference, IMF, Washington, DC, January.

Shleifer, Andrei (2003), 'Will the Sovereign debt market survive?', mimeo.

Wallace, Neil (1988), 'Another attempt to explain an illiquid banking system: the Diamond and Dybvig model with sequential service taken seriously', *Federal Bank of Minneapolis Quarterly Review*, Fall, **12** (4).

Zettelmeyer, Jeromin (2000), 'Can official crisis lending be counterproductive in the short-run?', *Economic Notes*, **29** (1), 13–29.

294- 306

# 15.  Towards a code for sovereign debt restructuring[1]

**Pierre Jaillet**

## INTRODUCTION

Since the adoption of the 'Prague framework' by the International Monetary and Financial Committee (IMFC)[2] in September 2000, the international official community has pursued and intensified its efforts to strengthen crisis prevention and resolution, in particular, ensuring that greater private sector involvement has been at the center of international discussions. Recently the focus has increasingly been on addressing sovereign debt restructuring and identifying ways to make it more orderly.

More generally, preventing excessive public debt accumulation has become a major concern of the international community as ill-conceived public policies have been clearly identified as a major cause of recent financial distress in emerging economies.

Recent experience has demonstrated that the risks of sovereign debt crises should not be overlooked. Sixteen months after defaulting on its external debt, Argentina embarked on the largest debt restructuring ever; Uruguay is currently planning to swap US$5.3 billion of bonds for new securities with a view to restoring medium-term debt sustainability.

While in the 1980s sovereign crises used to involve mostly bank loan rescheduling, recent episodes have increasingly entailed the renegotiation of sovereign bonds, reflecting the evolution in the external financing of emerging economies. (See Tables 15.1 and 15.2.)

So far, experience with sovereign bond restructuring suggests that collective action problems (that is, the difficulty of identifying bondholders, coordinating meetings with creditors and reaching an agreement supported by a large majority of creditors) are not as severe as many had feared. However, restructuring agreements have sometimes been difficult to achieve.

In some cases, the limited impact of catalytic official financing and/or the unwillingness of the official sector to envisage bailing out may lead a country to seek a partial or comprehensive debt restructuring consistent with the restoration of debt sustainability. The international community

*Table 15.1   Outstanding emerging market sovereign bonds*

| Applicable law | Issuer[1] | | | | | | Currency[2] | | | |
|---|---|---|---|---|---|---|---|---|---|---|
| | All EME | | Asia | Europe | Latin America | Middle East | US$ | € | DM | ¥ |
| | US$ | bn | | | | | | | | |
| Total | 555 | 269 | 62 | 156 | 274 | 63 | | | | |
| New York | 270 | 151 | 30 | 34 | 169 | 37 | 91 | 8 | 0 | 0 |
| English | 158 | 72 | 18 | 77 | 47 | 16 | 34 | 54 | 0 | 3 |
| German | 72 | 29 | 1 | 27 | 43 | 1 | 0 | 53 | 46 | 0 |
| Japanese | 55 | 17 | 13 | 18 | 15 | 9 | 0 | 0 | 0 | 100 |

*Notes:*
1. Number of bonds outstanding (unless otherwise specified).
2. Percent of total number of bonds outstanding issued under the same applicable law.

*Source:*   IMF.

*Table 15.2   Recent sovereign debt renegotiations*

| | Russia | Ukraine | Ecuador | Pakistan | Argentina |
|---|---|---|---|---|---|
| Old bonds involved | 3 | 5 | 5 | 3 | 152 |
| New bonds issued | 2 | 2 | 2 | 1 | – |
| Applicable laws | 1 | 3 | 2 | 1 | 8 |
| Amount restructured (US$ bn) | 31.6 | 2.6 | 6.6 | 0.61 | |
| Participation rate to the exchange | 98% | 95% | 97% | 95% | |
| Months between default and achievement of renegotiation | 18 | 3 | 10 | 2 | |
| Face value reduction | 36% | 0% | 40% | 0% | |
| Maturity extension | yes | yes | yes | yes | |
| Coupon reduction | no | yes | no | yes | |

*Source:*   Marx (2003).

has therefore an obvious interest in framing procedures that will ensure an optimal restructuring process, in order to minimize the cost of adjustment for the debtor and its creditors and also to prevent contagion at the regional or systemic level.

In view of its prominent role in crisis resolution and given identified short-comings, the IMF, in the 1990s, amended its internal process – procedures and access limits – for providing official support in crisis situations. The lack of a clear and predictable framework for crisis resolution has been perceived as increasing the risk of difficult and protracted negotiations, against the back-ground of subdued capital flows to emerging markets. Although in most cases the interest of private creditors is to enter into negotiations with sovereign debtors to protect their assets, creditors might delay negotiations for several reasons.[3] First, the heterogeneity of the creditors' group could result in coordi-nation difficulties, complicating the task of assembling a representative group. Second, not all creditors necessarily have an interest in maintaining long-term and/or commercial relationships with the debtor.

Until recently, the international debate has focused on two possible approaches for facilitating debt restructuring: the so-called 'contractual approach', based on the generalized inclusion of collective action clauses (CACs) in bond contracts (Box 15.1); and the 'statutory approach', that is, the IMF proposal of a Sovereign Debt Restructuring Mechanism (SDRM).[4] Not only are these two approaches different from a legal view-point, but they also differ with regard to their nature: (i) CACs are inserted in contracts *ex ante* with a view to facilitating the restructuring process of sovereign bonds; (ii) the SDRM would provide a comprehensive frame-work to deal *ex post* with sovereign debt problems, which relies on various statutory 'instruments' (for example, aggregation of claims, targeted stay on litigation, Dispute Resolution Forum).

---

### BOX 15.1   COLLECTIVE ACTION CLAUSES: RECENT DEVELOPMENTS

In September 2002, the G10 working group on CACs, chaired by R. Quarles (US Treasury), made recommendations to ministers and governors on the design of CACs (Group of Ten 2002). These recommendations aim at achieving three goals:*

1.  *Foster early dialogue, coordination and communication between parties through:*

    - a bondholder representative acting as an interlocutor with the sovereign during the life of the bond;
    - a mechanism for the election of a special bondholder rep-resentative. This representative should be empowered to

engage in restructuring discussions with the sovereign without undue delay;
- information sharing.

2. *Provide for effective means for parties to recontract, without a minority of debtholders obstructing the process:*

- a supermajority (typically 75 percent) of bondholders should be empowered to amend payments terms. The basis for the calculation of such a majority could vary according to applicable law and market practices;
- bonds directly or indirectly owned or controlled by the sovereign issuer and its public sector instrumentalities should be disenfranchised;
- a supermajority (typically 75 percent) of bondholders should be empowered to accept an exchange of the bonds for new instruments.

3. *Ensure that disruptive legal action by individual creditors does not hamper a workout that is underway:*

- a minimum of 25 percent of bondholders should be needed to accelerate repayments and another majority (with a maximum of 66.6 percent of vote) should be allowed to deaccelerate;
- the power to initiate litigation should be granted to the bondholder representative and individual enforcement should be explicitly prohibited;
- proceeds recovered by any bondholder should be distributed pro rata.

Following G10 recommendations, in February 2003, **Mexico** successfully issued bonds with CACs under New York law without incurring a significant penalty premium, thereby signalling that there might be room for wider use of such clauses by sovereign issuers. In addition, **European Union member states** indicated that, as of June 2003, CACs will be included in central government bonds issued under foreign jurisdiction.

*Note:* *The Report of the Group was published in March 2003.

The IMF initiative has served to promote a better understanding of the issues to be addressed in dealing with the resolution of crises. However, the IMFC stated that it is not feasible now to move forward to establish the SDRM, while recognizing that work should continue on issues that are of general relevance to the orderly resolution of crisis.[5]

Against this background, the international community has expressed interest in developing a non-statutory framework for addressing debt-servicing problems, based on a proposal of a 'code of good conduct' put forward by Governor Trichet.

We first examine the rationale for a code, before addressing its main features and the prerequisites for its effective implementation.

## THE *RAISON D'ÊTRE* OF A CODE OF GOOD CONDUCT

The key benefit of a code of good conduct would be to provide a comprehensive non-statutory framework to address debt-servicing problems while preserving, to the maximum extent possible, contractual agreements. Indeed, a code would spell out what is expected from all parties in times of sovereign financial distress and thus would provide a pragmatic way for stakeholders to optimize their behavior. This framework would provide common principles while ensuring the flexibility required for their implementation. In addition, a code of good conduct is intended to incorporate, or refer to various instruments and 'best practices'. For example, the widespread inclusion of CACs in debt contracts would facilitate the implementation of the code, although the code could be useful, in principle, in the absence of a CAC (for example, where not all bond contracts include CACs and/or other forms of debt have to be dealt with).

A code would list agreed-upon best practices on operational matters. By providing various options, it would ensure that creditors and debtors can adapt to the 'logic of circumstances' (see Box 15.2). Admittedly it is difficult to assess whether or not the debt is sustainable in the medium term. Experience indicates that making a judgment is rather complex and that temporary problems in servicing debt can turn into a major debt crisis.

## THE MAIN FEATURES OF A CODE OF GOOD CONDUCT

Basically, a code of good conduct seeks to clarify and improve the debt renegotiation process and/or provide elements on the interaction with the official sector, that is, the international financial institutions (IFIs).

---

## BOX 15.2 STYLIZED SCENARIOS FOR THE IMPLEMENTATION OF A CODE OF GOOD CONDUCT

As debt situations faced by countries are diverse and evolve rapidly, a code should be designed so as to deal with a broad range of situations that can be typified by three scenarios:

- In a first scenario (*alleviating tensions on sustainable debt*) characterized by sustainable debt over the medium term, a country faces short-term financial pressures and there are increasing expectations that the situation could deteriorate further. In order to prevent an unsustainable debt-dynamic from developing, proactive debt management or debt renegotiation might be contemplated by the debtor. In this context, creditors and debtors could usefully implement several principles of a code.
- In a second scenario (*renegotiating unsustainable debts, while remaining current*) characterized by unsustainable debt, the debtor triggers a debt renegotiation process, while still being able to service debt payments. An IMF program aiming at restoring debt sustainability over the medium term is designed. The principles and best practices of a code are expected to provide a comprehensive framework which would allow debtor and creditors to renegotiate new terms and conditions expeditiously, before the situation of the debtor deteriorates further.
- In a third scenario (*renegotiating unsustainable debt under a payment standstill*) characterized by unsustainable debt and a temporary payment standstill, the code would aim at reducing the risk of a non-cooperative debt restructuring process. Its implementation aims at ensuring the debtor's good faith and fair burden sharing among participants. The combination of an IMF adjustment program and lending into arrears is to be used as a critical instrument to reduce the severity of the crisis and ensure fair implementation of the code, including the good faith criterion.

---

**General Principles**

A code should first set general principles to be complied with building on earlier work,[6] seven principles have been identified as core elements of the code:

- *Early and regular dialogue based on trust among debtors and creditors* In order to reduce market overshooting following the debtor's decision to open negotiations about a restructuring, it is expected that a close and ongoing dialogue with its creditors, together with the provision of comprehensive and accurate information, will allow an early detection of debt-servicing difficulties. It will also help to achieve a broad creditors' participation in restructuring deals at a later stage, even though the initiative of the restructuring rests with the debtor.
- *Transparency of information*   Interested parties should ensure that fair information-sharing mechanisms are in place. Participants should be in a position to make an informed assessment of the economic and financial situation of the country, in particular to concur with the debtor on the unsustainability of the sovereign debt.
- *Fair representation of creditors*   Once the debt renegotiation process has been initiated, a fair representation of creditors will be key to agree on the terms of a restructuring.
- *Comparable treatment of the different creditors*   Once a debt renegotiation process has been initiated, specific procedures should ensure comparable treatment among creditors. This principle is essential since creditors will be reluctant to participate in a non-statutory cooperative process unless they are confident that free riders will not be rewarded. At the same time, there is a difficult balance to strike between an uncompromising implementation of the principle of comparability of treatment and the need to foster a deal agreeable to a majority of creditors, which require some flexibility in its implementation. In the same vein, the financing of critical activities might call for the exclusion of some categories of claims from the renegotiation process.
- *Economic and financial conditionality of debt rescheduling*   An efficient renegotiation process should primarily aim at enhancing or restoring, as soon as possible, a country's debt sustainability over the medium term. By committing themselves to working out a long-lasting solution, the creditors accept the principle that an agreement that would not restore debt sustainability is not viable and therefore that the net present value of their asset cannot be guaranteed.

- *Fair burden sharing between the different stakeholders* Debtor and creditors should commit themselves to seeking a fair burden sharing of debt restructuring costs.
- *Preservation, re-establishment or strengthening of normal financial relations between creditors and debtors* In particular, participants in the negotiation should commit themselves to negotiating in good faith. While seeking a solution to restore debt sustainability, the debtor should strive to minimize the cost incurred by creditors and to enforce contracts as long as possible. Similarly, creditors should recognize that the debt restructuring might require a writing down of their claims.

### Roadmap

A code should also provide a 'roadmap' by providing clear guidance to creditors and debtors. The roadmap should make it possible to determine the different phases of diagnosis and renegotiation, under various crisis scenarios. It should also spell out the role to be played by each party involved: debtor countries, private creditors (banks, bondholders and others) and official creditors. The key role of IFIs, in particular that of the IMF, in the different phases of renegotiation should also be specified.

A code would seek to protect contractual rights as far as possible. For the debtor, this would facilitate market re-access after the crisis. For creditors, the reference to the code is expected to reduce uncertainty about the restructuring process without increasing debtor moral hazard. Through ownership and appropriate incentives, it is expected to facilitate coordination among creditors, the debtor and the official sector so as to maximize the likelihood of success. Given the informal nature of the code, concerted agreement on standstills or stays will not bind rogue creditors. Yet, by establishing internationally recognized practices, a code could reduce creditors' incentives to hold out by raising the reputational risk of not acting cooperatively.

### Toolbox

A code should provide a 'tool box'. As the above principles can be implemented in a variety of ways depending on circumstances, a code should provide a whole range of internationally agreed 'instruments' and 'best practices'. A CAC is an indispensable instrument (see Box 15.1), and other instruments or best practices should be referred to or developed:

- *Structures for dialogue* There should be regular dialogue during renegotiation. The dialogue could take place within 'ad hoc steering committees' or standing bodies (for example, the Paris Club).

Different options could be envisaged and be tailored to the needs of the negotiation process.

- *Template for information sharing*   (i) While preserving the confidentiality of market-sensitive information, the debtor would be expected to provide creditors with information on the circumstances that call for the renegotiation of its debts, on outstanding debt and prospects, and on the negotiation process (timeframe, treatment of claims not included in the negotiation, and so on); (ii) adequate safeguards should be in place to protect confidential information and to ensure equal level of information of all parties. Creditors could appoint experts to help them formulate their decisions.
- *Modalities for representation of creditors*   As each class of creditor faces specific constraints, flexible approaches, inspired by recent experiences and various fora, should be favored. Contractual provisions (CACs, especially majority clauses) should be activated where they exist. When they are absent, they should be seen as a benchmark for the resolution of issues such as (i) the appropriate level of representation, (ii) the mandate given to creditors' representatives, (iii) the majority required to endorse key decisions. On the third issue, the solution suggested by the G10 Report on CAC (Group of Ten 2002)[7] could be considered as a best practice.
- *Concerted standstills*   In some cases, a concerted standstill (that is, an agreement between a debtor and its creditors providing for a suspension of debt payments, possibly backed by a voluntary stay on litigation) is advisable to prevent creditors from holding out. Specific guidelines could be designed to form market best practices. In some extreme circumstances, it might be appropriate for the sovereign to resort to a unilateral standstill; guidelines should clarify the conditions under which it would be acceptable for the debtor to go down this route.
- *Voluntary Dispute Resolution Forum*   Setting up an institution to deal with operational issues (computation and registration of claims, voting procedures and related conflicts) would increase clarity and predictability with regard to the implementation of the code.
- *Guidelines for defining the scope of the debt to be dealt with*   When the Paris Club debt is substantial, there may be a presumption that it would participate in the burden-sharing process, on a case-by-case basis, in a manner which is consistent with its own assessment of comparability of treatment.
- *Modalities of restructuring*   In exceptional circumstances, creditors might be compelled to accept a reduction in the net present value of their claims consistent with the return to medium-term sustainability. In practice, experience of both the Paris Club and restructuring

of private claims suggest that a variety of technical solutions could be tailored to debtors' situations and creditors' concerns.

- *Mediator*  A third party could be appointed as a mediator to prevent mutual suspicion. A fresh pair of eyes could help identify points of divergence between the debtor and creditors and help to reach a consensus.
- *New money*  To stabilize capital flows and preserve market access, a cut-off date could be set, resulting in the exclusion of new money from the renegotiation process. The experience of the Paris Club might be useful when determining best practices.

## THE CONDITIONS AND INCENTIVES FOR A SUCCESSFUL CODE OF GOOD CONDUCT

The preconditions for an effective resolution of debt-servicing problems and, hence the implementation of a code, are twofold:

- *Early identification of debt unsustainability*  IMF surveillance should help the debtor and creditors to determine the appropriate timing for activating the code. In particular, debt sustainability analyses which are to be routinely undertaken by the IMF will play a crucial role in the activation as they will allow the debtor and its creditors to identify situations where debt renegotiation might be required.
- *Appropriate IMF conditionality*  An IMF program is likely to be designed in conjunction with the implementation of a code. This program will provide parties involved in the renegotiation process with two 'public goods': information (for example, macroeconomic situation, financing gap, optimal debt structure), and leverage to ensure the sovereign's economic policy is consistent with restoring debt sustainability.

A strong incentive structure is necessary to ensure an effective implementation of the code.

- *Enhanced discipline in IMF financial assistance*  The code could not work properly unless the conditions for accessing IMF resources policy are clearly spelled out. Indeed, clear and firm access limits are a key incentive in triggering early debt renegotiation instead of waiting for further financial assistance.
- *Support and ownership from all stakeholders*  The code needs to be agreed upon and endorsed by all parties to debt renegotiation.

Ownership, which is a common feature of other codes and standards, is seen as one of the main incentives for adhering to and then implementing the code. Therefore, the code should be jointly drafted by representatives of the three constituencies involved: the private sector, the emerging countries and the official sector. It also has a bearing on its endorsement, which needs to be achieved by representative groups from these three constituencies.

- *Market incentives*  The experience of international standards and codes points to the effectiveness of an approach that relies on internationally agreed-upon principles and best practices. The same positive results can reasonably be expected with a code as peer and market pressures should contribute to deterring stakeholders from departing from its recommendations.

- First, on the debtor's side, peer pressure from other emerging market economies will ensure that an increase of investors' risk aversion *vis-à-vis* all emerging markets will be avoided. In addition, the market expectation that the debtor will act according to rules agreed upon should reinforce market discipline; indeed, a non-cooperative attitude on the part of the debtor would be rapidly censured by markets as it would be seen as a deliberate breaching of best practices. The market reaction would entail higher costs for the debtor resulting from sharper economic adjustment than otherwise necessary, together with a lasting loss of market access. Conversely, a cooperative process would greatly facilitate the return of the debtor to the market after the crisis is over.

- Second, on the creditors' side, there is interest in maintaining the contractual relationship with the debtor for as long as possible to increase the recovery value of their debts. In addition, creditors would have an interest in following the code as it would reduce uncertainty about the restructuring process without increasing debtor moral hazard. Finally, cooperative procedures and non-binding principles would rein-in creditors' incentives to engage in litigation.

## CONCLUSION

There is widespread recognition that the current framework for dealing with sovereign crisis needs some improvement. In other words, the status quo is not an acceptable option. Both the international official community and the private sector seem to agree on the merits of a non-statutory approach to addressing sovereign crises. That said, there are differences in opinion on the objectives and modalities of this approach.

At the present juncture, a code of good conduct seems to offer a promising avenue. The international official community has expressed interest in assessing further the potential benefits of this approach. The G7 officials are expected to prepare a report on the code, in consultation with issuers and the private sector by the Fall, 2003.

The inclusion of CACs by Mexico and possibly by other issuers in the foreseeable future, points to growing awareness of the benefits expected from the adoption of contractual provisions aimed at tackling debt resolution. This important step will make it easier to move towards the adoption and implementation of a code of good conduct.

## NOTES

1. This chapter is an abridged and revised version of, 'Towards a code of good conduct for sovereign debt renegotiation', prepared for the IFRI/IIE (Institut Français des Relations Internationales/Institute for Internal Economics) seminar on Sovereign Debt Restructuring, Paris, 9 March, 2003.
2. See IMFC (2000).
3. IMF, (2002a).
4. See Krueger (2001) and IMF (2001, 2002b, 2002c).
5. See IMFC (2003).
6. See Council on Foreign Relations (1999).
7. That is, leaving it to the creditors to choose between a qualified majority (typically 75 percent) with provisions to set up quorum rules, and the so-called 'outstanding principal' approach (with a reasonable threshold of 75 percent).

## BIBLIOGRAPHY

Bartholomew, Ed, E. Stern and A. Liuzzi (2002), *Two-Step Sovereign Debt Restructuring*, JP Morgan, 24 April.
Buchheit, Lee C. and G. Mitu Gulati (2002), 'Sovereign bonds and the collective will', Working Paper Series, Georgetown University Law Center, Washington, DC, March.
Council on Foreign Relations (1999), *Roundtable on Country Risk in the Post-Asia Crisis Era: Identifying Risks, Strategies, and Policy Implications*, Key recommendations from Working Group Discussions, 10/99–9/00, New York.
Gitlin, Richard A. (2002), 'A proposal: Sovereign Debt Forum' paper presented at the UN International Conference on Financing for Development, Monterrey, Mexico, 19 March.
Group of Seven (1999), *Report of G7 Finance Ministers to the Köln Economic Summit*, Cologne, 18–20 June.
Group of Seven (2003), *Statement and Action Plan of G7 Finance Ministers and Central Bank Governors*, Paris, 12 April.
Group of Ten (1996), *The Resolution of Sovereign Liquidity Crises*, Basle, May.
Group of Ten (2002), *Report of the G10 Working Group on Contractual Clauses*, Washington, DC, 26 September.

Group of Twenty (2002), *Communiqué of Finance Ministers and Central Bank Governors*, Delhi, 23 November.

Haldane, Andrew and Mark Kruger (2001), 'The resolution of international financial crises: private finance and public funds', Bank of Canada Working Paper 2001–20, Ottawa, November.

Hubbard, R. Glenn (2002), 'Enhancing sovereign debt restructuring', remarks made at the Conference on the IMF's Sovereign Debt Proposal, American Enterprise Institute, Washington, DC, 7 October.

Institute of International Finance (2003), *Draft Code of Conduct and Collective Action Clauses*, Washington, DC, January.

IMF (2001), *A New Approach to Sovereign Debt Restructuring: preliminary consideration*, 30 November, IMF.

IMF (2002a), *Fund Policy on Lending into Arrears to Private Creditors – Further Consideration of the Good Faith Criterion*, 30 July, prepared by the International Capital Markets, Policy Development and Review and Legal Departments, www.inf.org/external/pubs/ft/privcred/073002.htm.

IMF (2002b), *Sovereign debt restructuring mechanism: further consideration*, 14 August, IMF.

IMF (2002c), 'The design of the sovereign debt restructuring mechanisms – further considerations', unpublished, 27 November, IMF.

International Monetary and Financial Committee (IMFC) (2000, 2001, 2002, 2003), *Communiqué*.

Krueger, Anne O. (2001), *International Financial Architecture for 2002: A New Approach to Sovereign Debt Restructuring*, Washington, DC: American Enterprise Institute, 26 November.

Marx, Daniel (2003), 'Sovereign debt restructuring: the upcoming case of Argentina', www.rbwf.org/2003/madrid/marx.pdf.

Rogoff, Kenneth and Jeromin Zettelmeyer (2002), 'Bankruptcy procedures for sovereigns: a history of ideas, 1976–2001', IMF Working Paper WP/02/133, International Monetary Fund, Washington, DC, August.

Roubini, Nouriel and Brad Setser (2003), 'Improving the sovereign debt restructuring process: problems in restructuring, proposed solutions, and a roadmap for reform', mimeo, Institute for International Economics, Washington, DC, February.

pg 294 Title:

# Comments

## Andrew G. Haldane, Robert Gray and Henk J. Brouwer

## ANDREW G. HALDANE*

I have four points to make: on progress to date on crisis resolution; on where next for the Sovereign Debt Restructuring Mechanism (SDRM); on the resolution of non-sovereign and non-solvency crises; and on moral hazard.

### On Progress to Date

The title of Part V is 'The aftermath of the SDRM debate'. 'Aftermath' makes it sound like a time for tending the sick and wounded following some bloody and destructive battle. In fact, the war of words has been a fairly constructive one. Certainly, this debate has helped catalyse change on the crisis resolution front, which had not been much in evidence in the preceding five or so years. It is possible to speak of tangible progress in a way that would have been unimaginable two years ago.

International public policy has three stages: the ideas stage; the turning of those ideas into words (or policies); and applying those policies in practice. On that basis, and over the past 6–12 months, tangible progress has been made on:

1. *Access* Agreement has been reached at the IMF on new criteria and procedures to accompany any lending above the normal (100/300 percent of quotas) IMF lending limits. Exceptional lending should, in future, require an exceptional level of justification. So we have gone from ideas (for example, Haldane and Kruger 2001) to policies. And the next step is to go from policies to actions in live country cases;
2. *Collective action clauses (CACs)* Here we have also gone from ideas to words – specifically, the G10 and 'Gang of Six' private sector trade associations' draft clauses. But, most recently, we have gone further from words to actions – the inclusion of CACs in international bonds

in Mexico, Brazil, Uruguay and South Africa. In short, this reform has gone quite a long way in a short time. This is atypical in an architecture context.

3. *SDRM*  A vigorous – and more importantly, rigorous – debate has been taking place over the past 18 months. A concrete proposal for the SDRM was tabled by the IMF at the IMF Spring meetings in 2003. Although the formal proposal itself has been mothballed for now, some of the accompanying issues remain live.

4. *Code of conduct*  Again, we have gone from ideas to words – draft codes have been put forward by, among others, the Council on Foreign Relations, the 'Gang of Six' and the Banque de France. And at the IMF Spring meetings in 2003, it was made clear by the official sector that further action lies ahead.

So for many years, the rhetoric has been that good progress has been made on crisis prevention, but little progress on crisis resolution. It may be time to change that rhetoric. See Roubini and Setser (2003) for a summary of the various proposals.

**On SDRM: Too Much, Too Little or Just Right?**

Clearly, the SDRM recipe presented at the Spring meetings was not 'just right'. It failed to attract the support of the requisite supermajority of the IMF's membership to change the IMF's Articles of Agreement, which was necessary to bring the SDRM into force.

Some have concluded from this that the SDRM idea was 'too much'. For some, the SDRM was 'too big' an idea to be put into practice; for others, it was a bad idea in the first place. My conclusion is in fact the exact opposite – that the SDRM may actually have been 'too little', certainly by the time it had reached its final proposal. Why do I say this?

The SDRM, or mechanisms like it, is invoked when sovereign debt needs to be written down. Sovereign debt restructuring gives rise to coordination failures at two levels: (a) intra-creditor coordination problems, which might manifest themselves as holdout creditors and/or cross-instrument aggregation problems; and (b) debtor–creditor coordination problems, which might manifest themselves as stand-offs and/or delays in the restructuring process. Both such coordination problems can potentially generate inefficiencies in debt restructuring. Haldane et al. (2003) provide a theoretical treatment of these two types of coordination failure.

The SDRM proposal focused squarely on the first set of problems; it dealt principally with intra-creditor collective action problems. But there was, and is, no widespread acceptance that these problems are really that acute – or at least they have not been that acute in the past. For example, holdout problems have been few and far between. And aggregation problems have been non-existent (see Bingham 2002).

An SDRM built as a solution to a potentially non-existent problem was always going to be on shaky ground. Certainly, the perceived benefits of such a proposal were likely to be dwarfed by the political and practical costs of changing the IMF's Articles and enacting national legislation in many jurisdictions. Give or take, this was pretty much the judgment reached by the IMFC at their Spring meetings in 2003.

Is it possible to envisage an SDRM-type mechanism whose benefits might justify the costs of change? This is where the second coordination problem – that between the debtor and its creditors – comes in. This, for many people, is where the real inefficiencies in the restructuring process have resided historically. Witness the ongoing situation in Argentina, experience in Ecuador a few years ago and the earlier protracted workouts involving Latin American countries in the 1980s.

In situations of sovereign default, debtors have the whip hand. Their reputation is already ruined. Because of this, there are few incentives for them to cooperate. The upshot is delay, stand-off and disagreement. Solving this coordination problem calls for a quite different SDRM – a mechanism with some degree of third-party enforcement of decisions over both creditors *and* debtors. It would have more of the features of a bankruptcy procedure, with a court as the ultimate third-party enforcement agent. It would look more like the Krueger (2001) proposal, than the later watered-down, decentralized vintages. Different from these proposals, however, it would not have the IMF as judge, jury and executioner. That would be a role for an objective and independent arbiter.

What would this proposal amount to in practical terms? The SDRM model presented at the IMF Spring meetings proposed a Sovereign Debt Dispute Resolution Forum (SDDRF). The SDDRF's functions were, however, heavily circumscribed under the IMF model; its tasks were essentially administrative. Nevertheless, it is possible to envisage such a forum taking on a more ambitious set of tasks: for example, arbitrating between the debtor and creditors during the course of a workout negotiation; and, ultimately, adjudicating on whether the sharing of the spoils between them is an efficient and equitable one.

This would be a very different SDRM model from the one conceived by the IMF. It would tackle, for many people, the real friction in debt workout situations – debtor/creditor interactions and externalities, rather than intra-creditor ones. It would borrow more from domestic bankruptcy procedures, accepting some differences because of the specialness of sovereigns. And in this way, it would have a chance of offering enough by way of incremental benefit to justify the incremental cost of change, in a way the current SDRM proposal does not.

Some would argue that such a proposal was a bridge too far. For example, some have observed that the bankruptcy analogy is faulty for sovereigns (for example, Shleifer 2003). Because sovereigns are sovereign, the balance of bargaining power always rests with the debtor rather than with the creditors. An SDRM which further diluted and homogenized creditor rights would, according to this thesis, tilt the balance of bargaining power in the direction of the debtor to an even greater extent, thereby risking collapse of the sovereign debt market.

But the new SDRM proposed above would not fall foul of that critique. Its defining feature would be the need to retain an appropriate balance of bargaining power between the debtor and its creditor, recognizing that the debtor may ordinarily be holding all of the aces in a workout situation. That is where third-party enforcement comes in. More generally, rejection of the IMF SDRM model should not be seen as rejection of improved sovereign bankruptcy procedures *per se*. Alternative models hold out more hope.

The gestation period for such a expanded SDRM proposal would certainly be lengthy – just as it was with domestic bankruptcy procedures. And doubtless there would be loud and lengthy complaints from the private sector and/or debtors – again, just as there was following the introduction of domestic bankruptcy procedures. But whatever its gestation period, there may be merit in working up this alternative model if it is believed to tackle a genuine externality.

### On Dealing with Non-sovereign and Liquidity Crises

At the same time, both the SDRM and CACs can only ever be a part – possibly only a small part – of the crisis resolution toolkit. For example, they do nothing to help resolve crises sourced in the private sectors – as during the Asian crisis. And they do not help much in crisis situations where it is not believed that the debt needs rescheduling, that is, in liquidity crises. These are two areas where relatively little progress has been made on the crisis resolution front over recent years. This is a serious gap, for these types of crisis are very much the norm rather than the exception.

On managing *non-sovereign crises*, a particular lacuna concerns the management of banking crises. Resolving these has proven troublesome in the past, in particular when they have combined with sovereign sustainability problems – as for example in Turkey, Uruguay and Indonesia. The IMF's preferred response in these situations often involves extending a blanket deposit guarantee to the banking sector. This often helps stabilize the situation. But it also has potentially adverse side-effects on the incentives of bank depositors and bank managers. It also risks undermining limits on access to IMF resources. Further work on banking crisis resolution, in a world of limited official financing and weighing moral hazard concerns, is needed as a matter of urgency.

Another priority area for further work is the management of *liquidity or pseudo-liquidity crises*. Many, perhaps most, crises are neither at the pure liquidity nor at the pure insolvency ends of the crisis spectrum, but rather in the grey zone in between. In the past, the official sector has taken a rather schizophrenic attitude to the management of these grey-zone crises, sometimes filling financing gaps entirely with official monies, at other times making debtors or creditors shoulder more of the burden.

What is the appropriate scale of official financing in these situations? This requires us to take a view on what has become known as the catalytic finance doctrine – to what extent is official sector money able to catalyse the reflow of private finance? Murray (2003) calls this the 'loaves and fishes' miracle. But miracles do not come easily. And existing empirical evidence, and crisis experience, paints a rather dismal picture of the catalytic finance doctrine (Cotarelli and Giannini 2002; Hovaguimian 2003).

Rarely has the reflow of private capital lived up to expectations. This can be seen from the projected errors on the capital account for a number of systemically important IMF program countries. These capital account program errors have often been large, averaging 6 percent of GDP and in some cases reaching as high as 18 percent of GDP (Ghosh et al. 2002). But more important than their size is the fact that these errors have been systemically biased in the same direction: capital inflows have always fallen short of expectations. The anticipated catalytic effect has not been forthcoming.

So the empirical record of catalytic financing is a poor one. Can theory ride to the rescue? My reading of the literature is that it cannot – or at least has not yet. In standard bank-run-type models, last resort lending needs to be potentially limitless to work. In practice, the IMF can only act as a partial last resort lender because access is limited. And a partial last resort lender is potentially worse than no last resort lender at all (Zettelmeyer 2000).

More recent vintages of crisis models, for example, Morris and Shin (2003), Penalver (2003) and Corsetti et al. (2003), can generate a sort of catalytic effect. Within some range of fundamentals, partial amounts of IMF money can positively shift the rollover decisions of creditors; IMF loans shift the trigger point for a run. They may also catalyse the debtor to put in greater effort than they would otherwise. Through these routes, an increase in private financing may be secured.

Even these models suggest, however, that the window of opportunity for such a catalytic effect is a very narrow one. For example, too much official money and debtor incentives to adjust policy are blunted, not sharpened; too little money and creditor rollover decisions and debtor policy incentives are unaffected. Too adverse a shock and neither creditors nor the debtor have an incentive to behave well.

This theory tends to corroborate empirical evidence on the catalytic effect. Are catalytic effects impossible? No – but nor are they probable. The gap between this rather negative empirical and theoretical evidence on the catalytic effect on the one hand, and policy practice which often relies on the catalytic effect on the other, needs at some stage soon to be bridged. For example, it may call for a further refinement of the quantitative criteria for exceptional access to IMF resources.

## On Moral Hazard

One reason for avoiding large IMF packages is because the catalytic effect may not work. Another is that, even if it did work, it may have adverse side-effects. One (but only one) such adverse side-effect is moral hazard.

Moral hazard, or adverse incentive effects more generally, are hard to identify, much less quantify. For the most part, distorted decisionmaking is hidden and slow moving. Crises, by contrast, are easy to identify, visible and fast moving. Faced with certain costs of crisis, but uncertain side-effects of resolving them through a large-scale IMF loan, it is not surprising that policymakers have typically reached for the check book. Their motto has been: 'when in doubt, bail out'.

To question seriously this approach, we need concrete quantitative evidence that moral hazard is a clear and present danger. Existing empirical work, including at the IMF, has failed to find much evidence of such a risk. For instance, looking at the behavior of borrowing costs, the literature has found some evidence consistent with dwindling moral hazard in the past – for example, the increase in spreads and the widening in their distribution following the Russian crisis (Dell'Arricia et al. 2002). But overall, the evidence of moral hazard is patchy, especially when looking at the behavior of capital flows and prices over recent years (Kamin 2002).

The Bank of England has recently looked at some new data to gauge whether this reading of the runes is a correct one (for a summary, see Haldane and Taylor 2003 and the references therein). For example, an examination has been made of the behavior of creditor banks following IMF interventions. Is the market valuation of these banks boosted by large-scale IMF loans, in ways that cannot be explained by falls in the real hazard of crisis? And is this boost greater for creditors with a larger overall emerging market portfolio, as the market anticipates further bail-outs in the future?

The answer to these questions, at least for UK banks, is yes. Yes, there is a significantly positive boost to the market value of creditor banks following IMF interventions. Yes, this boost cannot be explained by falls in the real hazard of crisis. And yes, this effect is larger, the larger is the creditor banks' emerging market portfolio. In short, there is a creditor moral hazard case to answer.

We have also looked more directly at debtor moral hazard – whether there has been a greater tendency to seek an IMF program, for given fundamentals, following the extension of the IMF safety net in the late 1990s through the New Arrangements to Borrow (NAB) and the Supplemental Reserve Facility (SRF). The answer again is yes. Controlling for the fundamental determinants of a country seeking an IMF program, the late 1990s did witness a sea-change among debtors, with a greater willingness to seek IMF financing. In short, there may be a debtor moral hazard case to answer too.

Taken together, this evidence is not proof positive that moral hazard is so pervasive that it presents an overwhelming case against large-scale bailouts. It does, however, suggest the need to be cautious about ruling out moral hazard as a hypothetical possibility without quantitative backing. It is a danger that is ever present, if not always clear.

## ROBERT GRAY

I shall not address the code of good conduct issue as agreements are in place with the official sector on the merits of a code. However, I shall comment in greater detail on the subject of collective action clauses. The title of Part V refers to collective action clauses in practice, and without Mexico's courageous espousal of CACs, the words 'in practice' would not resonate today.

In terms of CACs, most attention has been focused on qualified majority voting, but another key collective action clause is the acceleration clause, governing the acceleration and deacceleration of debt obligations. This clause can do a great deal to shackle the rogue creditor, and reduce the risk of precipitous litigation where it might otherwise exist, because it limits the ability of a single rogue creditor to accelerate the bond without support from other creditors.

What has been the general issuer reaction (judging by the cases of Mexico, Brazil and Uruguay) to the model CACs that were prepared by the 'Gang of Six' trade associations? It is not surprising that the information covenant has been thought demanding; although issuer compliance with Special Data Dissemination Standard Site (SDDS) seems reasonable. The real disappointment is that issuers have not (yet at last) accepted the engagement clause which provides for issuer recognition of the legitimacy of a properly constituted bondholder committee after a bond is in default or restructuring discussions have started. This is a principle that the private sector will certainly expect to see incorporated in any future code of good conduct. So where do CACs go from here? To date, borrowers have simply adopted the market conventions for the market in which they are issuing at any particular time: as a result, the same borrower will include a unanimity provision in its New York law contracts while including qualified majority voting provisions in its English law contracts. The precise form of clauses has not figured in pre-mandate negotiations between issuer and underwriter; or even in that period between when a bond issue is mandated and launched. It has been assumed that such matters will be left to each party's legal counsel.

The decision by Mexico to include a qualified majority provision in a New York law bond contract has changed all that. Issuers will have to be proactive in deciding whether or not to include qualified majority and other collective action provisions in their bond documentation. Debt issuance programs provide them with a particular opportunity to standardize their bond documentation. The International Primary Market Association (IPMA), which I chair, will follow its normal practice of including standardized clauses in its handbook. Where an underwriter deviates from IPMA's standard clauses, it is required to disclose such at the time the issue is launched.

Why do I believe in the importance of uniform CACs? Mainly because in the timeframe in which bond issues are launched and sold, there is little time for investors to judge the pros and cons of different provisions. Their priority is on judging whether the bond in question represents good value relative to other investment opportunities. I would not welcome a world in which an issuer yield curve is based on the relative strengths and weaknesses of the level of CAC protection. An even less desirable outcome would be if the form of a particular issuer's collective action clauses became a source of competition: for example, if an underwriter marketed itself to an issuer as being able to launch an issue with a lower qualified majority level than its competitors; or if an issuer argued that a lower percentage of bondholders should be allowed to amend its bond terms because it was a stronger credit than other issuers.

What we now need is for other emerging market issuers from a broad credit spectrum to follow the recent cases. However, I am not convinced that issuers should be given financial incentives by the official sector, including the IMF itself, to introduce collective action clauses. If issuers have to be incentivized to adopt these clauses, that sends a strong signal that they may be undertaking something that is not in their interest. From their side, investors would view a system of incentives as official interference in the workings of the market. Far better that collective action clauses should be adopted because they represent a 'win–win' situation to both issuers and investors: for issuers because they will be less vulnerable to the risk of rogue investors, and for investors because workouts should be more predictable and less protracted.

Underwriters may have to temper their competitive enthusiasm and remain resolute in their encouragement of issuers to maintain standards of documentation and disclosure. The competitive enthusiasm of underwriters was one reason why the use of trustees has virtually disappeared from market practice. To save the issuer a small amount of expense, underwriters failed to stress to issuers the value of appointing trustees. The benefit of a trustee is twofold. First, a bondholder trustee offers the best opportunity for effective creditor coordination. For a start, no bondholder can take unilateral action without involving the trustee. Litigation must be carried out by the trustee, and any recoveries through litigation are shared on a pro rata basis among all the bondholders.

Without a trustee, sharing is impractical. Without a trustee at the center of the process, it would be difficult to either induce a creditor that had made a disproportionate recovery to disgorge the excess or to determine which bondholders would be entitled to share. Would it be those holding the bonds when the issuer agreed to pay, those holders when the issuer actually paid or those holding if a collecting bondholder actually disgorged his/her excess share?

Lee Buchheit of Cleary Gottlieb sees an analogy between bondholders and a group of theatergoers: would it be those who stayed to the end of the play, those who left at the interval or those who paid for their tickets but never showed up? The second benefit of a trustee is that it provides a useful channel for communication between the issuer and the bondholders, bearing in mind that, legally at least, neither the lead manager nor a fiscal and paying agent has any responsibility to do so. There is clearly some antipathy among many US investors to the use of trustees. This appears to be grounded in the belief that US trustees have been very passive. Trustees will certainly stick closely to the text of the indenture in deciding what they are authorized to do. This does not seem to be valid criticism of the trustee concept, more one of how trustees have been allowed to behave in practice. Trustee timidity need not be a fact of life. In the international market, trustees have been seen to take unilateral action in putting a debtor into default without prior consultation with bondholders because it believed that the circumstances justified such action.

A challenge in the Eurobond market, and perhaps to a lesser degree in the US one, is one of how to bring the bondholders to the negotiating table. It is difficult to identify and mobilize holders of bearer bonds, which are still a feature of the market. Where holders of bonds need to be lobbied, it has to be done through the international clearing systems (Euroclear and Clearstream) and through advertisements in the financial press. The international clearing systems will not disclose to the issuer or its advisers the identity of the participants that have positions in the bonds. (The position on this is different in the United States, in the way that the Depository Trust Company works.) Notices or requests for proxies are given to the clearing systems, which pass them on themselves to their participants. These participants are themselves typically custodians who in turn are then expected to pass all communications to their beneficial owners. The issuer or its advisers are unable to check on whether that has actually happened. Should the beneficial owner wish to vote its bonds the same chain operates in reverse.

The situation can be even more problematic if the issuer is already in default. If an issuer is in default, the clearing systems will seek to have defaulted bonds withdrawn from their system and held by the beneficial owner directly. Unwieldy as this all sounds, it is a system that can be made to work. The exchange offers for Ukraine and Ecuador certainly attracted high levels of bondholder support, well in excess of 95 percent. This high response level was due to a combination of factors: the energetic efforts of the banks executing the exchange offers and the effectiveness of the 'exit consent' mechanism. But equally important was the flexibility, which allowed the bondholders to vote their bonds through written proxies and by use of the internet. Uruguay's requirement for its exchange that letters of transmittal be submitted electronically is another step in the right direction.

I leave until last the key issue that the private sector will have to address on CACs: incorporating the idea of aggregation on an *ex ante* basis. It would be dangerous to extrapolate too much from the Uruguay case. One of the reasons for the market's dissatisfaction with the IMF proposal for the SDRM was the prospect for the aggregation of a broad range of claims within a single voting framework. Many bond investors and bank lenders remain uncomfortable with the aggregation concept. It is certainly a two-edged sword. On the one hand it could be argued that it is good for investor protection because it limits the vulnerability of a well-intentioned creditor to having a specific bond controlled by a rogue creditor; but on the other hand it could be argued that aggregation weakens investor rights because the well-intentioned creditor may be outvoted by holders of other debt securities (or bank lenders) which may have different motivations. Further work will be required before the industry position on aggregation becomes clearer. However, it is clear that if the market did adopt some form of aggregation as the norm, this would be the last remaining nail in the coffin of the SDRM; perhaps a worthy enough objective in and of itself.

# HENK J. BROUWER

Part V has provided an extensive overview of the issues that play a role in the 'aftermath of the SDRM debate'. Instead of commenting in detail on all the various contributions, I shall touch on a few key policy items.

**Surveillance**

First, I shall underscore the importance of Fund surveillance. IMF surveillance should provide a preventive mechanism capable of signaling risks on the economic horizon and anticipating the necessity for timely policy action. The Argentine case clearly illustrates that the Fund has still some work to do to strengthen its surveillance activities. In this context, it will be a challenge for the Fund to remain firm in its policy advice when the economy of an emerging market performs relatively well. Countries should be urged to use the 'good times' to improve their policies further and to build up buffers, so that their systems become less susceptible to shocks.

**Access Limits**

A discussion on crisis management instruments is intertwined with the issue of access limits. In my view, it is essential that the Fund is clear and predictable with regard to the financing it will provide in order to reduce uncertainty and moral hazard. In the absence of a sound framework for official financing, the efforts of the international community to enhance the instruments for crisis management may not provide sufficient incentives for debtors and their creditors to work out debt restructurings in a timely way. Lack of clarity and predictability will leave debtors and creditors in limbo, and may make them wait for the official sector to bail them out.

I cannot but agree with Giannini (Chapter 14) who states that the Fund's renewed framework for exceptional access in capital account crises represents very important progress over the past practice. This framework establishes substantive criteria, including a clearly sustainable debt and stronger procedures for decisionmaking on exceptional access proposals. The member's best efforts to secure private sector involvement in program financing are also an important consideration for justifying exceptional access. This new approach needs to be tested now in concrete circumstances.

**Debt Sustainability Analyses**

In order to determine whether a country's debt is sustainable or not, the new debt sustainability analyses of the Fund are important. They are especially valuable in highlighting the linkages between exchange rate fluctuations and debt dynamics, which reflect a common feature of most countries under stress in, for example, Latin America.

The new analyses should make better-informed judgments possible. In my view, they may be enriched by taking other aspects that are relevant for debt sustainability into account, such as maturity, currency decomposition, indexation and holdership of the debt. Moreover, liquidity aspects of sustainability, particularly debt servicing, need to play a more central part in the analyses. Also, examination of movements in asset prices, changes in countries' access to markets, and changes in the composition of capital flows are critical to a clear understanding of debt sustainability. The challenge for the IMF is to present these aspects in a comprehensive, easily accessible and systematic way.

**Collective Action Clauses (CACs)**

CACs are not new. Since the second half of the 19th century, majority action clauses have constituted a regular feature of both corporate and sovereign bonds governed by the law of England. Currently, the outstanding stock of foreign sovereign bonds issued with CACs amounts to roughly one-third of the total.

For some time, the international community has been promoting a wider use of CACs, particularly in the New York market where CACs are generally absent. The Rey Report (Group of Ten 1996) recommended the adoption of CACs in sovereign bond contracts as part of an integral framework for debt resolution back in 1996. Six years later, the Quarles Report (Group of Ten 2002) followed up on this G10 work, and produced concrete drafting proposals for model CACs. Recently, Mexico and Brazil moved to include CACs in their bond issues governed by New York law, and Uruguay signaled its intentions to do so. In a way, this lead-time of CACs underlines that changes in the international architecture do not happen overnight, or – as Zettelmeyer (Chapter 13) rightly points out – history and inertia matter. At the same time, the lead-time of CACs may also suggest that there is still hope for the SDRM.

Following up on the recent movers, note that Brazil opted for a majority amendment clause of 85 percent, and not of 75 percent as Mexico opted for. Obviously, every sovereign is free to choose whatever clauses it prefers to include in its debt, but a majority amendment clause of 85 percent is somewhat less ambitious when it comes to facilitating debt workouts. One could even argue that Brazil's move plays into the hands of the Gang of Six – which wants this higher threshold – and that a golden opportunity to end the debate about the voting threshold seems to have been missed.

But apart from this specific point, Mexico's and Brazil's moves to include CACs should be welcomed, as well as Uruguay's intentions. The first-mover problem has been successfully solved. It is now important that the momentum for adopting CACs is maintained and that a real shift in market practices is achieved. For this purpose, efforts could be made to include CACs in good practices and guidelines on debt management of various countries. The inclusion of CACs may also be discussed in IMF Article IV surveillance, which could track and publicize the use of CACs as a recommended feature of bond contracts and good governance.

**Code of Good Conduct (CGC)**

As is clearly demonstrated by Jaillet (Chapter 15), a CGC comprising best practices of debtor–creditor coordination could usefully underpin the use of CACs and our efforts to increase private sector involvement. Ideally, it should reduce the uncertainties pertaining to debt restructurings. I therefore support the work that the Banque de France is undertaking with private sector parties to develop such a roadmap.

In this context, it may be worthwhile considering the following. The contractual clauses in each instrument may not be able to address disputes among holders of different bond issues or different classes of creditors such as bondholders, banks and international financial institutions. In order to address this coordination problem, a voluntary forum of debtors and creditors could be established, a so-called 'Club of New York'. In this forum, debtors and creditors can cooperate on dispute resolution and work out debt restructurings. The forum may be embedded in the CGC.

Finally, I shall return briefly to the SDRM. At the moment, much of our efforts will go into the promotion of CACs and the development of a CGC. If these two instruments of crisis management prove to be successful, then there may be no need for a fully-fledged SDRM. However, in case they fail and disorderly workouts remain with us for quite some time, one may argue that the case for an SDRM becomes stronger. Time will tell.

## NOTE

* The views expressed are personal ones and are not necessarily those of the Bank of England.

# REFERENCES

Bingham, G. (2002), 'Sovereign debt resolution mechanisms: recent proposals', mimeo, Bank for International Settlements, Basle.

Corsetti, G., B. Guimaraes and N. Roubini (2003), 'The tradeoff between an international lender of last resort to deal with liquidity crises and moral hazard distortions. A model of the IMF's catalytic approach', mimeo, New York University.

Cotarelli, C. and C. Giannini (2002), 'Bedfellows, hostages or perfect strangers? Global capital markets and the catalytic effect of IMF crisis lending', IMF Working Paper WP/02/193, International Monetary Fund, Washington, DC.

Dell'Arricia, G., I. Schnabel and J. Zettelmeyer (2002), 'Moral hazard and international crisis lending: a test', IMF Working Paper WP/02/181, International Monetary Fund, Washington, DC.

Ghosh, A., T. Lane, M. Schulze-Ghattas, A. Bulir, J. Hamann and A. Mourmouras (2002), 'IMF-supported programs in capital account crises', IMF Occasional Paper 210, International Monetary Fund, Washington, DC.

Group of Ten (1996), *The Resolution of Sovereign Liquidity Crises* ('Rey Report'), Basle, May.

Group of Ten (2002), *Report of the G10 Working Group on Contractual Clauses*, Washington, DC, 26 September.

Haldane, A.G. and M. Kruger (2001), 'The resolution of international financial crises: private finance and public funds', *Bank of England Financial Stability Review*, December, pp. 193–202.

Haldane, A.G., A. Penalver, V. Saporta and H.S. Shin (2003), 'The analytics of sovereign debt restructuring', *Journal of International Economics*, forthcoming.

Haldane, A.G. and A. Taylor (2003), 'How does IMF lending affect debtor and creditor incentives?', *Bank of England Financial Stability Review*, 122–33.

Hovaguimian, C. (2003), 'What is the catalytic effect of IMF programs? And when might it work?', mimeo, Bank of England, London.

Kamin, S. (2002), 'Identifying the role of moral hazard in international financial markets', Federal Reserve Board International Finance Discussion Paper 2002–736, Washington, DC.

Krueger, A. (2001), 'International financial architecture for 2002: a new approach to sovereign debt restructuring', speech at the American Enterprise Institute, New York, November.

Morris, S. and H.S. Shin (2003), 'Catalytic finance: when does it work?', mimeo, London School of Economics.

Murray, J. (2003), 'Comments on "Reflections on moral hazard and private sector involvement in the resolution of emerging market financial crises"', mimeo, Bank of Canada, Ottawa.

Penalver, A. (2003), 'How can the IMF catalyse private capital flows? A model', mimeo, Bank of England, London.

Roubini, N. and B. Setser (2003), 'Improving the sovereign debt restructuring process: problems in restructuring, proposed solutions and a roadmap for reform', mimeo, Institute for International Economics, Washington, DC, February.

Shleifer, A. (2003), 'Will the sovereign debt market survive?', NBER Working Paper no. 9493, National Bureau of Economic Research, Cambridge, MA.

Zettelmeyer, J. (2000), 'Can official crisis lending be counter-productive in the short run?', Economic notes, **29**, 13–29.

PART VI


Governance of the
International Financial System:
The IMF, the G7, G10 and G20

323- 38

# 16. The governance of the international financial system

**Lorenzo Bini Smaghi***

## INTRODUCTION

The issue of governance is increasingly being raised in economic life, especially when major failures occur in the functioning of markets and institutions. As far as the international financial system is concerned, the Asian crisis of the second half of the 1990s was one of those cases which led to a reassessment, in particular with respect to the Bretton Woods institutions.

The Cologne G7 Summit (G7 1999) contained some suggestions with respect to improving the governance of the international financial institutions (IFIs). In particular, the governing body of the IMF was strengthened and the Group of 20 was created, to enlarge the sphere of consensus building between industrial and emerging market countries. The Financial Stability Forum, an emanation of the G7, was also created to oversee the work of the various groupings in charge of monitoring the stability of financial markets.

These developments have not stopped the critics of the current system of governance. The meetings of the IFIs since 2000 have given rise to various demonstrations, and the intensity has been attenuated recently only due to the emotions post September 11. Criticisms come from all parts, starting from the academic world (even when there is close involvement with the working of the institutions, as in the case of Joseph Stiglitz), nongovernmental organizations, but also the political world. In the United States, for instance, the IFIs are under serious scrutiny by Congress. The refusal by the US administration to bring to Congress any institutional issue regarding the IFIs, for fear that Congress would take that opportunity to ask for substantial and unpredictable changes in the functioning of the institutions, has been a major obstacle to change.

Criticisms should not be rejected without close scrutiny. What is important, however, is to distinguish criticisms related to the governance itself from others related to the performance of the institutions and their mission. Some of the most frequently expressed criticisms of some institutions like the World Bank or the IMF are those of 'mission creep' or being subject to a monolithic culture (the so-called 'Washington Consensus'). These are not issues related to governance *per se*, and can be addressed in the context of the current governance system.

This chapter tries to limit the analysis to issues of governance. When considering the international financial system, the issue of governance can be examined on two levels: the first is the level of the system itself; the second is that of the single components of the system.

Assessing the governance of the system itself implies asking whether the structure of institutions and groupings which govern the international financial system is appropriate. Is there any duplication? Is there something missing? This is the type of question that was addressed at the Cologne Summit with the creation of the Financial Stability Forum.

This is not a major issue today. The voices demanding reform are not seeking the creation of new institutions or groupings, or the suppression of any of the existing ones.

The main issue related to governance that is of interest today, nearly five years after the Cologne summit, is the Governance of the institutions and groupings that support the international financial system. With the increased integration of financial systems, the emergence of new players in the world economy, and the development of corporate governance practices in the private and public sectors, it is legitimate to ask whether the existing structures and institutions are adequate, can deliver the expected results and can reach their intended recipients.

In this chapter I concentrate on the issue of governance of the IFIs and groupings. I shall consider separately:

- the Bretton Woods institutions: the IMF, the World Bank and the World Trade Organization (WTO); and
- the groupings of the most powerful nations, in particular through the group of the seven most industrialized countries (G7), as well as by other 'informal' groups such as the G20.

The issue of global governance is strictly linked with the provision of public goods, which requires specialization – that is, a specialized institution – to reap the benefits of efficient allocation of resources. It is not by chance that both the IMF and the World Bank were established as specialized institutions, each with its own mandate, its own instruments and its own form (a Fund and a Bank) to deal, respectively, with monetary and financial stability and with development issues. Their specialization made it easier to establish representation at the highest possible level, while preserving efficiency.

Representation and specialization need to be compatible with efficiency, and thus effective decision-making. This is not an easy task. There are obvious tensions between specialization and representation, between representation and efficiency and between specialization and efficiency. In particular, specialization prevents exploiting issue linkages in decision-making and thus limits the scope of possible solutions.

Informal institutions such as the G7 can support the action of formal institutions. They can provide viable solutions to leadership of global governance. However, the restricted number of participants in these groups raises the question of the legitimacy of a small number deciding on broad issues of interest for the world, such as the fight against poverty, the environment and food safety or international security. This has been subject to increasing criticism. In Monterrey,[1] in March 2002, while rejecting the need for a new overarching body, the need to improve international cooperation and to broaden and strengthen the participation of developing countries in international economic decision-making and norm-setting was emphasized.

In this chapter I shall assess the current system of governance of existing institutions and groupings and look at proposals to improve it, so as to address to the expectations raised in Monterrey and other fora. Some of the changes required need strong political vision and leadership. This sets the frame for this chapter in the medium- to long-term horizon. However, postponing indefinitely the solution to the problems of governance may exacerbate tensions in the international system and may open even wider problems of governance than those that may appear today. There is no doubt that the respective roles of the different institutions and groupings, in particular the more recently created G20, depend on the adaptation of the governance of each one of them to the requirements of their respective tasks.

## THE PARAMETERS

Weaknesses in the current arrangements have pointed in particular to: the discrepancy between the needs of a globalized world and the national character of policy-making (the jurisdictional gap); the lack of participation of many marginal and voiceless groups of countries or in civil society (the participation gap); and the lack of incentive for both developing and industrial countries in implementing international agreements and making international cooperation fully operational (the incentive gap) (Kaul et al. 1999).

In looking at how the different institutions and groupings fulfill their governance requirements, I shall use the following parameters:

1.  *legitimacy*   decisions should be taken in accordance with the mandate of each institution/organization and with the participation of those who are mainly affected by these decisions (ownership);
2.  *efficiency/effectiveness* governance in institutions/organizations should ensure that the decision-making process will be speedy and effective and therefore that wider benefits would be achieved at a lower cost;
3.  *representation*   decision-making should involve all parties entitled to take decisions. They should therefore be adequately represented in governance bodies (the shareholder principle); and
4.  *accountability*   decisions should be transparent and decisionmakers should be responsible for their decisions toward public opinion (the stakeholder principle).

The coexistence of these criteria in governance structures implies trade-offs. In particular, trade-offs occur between the efficiency criteria, on the one side, and the other criteria on the other:

-   the equity criteria cannot be fully satisfied by granting general representation without hampering the efficiency of decision-making;
-   a full application of the legitimacy criteria can contrast with the need to ensure the efficiency of the decision-making process; and
-   a full application of the accountability criteria, giving full transparency to the decision-making process, may prove to be at odds with the need for confidentiality required by an efficient decision-making process.

The larger and more specialized is an institution the greater its capacity to benefit from economies of scale and to internalize externalities; but, on the other hand, the larger the institution, the less its decisions can match the tastes and preferences of all its shareholders (Drazen 2001). Trade-offs are therefore necessary. When, within formal institutions, it is not possible to reach decisions located on the trade-off frontier, we are confronted with institutional failure. In such a case the institutions should be reformed.

## THE BRETTON WOODS INSTITUTIONS (BWIS)

Changes in the economic framework imply a change in perspective and organization within the BWIs, particularly in the IMF and the World Bank and in the way they concur to ensure financial stability on the one hand, and to promote development and poverty reduction on the other. Both institutions, therefore, have included in their mandate objectives to provide resources, services, systems of rules and policy regimes with substantial cross-border externalities that respond to the definition of global public goods, and that can be produced in sufficient supply only through cooperation and collective action by developed and developing countries (World Bank 2000).

The BWIs have already amended their mandates, roles and expertise. However some countries, mainly developing ones, did not consider the changes that have taken place as sufficient to meet the new challenges. 'A key issue is whether the mandates of the existing organizations remain relevant, and their legitimacy and governance structure are adequate to serve the needs of the global community in the early twenty-first century' (van Houtven, 2002, page 2). I shall address this topic using the above mentioned parameters.

## Legitimacy

Legitimacy of BWIs is fulfilled by membership. Broad membership ensures adequate representation of all interests involved. Indeed, the legitimacy to decide and operate in different fields, in accordance with the mandate, is conferred on these institutions by their very nature, and in particular by their broad membership.

Legitimacy can be examined from two different angles: the mandate of the institution and the ownership of decisions by the executive board.

The case of the IMF mandate is emblematic. It has evolved over time to respond to the new challenges posed in part of its constituency. This encompasses:

- a new role of the Fund in preserving macroeconomic and financial stability through its activity for crisis prevention and resolution; and
- an increased involvement of the Fund in developing countries and transition economies, in particular to promote growth and poverty reduction in low-income countries.

There has been a progressive adaptation of the IMF mandate to new conditions. The Fund has preserved its legitimacy, while broadening its sphere of competence. However, both the Fund and the Bank have often been accused of 'mission creep' and of extending their activities in fields that go beyond their respective mandates. The issue has been raised in the Fund during discussions on streamlining conditionality, while the criticism of the Bank has been made in terms of 'losing effectiveness and becoming a bloated bureaucracy' (Passacantando 2002 p. 2)

The second way to assess the legitimacy of the institution is through its decision-making bodies, the executive board and the management. Issues such as the ownership of decisions, the right of initiative of the management, and the involvement of the board in approving programs and proposals have to be addressed.

The management has the right to take initiatives. Management, therefore, can choose topics and ask staff to undertake analysis. However, at present the criteria for setting priorities are not well established, while the role of the board is often limited to a simple ratification of management initiatives. Hence, the board is not always able to be proactive and cannot provide the necessary feedback. There is a risk that decisions are taken as an 'act of faith', without a true sense of ownership.

Such is the case when the management takes the initiative to start negotiation and demands *ex post* board approval, whereas an earlier board involvement would be warranted. A comparison with the analogue procedure in the private sector may shed a different light on the legitimacy of the process. When a company starts to analyse a relevant financial operation, the management needs to have permission from the board to negotiate a possible deal with the counterpart. Management reports to the board at the various stages of the negotiation, until a deal is agreed. The method adopted at the World Bank/IMF too often does not involve the board until proceedings have reached a 'take-it-or-leave-it' stage. The board should be involved *ex ante* and retain the right to participate in the negotiation, as is the case in any private financial institution. Confidentiality is often given as an excuse for not involving the board and restricting the information to a subset of the shareholders. But this is not very convincing.

The new procedures for granting exceptional access to the IMF resources represent a case for testing whether early board involvement can be implemented. The recent experience is encouraging, for instance in the case of the decisions concerning Argentina (2003) or Brazil (2002). But there are also negative examples, such as the decisions taken in the case of Uruguay (July 2003), when the board opinion was crowded out by public declarations from the managing director and the US treasury secretary.

**Efficiency/Effectiveness**

The restricted composition of the board ensures the efficiency of the decision-making process in the BWIs. However, this implies a trade-off with representation, since not all members take part in the board discussion, but most of them (160 over 184) are indirectly represented through their participation in countries' constituencies. Decisions may not always be satisfactory for the whole membership. On the one hand, the Fund has progressively lost its role as a credit union (Kenen 1986) and an increasing divergence of interest has emerged between members that became permanent creditors and those that are permanently in a debtor position. On the other hand, the Bank has been criticized on the assumption that financial allocation responds excessively to the strategic interests of the large shareholders and is not sufficiently sensitive to local political realities.

The efficiency/effectiveness of the decision-making process involves the board's participation in the decision-making process as well as in the voting system.

To be effective, the board should be informed in due time to enable it to make timely and appropriate decisions. This is particularly relevant with regard to the IMF's crisis prevention and crisis resolution functions. To perform its role in crisis prevention the board should be provided with a candid, comprehensive and authoritative report of the Fund's surveillance. IMF surveillance should ensure independent assessment of economic conditions and policies in member countries and, if a program is in place, it should provide the board with the opportunity to reassess a program strategy. If these conditions are not met, early information, and thus capacity to influence decisions, are unlikely to be allocated equally among shareholders. Not that this necessarily means that G7 countries will 'impose their views', as other groups – for instance, the informal G11 coordination in the Fund – might be just as effective, or even more, in this process. What matters, of course, is that G7 countries are on the 'creditor side' while the G11 countries are mostly on the debtor side. We shall return to this issue below.

Efficiency of decision-making is crucial in the case of crisis resolution. During the Asian and Brazilian crises, G7 countries played a decisive role, in particular by supplementing IMF resources with bilateral loans. In contrast, in the case of Argentina and Turkey, the G7 decided to leave entirely to the Fund the financial burden of supporting the crisis countries. More recently the G7 strategy has been oriented toward the definition of a framework for crisis resolution and the involvement of private creditors. The Fund has contributed to the development of this framework, in particular, exploring solutions to make more effective the process for restructuring unsustainable sovereign debt.

In this context, the Sovereign Debt Restructuring Mechanism (SDRM) was designed to provide an orderly and predictable framework for sovereign debt restructuring, thus helping to create incentives for early actions by creditors and debtors and to reduce pressure for large official bail-out packages. The SDRM should be part of a strategy, together with a more rigorous policy for access to IMF resources. The opposition of the United States and some emerging market economies (EMEs) (in particular Latin American countries) and the negative reactions of the creditor community slowed down work on the SDRM. This has had negative implications on efficiency: the IMF cannot count on the necessary instruments to perform its tasks in accordance with its mandate and on the G7 which risks being involved again in supplementing bilateral resources.

The efficiency of the institutions also depends on the time-frame within which the executive board takes decisions. In the IMF, decision-making is generated by consensus, based on the fact that 'the Chairman shall ordinarily ascertain the sense of the meeting, in lieu of a formal voting,' (Rule C10 of IMF Rules and Regulations). Consensus means unanimity, although for many decisions it is sufficient that a large majority agrees (van Houtven 2002).

The consensus procedure is a good illustration of the trade-off between efficiency and representation: decisions by consensus need to take account of all positions, including those of minority shareholders. In this case, the quota share is not as important and the implicit voting is skewed toward a 'one head, one vote' system. Decisions can be delayed until a 'consensus' is found; this implies that developing countries, although holding a minority position, have a potential veto power. In contrast, where differences are too large, the need for consensus would not be appropriate. Efficiency would require a change in the voting practices and would imply more frequent voting. But implications in terms of ownership of these decisions may become quite relevant.

### Representation

This parameter calls into question the ways in which members are in a position to take direct part in the decision-making process and the ways in which they can influence the decisions of the board. Technically the problem is linked with the ways in which member countries' quota shares and voting powers are determined.

The problem has three facets: (a) quotas and voting shares, (b) the role of low-income countries, and (c) from a different angle it also concerns the issue of the representation of the European Union (EU) in the BWIs.

### Quotas and voting share

BWIs are different from the UN system where the principle of 'one head, one vote' prevails. Countries are (or should be) represented in the BWIs in line with their relative importance in the world economy. This is measured by the quotas calculated on the basis of specific formulas. However, current quotas ('actual quotas') differ from those determined by using formulas ('calculated quotas'). This means that the allocation of quotas and voting rights too often reflects the past rather than the current economic weight of member countries. For some countries, calculated quotas are substantially above their actual ones, meaning therefore that they are formally under-represented with respect to their economic importance. This concerns, in particular, individual EMEs (but also some industrialized countries). In contrast, this is not a general problem of developing countries as a group. Indeed, the ratio between actual and calculated quotas is about 60 percent for the developing countries while it is only 32.5 percent for the industrial countries (van Houtven 2002). The developing countries (including transition economies) which represent about 85 percent of the membership (160 developing and 24 industrial countries) hold around 35 percent of the total quota share while their voting power is around 40 percent of the total.

**The role of low-income countries**
For the low-income countries, the representation issue coincides with the problem of strengthening their participation in the decision-making process, as set out in the Monterrey consensus. In this case the problem is not an issue of increasing representation in terms of voting power (although an increase in basic votes would contribute to substantially increase their voting share). The main concern of this group of countries is to have a stronger voice, especially on issues of primary interest to them. This problem rests more on the quality of countries' representation than on the quantity of their voting power. The true issue in this case is to increase these countries' ownership of projects and programs and to help them to build their capacity to participate effectively in multilateral institutions and fora. Any revision of the quota system can hardly be a solution. However, it could have 'an important symbolic value and help preserve, in the long run, the legitimacy of the institution[s] in the face of major changes in the distribution of world economic power and persistent global inequities' (Passacantando 2002 p. 5)

**Representation of the EU**
The issue of EU representation in the BWIs is completely different in nature. The problem concerns the role that the EU as a regional body can play to mediate between the national and the global levels. Coordination on key issues is necessary to influence decisions in the Fund and in the Bank. The current voting power of the EU countries in the IMF board is nearly 30 percent of the total; however, as a group the EU has far less political influence than the United States, who hold 'only' 17 percent of the voting power. The EU problem here does not lie in the method for calculating quota shares and voting power, but in the weak coordination among EU countries. The problem is further exacerbated by the fact that EU countries participate in nine different constituencies.

EU countries have only recently developed a coordination process. There is scope for further improving such cooperation. Yet, there are natural limits to what can be achieved within the existing cooperation framework. If EU countries want to truly improve their collective influence on international issues and on the IMF, some institutional change in the way European interests are represented and pushed forward may be necessary. Several solutions could be envisaged. The spectrum of options ranges from, at one end, the strengthening of *ex ante* coordination on some crucial issues to, at the other end, the extreme hypothesis of the creation of a single EU chair with different intermediate options to regroup EU countries in 'pure' EU constituencies. (Bini Smaghi 2004). It should be noted that any move towards a more unified EU representation in the BWI would go a long way in internalizing the role of the informal groups in the formal institutions, thus offering a major contribution to the reform of global governance.

**Accountability**

This parameter implies that decisions should be transparent and accessible to the general public. In addition, it requires that the management of the institutions should be accountable to the shareholders.

The BWIs are (and should remain) government-based institutions. Indeed, this should not be an obstacle to improving transparency and achieving greater accountability towards civil society at large, even more so given the rapid privatization and decentralization of economic processes that have taken place in the last decades at the national level. This is also essential to fulfill the criteria of legitimacy and representation.

The criterion of accountability could be applied under different perspectives. I shall limit the discussion to two main issues, namely the policy of transparency and the procedure for the appointment of the managing director/president.

Considerable progress has been achieved toward greater transparency. In particular, the IMF is moving from a situation in which it was a 'secret' institution to one where most documents and decisions are published promptly and are available to the general public on the web. There are areas, however, where more progress is needed, for example concerning the publication of Article IV reports. Nevertheless, there is another trade-off: publicity may reduce staff candor or in some cases may impede the disclosure of sensitive information, and this would damage relations between the IMF and member country authorities. Also in the World Bank there are trade-offs between the confidential nature of the financial transactions and the need for accountability and policy disclosure.

An area where the issue of accountability has not yet found an appropriate solution concerns the procedure for the appointment of the IMF managing director and the president of the World Bank. Neither the Bank nor the Fund have specific formal selection procedures for such appointments. A set of principles and procedures aimed at increasing the transparency and accountability of the exercise has been identified. It remains to be seen how they will be implemented.

## THE INFORMAL GROUPS

Globalization requires both specialized institutions and global vision. A global vision is the capacity to establish the necessary linkages among different issues. Bretton Woods institutions provide specialization; the global vision is provided by an informal kind of institution. These are the G7/G8, grouping the most powerful and wealthy nations, the G10 (the G7 countries plus Belgium, the Netherlands, Sweden and Switzerland), and the G20, created in 1999 with the participation of the G7 countries, Russia (the G8), Australia and the main EMEs (Argentina, Brazil, China, India, Indonesia, Korea, Mexico, Poland, Saudi Arabia, South Africa and Turkey). There is also the G11, an influential group internal to the IMF and composed of the directors of 11 constituencies, who coordinate on issues judged of common relevance by its members (at present, constituencies are led by Argentina, Brazil, China, Egypt, Gabon, India, Indonesia, Iran, Saudi Arabia, South Africa and Venezuela).

Examining governance issues at the group levels requires changes in the above-mentioned criteria. Indeed, not all the criteria have the same relevance for the groups that they have when applied to formal institutions. This is due to their informal nature, to the absence of a statutory mandate and to their restricted membership which by the definition infringes the representation criteria. On the other hand, the rationale for having an informal structure of governance lies in the efficiency of the decisionmaking process and in the capacity of these groups to solve the collective action problems that arise in formal institutions. Indeed, in the BWIs, broad membership implies a great differentiation of interests. In contrast, at the group levels, the issue of legitimacy becomes of special relevance since a small number of countries, although controlling a large proportion of the world economy, is called upon to make decisions that will have an impact on the world population at large.

Cooperation among the major industrialized nations was established over 40 years ago with the creation of the G10 as a response to a serious threat to the international monetary system. In the past, the G10 – which is the oldest forum for cooperation among finance ministers and central bankers – has played, in cooperation with the IMF, an active role in the management of financial crises, in particular in the context of the General Borrowing Agreements (James 1996). In the years since the G10 was established, other groups such as the G7 and the G20 have come into existence and new specialized fora (such as the Financial Stability Forum) have been created to strengthen international cooperation on specific issues. The G10 therefore has progressively lost its political influence, to assume increasingly a more technical role in support of the activities of the G7 and also the BWIs, as in the case of the preparation of templates of collective action clauses in the recent discussion on mechanisms for sovereign debt restructuring.

The issue of legitimacy arises in particular when looking at the role played by the G7/G8 summit. The heads of state and government of the five most powerful nations met for the first time in 1975, in Rambouillet, with the objective of restoring economic and financial stability in the aftermath of the dollar/gold standard. They have continued to meet regularly since then, although the main themes of their deliberations changed through time. More recently, the focus of G7 and lately G8 summits has been on issues linked to the fight against poverty, the environment and food safety, as well as international security. Recently, the economic dimension has been sharply reduced. The change in focus led many to question the legitimacy of the G7 and the G8. How is it possible to discuss the fight against poverty without the poorest countries in the world sitting at the table? How can the G7 and G8 discuss the environment without taking into account the needs of the emerging economies whose primary objective is economic development? The broadening of the issues discussed at summits has led to a serious questioning of the legitimacy of the world's richest nations to discuss them in isolation.

The question of legitimacy, however, is less critical for economic issues, which are now largely addressed by finance ministers and central bank governors, meeting often and having the spare technical instruments to address the critical issues affecting the world economy. The legitimacy of the G7 – on economic and financial issues Russia is not yet a member of the club – derives mainly from the ability to solve problems and is therefore strictly linked with the efficiency of its decision-making. From the point of view of efficiency, indeed, the G7 model of coordination ensures timely decisions, favored by the fact that G7 countries share common goals and homogeneity of preferences, and have the ability to act and good political and bureaucratic control. This is also due to the method based on periodic gatherings of finance ministers (with the participation, on some issues, of the governors of the central banks) and on the intensive work of the deputies (and the deputies' deputies) who meet even more frequently and have conference calls every fortnight (or more often, if needed).

International financial stability involves all aspects that define global public goods (Allen 2002), with linkages between different issues and between national policies and international institutions. The role played by the G7 in ensuring international financial stability in cooperation with the BWIs, in particular the Fund, the national governments and the private sector, has evolved over time. In the mid-1970s, the main concern of the G7 was exchange rate fluctuations resulting from the different economic policies following the first oil shock. Eventually, coordinated foreign exchange intervention became increasingly rare (the latest event took place in October 2000 to counter the excessive depreciation of the euro against the dollar). In the 1980s, the main issues of concern for the international community shifted from the exchange rate to financial stability. The main threat became the emerging markets' debt crises. In the 1990s, the main shocks came from a series of crises involving important EMEs (Mexico in 1995, the Asian countries in 1997, Russia in 1998, Brazil in 1999, Turkey and Argentina in 2000–01) and threatening international financial stability.

The G7 plays an increasingly important role in addressing international financial instability by: (a) developing a strong and efficient coordination mechanism based on a strong commitment to achieve common positions when a crisis erupts; (b) sharing common views on the way to address a financial crisis thus avoiding the situation whereby different views (for example, concerning private sector involvement) would prevent the group from acting in a cohesive way when a crisis emerges; (c) representing an important reference to the IMF management and for the debtor countries in the course of crisis management and resolution; and (d) supplementing IMF financial support with bilateral loans. Finally, because most emerging market countries' creditors belong to the G7, the G7 authorities have some leverage to ensure that the solutions designed by the IFIs do safeguard their citizens' interests, but also involve the creditors in the resolution of crises.

These factors provide legitimacy to the G7 to adopt a leadership role towards the international institutions, the debtor countries and, although with less success, the private sector in managing crisis situations. They also provide guidance in addressing the issue of financial stability. The leadership can suggest reforms for the existing institutions, and particularly the way in which the IMF operates (Bini Smaghi 2004). The Cologne Report on the reform of international financial architecture marked the evolution of the IMF from the promotion of monetary stability through appropriate macroeconomic and exchange rate policies, to the development of sound domestic and financial markets. Indeed, the Asian crisis, showed that sound macroeconomic policies are not enough if financial markets are not sufficiently developed to support highly volatile capital flows.

However, by emphasizing the importance of strengthening domestic financial markets, the Asian crisis also showed that the G7 alone could not put in place a proper incentive structure to induce emerging market countries to strengthen macroeconomic policies and their financial system, implementing best international practices and adopting internationally agreed standards and codes. The Asian crisis experience encouraged the G7 to adopt more encompassing goals. The program strategy for this decade was clearly stated in the Cologne Report:

> Our overall strategy is to identify and put in place policies to help markets work properly and to provide the public goods necessary to achieve this objective. This requires public authorities to provide for enhanced transparency and disclosure, improved regulation and supervision of financial institutions and markets, and policies to protect the most vulnerable. It also requires that private creditors and investors bear responsibility for the risks they take, and are involved appropriately in crisis prevention and crisis management. In these respects, the establishment of internationally agreed codes and standards for policy-makers serves both as an incentive for better governance and as a yardstick against which to measure country risk. (G7 1999a, p. 2).

The need to increase the legitimacy of G7 initiatives to a larger part of the world (thus contributing also in increasing their effectiveness) leads to the idea of involving the main EMEs more directly and to share with them a project aimed at ensuring international financial stability. The useful suggestions for enhancing global economic security that emanated from the G22 and G33 processes demonstrated the potential value of a regular international consultative forum with a broader membership than the G7. This led to the set-up of a new group, the G20, which includes the G7 countries, Russia, Australia and the most important EMEs, with worldwide coverage. The creation of the G20 represents the next stage in the evolution of informal consultation among industrialized countries and emerging markets, necessary to bridge positions and promote mutual understandings, thus enhancing consensus. It is also an answer to the request coming from many sectors of the academic world and civil society for an increased involvement of the EMEs in the decision-making process, as was the case with Jeffrey Sachs's proposal to move from a G7 to a G16 (Sachs 1998).

The idea of an enlarged informal group can be traced back to the Cologne Report. Indeed the G20 was created 'as a new mechanism for informal dialogue in the framework of the Bretton Woods institutional system to broaden the dialogue on key economic and financial issues among systemically significant economies and to promote cooperation to achieve stable and sustainable growth that benefits all' (G7 1999b, p. 6). It is clear from its inception that the G20 has been created as a deliberative rather than a decisional body and was designed to encourage the 'formation of consensus' on international issues, with a particular focus on promoting international financial stability. Its program of work has been clearly designed by its first chairman, the Canadian Paul Martin, who suggested that the G20 should 'focus on translating the benefits of globalization into higher incomes and better opportunities everywhere' (Kirton 1999).

The G7 remains the key policy forum where macroeconomic policy and issues related to the stability of the international financial system are discussed. In other areas, while the G7 countries remain the dominant actors, efficiency considerations call for greater involvement of some major emerging and developing countries. These areas encompass crisis prevention and resolution, debt issues, financial crime and development.

Groups are also well equipped to develop their role and their instruments of action to match a changing economic environment. Increasingly, their role is complemented and supplemented by international institutions, primarily the BWIs. Both formal and informal gatherings, however, are pursuing a similar role, namely to provide governance without a government, while keeping their 'specialization' character, as for the BWIs, or their 'leadership' character, as for the groups.

## CONCLUSIONS

Increasing interdependence and faster globalization have posed new issues for the international governance system and have raised concern for a fundamental reform. In Michel Camdessus's words:

> An increasingly open system of world trade and an increasingly and prudently liberalized system of world finance are the two greater public goods that have been produced by the international community in the postwar era. The effort to reform the system is fundamentally to sustain and enhance these public goods. (Camdessus 1999)

The current set-up is based on the coexistence of the complementary functions played by some specialized institutions (mainly the BWIs), with an almost universal membership, and the leadership role played by a small number of major countries, mainly through the G7, which provides global vision, issue linkages and efficient decision-making. These are essential functions that any effort to reform the system should continue to preserve.

Should the EU increasingly act as a unified actor in the global system and speak with one voice in the BWIs, many of the externalities in global governance which require the support of informal institutions such as the G7 could be internalized. The operation of the BWIs would probably be improved with respect to all four criteria discussed in this chapter.

## NOTES

*    I wish to thank Vincenzo Zezza and Francesca Mercusa for their contribution. The views expressed are only those of the author.
1.   International Conference on Financing for Development, Monterrey, Mexico, 18–22 March, 2002.

## REFERENCES

Allen, Marc (2002), *Financing the Global Public Good of International Financial Stability*, Washington, DC: International Monetary Fund.

Bini Smaghi, L. 2004, 'A single EU seat in the IMF?', *Journal of Common Market Studies*, **42** (2), 229.

Camdessus, Michel (1999) '*International financial and monetary stability: a global public good?*' Remarks at the IMF Research Conference, International Monetary Fund, 28 May Washington, DC: IMF.

Drazen, Allen (2001), *Political Economy in Macroeconomics*, Princeton, NJ: Princeton University Press.

Group of Seven (G7) (1999a), *Report of the G7 Finance Ministers to the Köln Economic Summit*, Cologne, 18–20 June.

Group of Seven (G7) (1999b), *Statement of G7 Finance Ministers and Central Bank Governors*, Washington, DC, 25 September.

International Monetary Fund (IMF) (Various years) Fact sheets, News briefs.

James, Harold (1996), *International Monetary Cooperation since Bretton Woods*, New York: Oxford University Press.

Kaul, Inge, Isabelle Grunberg and Marc A. Stern (1999), *Global Public Good: International Cooperation in the 21st Century*, New York: Oxford University Press.

Kenen, Peter (1986), *Financing, Adjustment and the International Monetary Fund*, Washington, DC: Brookings Institution.

Kirton, John (1999), '*What is the G20?*', mimeo, University of Toronto, G8 Information Center www.library.utoronto.ca/g7/g20/g20whatisit.html, 30 November.

Passacantando, Franco (2002), '*Governance reforms at the World Bank*', mimeo Institute for Studies and Economic Analyses (ISAE), Rome, 19 November.

Sachs, Jeffrey (1998), '*Making it work*', The Economist, 12 September.

van Houtven, Leo (2002), 'Governance of the IMF', IMF Pamphlet series, no. 53, International Monetary Fund, Washington, DC.

World Bank (2000), *Poverty Reduction and Global Public Goods. Issues for the World Bank in Supporting Global Collective Action*, Washington, DC: World Bank.

# 17. Governance issues: the IMF, the role of the G7 and some related issues

**Wouter Raab\***

## INTRODUCTION: THE IMF AND THE INTERNATIONAL FINANCIAL ARCHITECTURE

Of the 184 member countries of the IMF, only a handful are powerful enough to defend or represent their vital international economic interests on their own. For most others, however, membership of an intergovernmental organization is essential to ensure that their views and interests are represented in the international arena. Having representation at international meetings to defend its interests is a vital element of a country's sovereignty. Therefore, a multilateral, rules-based organization is an indispensable cornerstone of the international monetary system. Rules and procedures, which give the same rights and obligations to every member country, provide the framework through which countries can commit to mutually binding actions and agreements. Such undertakings can on the one hand limit sovereignty of the individual member state, but on the other, by providing a multilateral framework for effective international action they will also enhance the capacity of all member countries together to deal with the cross-border impact of developments in major financial and goods markets.

The IMF is the core institution in the international financial system, primarily because of its mandate and its highly relevant actions in the fields of crisis prevention and crisis management. For my purposes, that is, discussing governance in the international financial system, a key element of the IMF is that it provides a general framework of rules: internal rules on the governance within the institution; and external rules on how countries should conduct their policies, and on the terms and conditions under which countries have access to IMF facilities. These rules make the behaviour of member countries and of the IMF predictable and consistent, and they provide for equal treatment and equal access to IMF instruments. They therefore foster legitimacy and stability in the international financial system.

I shall concentrate in the remainder of this chapter on the internal governance of the IMF. A unique feature of the IMF is its broad, almost universal membership and the fact that voting rights are related to a member country's weight in the world economy. The five biggest members are entitled to appoint their own representative on the executive board. The remaining 179 countries are grouped into 19 constituencies that each elect one executive director to represent the constituency on the board of directors. In total the board consists of 24 executive directors. Together these features of IMF governance ensure that one of the principles of efficient decisionmaking is generally met: an efficient decision should involve all those who decide, pay and benefit.

The IMF is often criticized for not being democratic because it does not apply the principle of 'one country, one vote'. Therefore the IMF is often called an instrument of the industrial countries to dominate the developing ones. This is a rather Machiavellian view of the IMF. Niccolò Machiavelli argues in his famous book, *Il Principe* (*The Prince*), published in 1532: 'contemporary experience shows that princes who have achieved great things have been those who have given their word lightly, who have known how to trick men with their cunning, and who, in the end, have overcome those abiding by honest principles'. Today, we do not believe in such a view. The IMF cannot be run in such a way. Therefore, it is important to find the right balance between equality and efficiency. The legitimacy of the IMF and the international financial architecture depend on it. Does the governance at the IMF succeed in finding this balance? Has it sufficiently adapted to changing economic circumstances in the world?

## INTERNATIONAL DEVELOPMENTS

The international financial architecture is a dynamic system. It has both fostered globalization and been influenced by it. The increased importance of capital as opposed to trade flows has had a significant bearing on the functioning of the IMF and its instruments. The advent of some emerging market countries in the world economy justify a larger say for these countries in the governance of the international financial architecture. The process of European integration has brought European representation on the executive board of the IMF onto the agenda. Another important development is the rise of various informal groups, most notably the G7, but also the G20. Has the IMF adjusted to these changes? In terms of its analysis, yes. Although some will say not fast enough and not without making mistakes. In terms of its governance, one cannot escape the conclusion that this has hardly changed over time, at least formally. As a consequence, informal get-togethers of major countries have developed around the IMF, in an attempt to respond to the changes in the external environment, mentioned above.

## WHAT ARE THE PROBLEMS WITH IMF GOVERNANCE?

Few people are content with the governance of the IMF: among the problems mentioned are:

- the executive board with 24 directors is too unwieldy;
- the composition of the board does not represent economic realities and there are too many Europeans;
- IMF management is really in charge of the institution;
- the United States is too powerful;
- the G7 has too much influence;
- decisionmaking is driven by political arguments rather than by economic motives; and
- the IMF is a rich countries' club.

In the remainder of the chapter I shall focus my remarks on the size and composition of the board, European representation and the role and influence of the G7.

## SIZE OF THE EXECUTIVE BOARD OF THE IMF

It has been argued that the size of the IMF board, with 24 executive directors, is too big and too unwieldy for efficient decisionmaking. This is a popular belief that in my view is nevertheless wrong. The IMF has 184 member states. Through its organization into constituencies, all have a say in IMF decisionmaking either directly or indirectly, related to their relative strength in the world economy. These are unique features. A balance is struck between representativeness, equity and efficiency; 24 is hardly excessive considering that the agenda has an important bearing on the global economy. If the board does not function as effectively as it should, this has more to do with its methods of organization and working practices than with the absolute number of directors. There are various ways in which the board could organize its work more efficiently and so limit the burden on staff, management and itself. For instance, is it always necessary to discuss Article IV reports with all 24 board representatives? Could the board not establish more committees, with limited but rotating membership? These committees could have in-depth and technical discussions, leaving the policy issues for the full board. Speaking times should be limited and strictly adhered to. The duration of full board meetings should be drastically cut, limiting the burden on management. To achieve this, greater resort to voting might be justified. The board should primarily discuss strategic issues.

Certainly, the number 24 is not sacrosanct. It could be less or more. But adding or cutting a few chairs would not make a dramatic difference as opposed to improving the working methods of the board. Twenty-four people seated around a table, representing 184 countries, when issues of key importance for the global economy are discussed, seems reasonable.

## COMPOSITION OF THE BOARD AND REPRESENTATION ISSUES

Regarding composition and representation, the following popularly-held beliefs are often expressed:

- emerging market economies are underrepresented;
- the voice of developing countries in the IMF is too weak; and
- Europe is overrepresented.

As politically motivated views, they may be self-evident truths (to those who want to believe in them), but they are not necessarily informed by facts. For instance, the above-mentioned categories are much too broad for a meaningful discussion of representation. On the basis of the principle that quotas in the IMF should reflect a country's position in the world economy, it is true that within the groups of emerging market countries and developing countries some are underrepresented, but most of them are not and some are even overrepresented. The various specifications of a simplified quota formula as tried out in the Cooper report[1] and the subsequent work by IMF staff[2] did not produce a higher quota share for developing or emerging market countries as a group. The fact is that if we use variables that measure position in the world economy, those countries appear not to be systematically underrepresented. The only countries really benefiting in those exercises are industrial countries, particularly the larger ones. This will hardly be the solution to solving the issue of representation in the IMF.

We should examine on a case-by-case basis which countries are seriously underrepresented, using the quota formulas for that purpose. These formulas are the expression of what the international community believes are the appropriate factors determining a country's position in the world economy. For those countries that are underrepresented and are interested in a larger quota share, an *ad hoc* increase is desirable. This is exactly what was done for China in 2001, when such a proposal was put forward by the board committee, chaired by the Dutch executive director.

If developing countries as a group need a stronger voice, then raising the level of basic votes for each member country is the most effective way to give them a larger share as a group. A stronger voice – as opposed to just a larger voting share – in the IMF can be achieved by making developing-country representation more effective. Improving working methods in the constituencies of developing countries, improving communication with capital cities and fostering greater ownership and understanding of the IMF (and its procedures) in those cities are then called for. The executive board has decided to provide the constituencies of developing countries with more resources to achieve this.

Finally, one problem in the field of quota distribution is the large and often persistent difference between actual and calculated quotas according to the formula. We need to think about ways of closing this gap.

If we are prepared to make these changes we shall have a more responsive and flexible system that reflects developments in the world economy. Tweaking the system on the basis of biased political perceptions will not create a stronger and more legitimate system, but rather the opposite.

## EUROPEAN REPRESENTATION

The process of political integration in Europe has not yet reached a stage that justifies concentration of the European chairs in the IMF. The European Union (EU) is not a federation, where normally external policies are decided at the federal level. In particular, the EU has no power in the fields where the IMF is active, except for monetary policy for the member states that have adopted the euro and the exchange rate of the euro, and to some extent for the fiscal policies of EU member countries. Fiscal policies, structural reform and issues of international finance are the primary responsibility of the EU member states, although they are coordinated in the EU as a matter of common interest.[3]

Further, would it be sensible for the EU countries to try to speak with one voice on the IMF Board? The answer is yes, for obvious reasons. In fact, EU member states are increasingly doing just that. Common positions are drafted on matters such as access policy and the Sovereign Debt Recovery Mechanism (SDRM). Should this lead to one chair for the EU? In the long run, yes, but how long is the long run? Discussions in the EU

Intergovernmental Conference (IGC), which is drawing up a new constitu-
tional treaty for the EU, do not point to a move to a more federalist or
communitarian approach that is believed to provide stronger safeguards for
the smaller member states against a concentration of power in the larger
ones. Against such a background it is difficult for the former to make concessions with regard to their representation in the IMF. Their sovereignty
is at stake both in the IMF and in the EU. Any changes that will be made
to European representation at the IMF need to be symmetrical with regard
to bigger and smaller member states. A scenario in which a few European
countries would have to give up their chairs, while others continue to
appoint their own executive director is not attractive. So while one EU chair
on the IMF board is conceivable, both economic and political integration
need to make further progress before that eventuality.

However, even one EU chair raises some problems with governance too.
What would it mean for the internal governance of the IMF if there were
two powerful blocs, the United States and the EU, on the IMF board? There
would be a strong tendency for the two to strike a deal between themselves
first, after which the other members would be informed about the outcome.
Even worse would be the situation where the two would hold such opposing
views that a quick and sensible compromise could not be reached. Tension
and incoherence within the international community would increase and
the IMF would pay a price for that, in terms of reduced efficiency and even
reduced relevance.

At present, constituencies which are led by an EU member country
consist of a mix of EU and non-EU member countries, sometimes not even
European countries. In the medium term, would a reorganization or concentration of European chairs into homogeneous EU chairs make sense?
The benefits are not self-evident. The formation of constituencies has so far
taken place voluntarily. The present formation, with only a few exceptions,
is no obstacle to EU coordination, certainly no more than the G7 process
is. It is not clear what benefits over the present situation would justify the
expulsion of the present non-EU member countries from those constituencies, leaving them on their own to find new partners. Rather, this
would again result in one grouping being pitted against others, and would
do nothing to build bridges among the membership of the IMF.

Contrast this with the experience of the so-called 'mixed' constituencies,
those that consist of both creditor and debtor countries.[4] The Dutch constituency is an example of this. The Netherlands has joined a constituency
with some other European countries outside the EU. None of them is in
the first wave of entrants to the EU, except for Cyprus. Cooperation is
enjoyed mutually. The Netherlands provides technical advice, financial
support, advice in their dealings with the IMF and the World Bank, and

speaks on their behalf in other fora as well. When the IMF board discusses an issue where creditors and debtors are pitted against one another, the Netherlands also sees the issue from the perspective of the debtors. As a result, mixed constituencies have a moderating influence in the IMF. They try to work constructively towards proposals that find a balance between the various interests at stake. Rather than breaking up these constituencies, we should try to emulate their positive experiences elsewhere.

## G7 AND OTHER INFORMAL GROUPS

Given the alleged inefficiency of the board, the increased tendency of the G7 to coordinate and to influence IMF policies seems to be just a normal reaction. Much is made, particularly by those in the G7, of the efficiency in its decisionmaking. However, other views can also be heard, for example:

- the G7 is losing sight of its original objective, that is, multilateral surveillance of their economic policies, and is focusing increasingly on matters outside its remit and control, such as AIDS and development finance;[5]
- the G7 is a rich countries' club whose recommended policies are biased and tend to promote primarily its own interests; and
- the exclusiveness of the G7 irritates members of the international community; both among traditional allies of the G7 and political opponents of industrialized countries, there is a feeling that G7 recommendations and policy orientations are inspired more by political considerations than by sound economic reasoning, to an extent that others, including IMF management and staff, do not feel comfortable with the fact that the G7 can often be seen to push policies agreed among themselves through the IMF board, negatively affecting the legitimacy of IMF policies and the general support for them.

In more general terms, one could say that whatever one's opinion about the efficiency or speed of G7 decisionmaking, its recommendations do not pass the more generic efficiency test: the link between deciding, paying and benefiting.

This is not to say that the G7 does not do useful or sensible things – it does, sometimes, but not always. A non-G7 country like the Netherlands essentially agrees with the general thrust of G7 recommendations, and subscribes to the economic thinking that is behind G7 policy. But what has the G7 achieved that could not have been achieved through more open consultation and discussion, primarily through the IMF board? The wording in

G7 communiqués is often so general that it generates little enthusiasm, let alone the motivation to raise objections.

The problem with the G7 is more at the practical and operational level. For example, its latest statement contained an action plan which describes how to strengthen crisis prevention and resolution: '[IMF] program documents for cases of exceptional access should always be published'.[6] This is completely right, but such detailed prescriptions should primarily be discussed by the IMF Executive Board

Another example is the case where the international community should consider what response to give to a crisis in a particular country. Other chapters in this book have cited the examples of Argentina and Turkey, where heavy-handed G7 intervention was applied. The result was frustration of good and open discussion by the IMF board, less-effective IMF policies, and less support for their policies overall. It also leads to less credibility and legitimacy of IMF policies. So there is an efficiency problem with G7 policy propositions: are they really sufficiently balanced to take account of all relevant angles and interests? Some propose other groupings, such as the G20, as more legitimate forms of informal grouping, primarily because of its wider membership which also includes various emerging market economies. However, there are two problems with this: first, membership of the G20 is even more arbitrary than that of the G7, where size is at least a relatively objective criterion; and second, the wider membership still does not address the fundamental problem of non-representation for those that are not present – for them, the legitimacy does not increase. The role of the G20 should remain one of consultation and of information sharing.

One could seriously question whether the G7 process weakens or strengthens the IMF. If some members have no confidence in the board, this seriously undermines its effectiveness. Who runs the IMF? According to the Articles of Agreement it is the executive board.[7] But who believes that? One could easily blame the management of the IMF for trying to circumvent the board or keep it in the dark. But even if this were true, somebody would lend them a hand. It is public knowledge that often G7 countries put pressure on the management of the IMF to limit the range of options presented to the board. The executive board should be the place where policy responses to international crises are discussed and considered. The debate should be open, inclusive and based primarily on economic argumentation. In the discussion above on the size of the executive board, it was indicated that the working method of the board may have to adapt to match the 'decisiveness' of the G7. The result should be policies that have a higher degree of legitimacy, find more general support worldwide and are seen to be less politically motivated. Given their quota shares, the G7 countries would still be the most influential members, but they would work more through IMF channels and with the other members. They would be surprised to find that their advocated policies would often win the day, not because of their self-proclaimed leadership but simply through the force and quality of their arguments. In a rules-based system, quality rather than power determines policy.

## CONCLUSION

I believe in a rules-based system and its long-run superior performance, rather than a view of legitimacy as just a question of finding the minimum number of countries that are needed to make a decision. All those that are involved with or affected by a certain decision should have a say in the decisionmaking process.

The IMF should be the central institution to deal with issues of global financial and monetary stability and global economic prosperity. The role of the executive board should be strengthened to bring its actual role more in line with its statutory powers. To enhance its efficiency and legitimacy, some adjustments may be required:

- the introduction of more efficient working methods, including more voting by board members;
- adjusting quota shares more quickly to adequately reflect developments in the world economy;
- the organization of countries into constituencies on a basis that seeks to maximize cooperation and compromise rather than pitting one group of countries against others (EU versus the United States, industrial versus developed and so on); and
- all member states should work through the executive board and not undermine it by working around it.

## NOTES

\* The author would like to thank Bilal Taner of the Ministry of Finance of the Netherlands for his help in writing this chapter.
1. 'Report to the IMF Executive Board of the Quota Formula Review Group', 28 April 2000, available on the IMF website, www.imf.org.
2. IMF, 'Twelfth general review of quotas, preliminary considerations and next steps', 22 January 2002, www.imf.org.
3. Monetary policy is the sole responsibility of the independent European Central Bank (ECB) which therefore is granted observer status on the IMF executive board; the exchange rate of the euro is a shared responsibility of the ECB and the Council (of EU finance ministers); fiscal policy is the primary responsibility of EU member states, but is

subject to a process of coordination (defined by the EU Treaty and the Stability and Growth Pact) under which, in some instances, the EU Council can make binding recommendations to member states and even impose sanctions.

4.  See also Leo van Houtven, 'Governance of the IMF: decision making, institutional oversight, transparency, and accountability'; 'Together, the seven mixed constituencies comprise 70 members; in Board discussions, they often hold the middle ground between the Group of Five major industrial countries and the 12 developing country groups (including Russia)' (p. 21), www.imf.org/external/pubs/ft/pam/pam53/contents.htm.
5.  Jeffrey Garten, 'Useless extravaganza in Evian', *Financial Times*, 26 May 2003.
6.  See 'G-7 action plan implementation, April 2003', www.g8.utoronto.ca/finance/fm041203.htm.
7.  According to the Articles of Agreement (Article XII section 3a) this power is delegated to the executive board by the board of governors.

# Index

floating exchange rate plus CAC
211–13
'Impossible Trinity' and bipolar view
206–9
India 219–22
intermediate exchange rate regime
plus CAC 213–14
intermediate exchange rate regime
plus capital controls 215–17
direct monetary controls, South Africa
239–40
discount bonds 75
disinflation 62
dollarization 42–9, 210, 255
Domestic Applicable Law, Argentina
116
domestic financial markets,
susceptibility to external shocks
33
domestic financial systems, stability of
12
domestic insolvency procedures,
international analogue to 275–6
domestic law, debt issued under 72
domestic policies
changes to 16
lack of confidence in 11–12
'domestic precommitment strategy',
adoption of 235
domestic sovereign debt markets 86–8
domestic tax base, preservation of
143
dual exchange rate system, South
Africa 241–2, 243

East Asia
capital account liberalization
154–60
exchange rate regimes 210, 220
economic growth, emphasis on 14
economic stability and democracy
168–70, 189–90
discussion 187–9
policy choice and speculative attacks
171–82
policymakers in democracies 182–7
sample and variable descriptions
191–3
Ecuador
bonds 316

debt restructuring 69, 73–6, 94, 309
exchange rate regime 211
effectiveness, IMF 16
Egypt
capital account liberalization 161
collective action clauses 70, 284
debt 80
debt default 83
electoral enfranchisement, effects of
172–5, 176, 178–9, 181–90
Electricity Generating Authority,
Thailand 78
11th September 2001 202
emerging market credits (EMCs) 131
emerging markets (EMEs)
'bipolar view' 209
capital flows to 147–8, 200, 202–3,
215
debt crises 335
effects of international commodity
prices 251
financial stability in 253, 336
national economies of 36
representation in decision-making
331, 340, 342–3
role capital controls 144, 250–51
special needs of 40–41, 334
emerging markets (EMEs), crises in
55–7, 83–4
use of capital controls 63–7
collateralized debt obligations
131–2
collective action clauses 70–79
creditor committees 79–83
effects of capital account
liberalization 140, 142
effects of pegged currencies 141
floating exchange rates 60–61
solutions of IMF 57–60, 67–70
surfeit of inflows 137
view on SDRM 289
*Empires of the Sand; The Struggle for
Mastery of the Middle East
1789–1923* 80
endogenous
default costs 263–5
politician problem 233, 234
engagement clause, collective action
clauses 314
Eurobonds 74, 75, 316